CAIRO

BEFORE THE AFTERMATH

A PHOTOGRAPHIC EXPLORATION

SCOTT SHAW

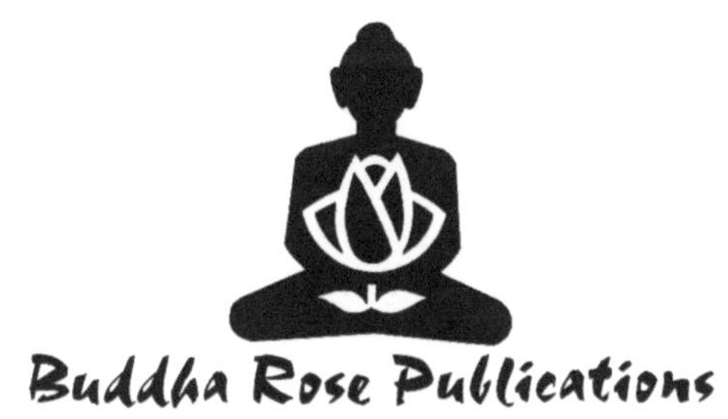

Cairo: Before the Aftermath

By Scott Shaw
www.scottshaw.com

First Edition 2013

ISBN: 1-877792-74-8
ISBN 13: 978-1-877792-74-8

Printed in the United States of America

CAIRO

BEFORE THE AFTERMATH

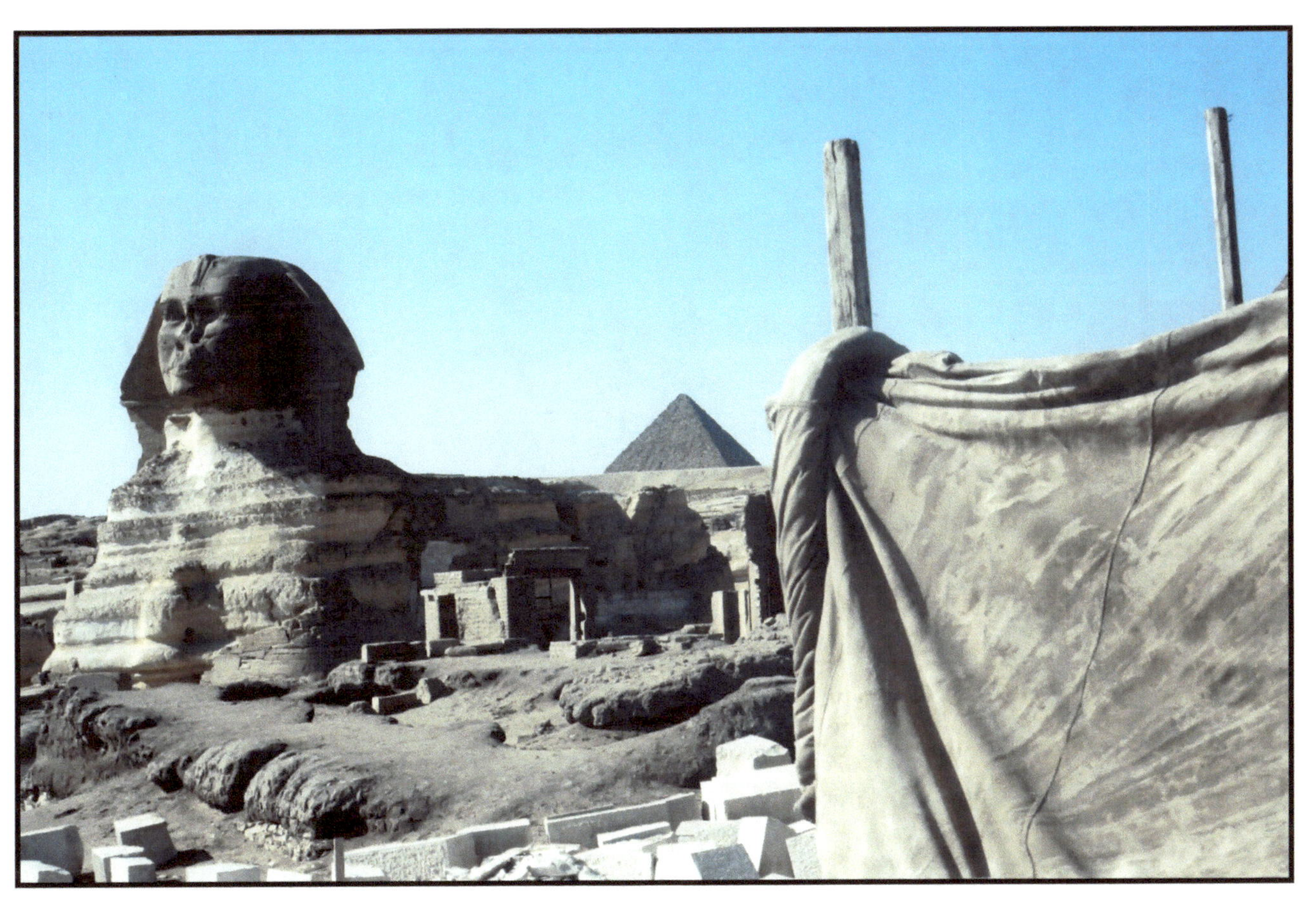

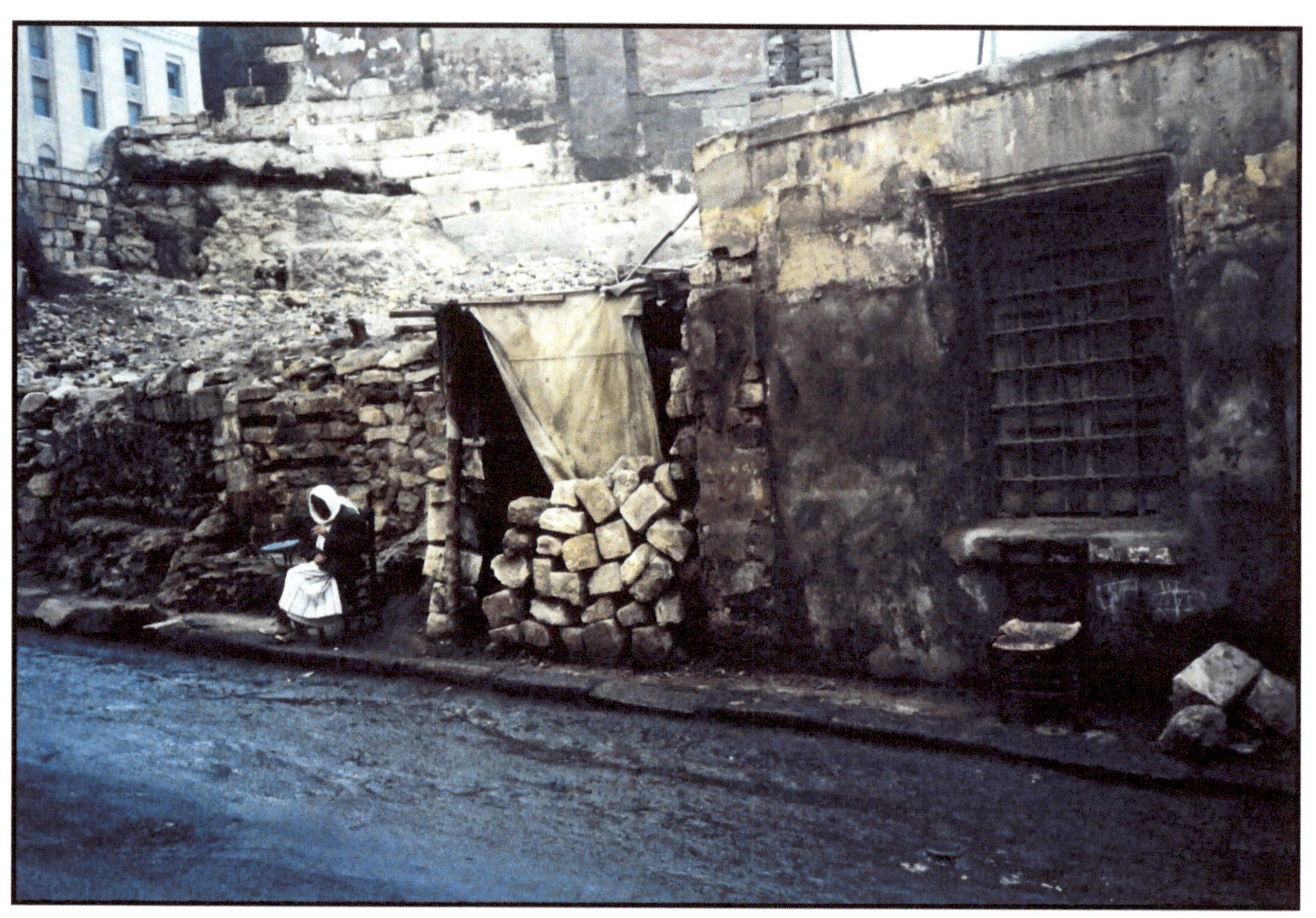

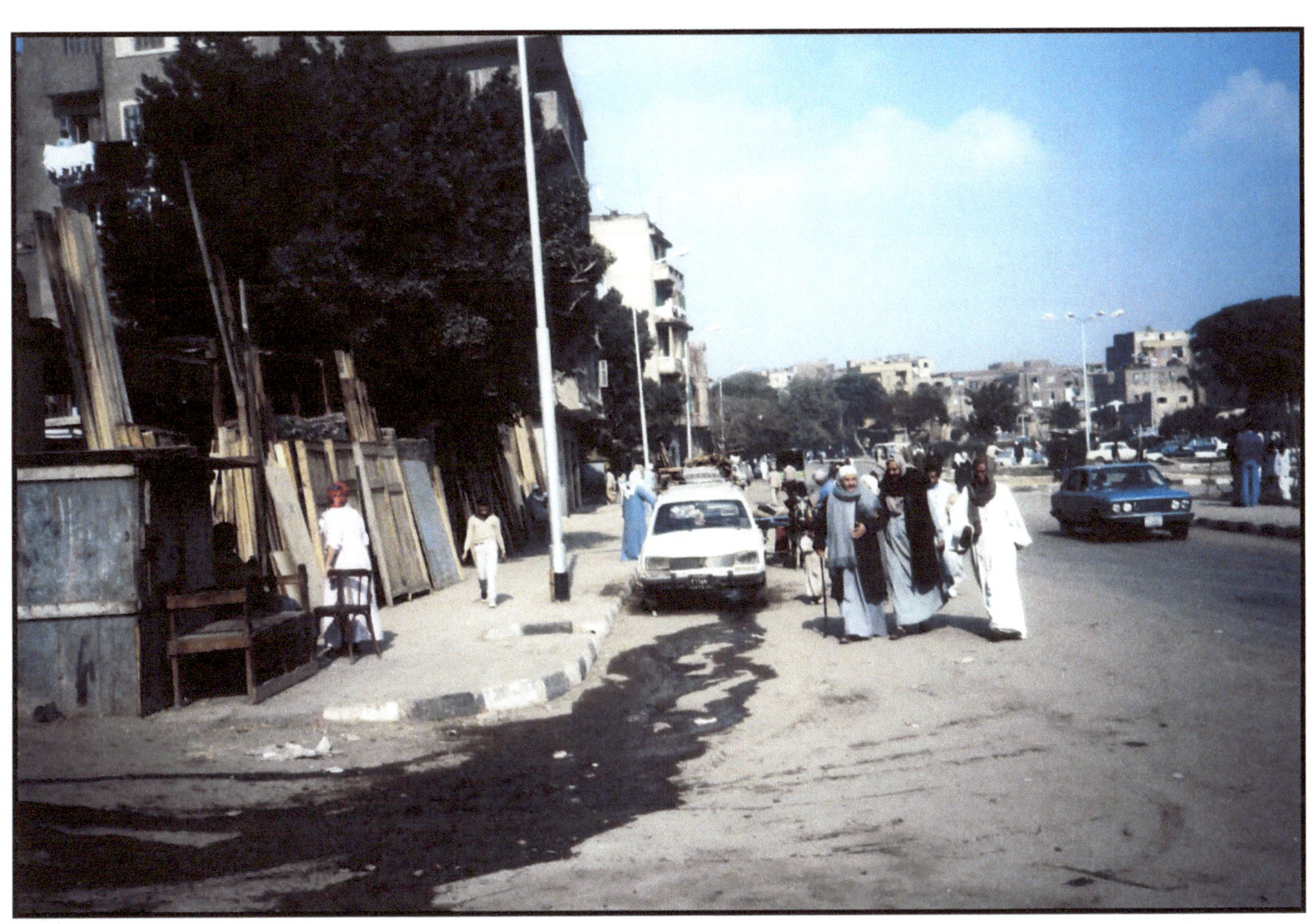

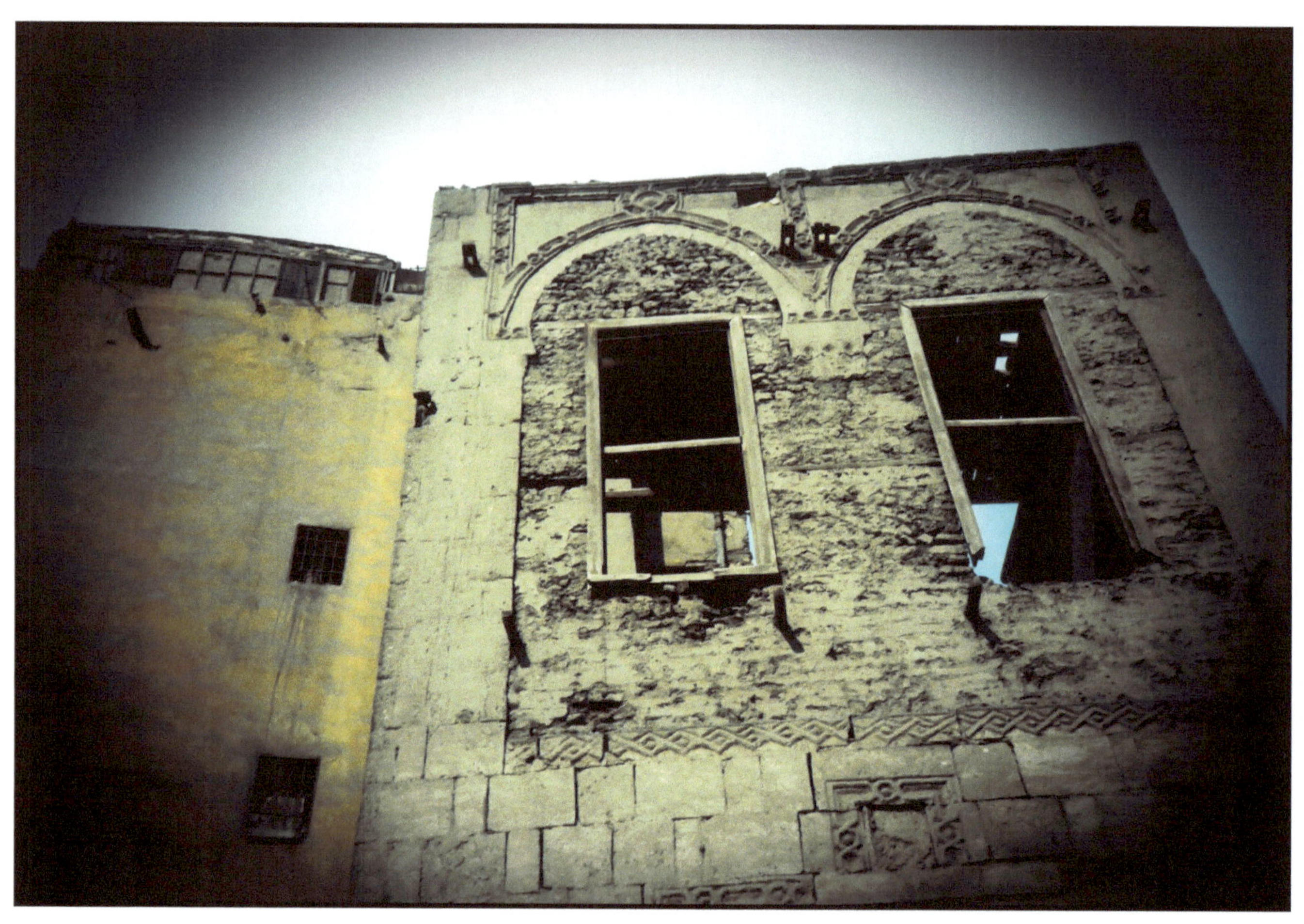

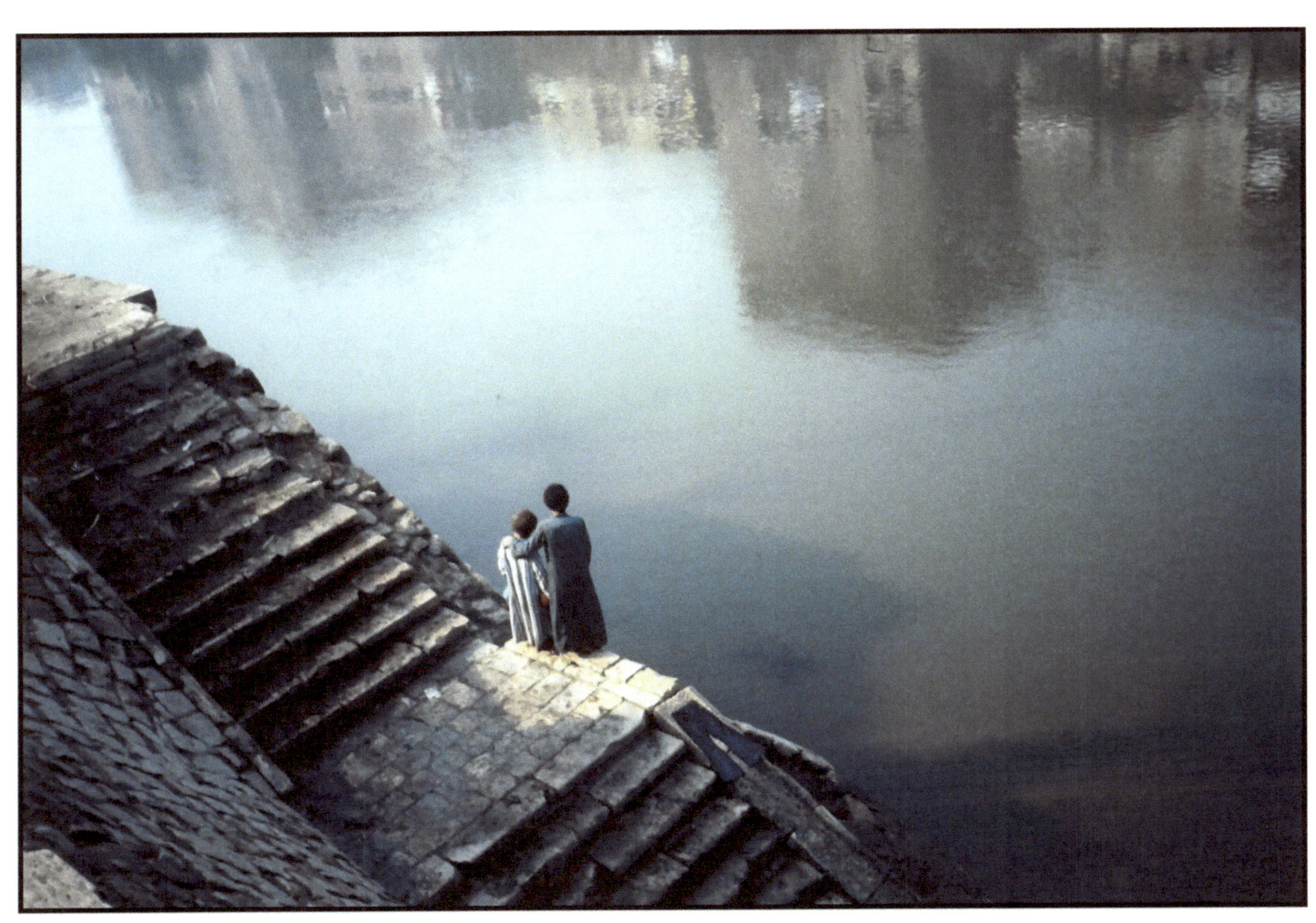

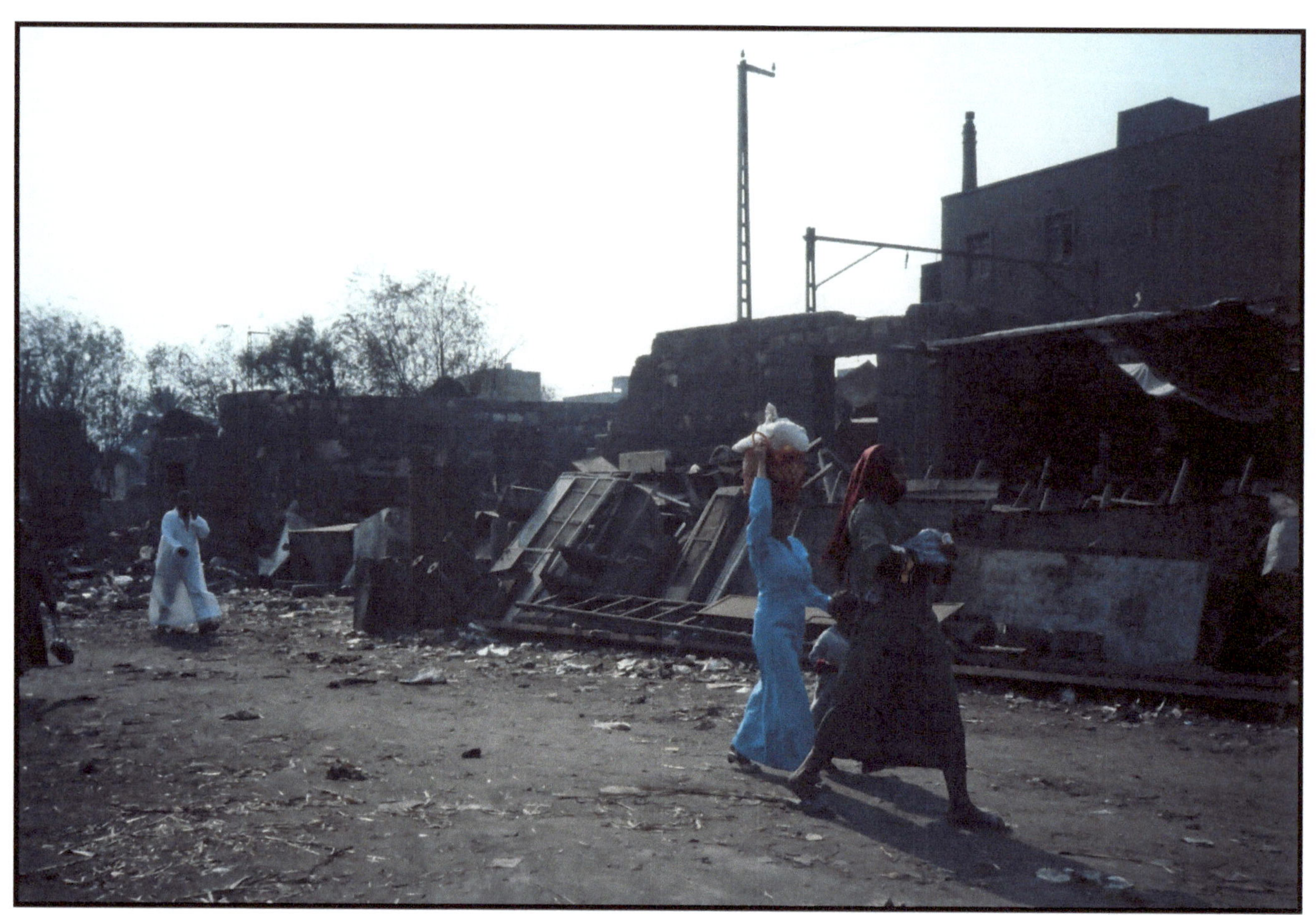

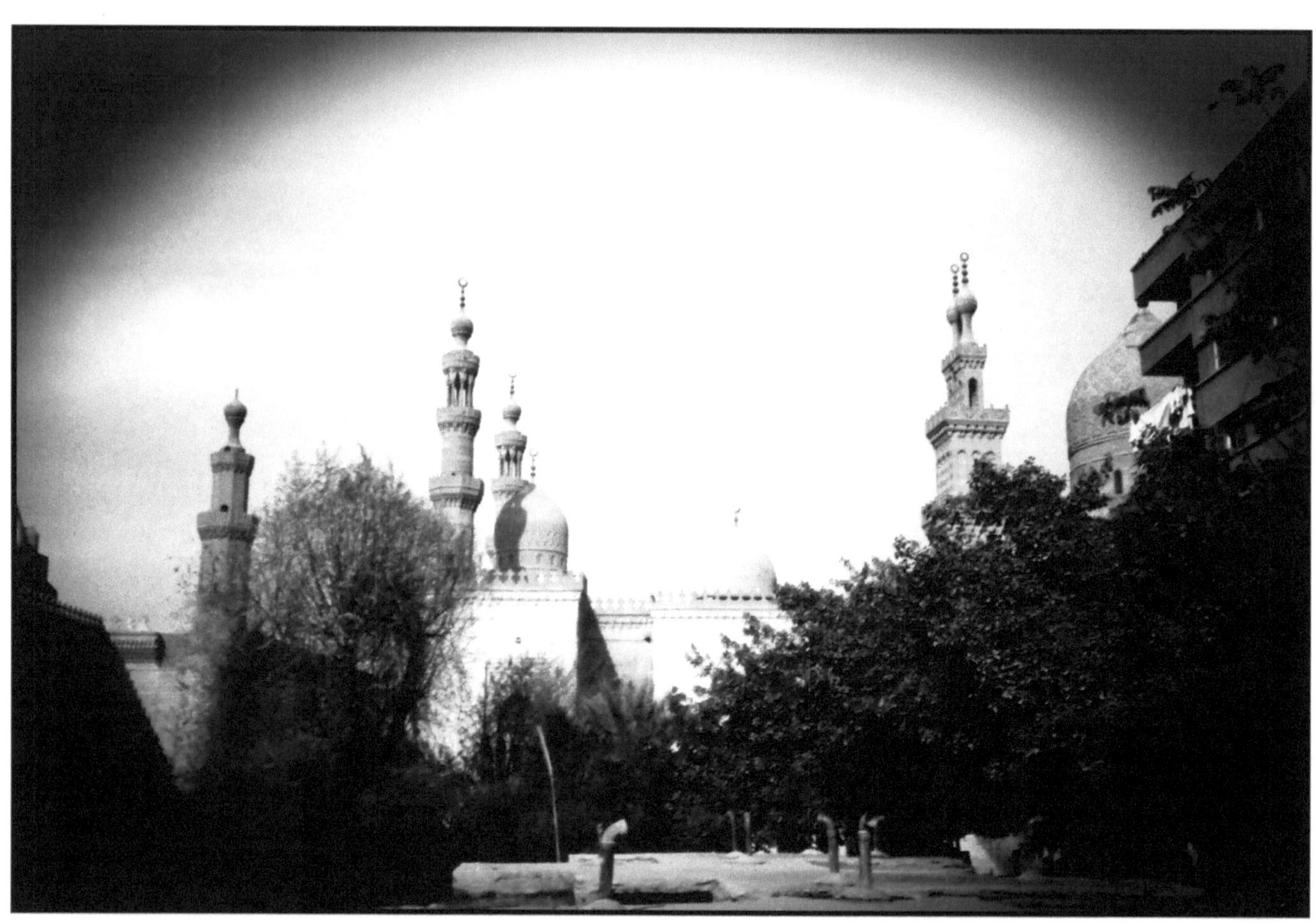

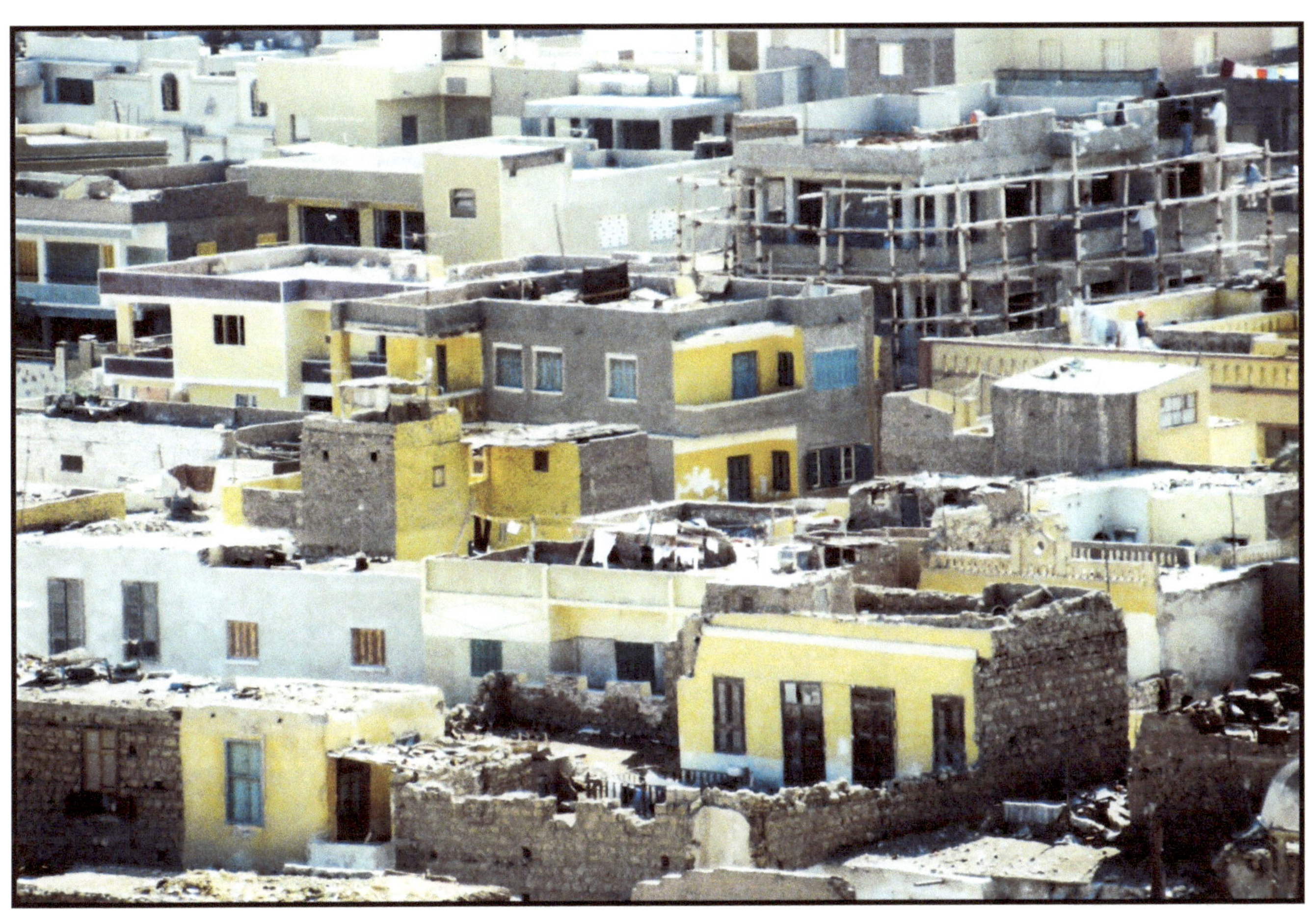

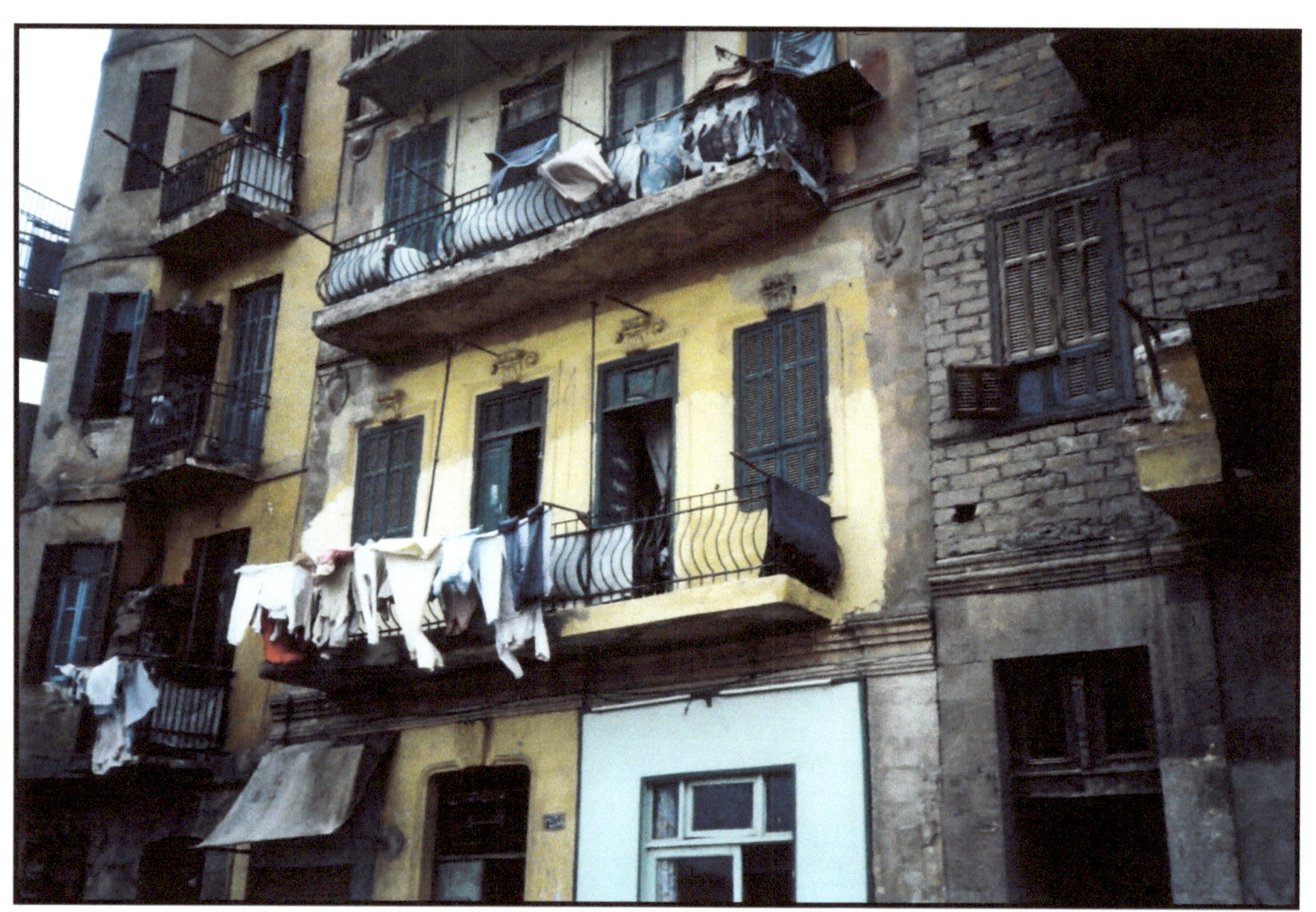

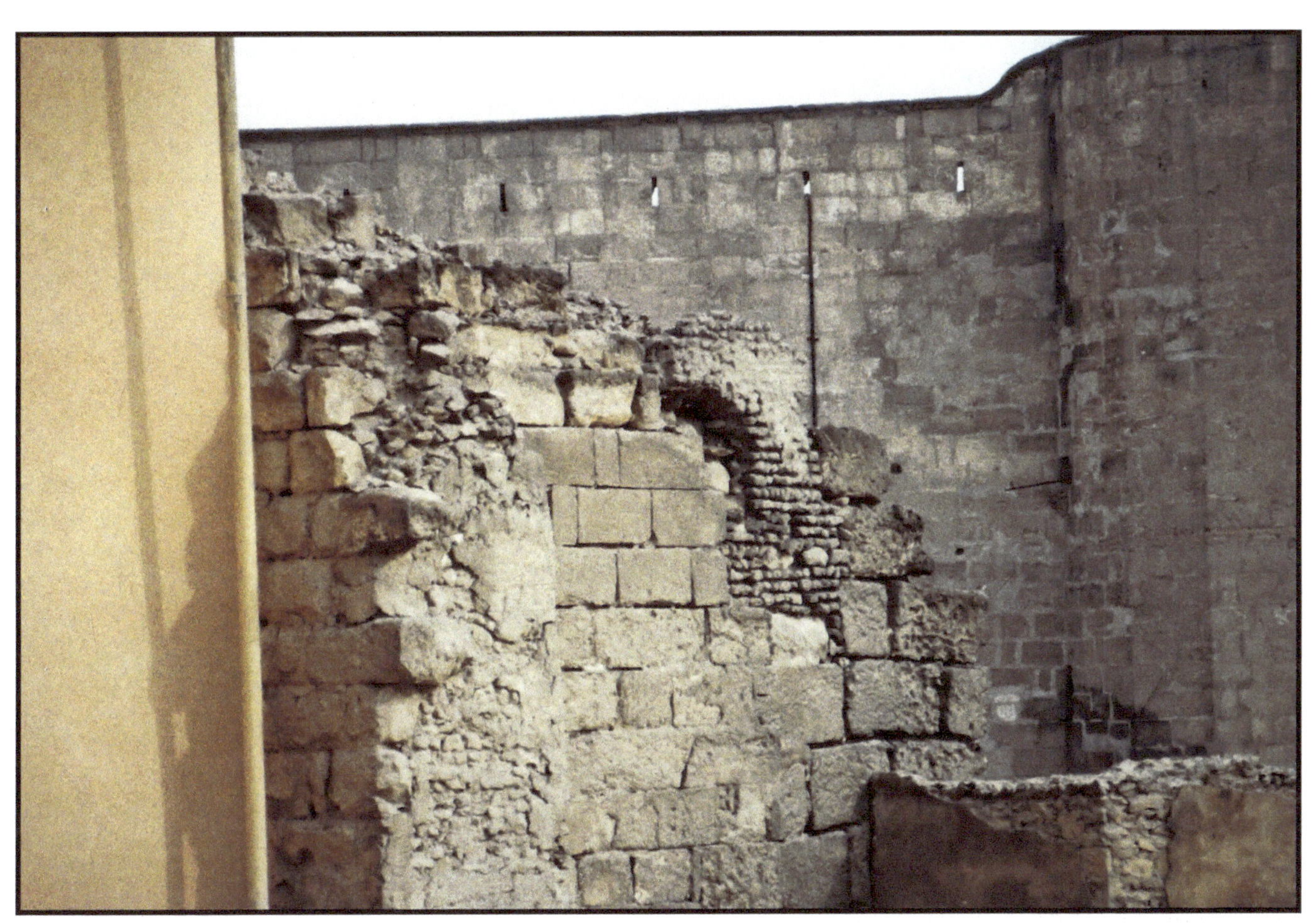

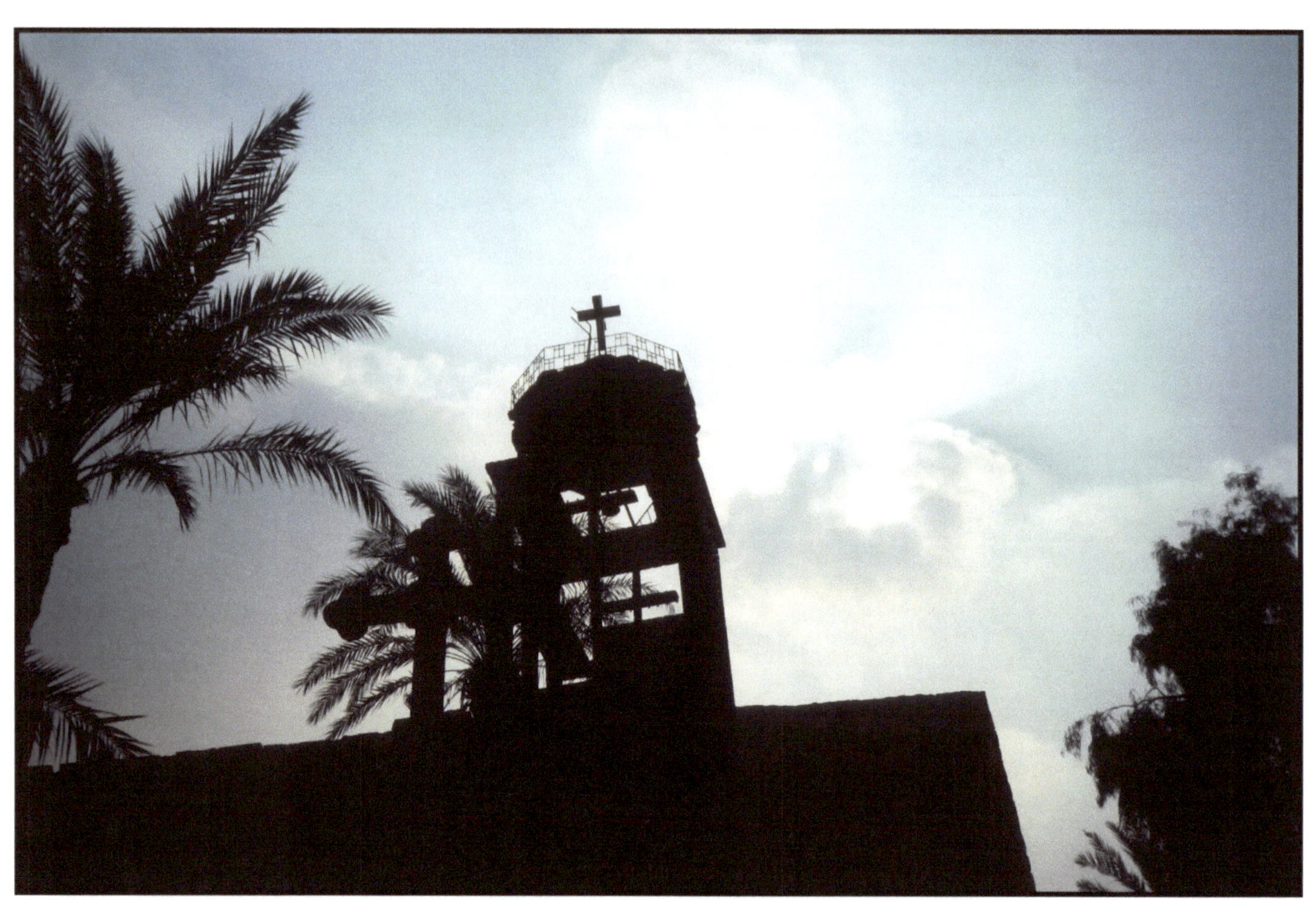

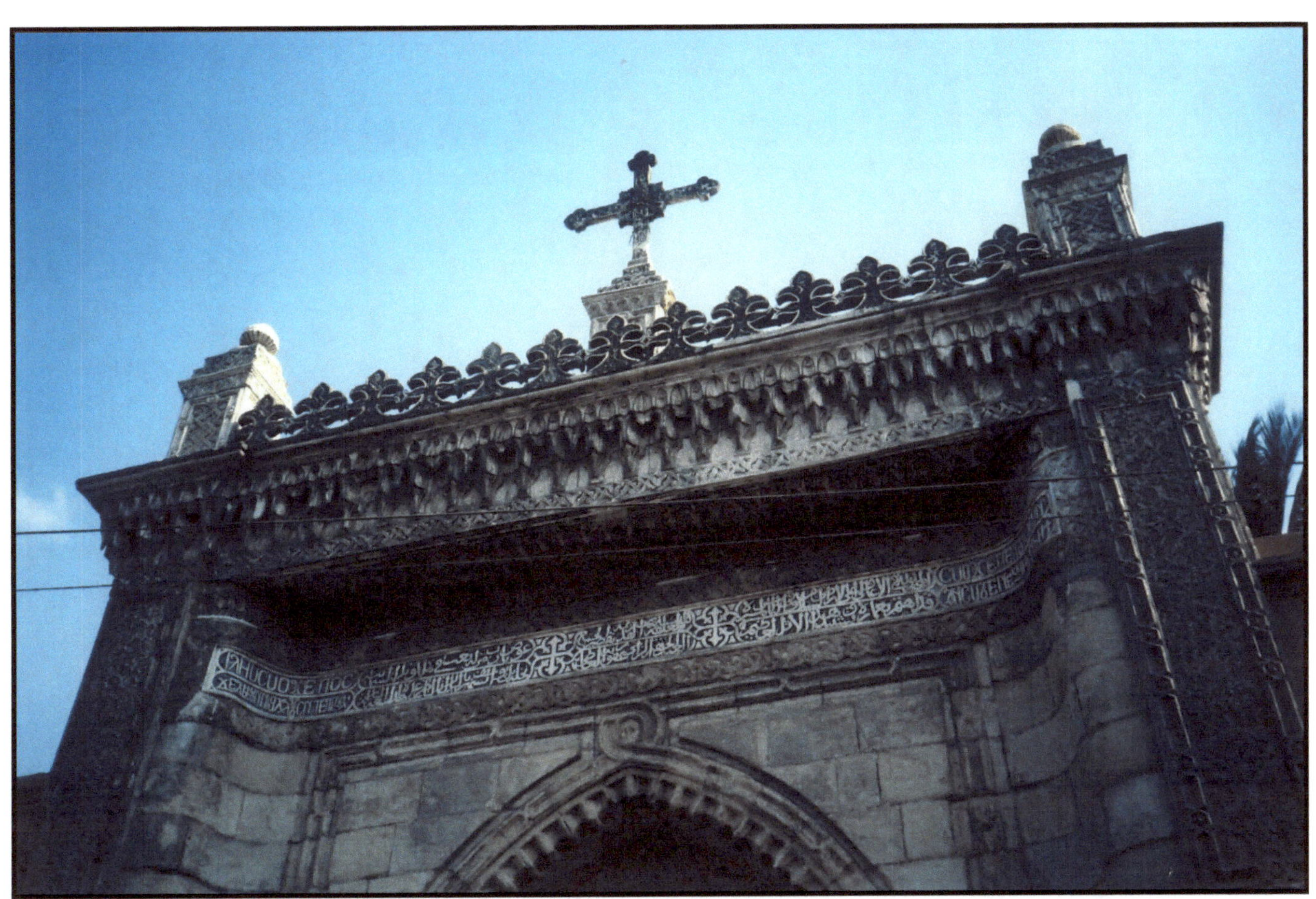

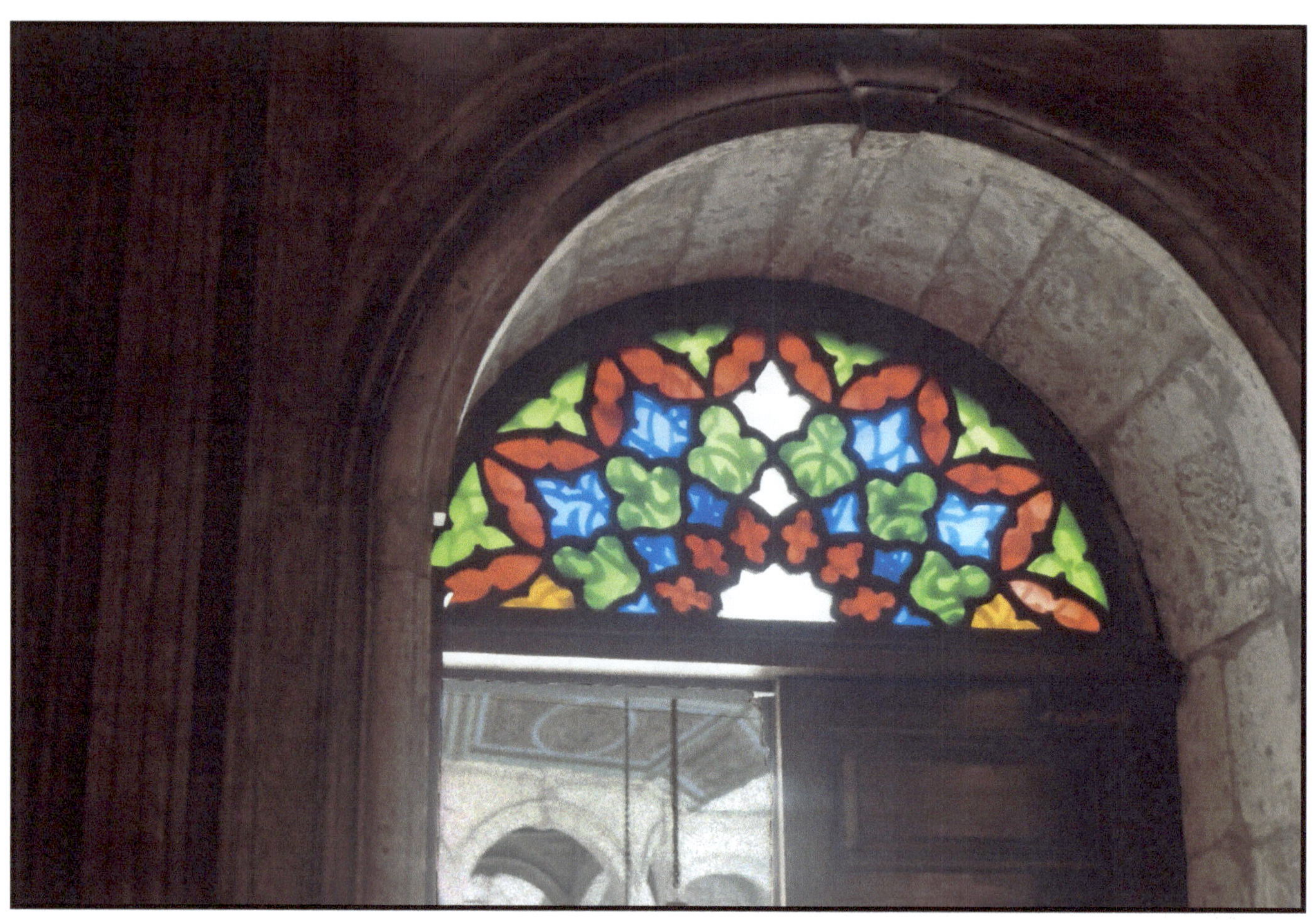

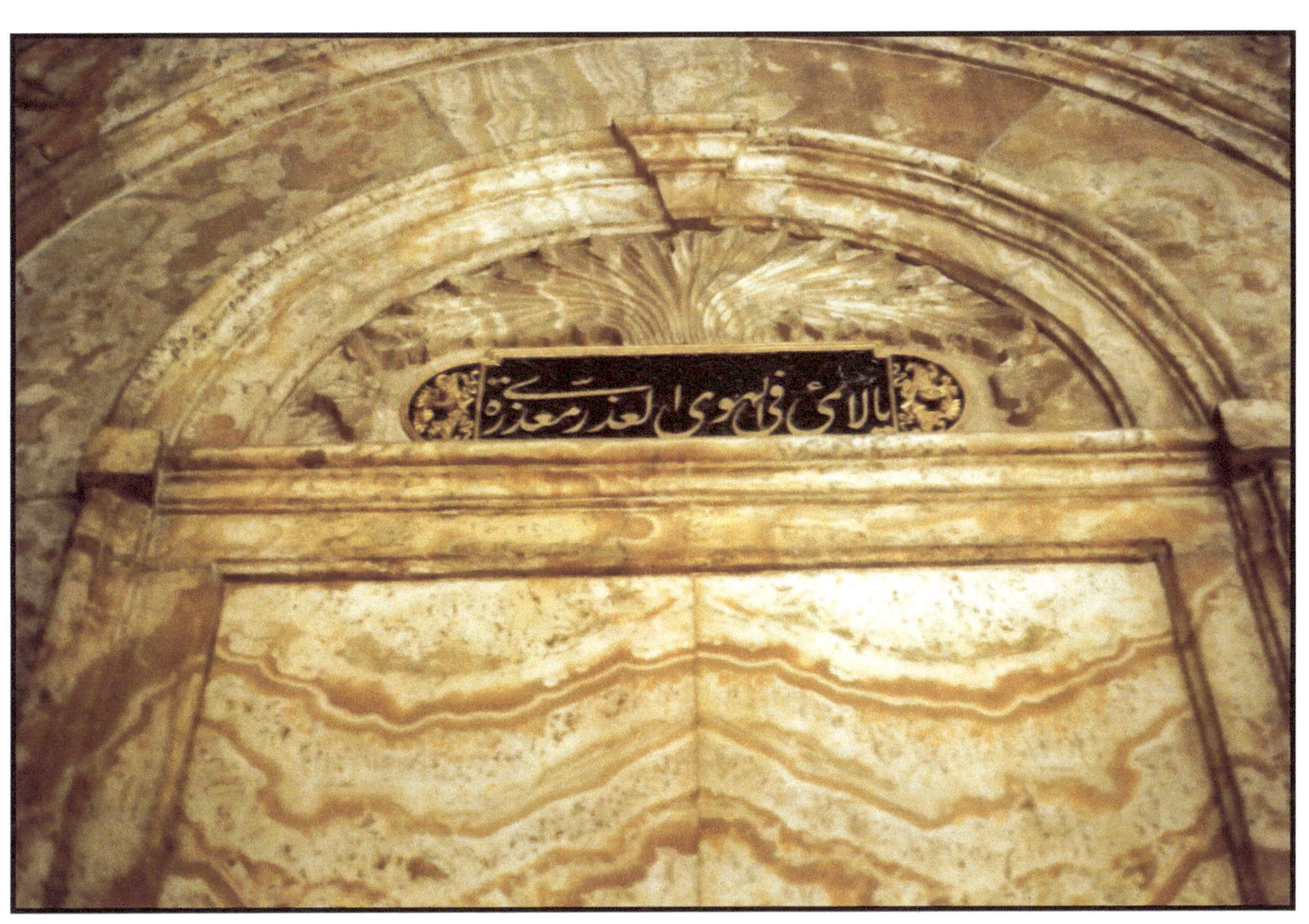
يا لائمي في الهوى العذري معذرة

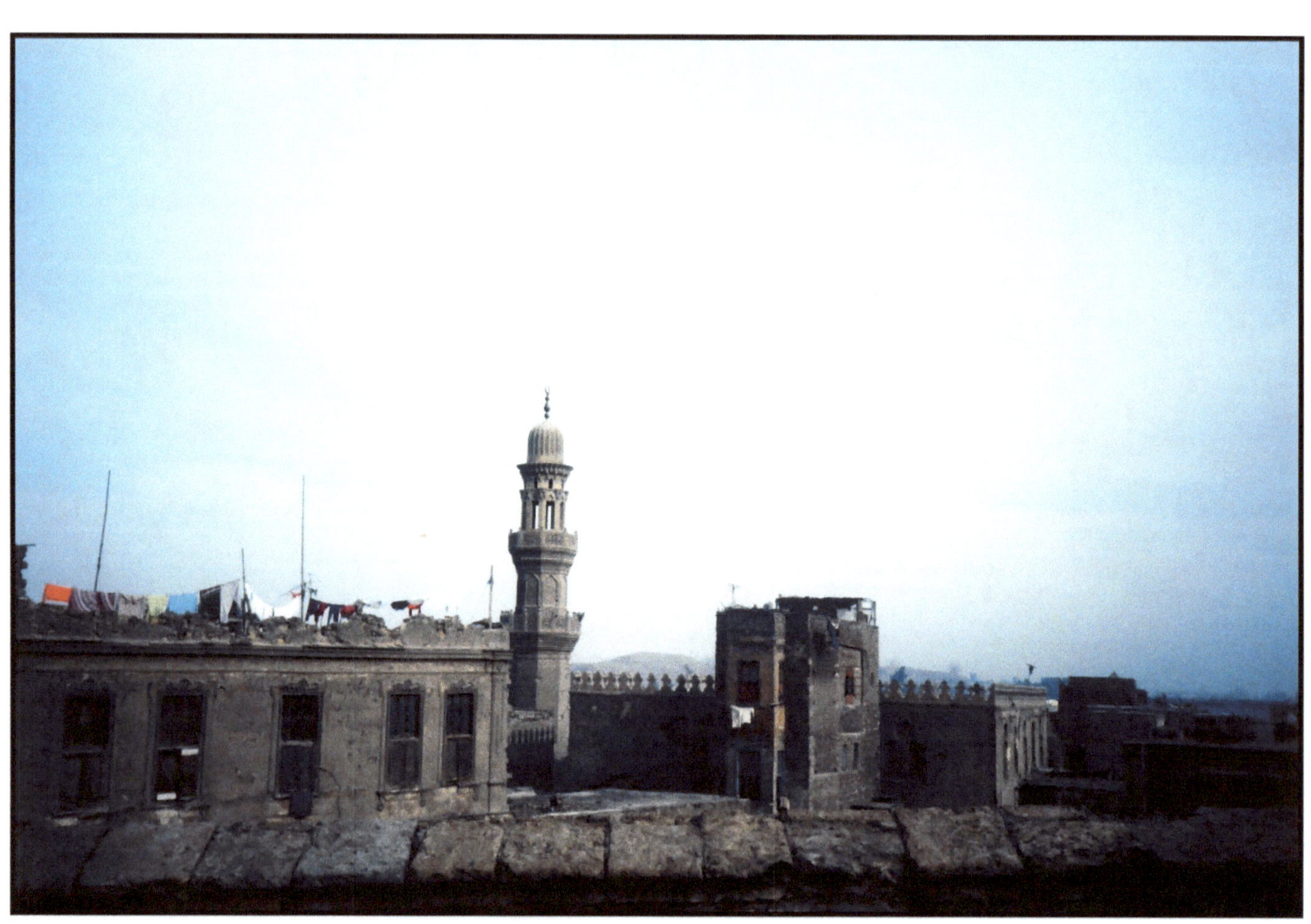

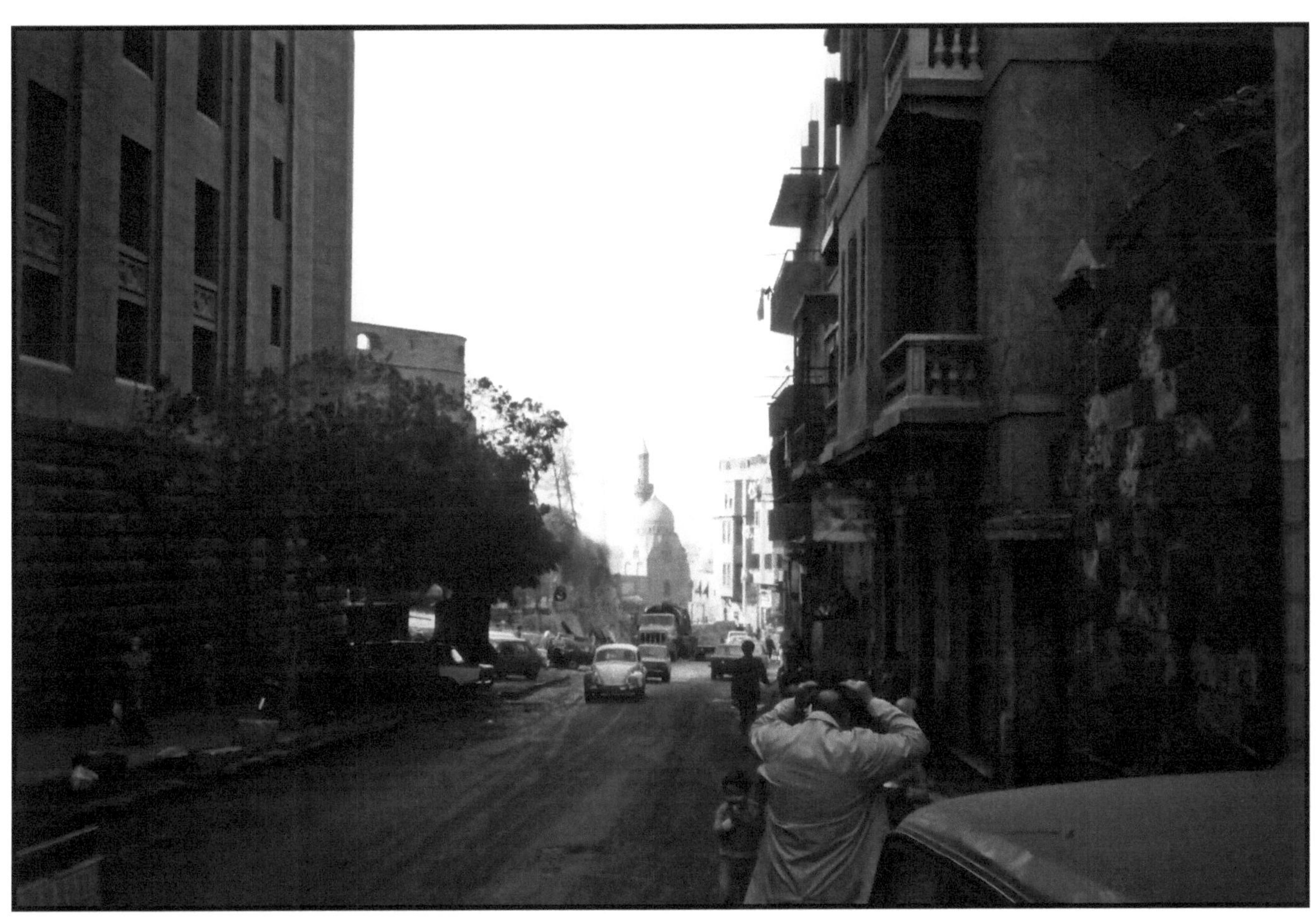

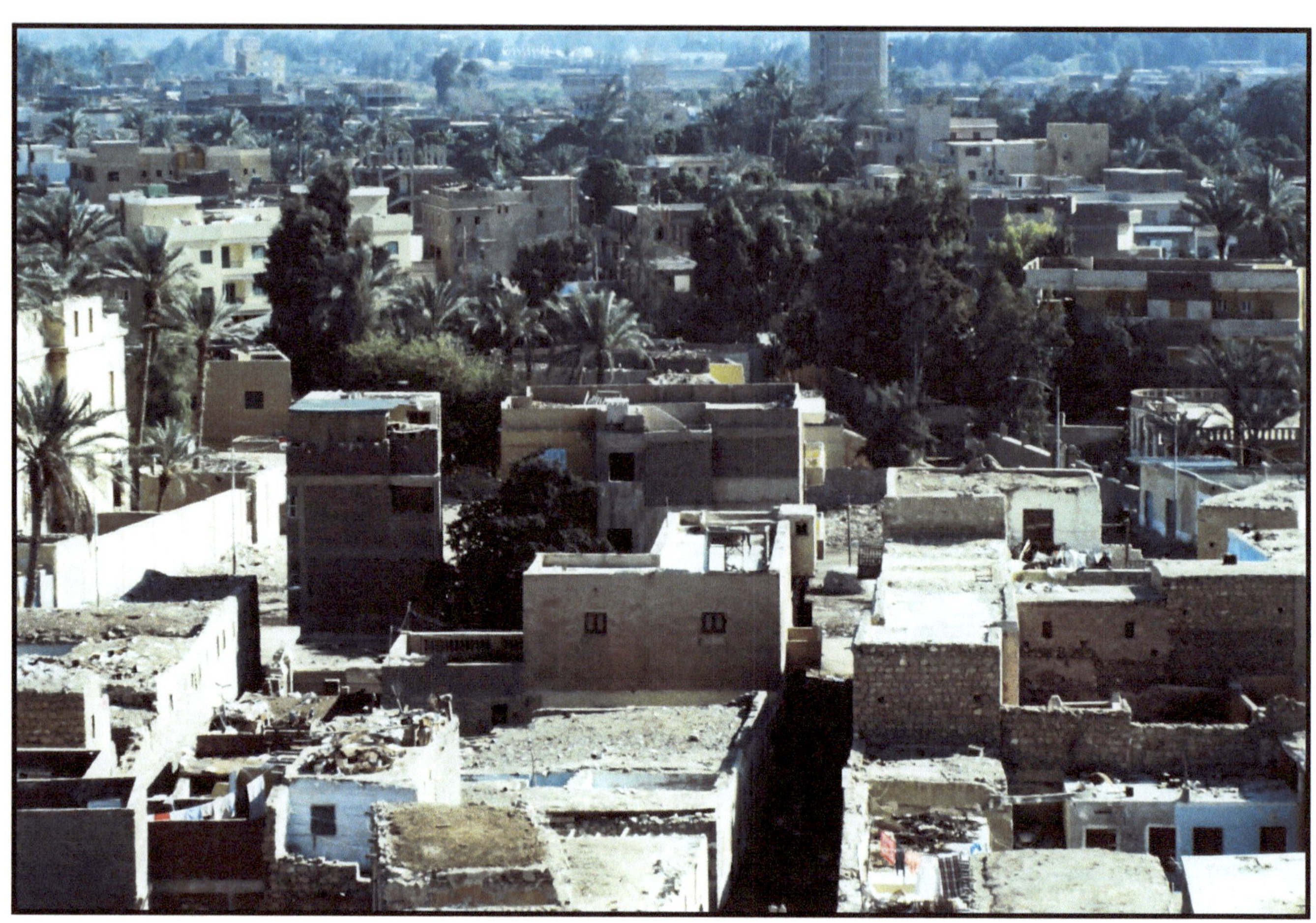

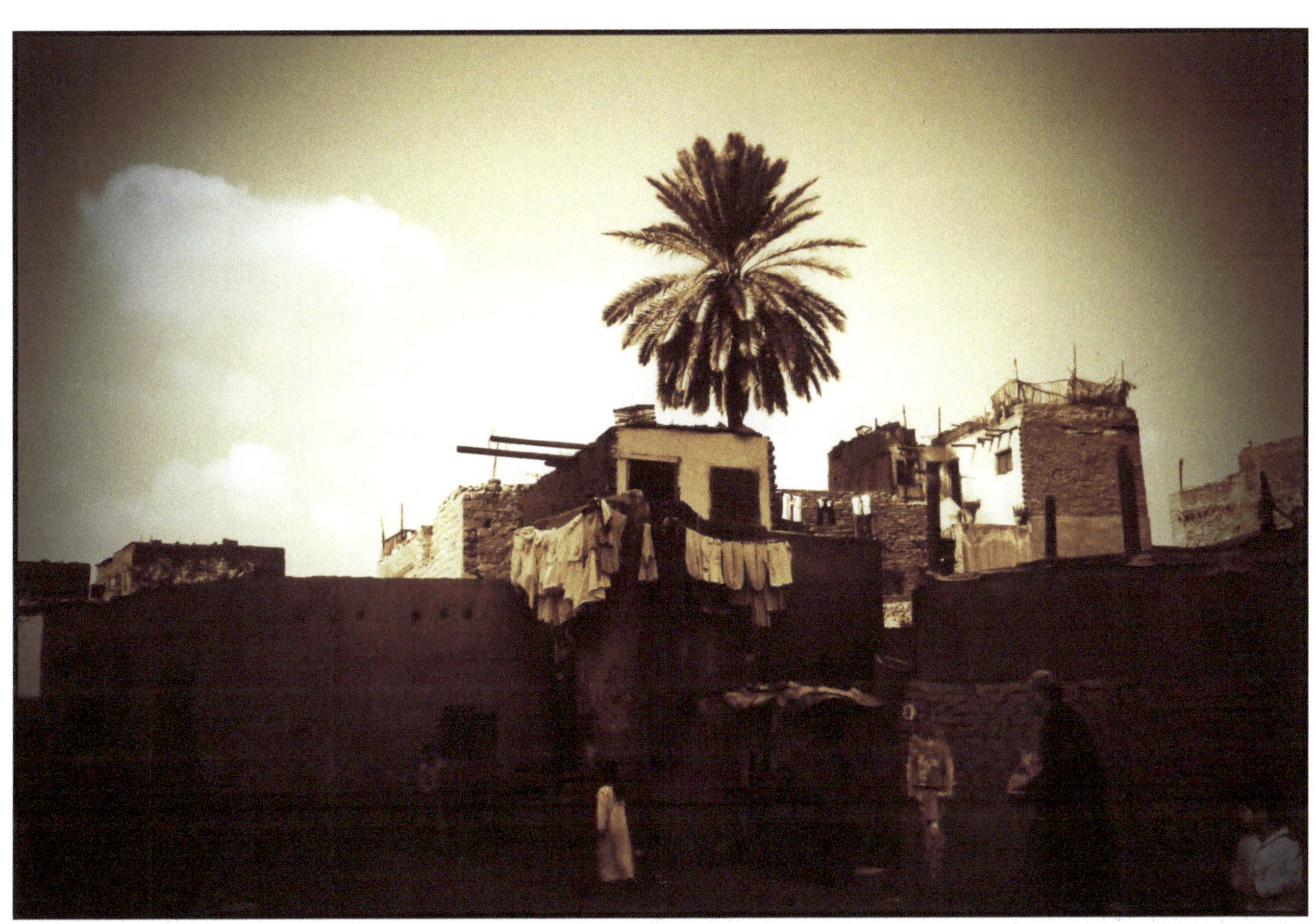

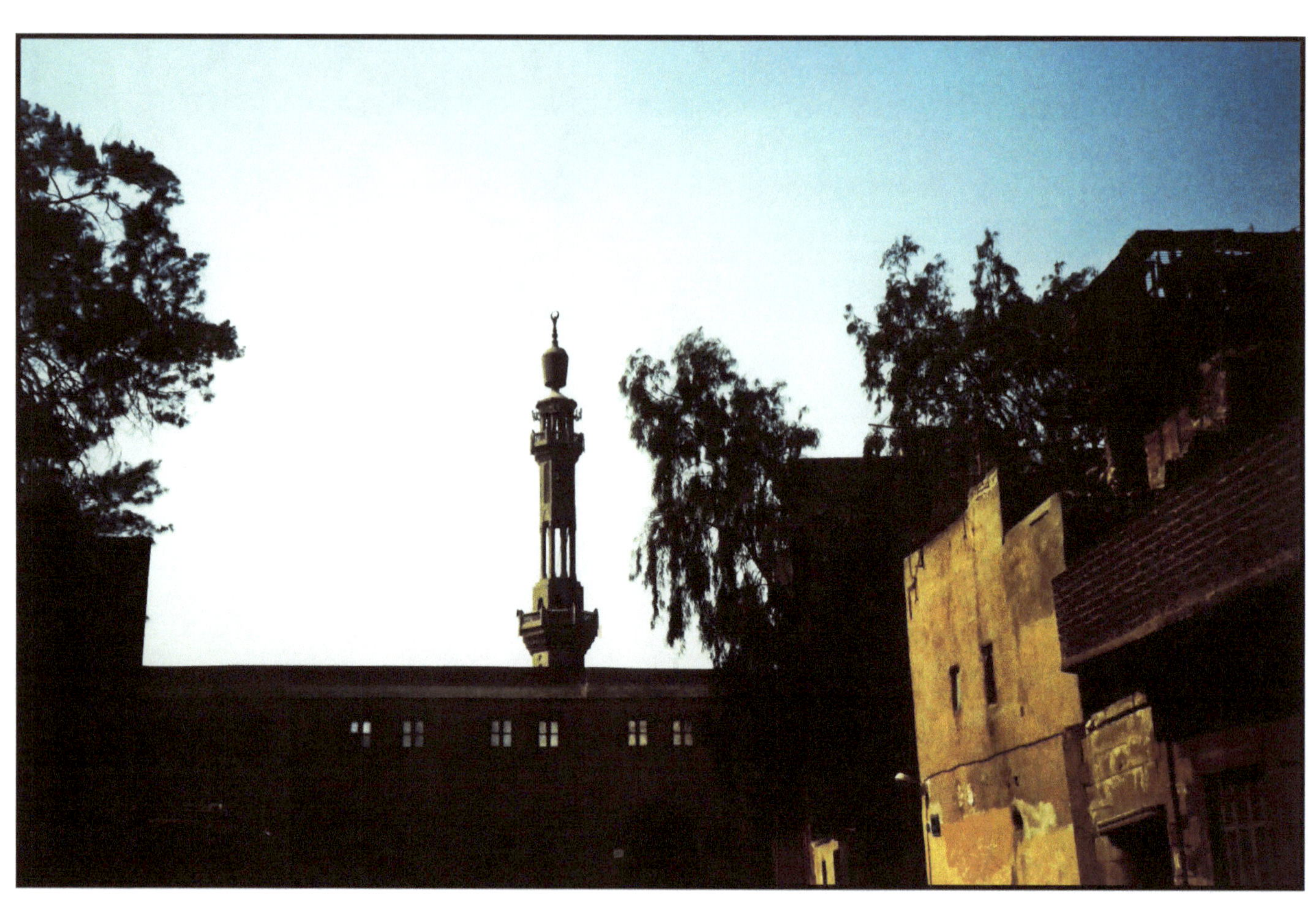

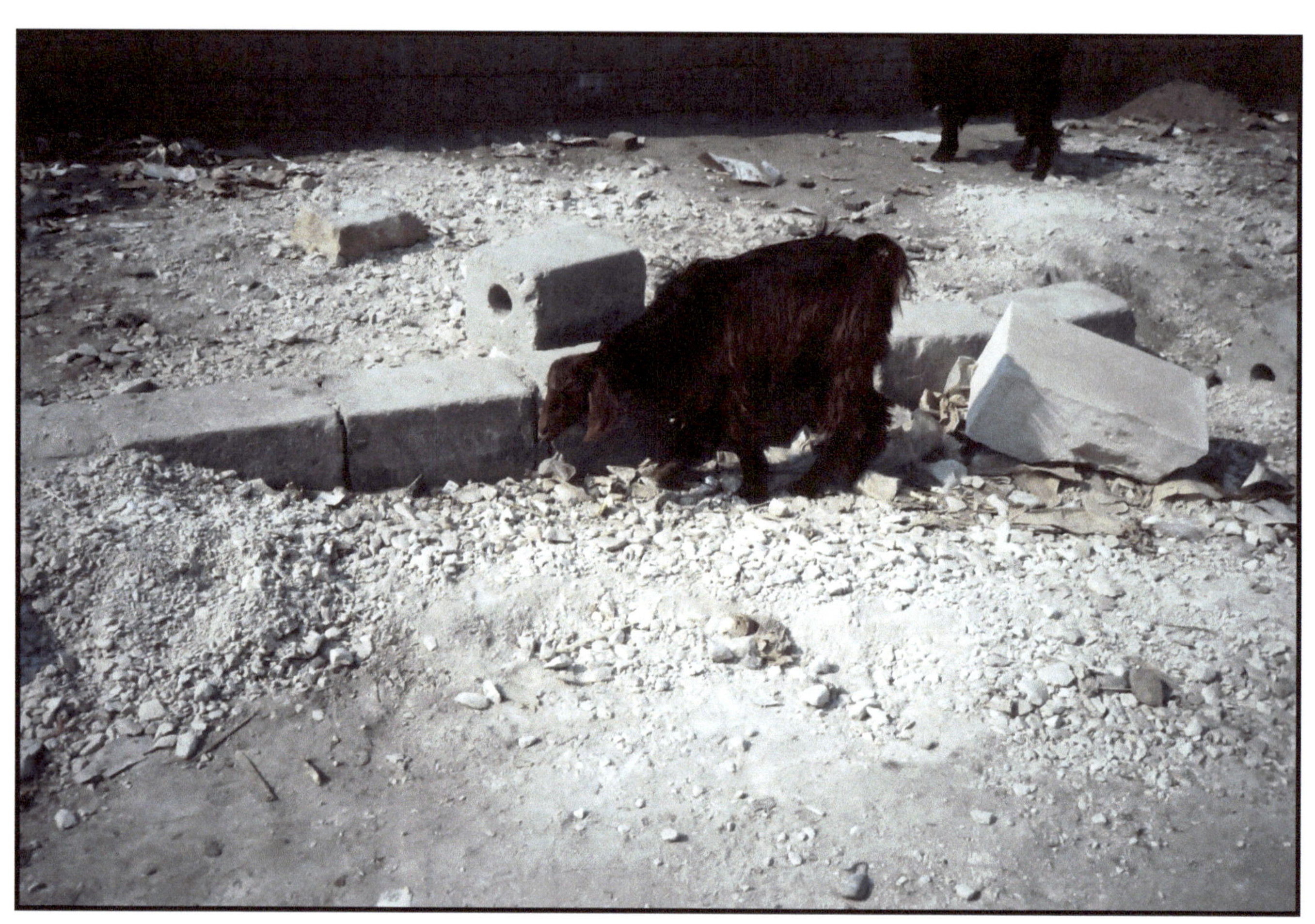

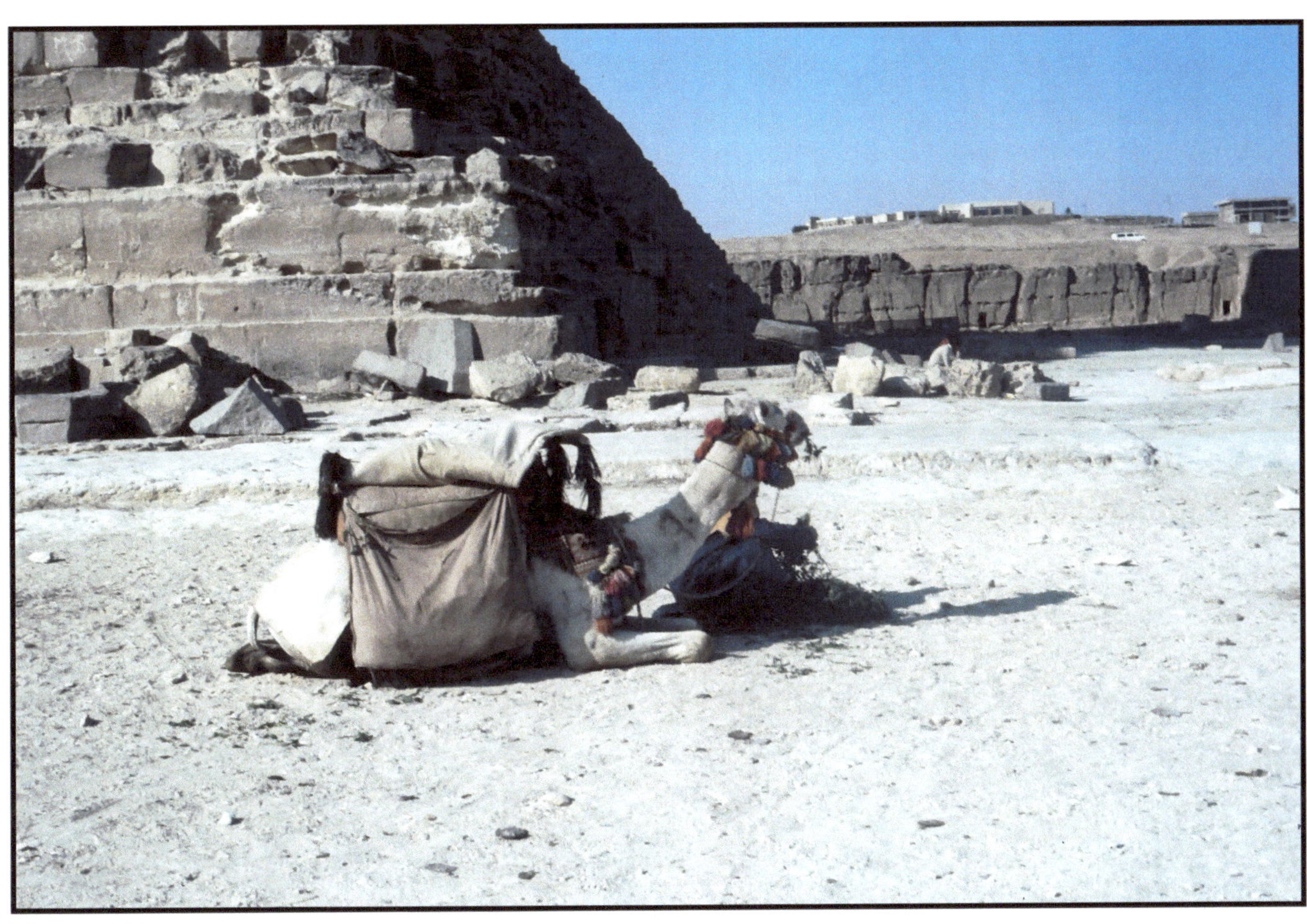

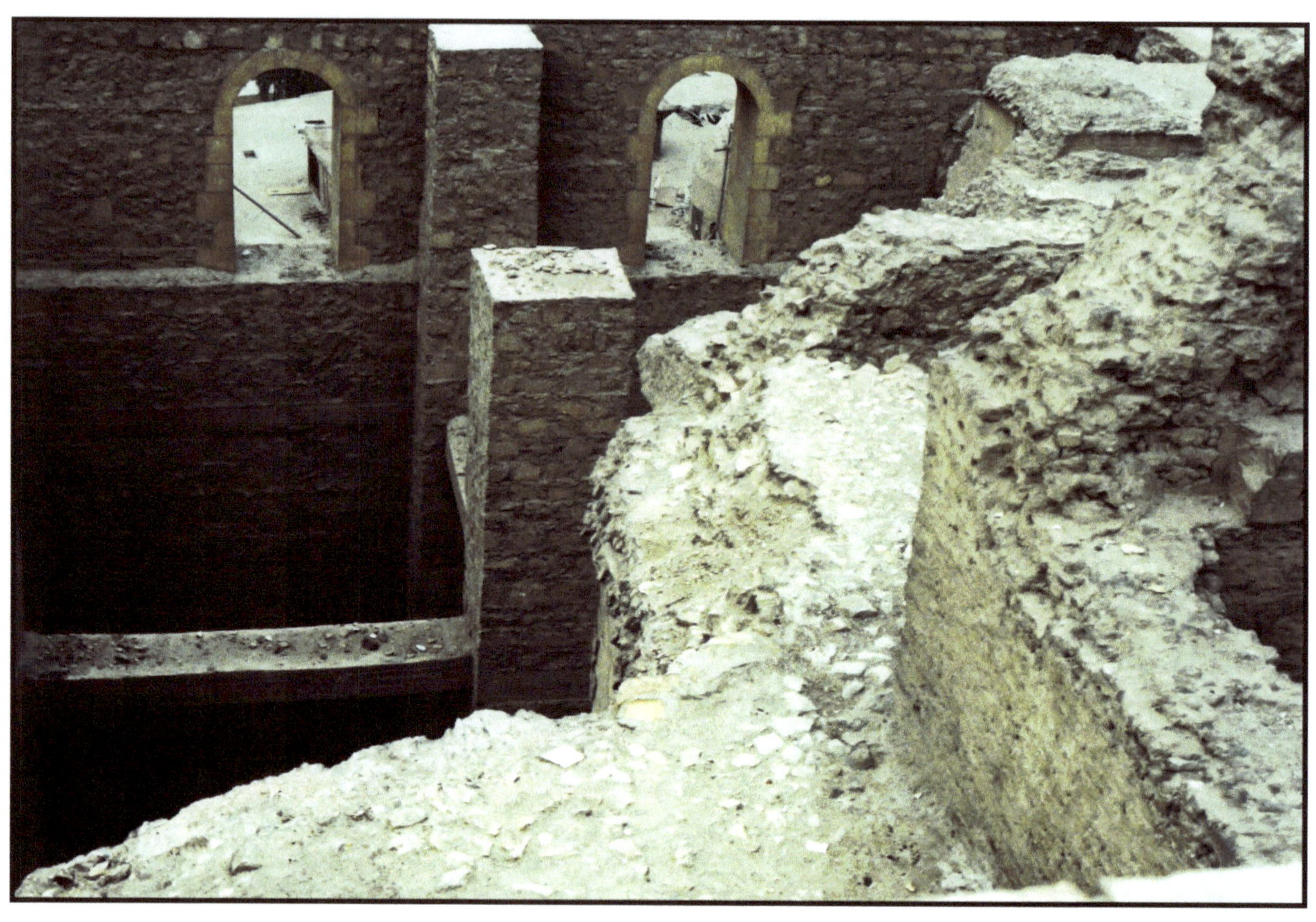

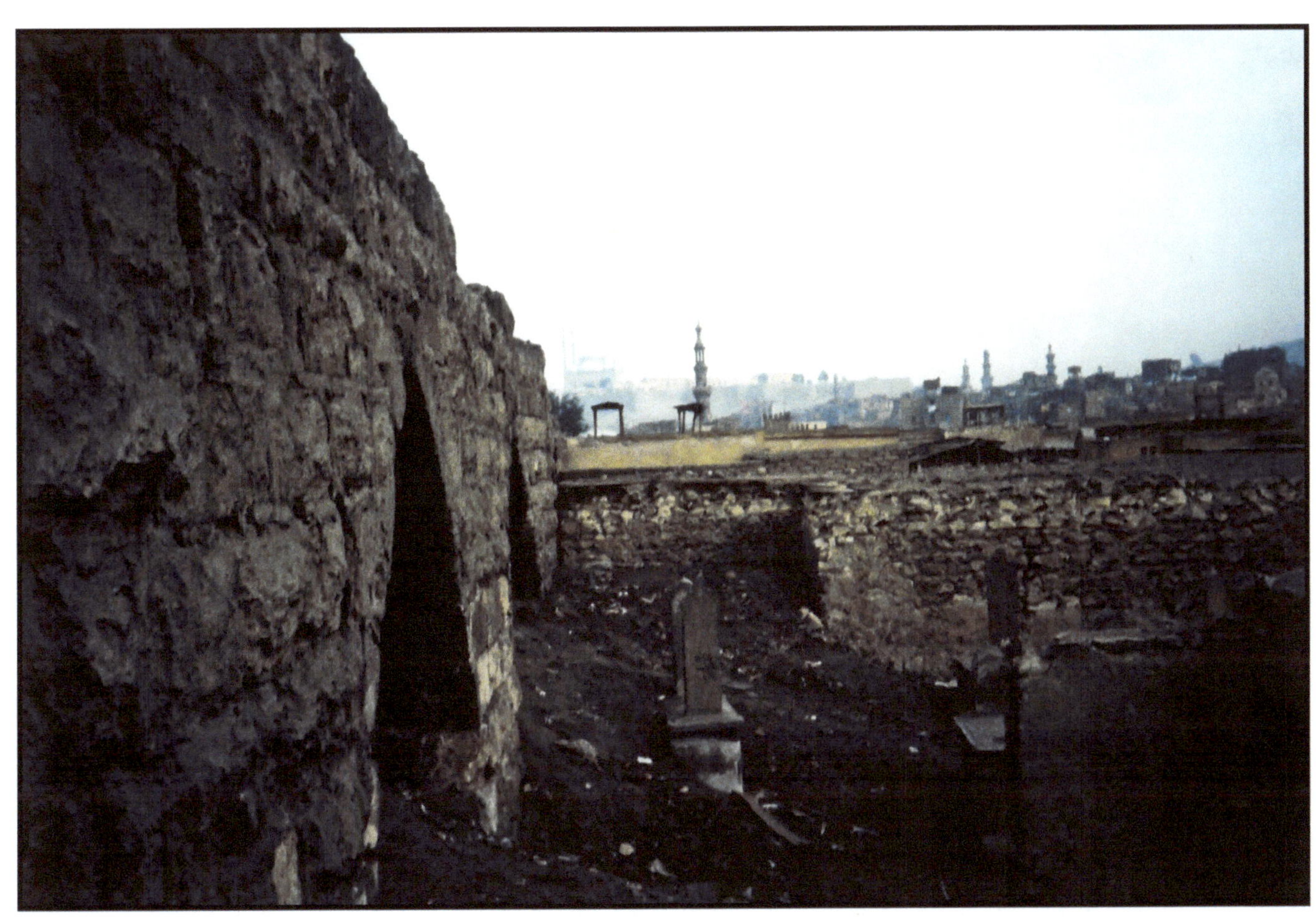

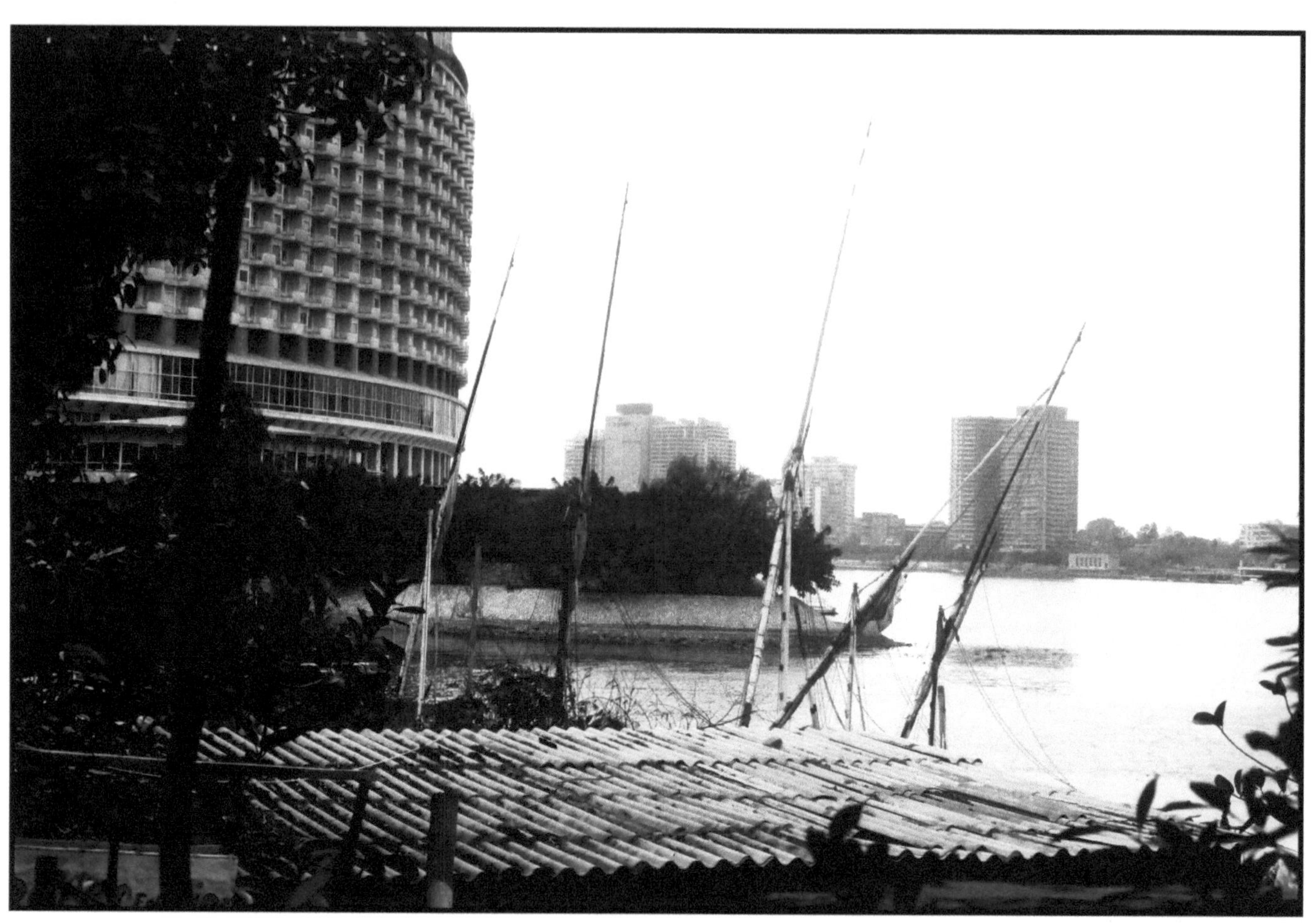

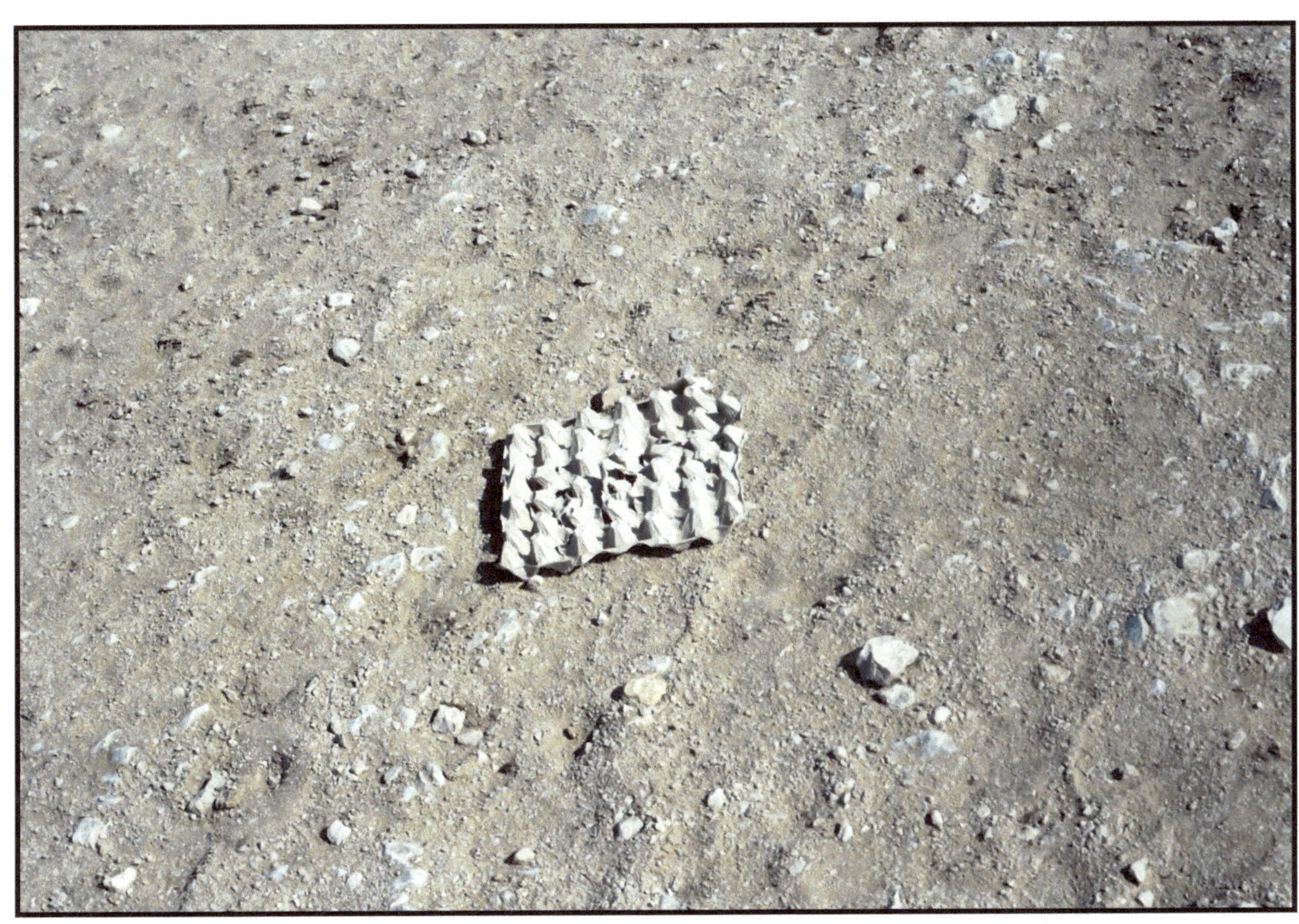

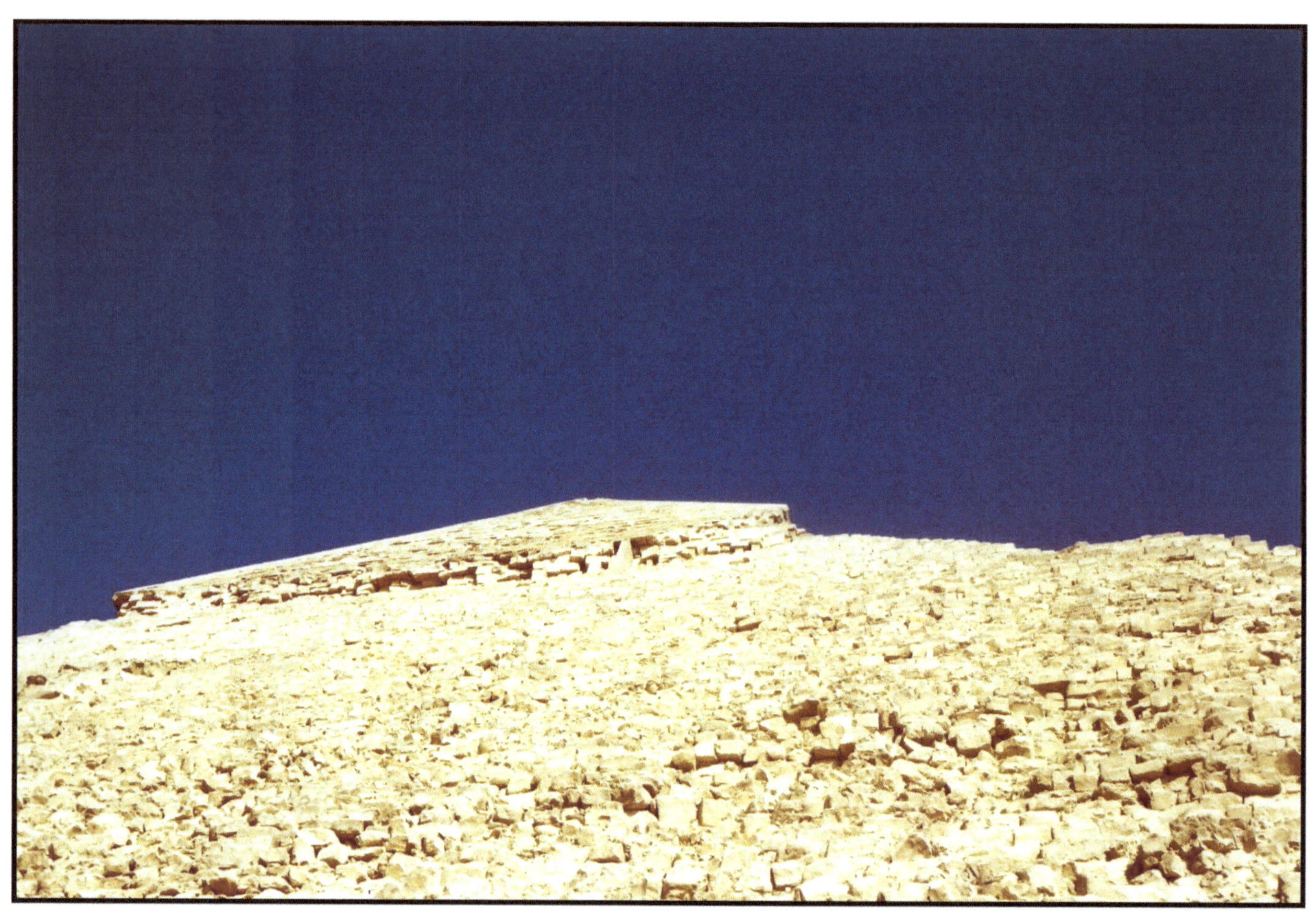

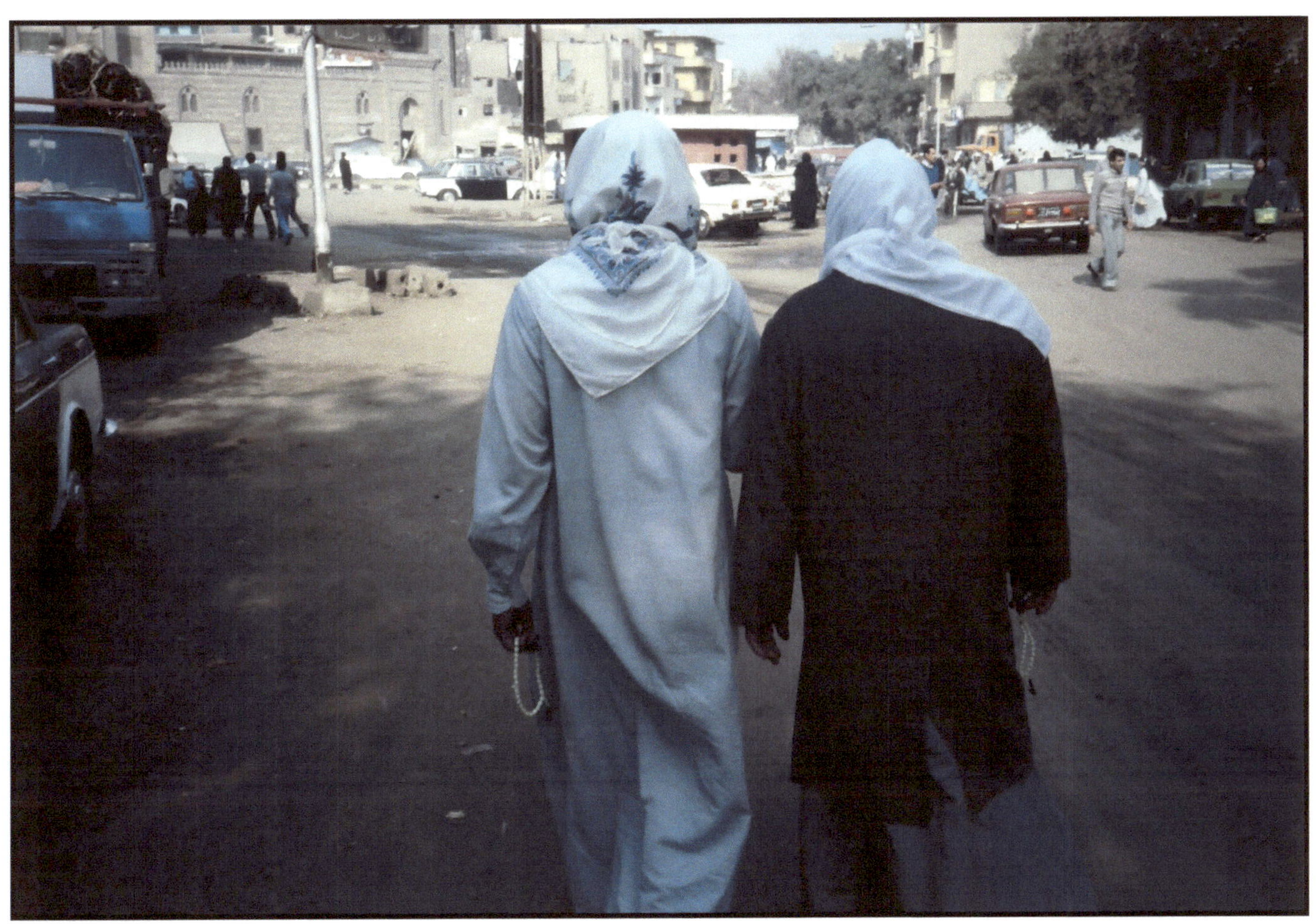

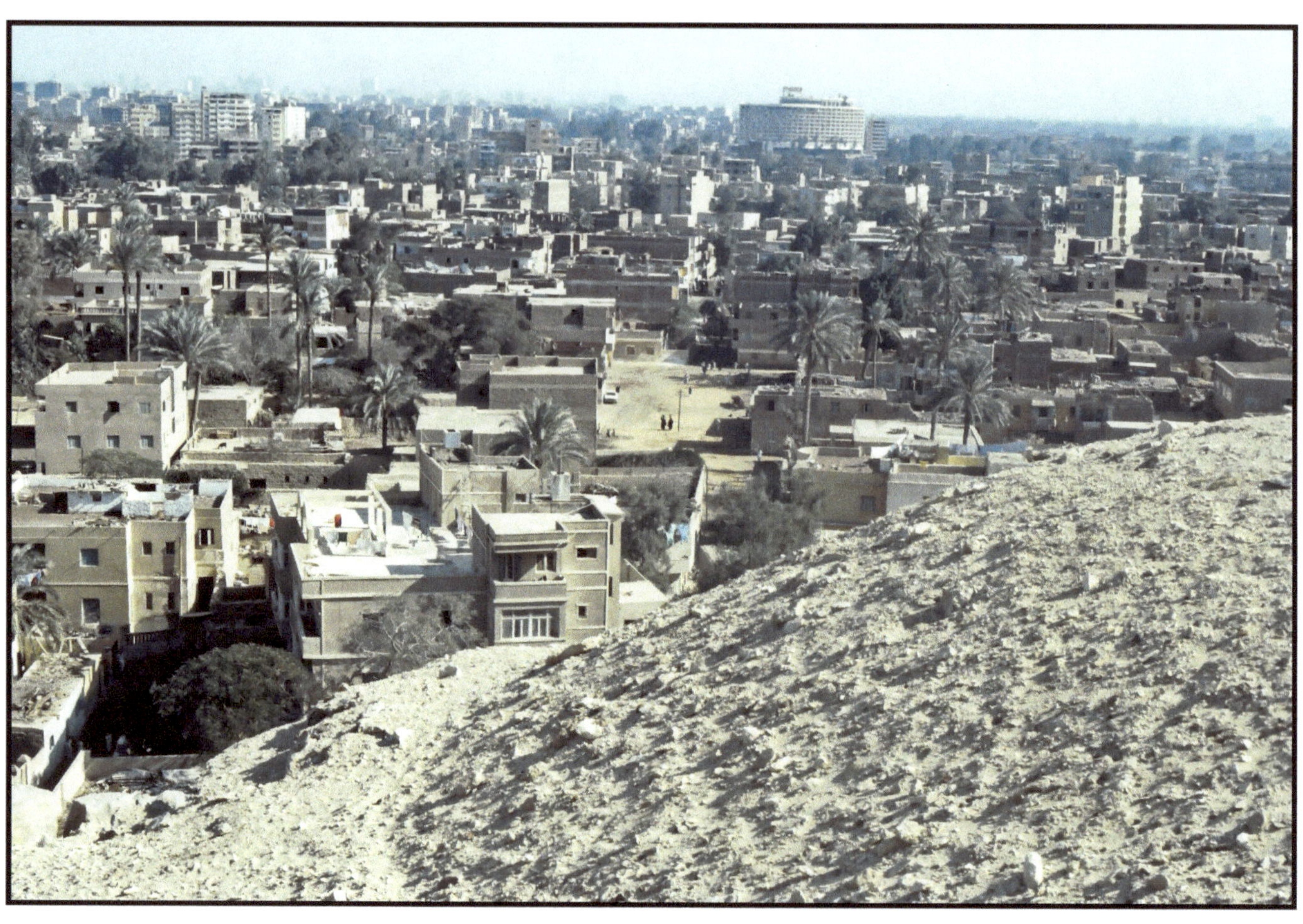

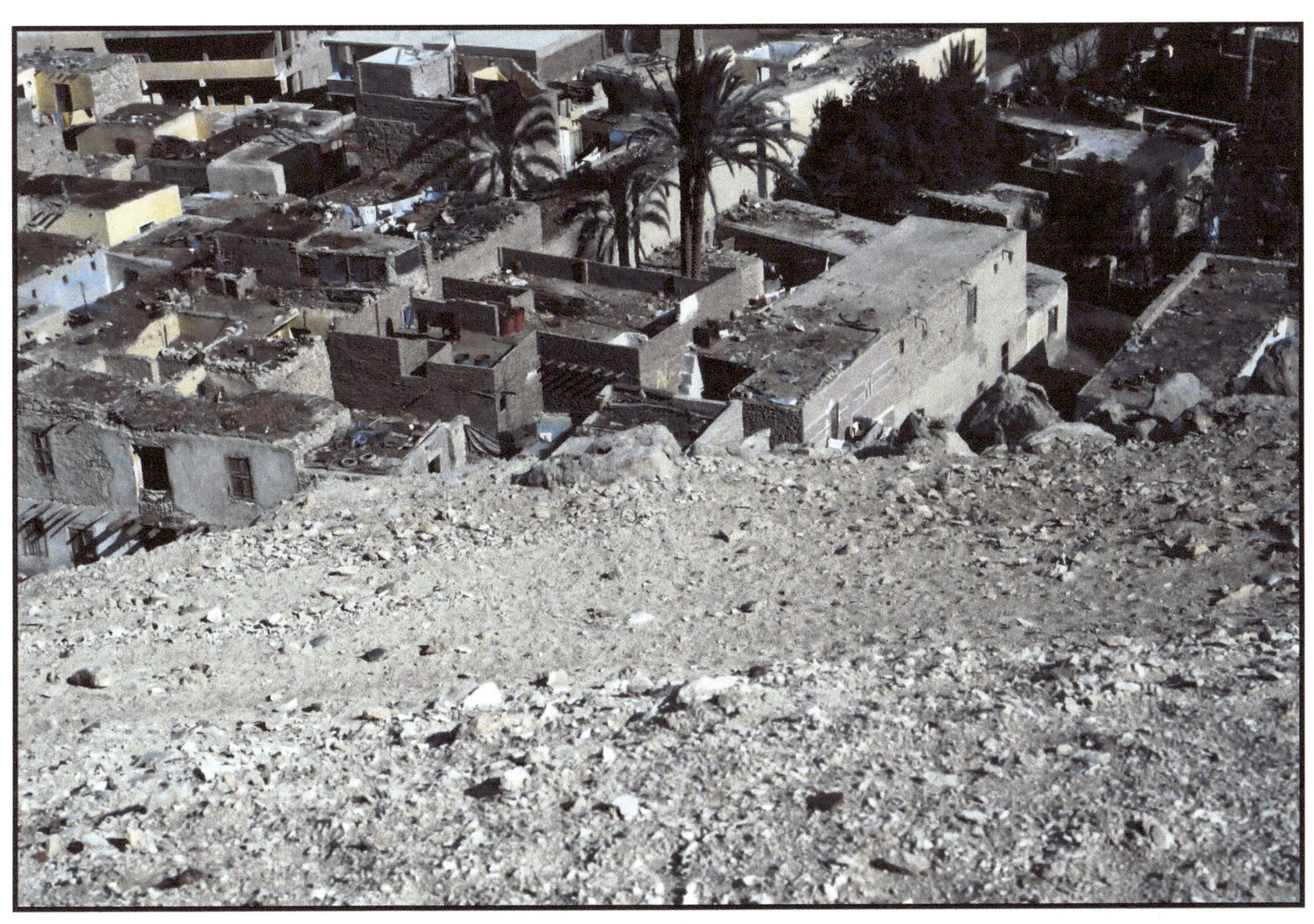

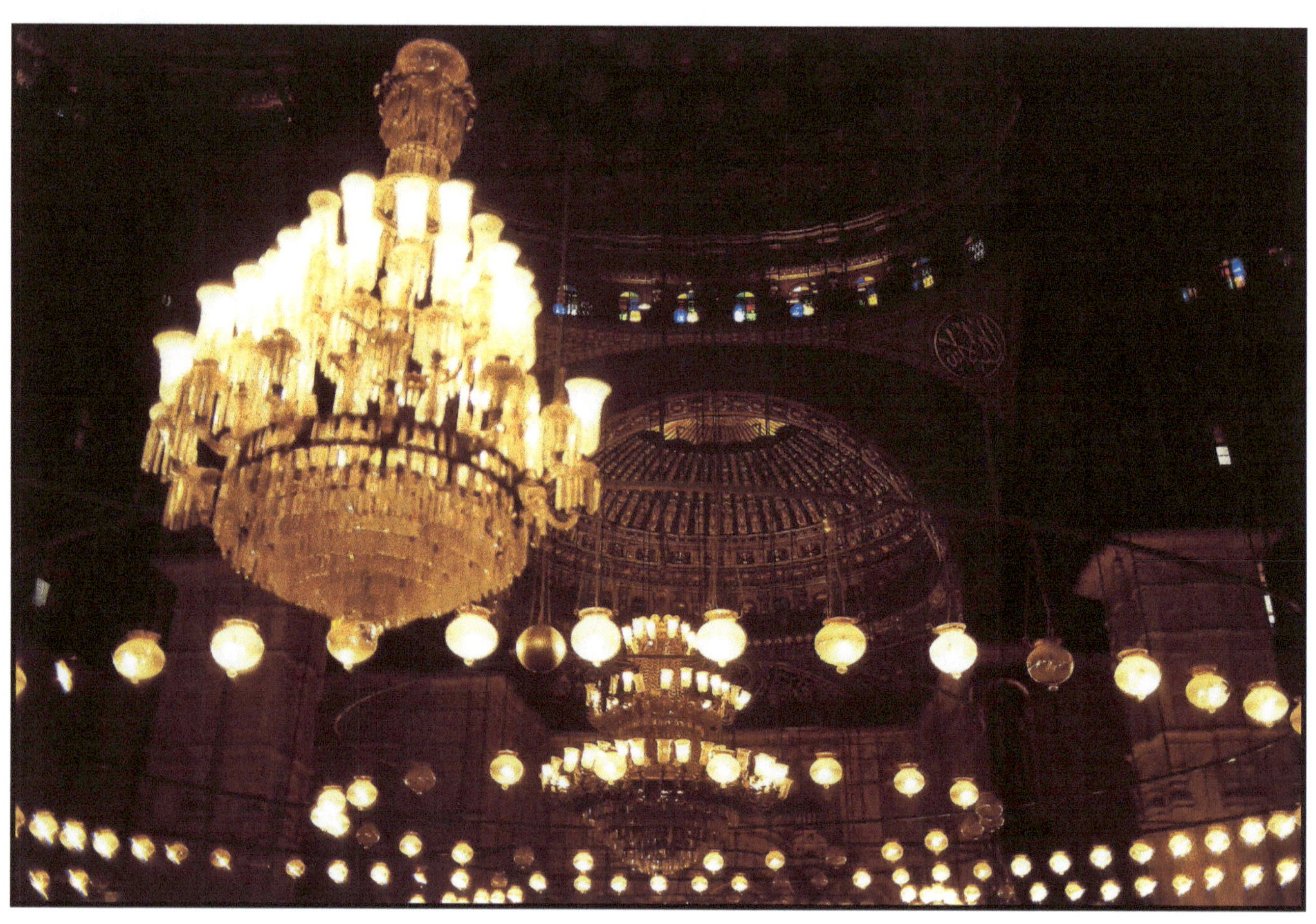

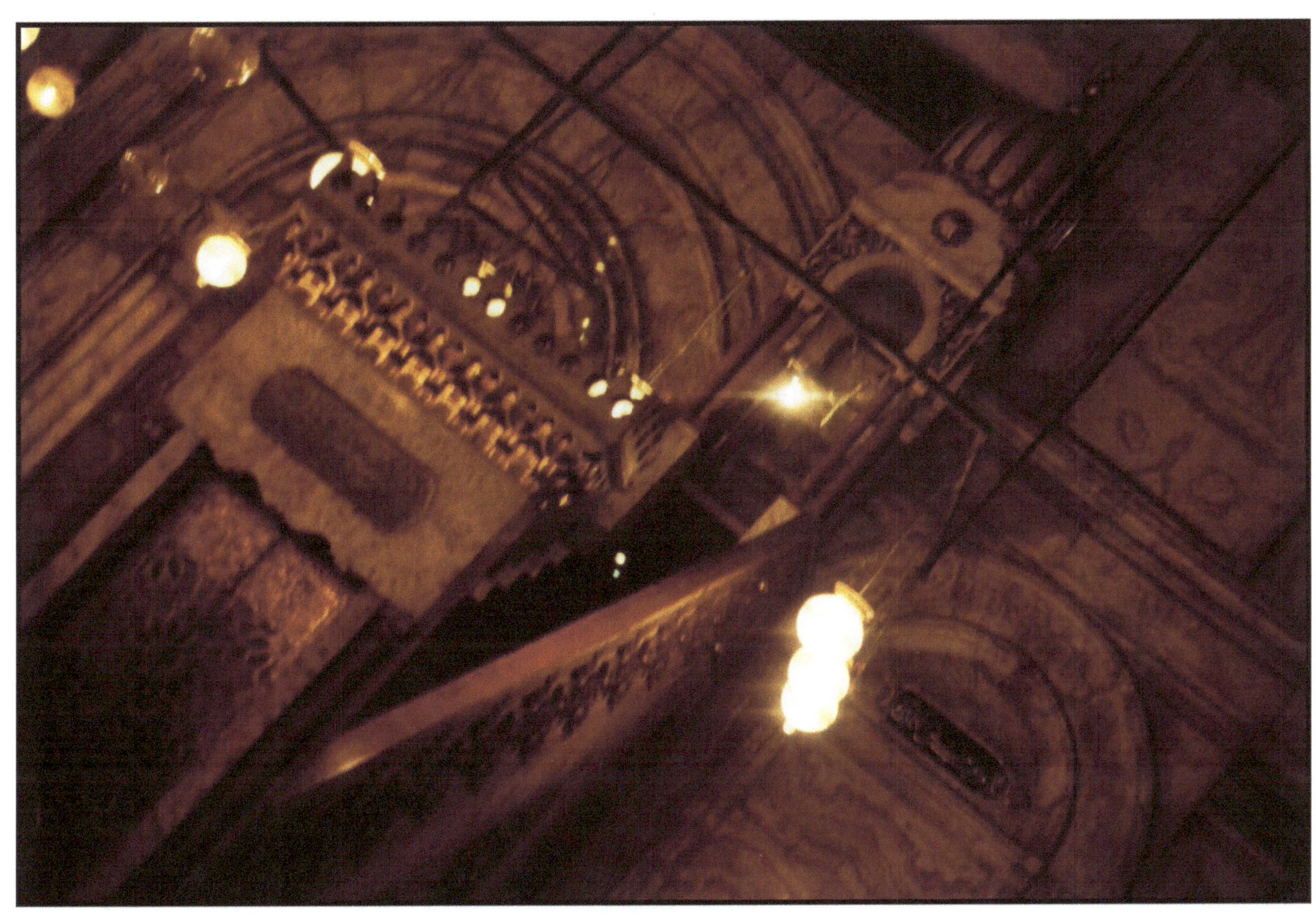

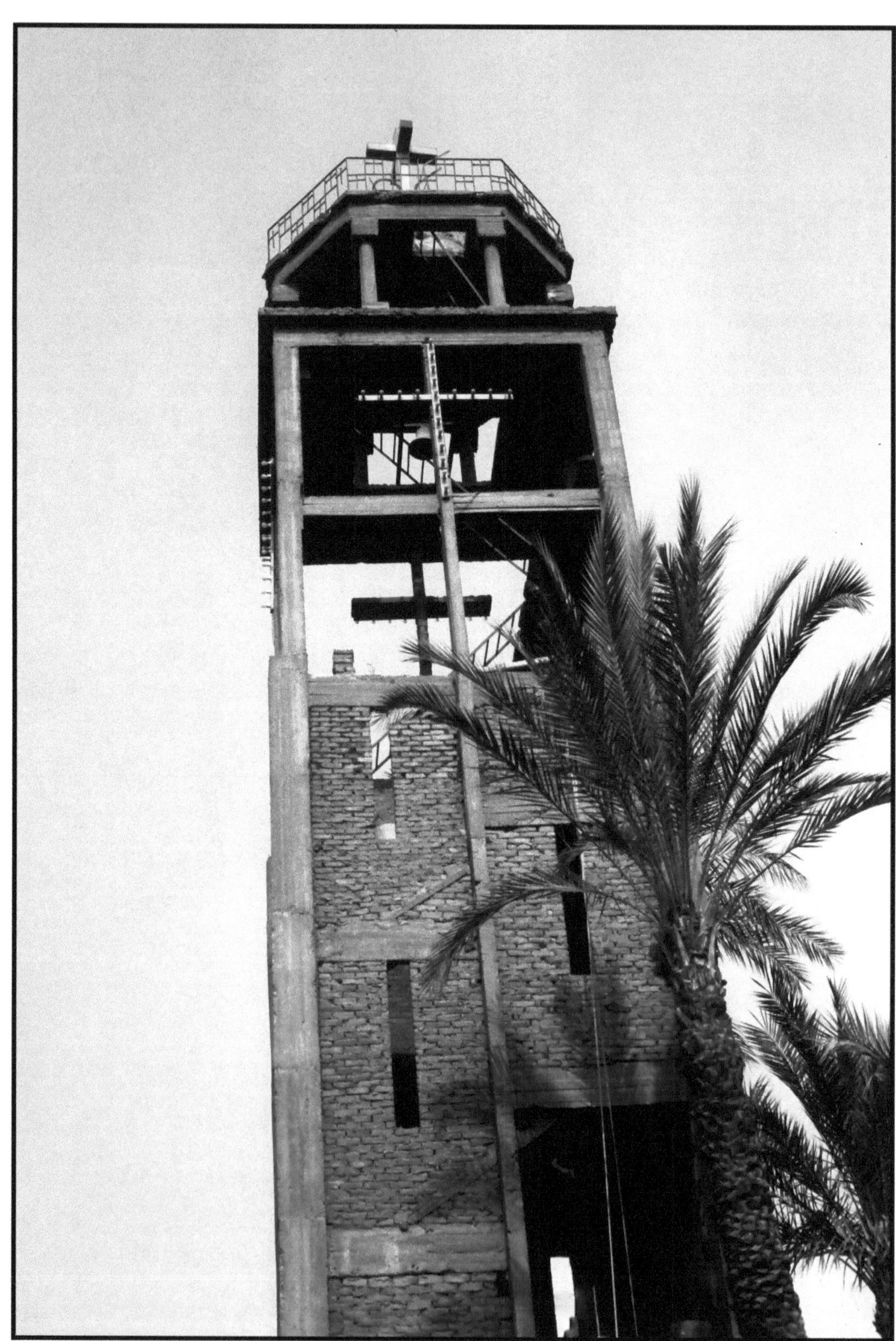

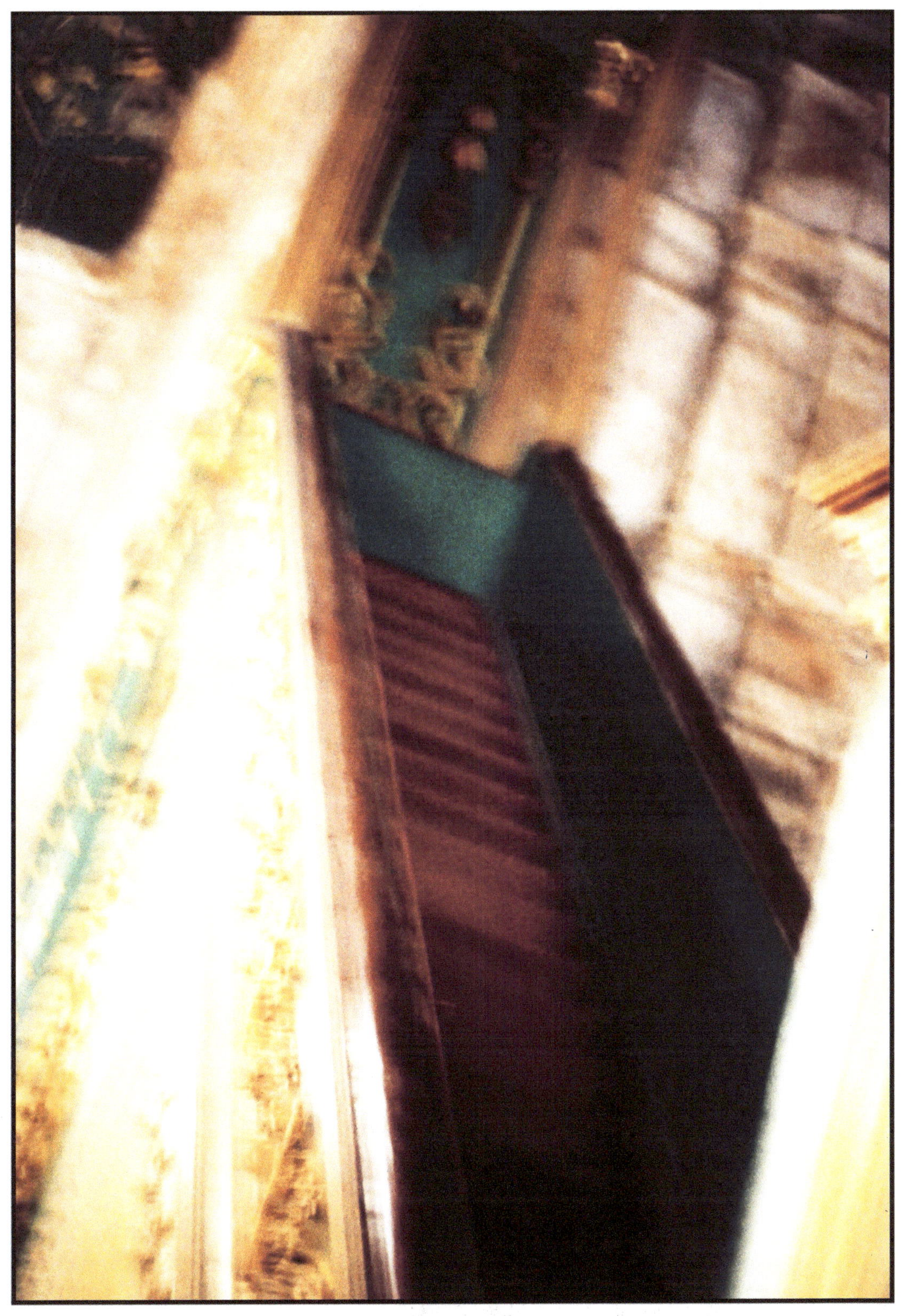

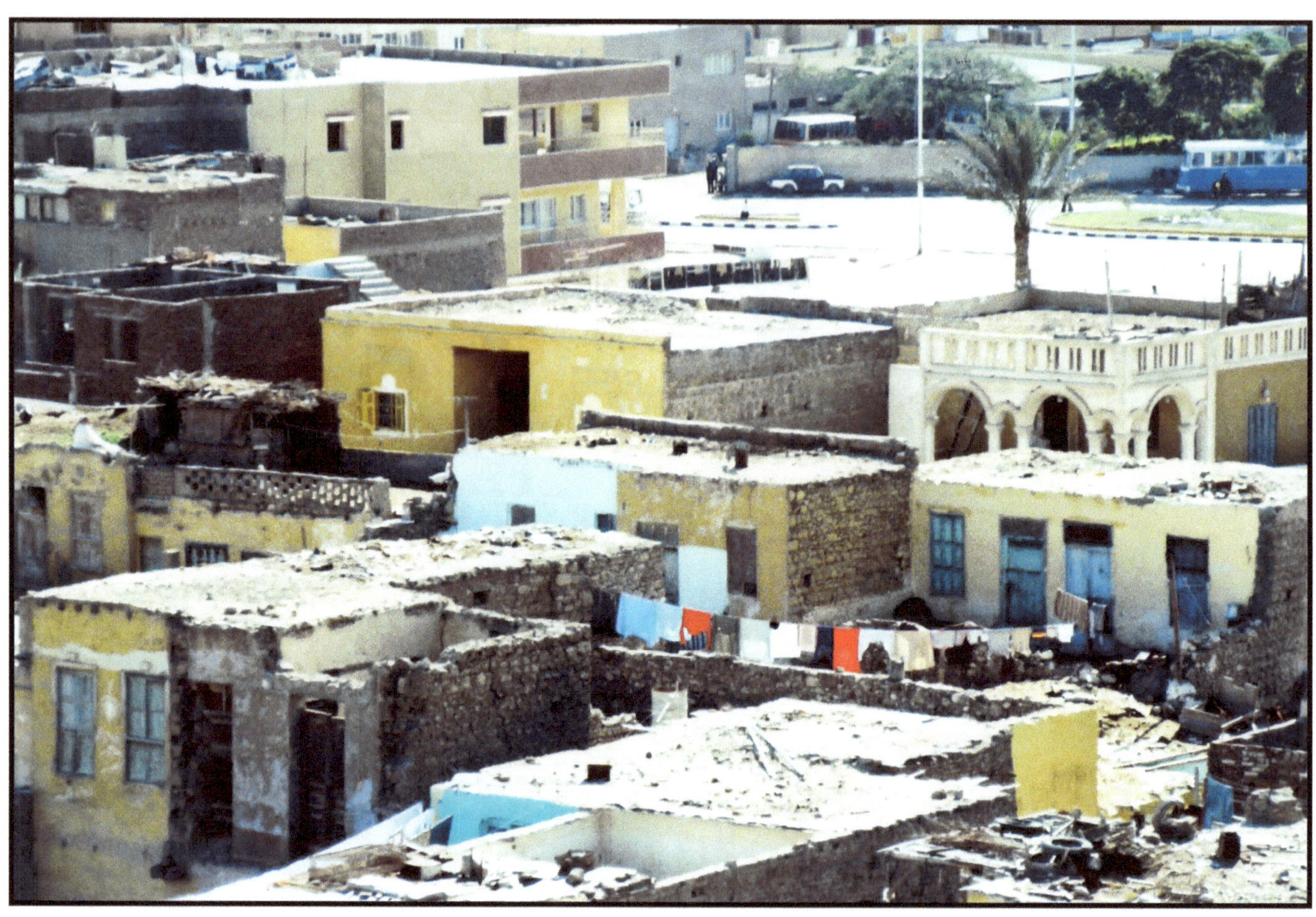

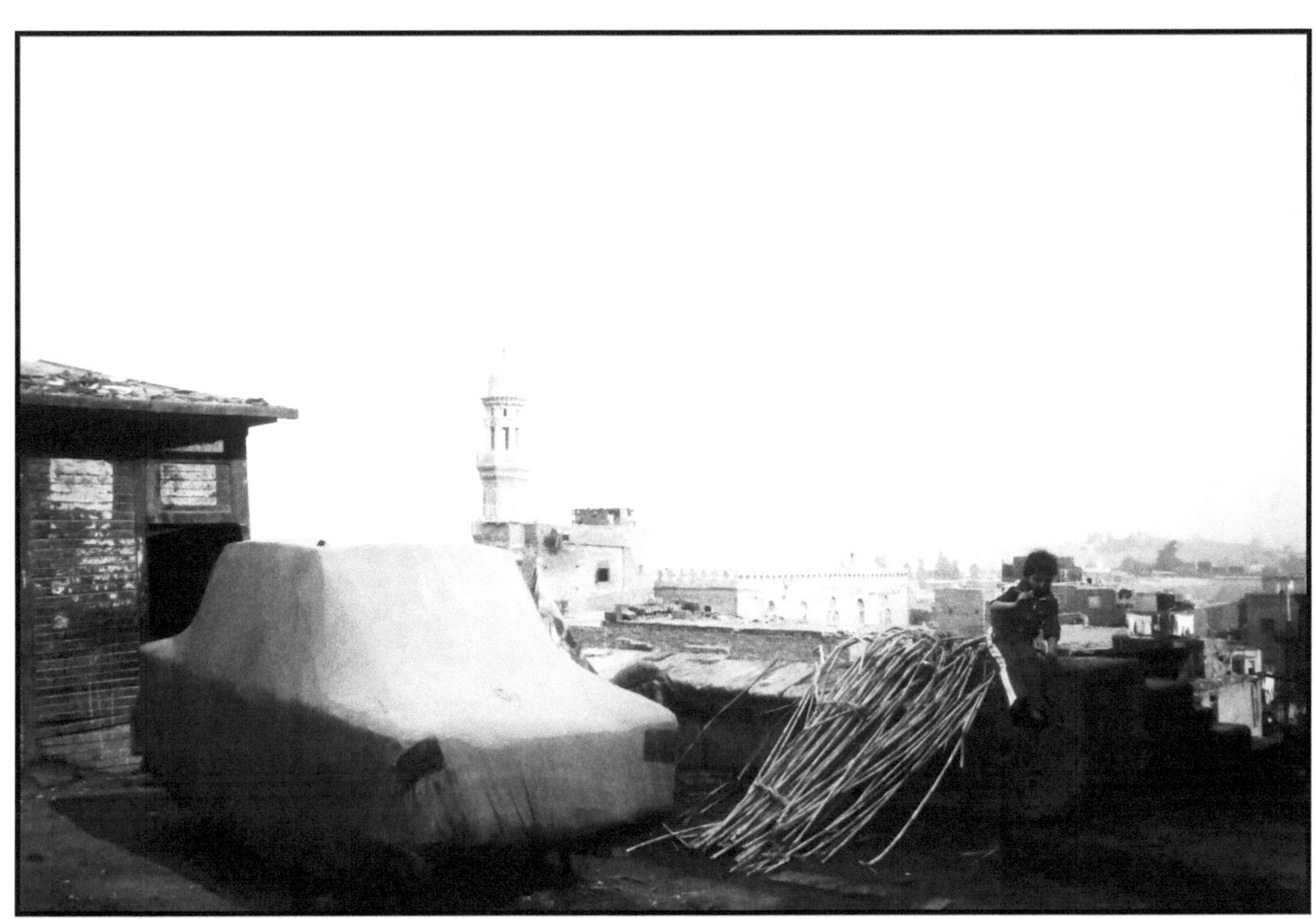

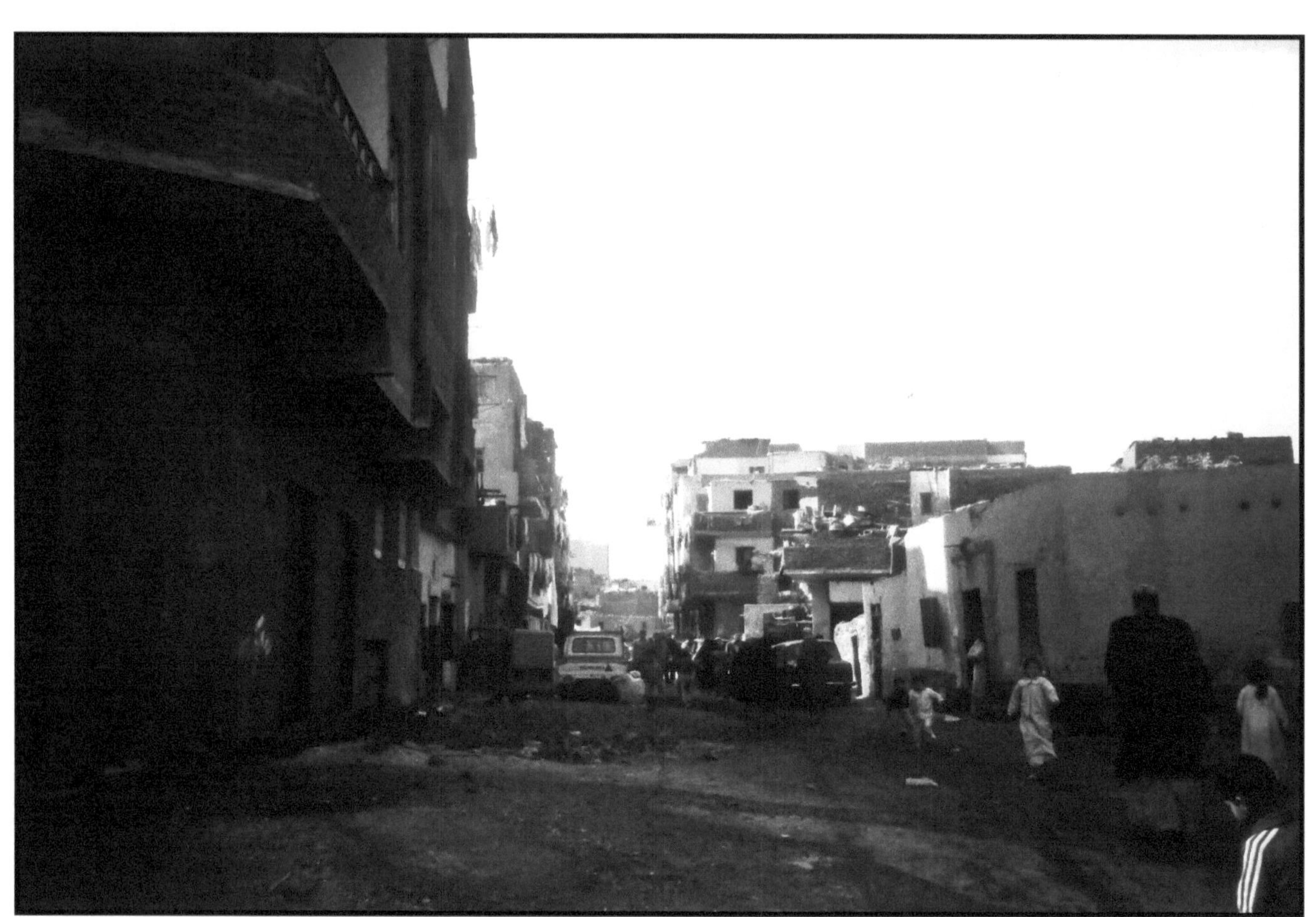

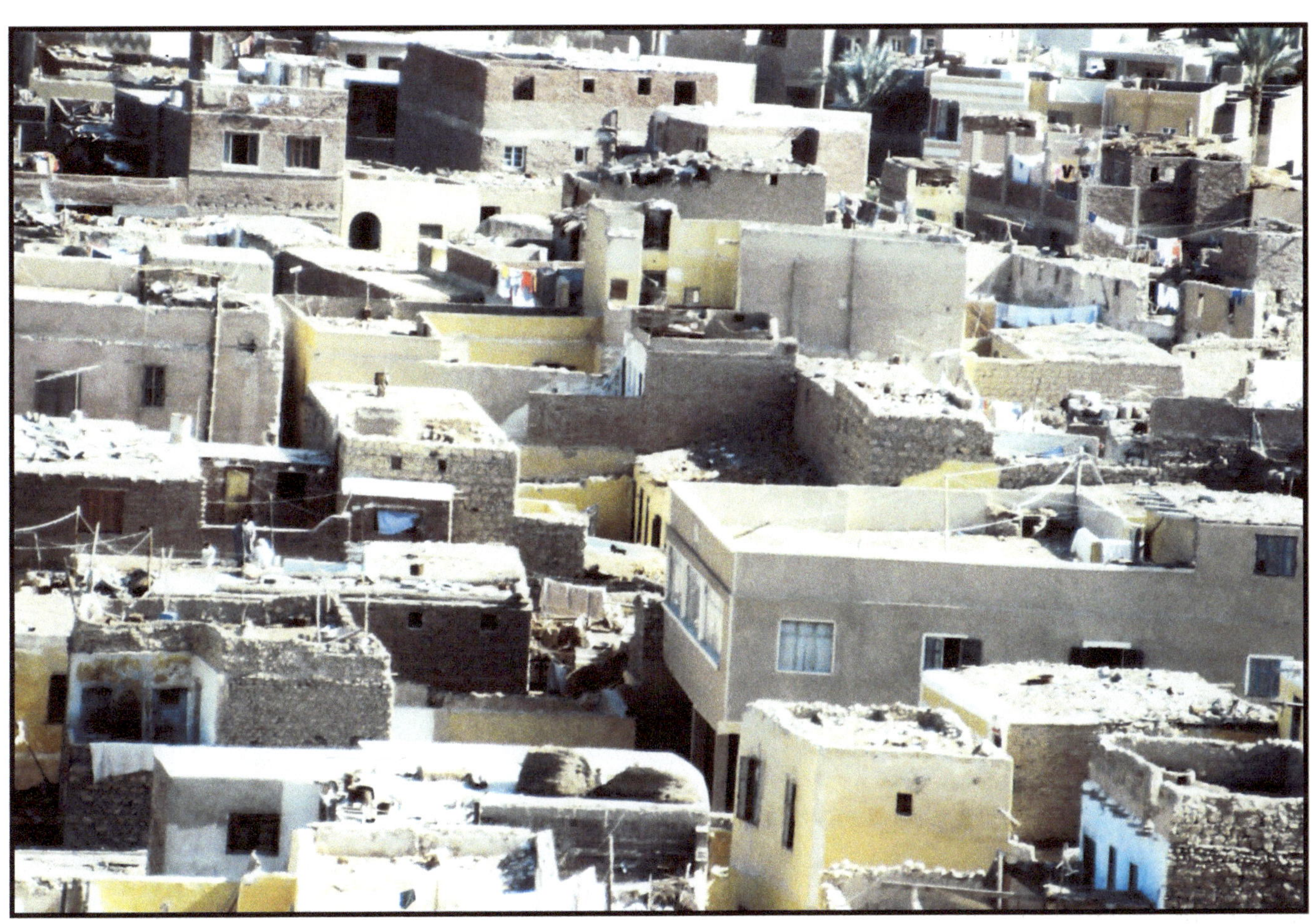

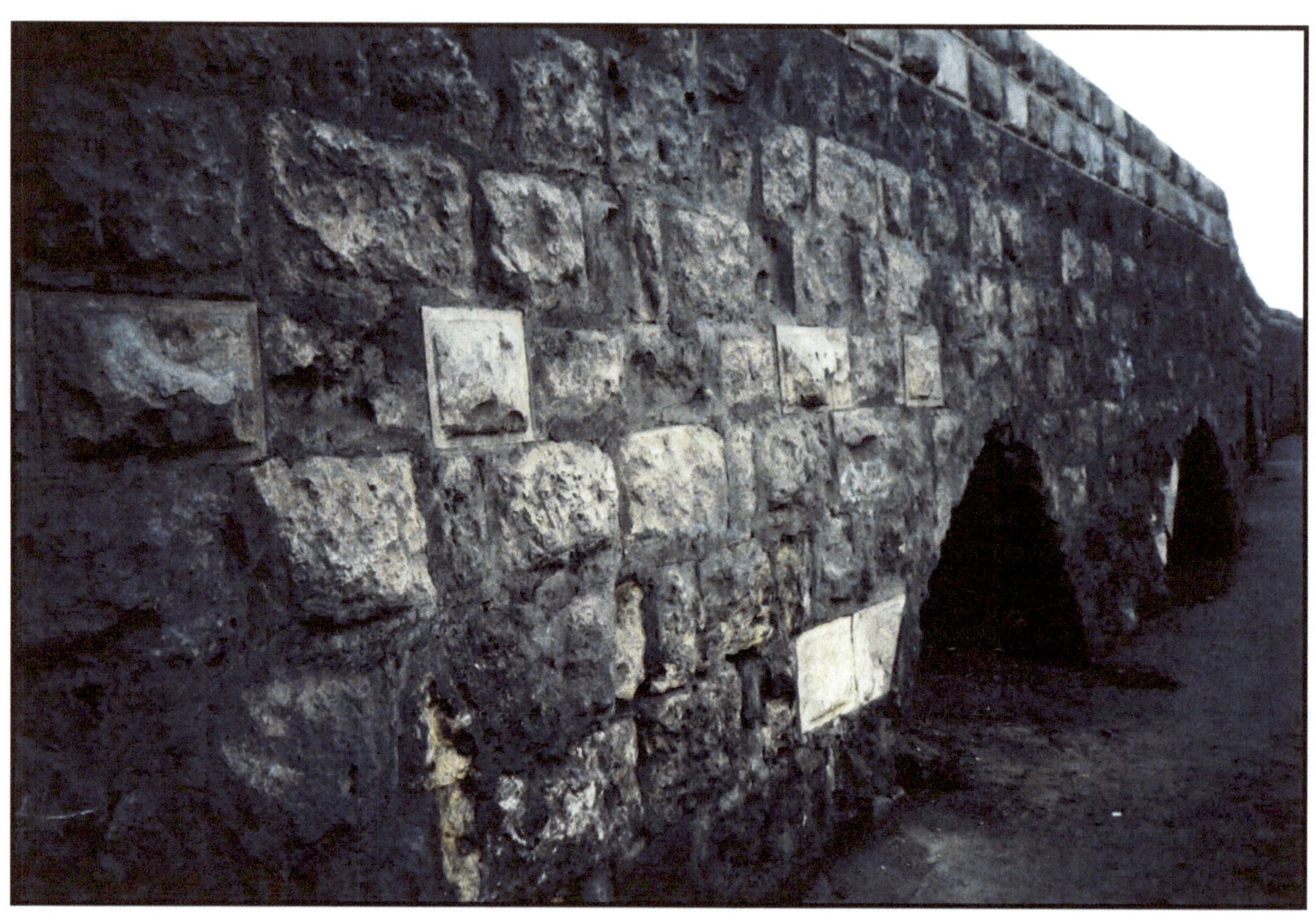

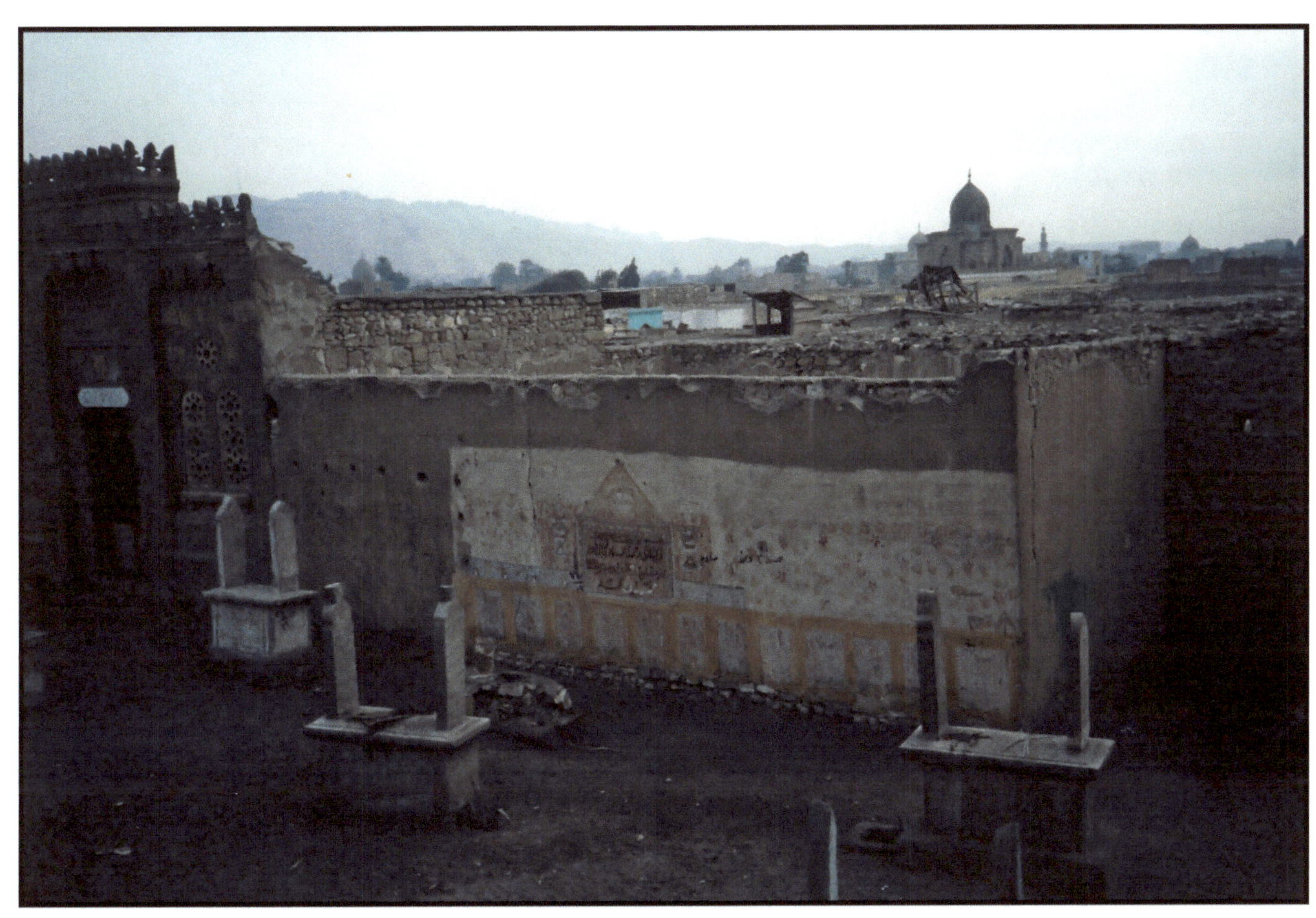

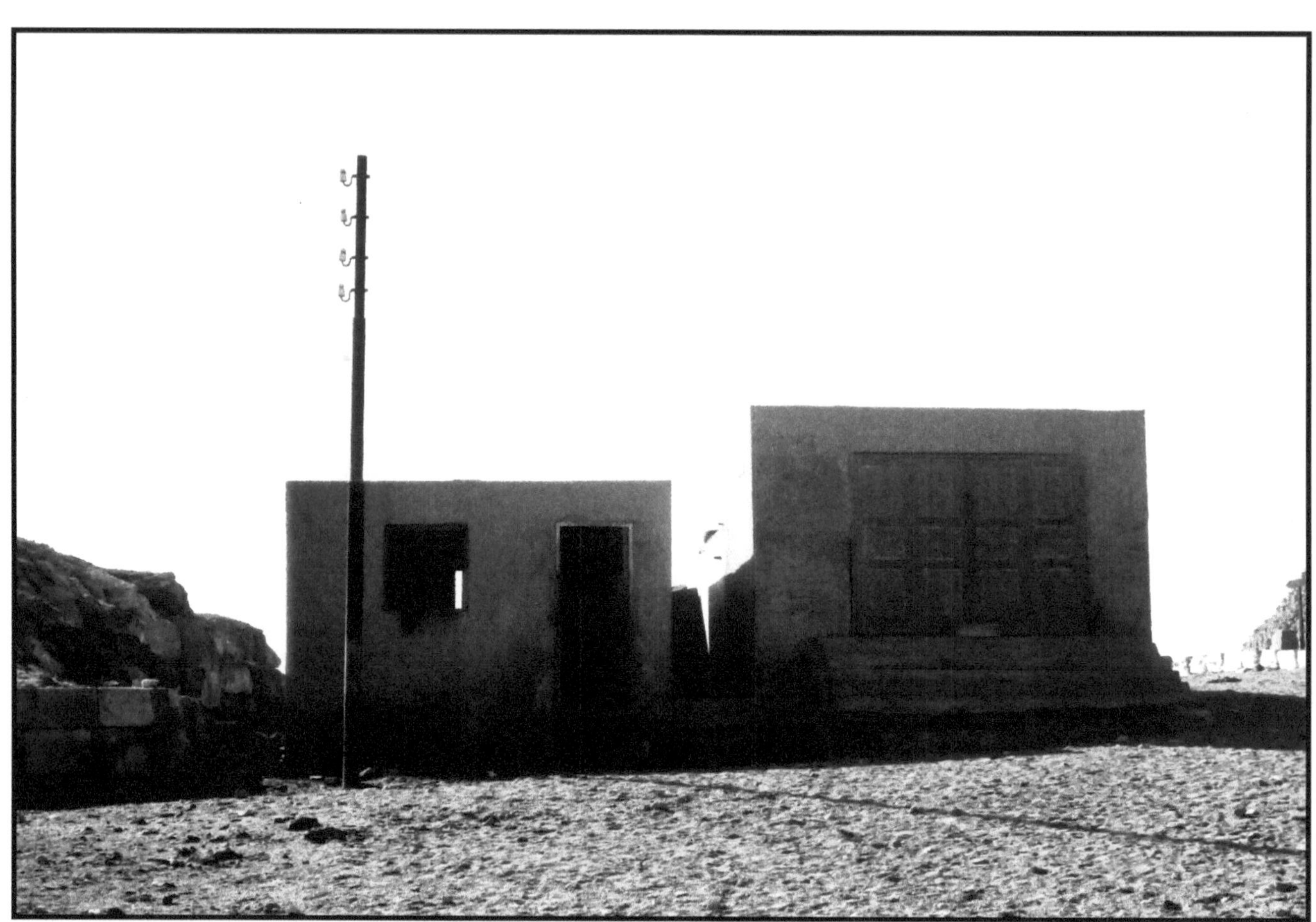

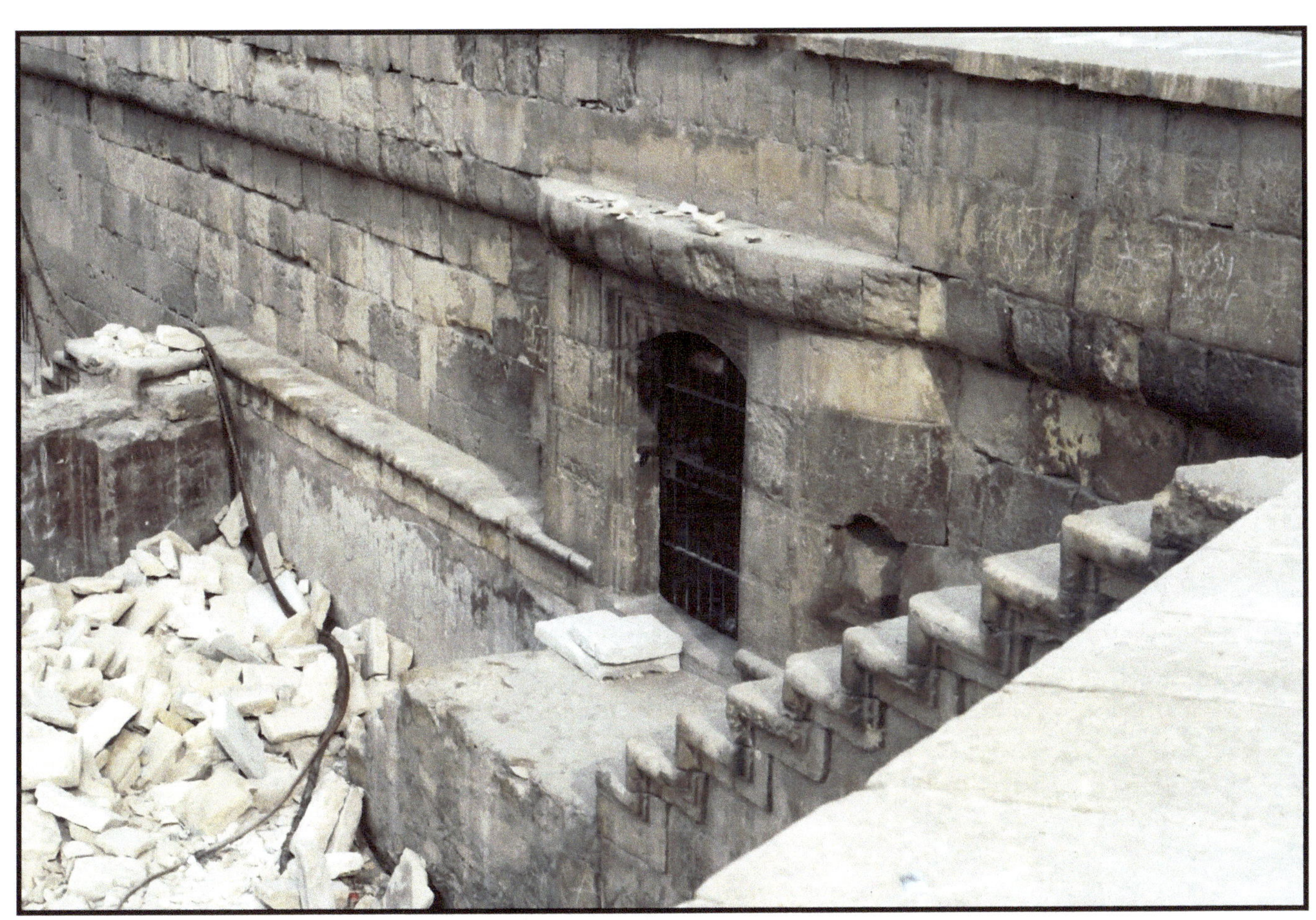

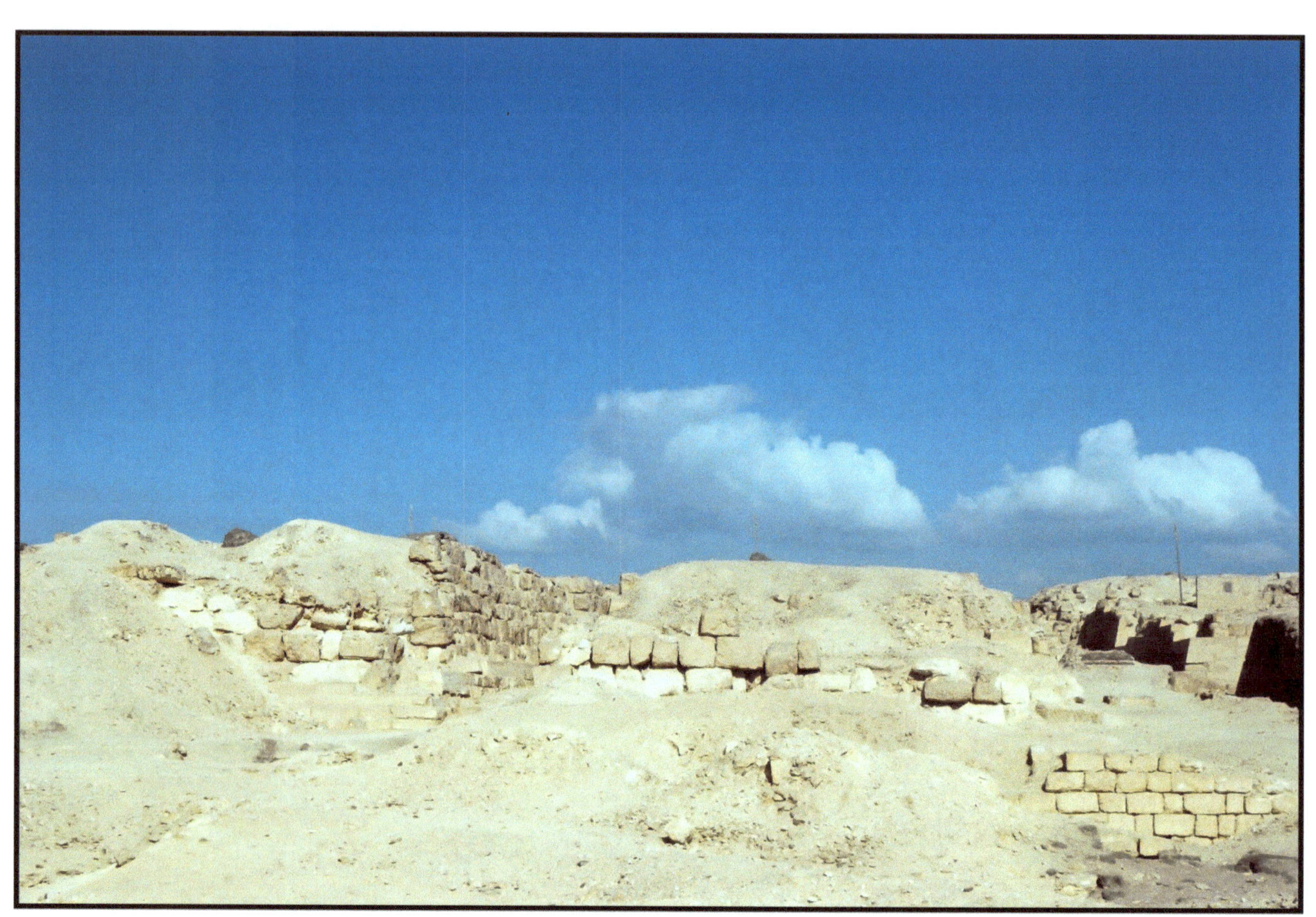

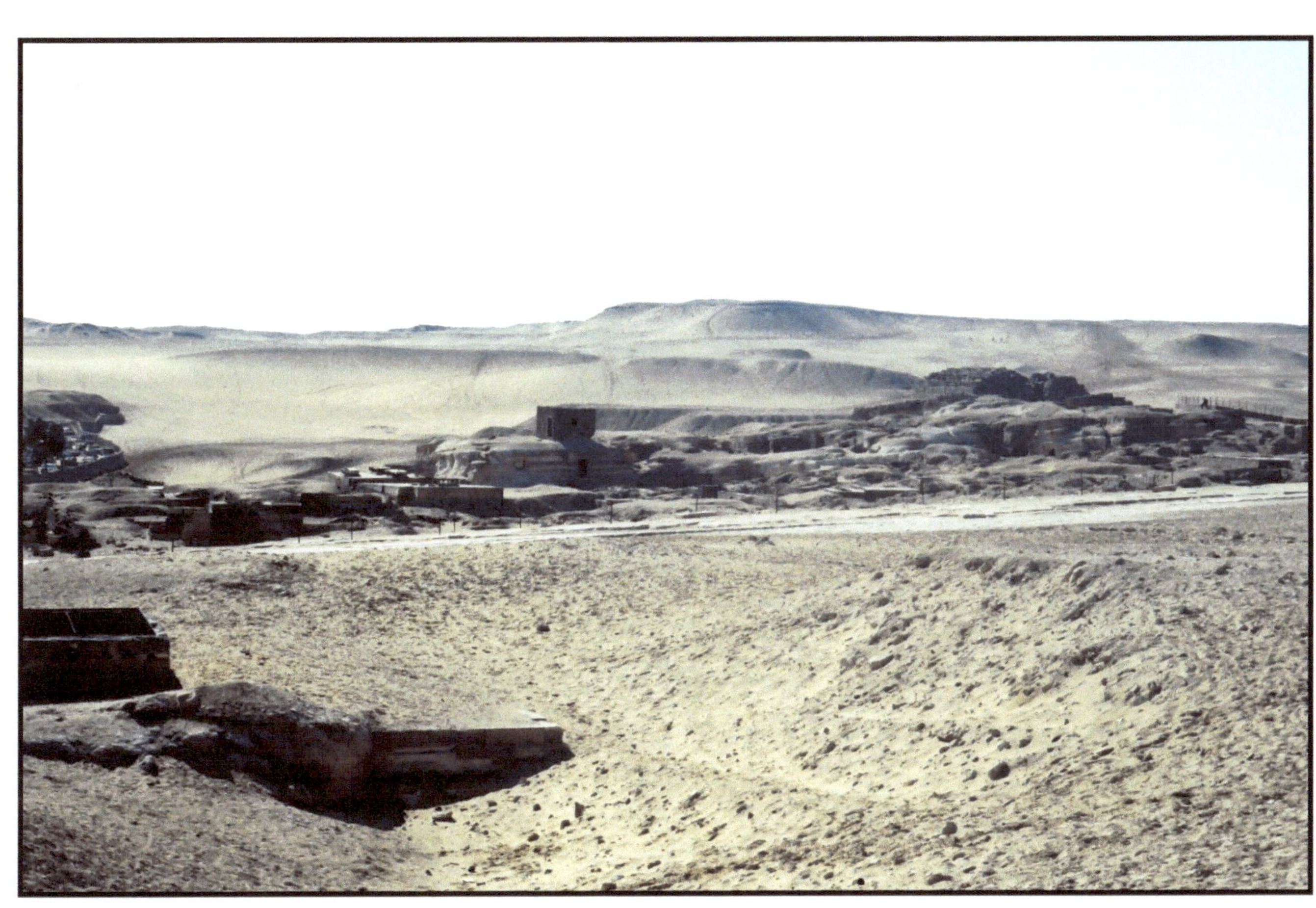

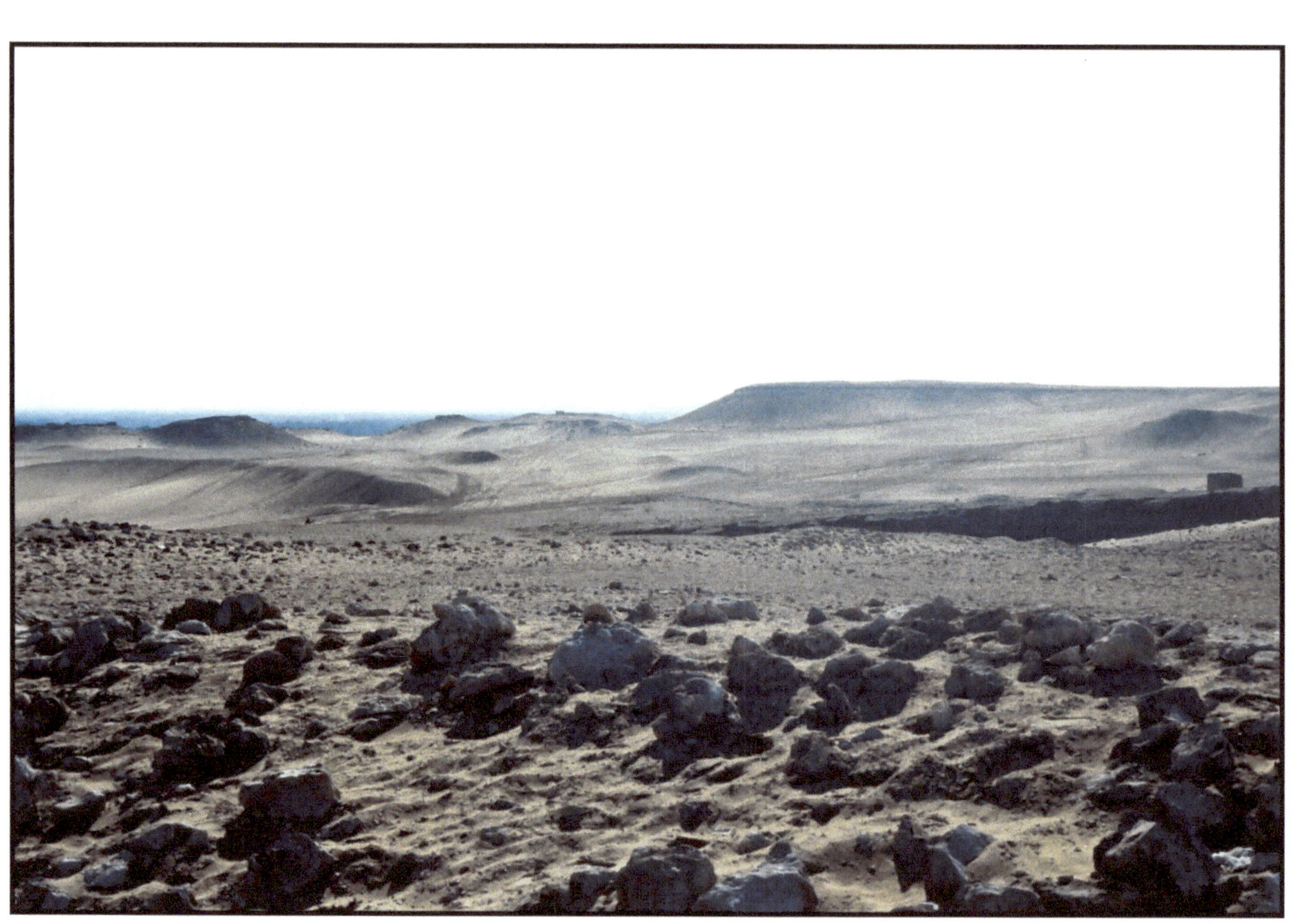

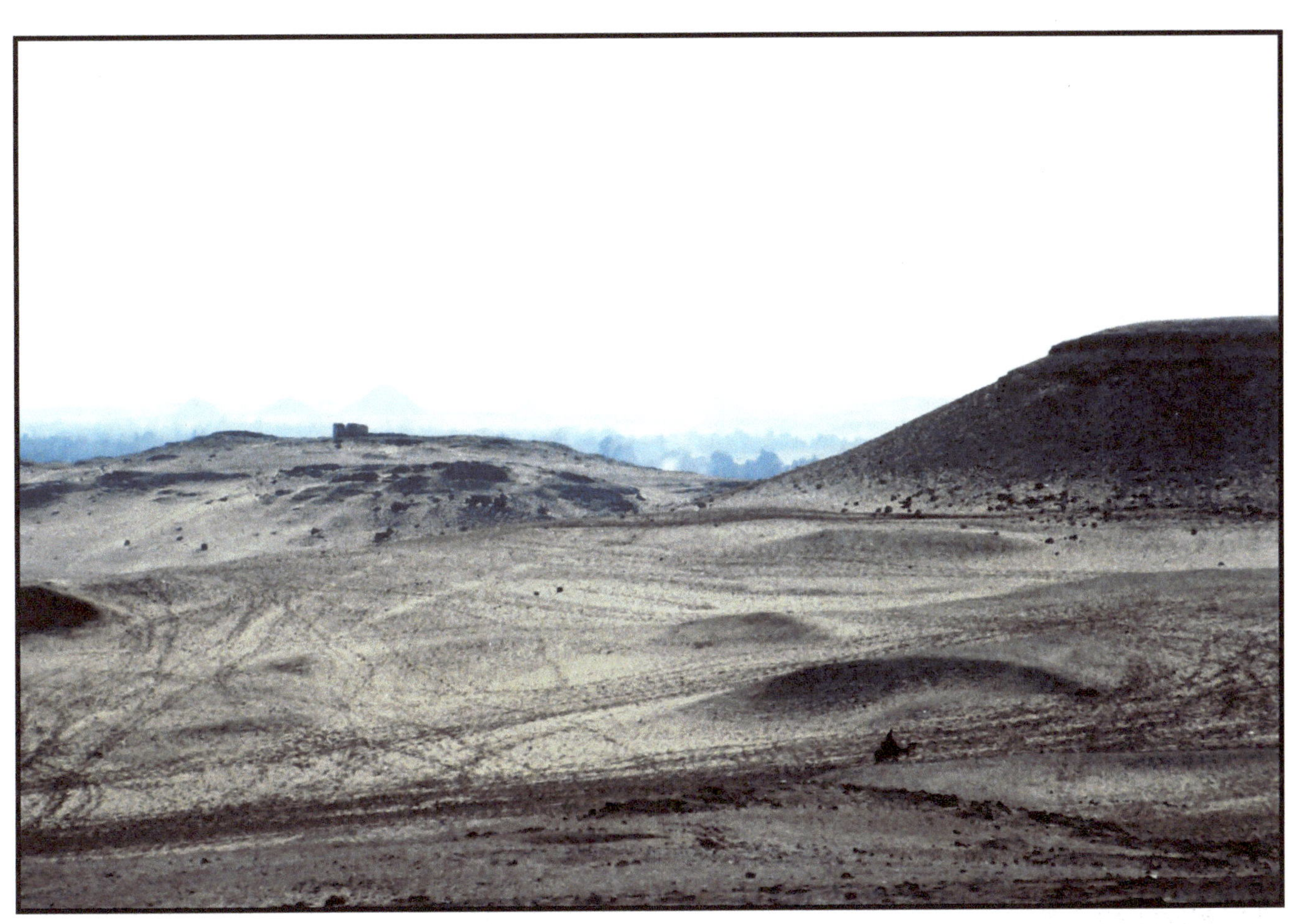

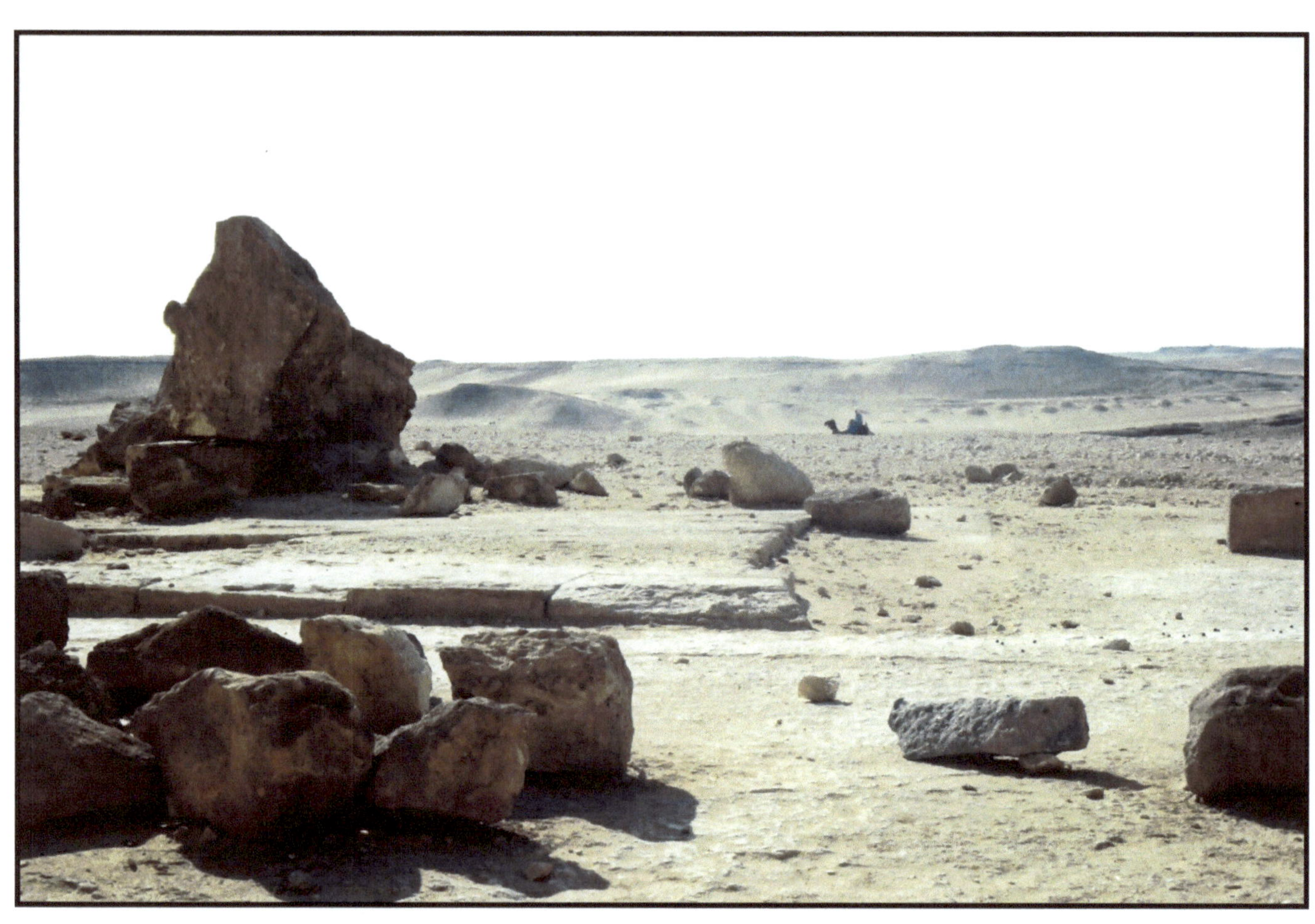

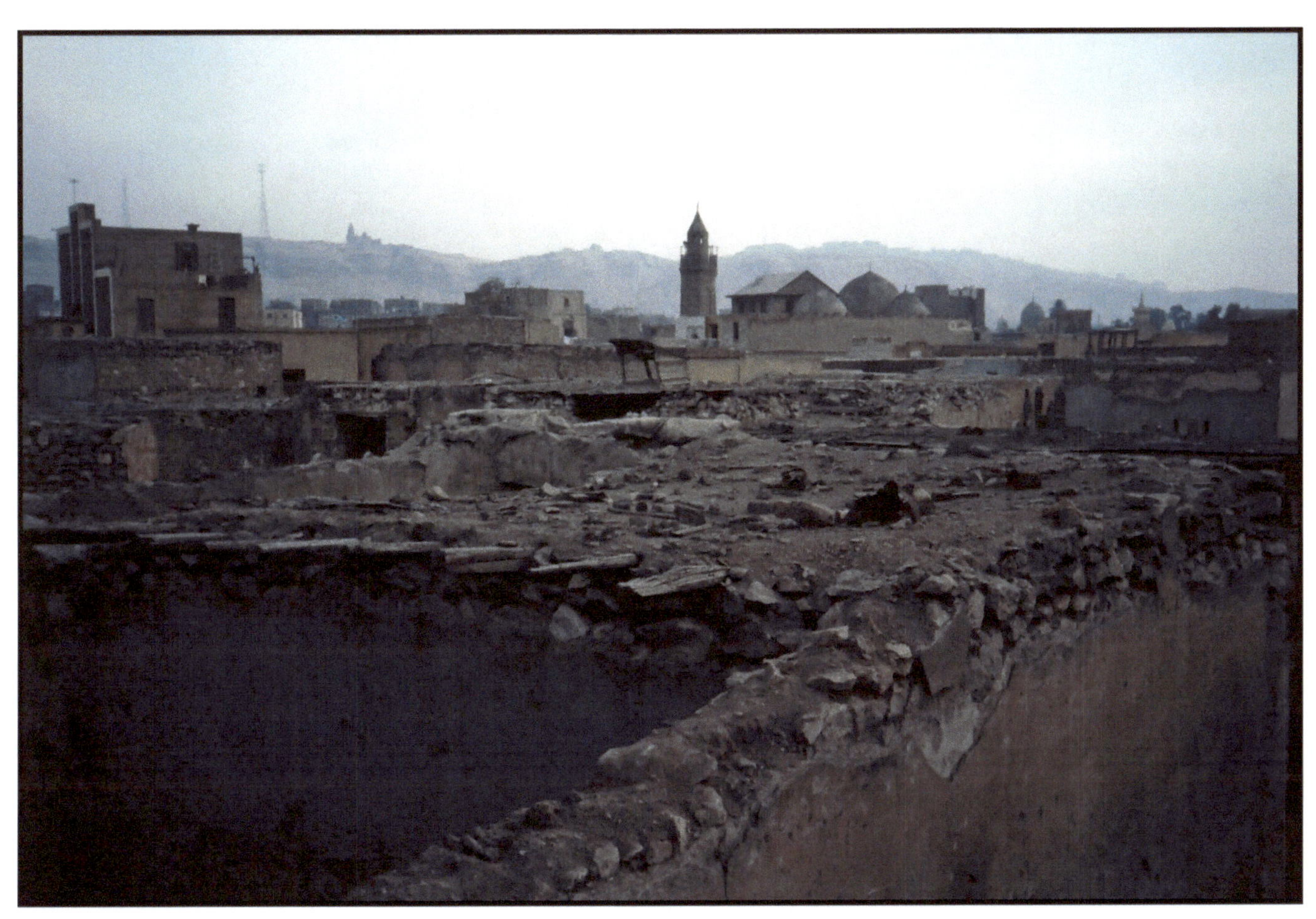

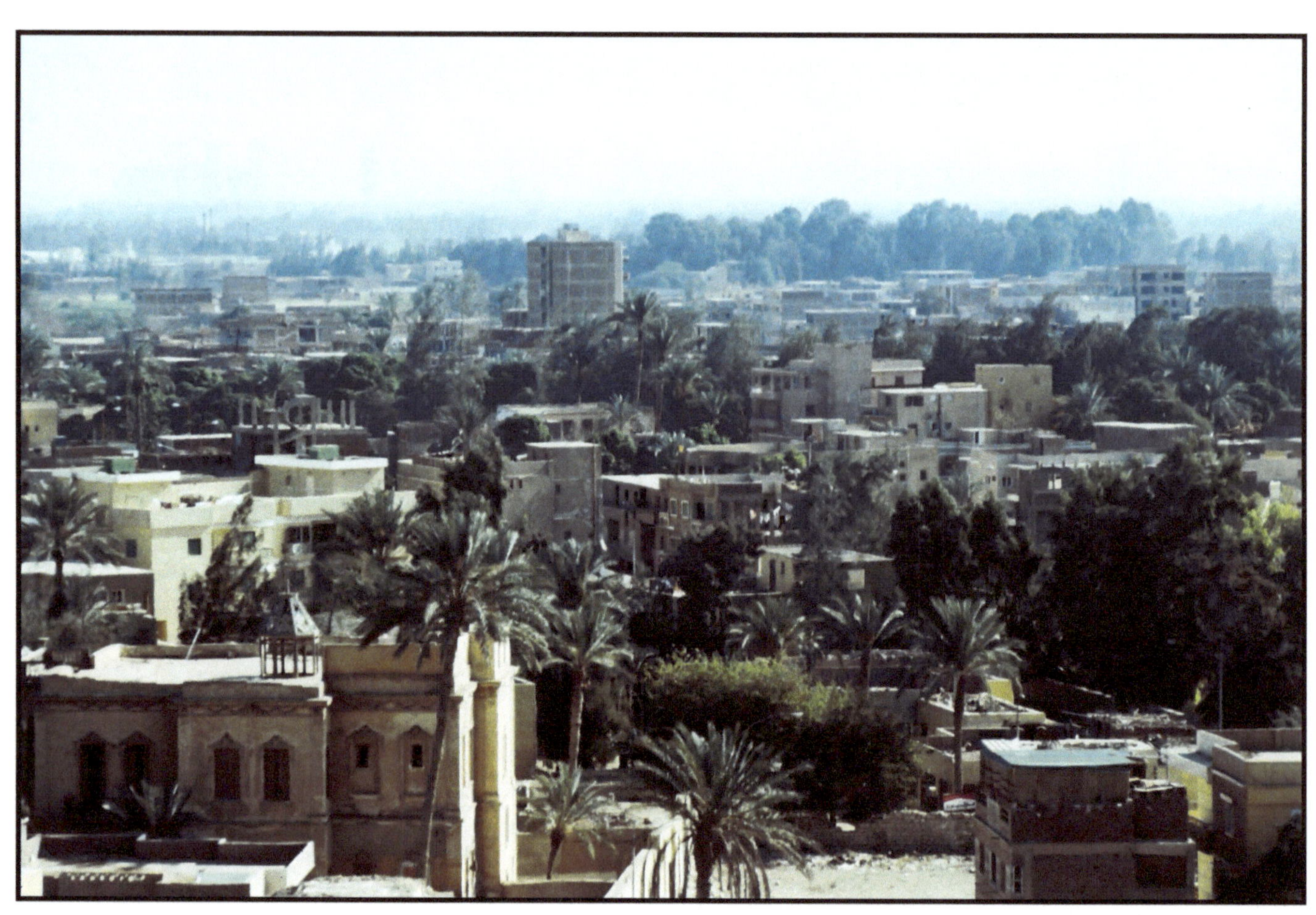

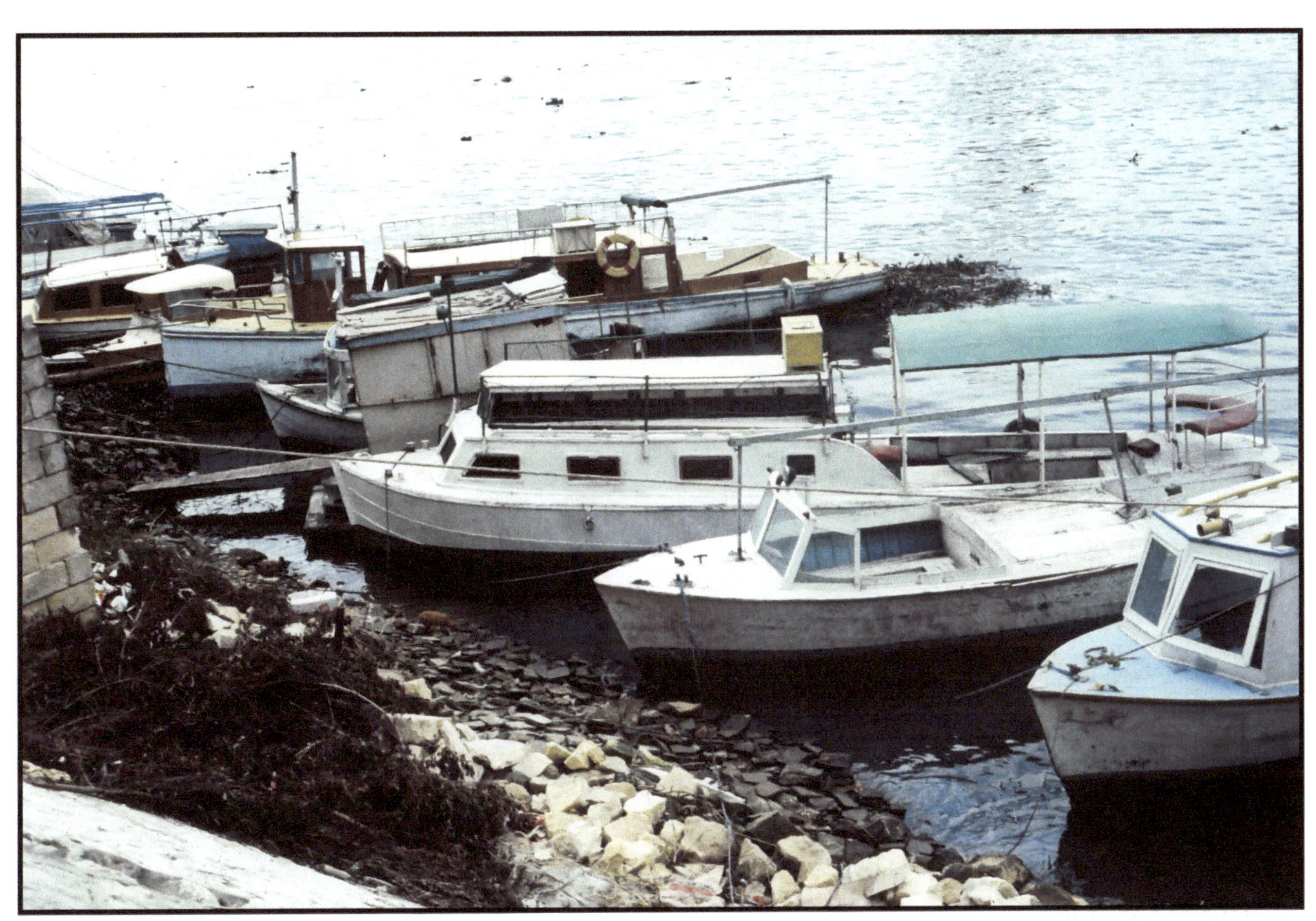

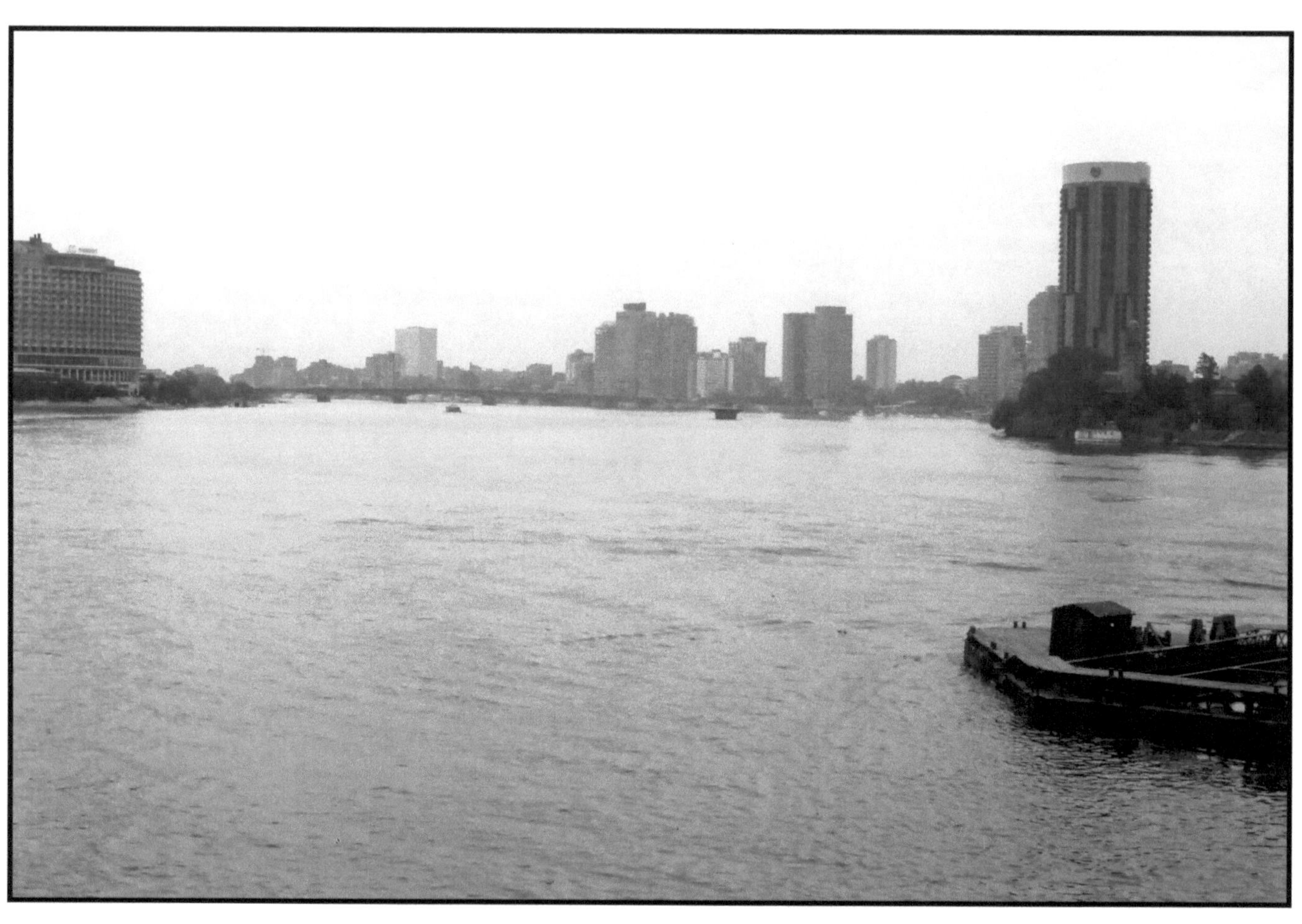

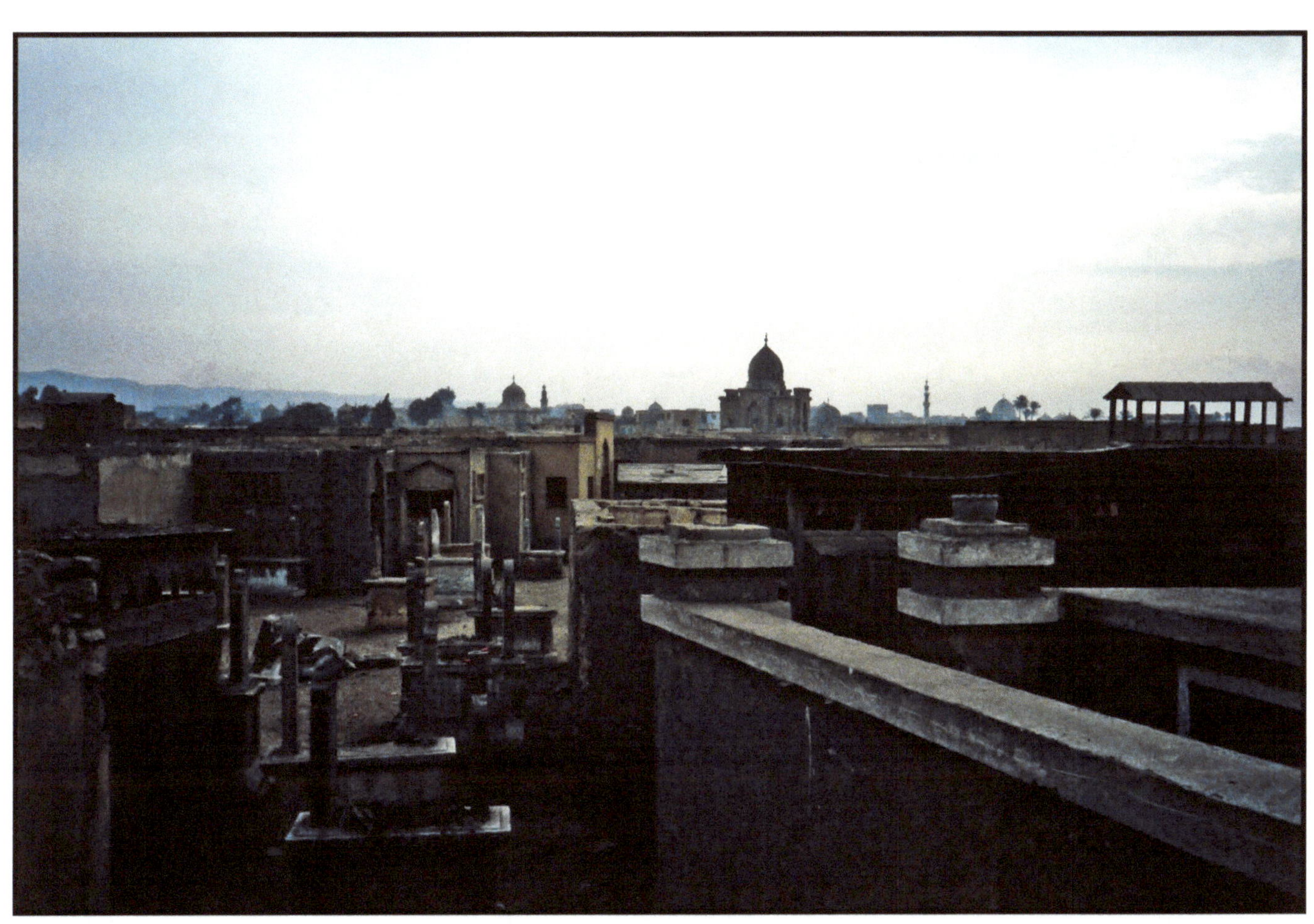

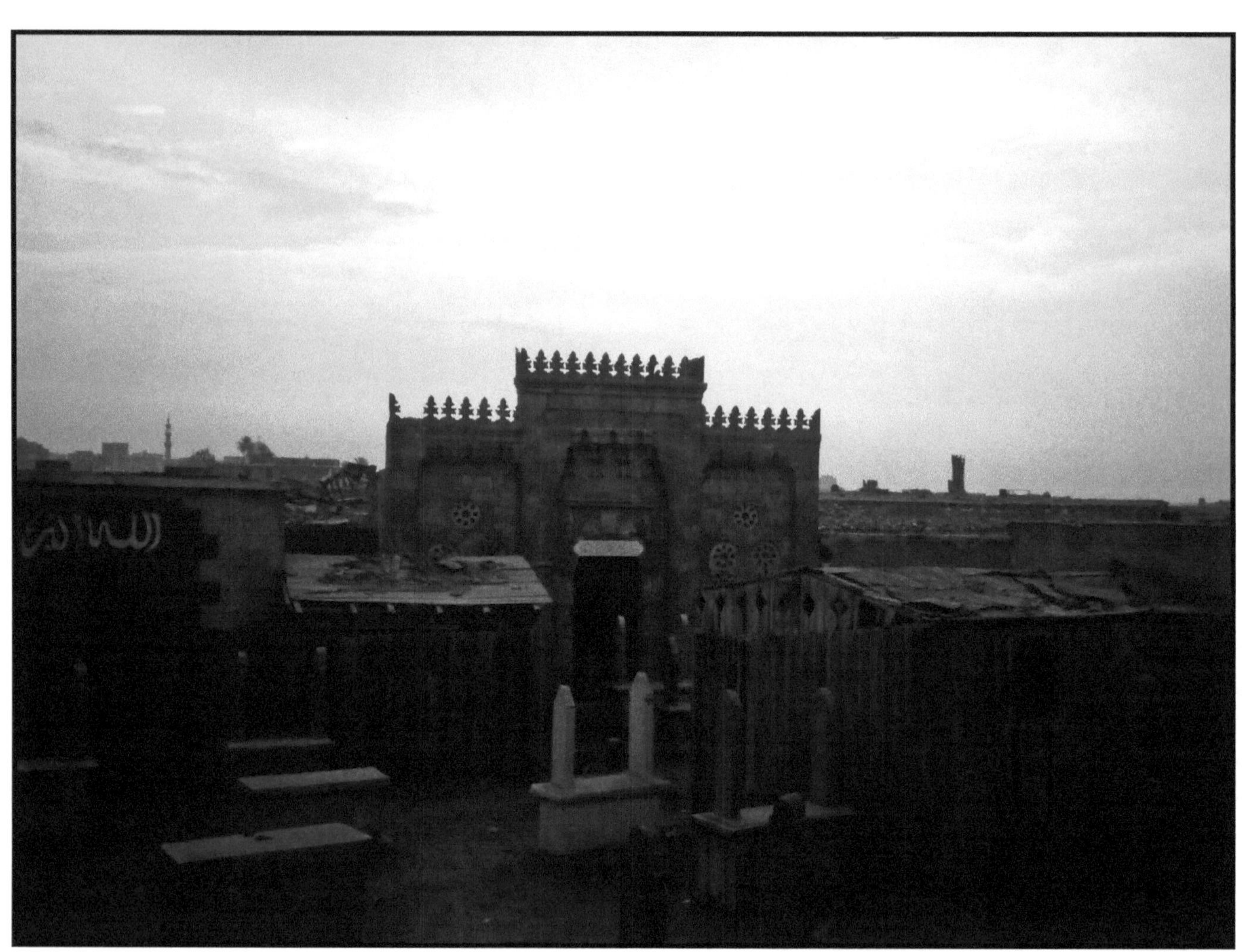

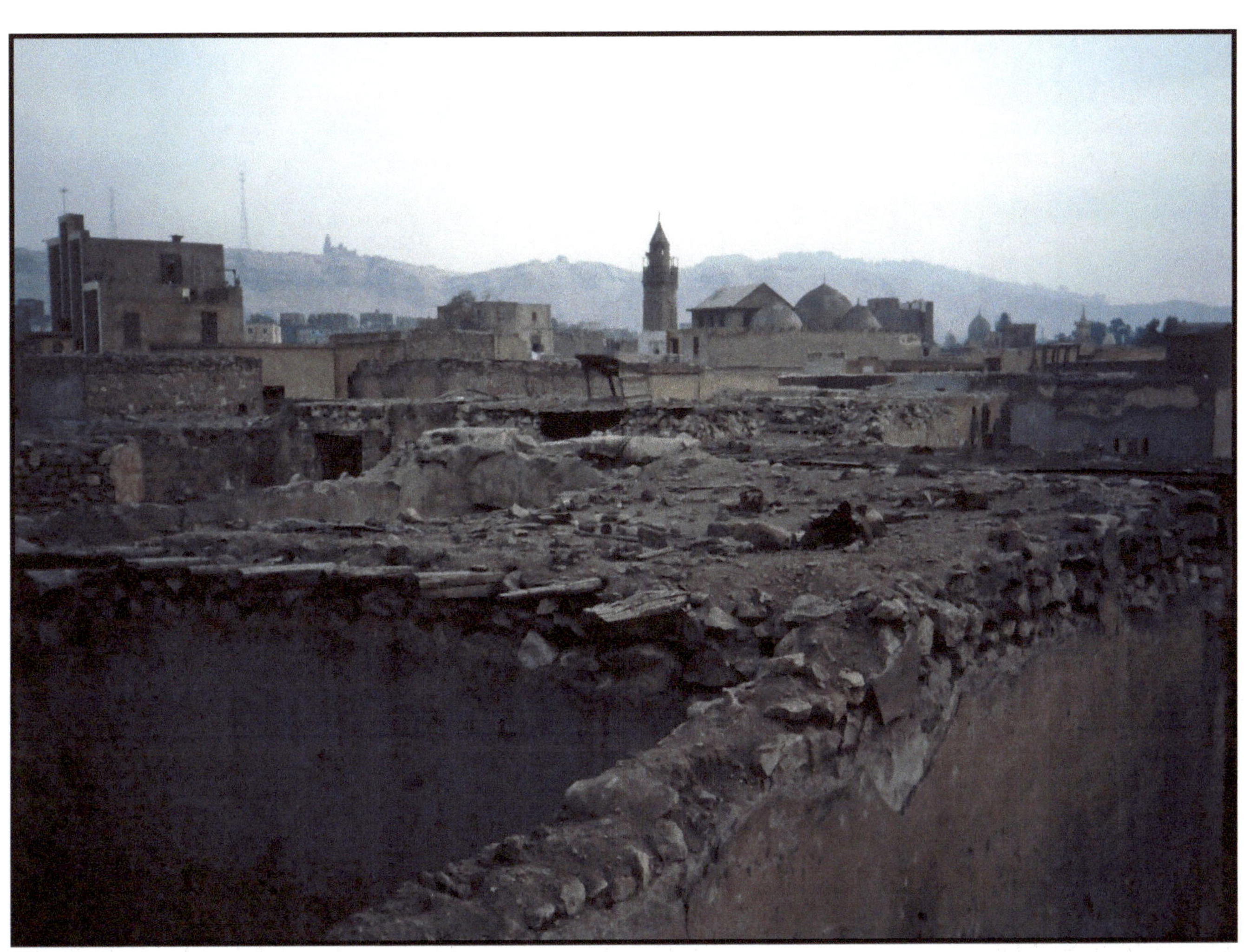

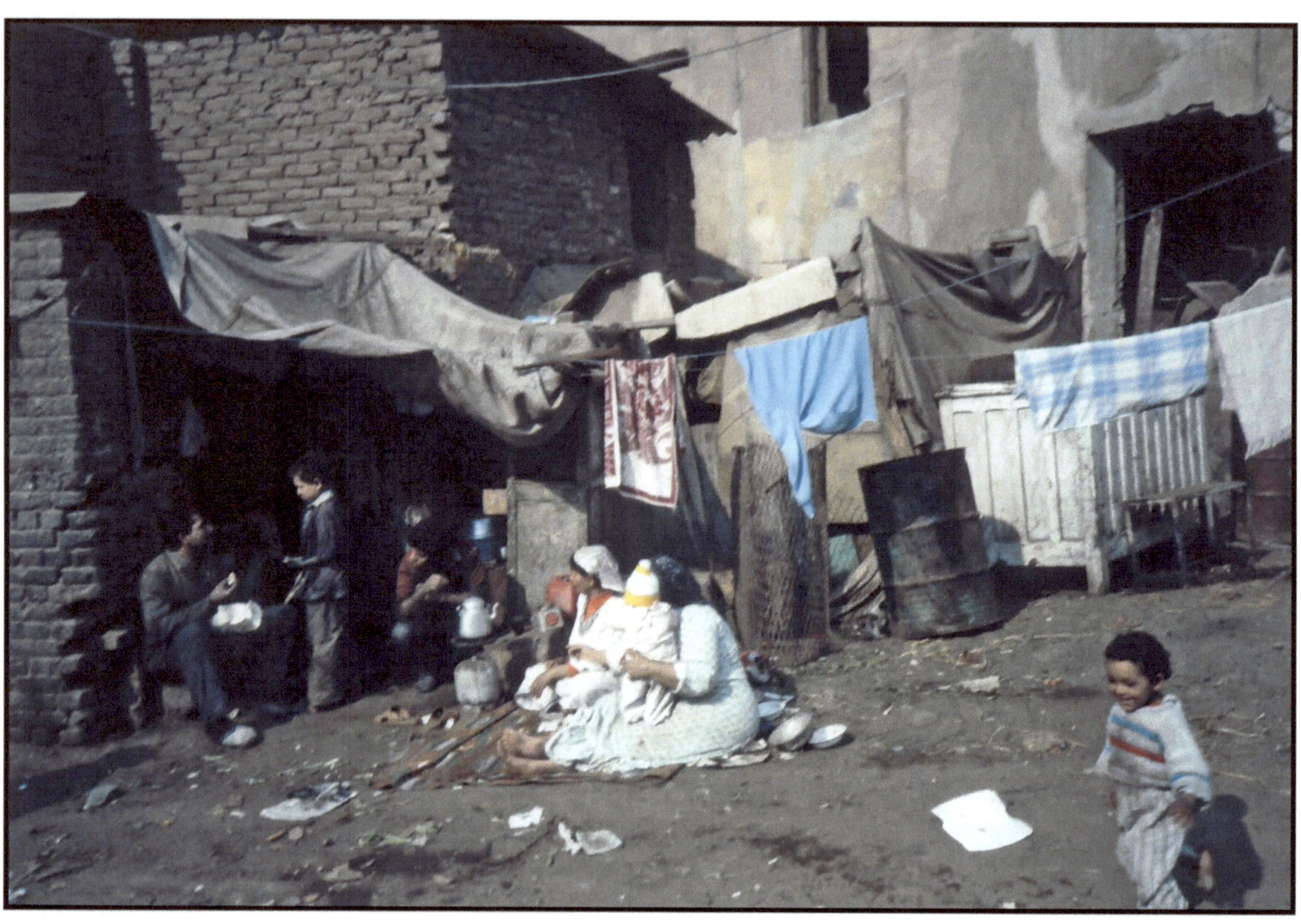

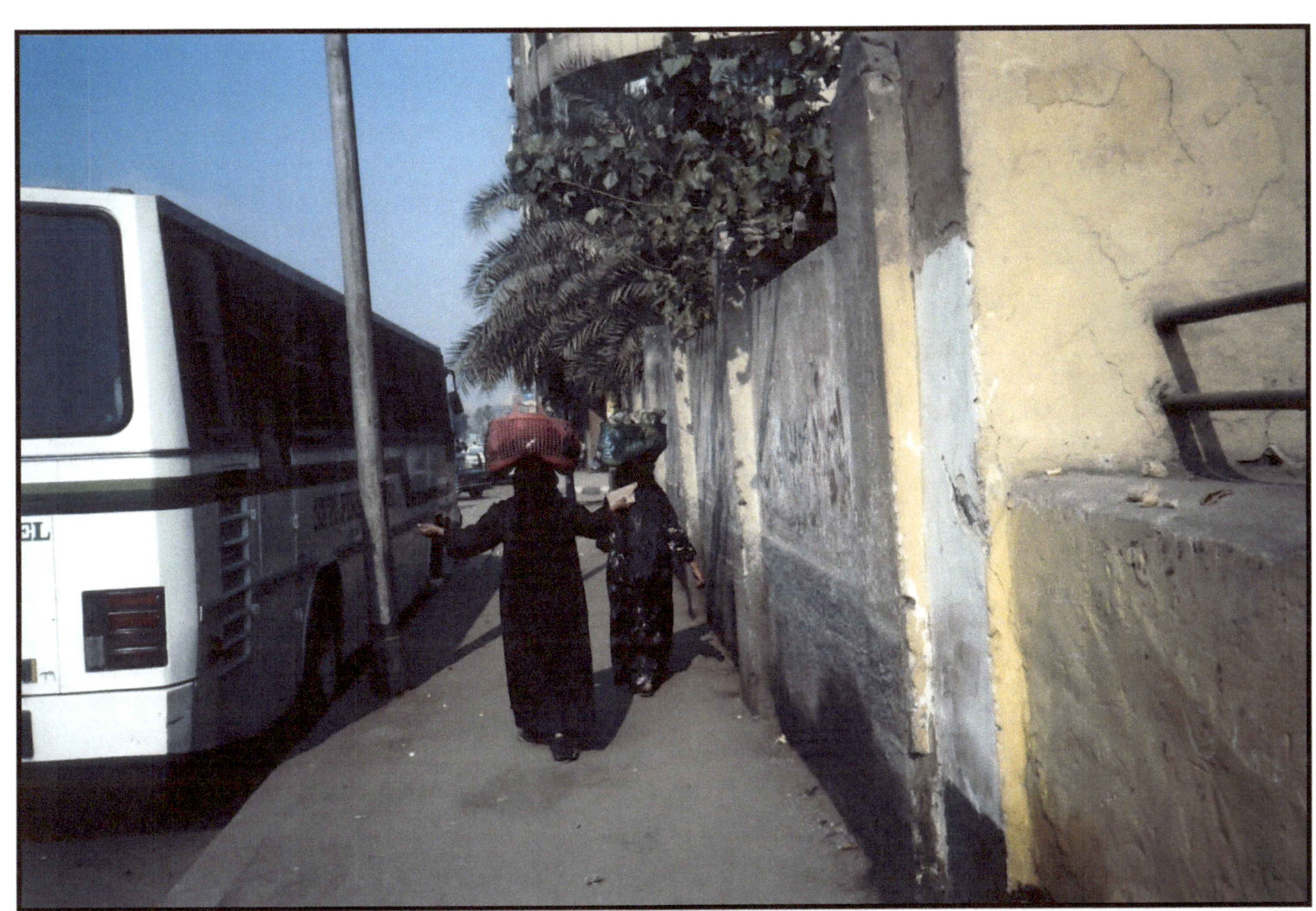

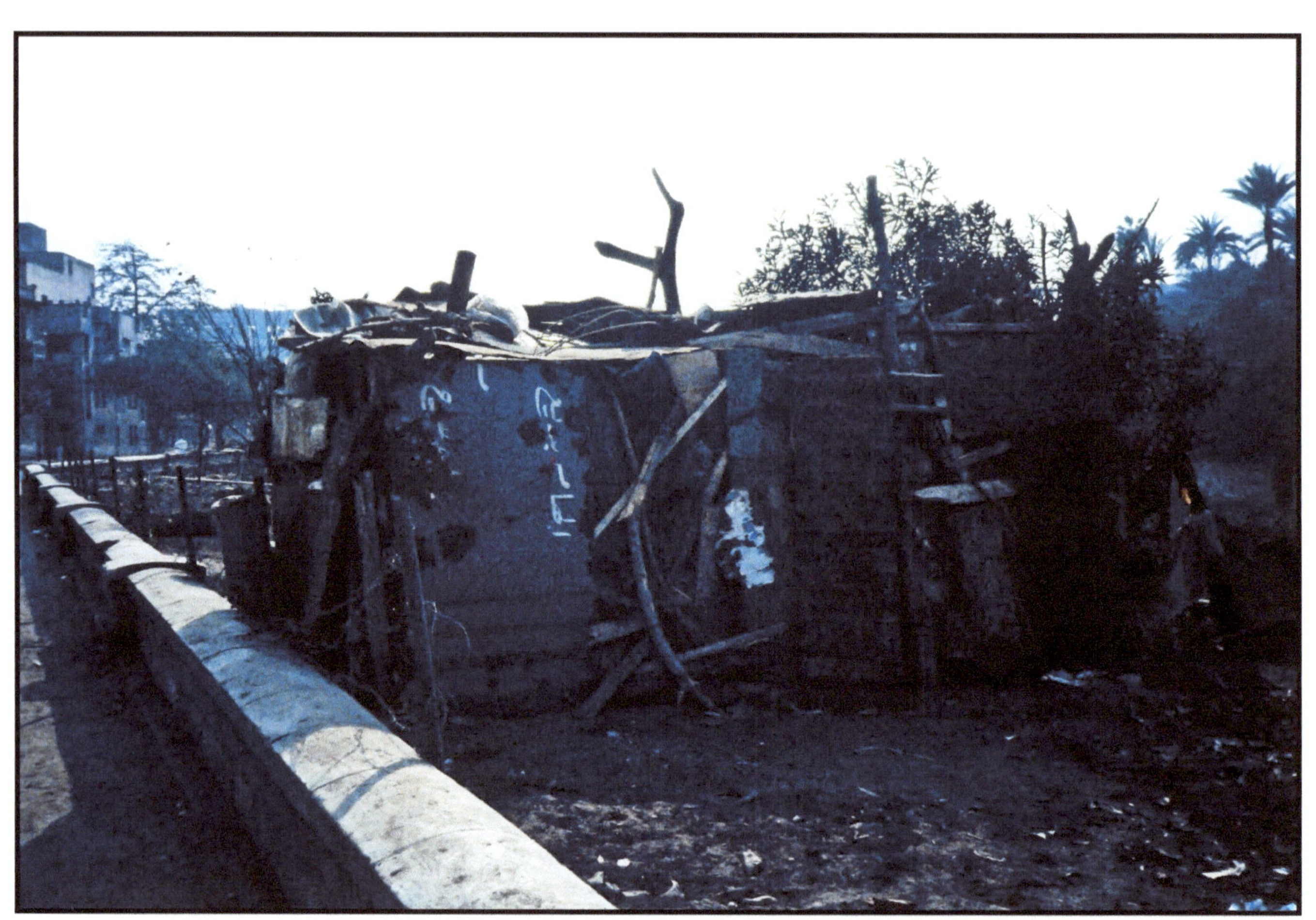

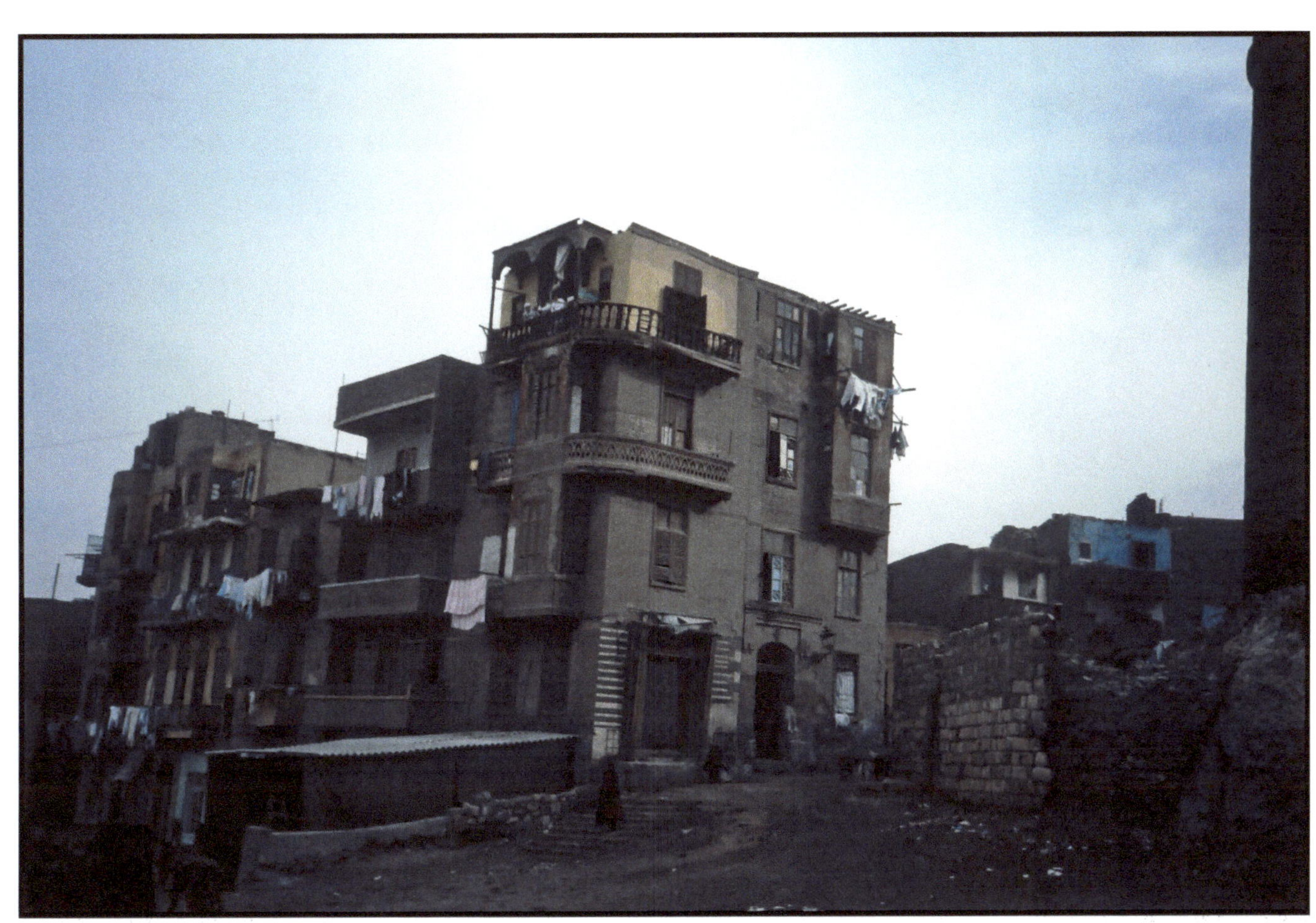

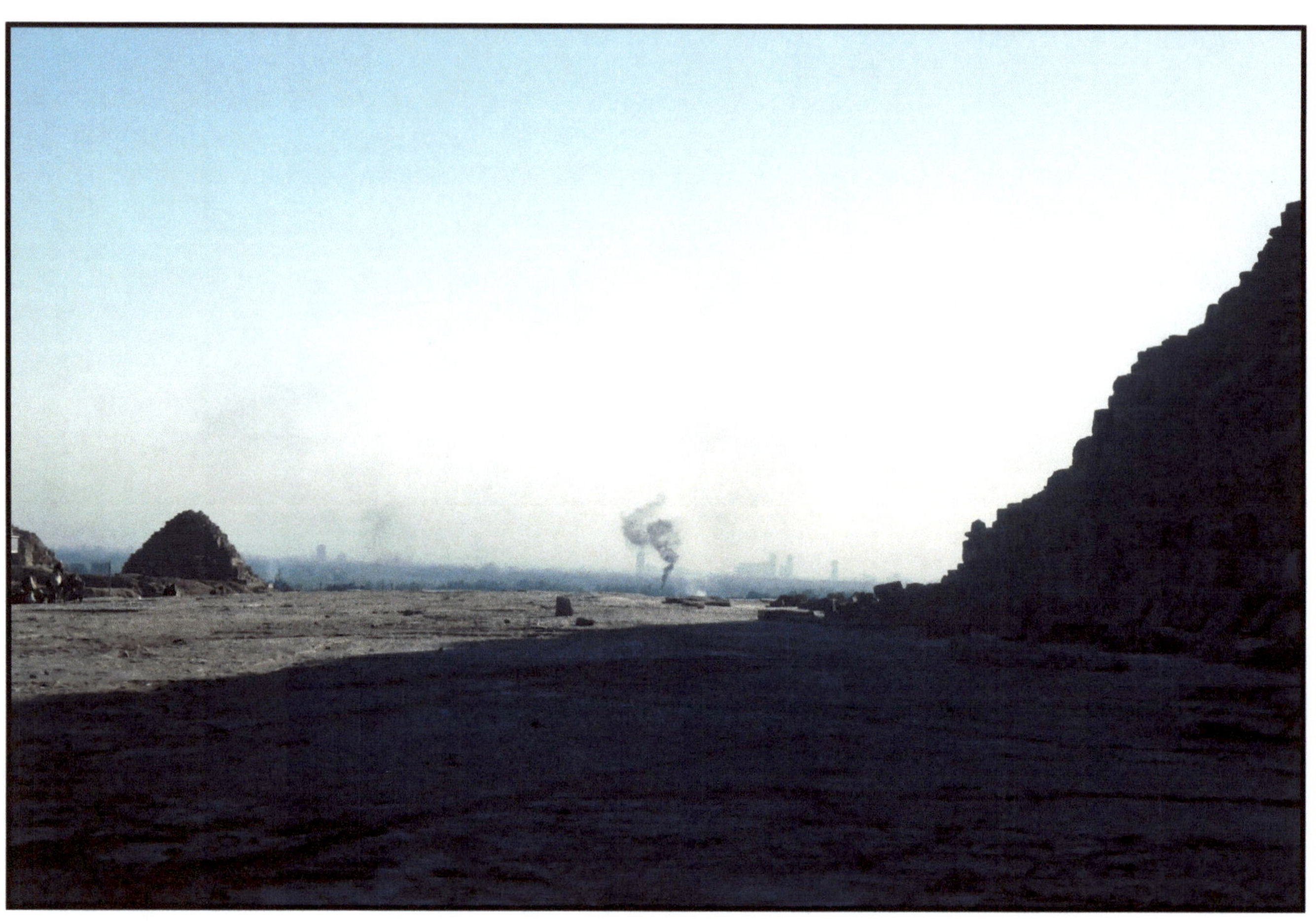

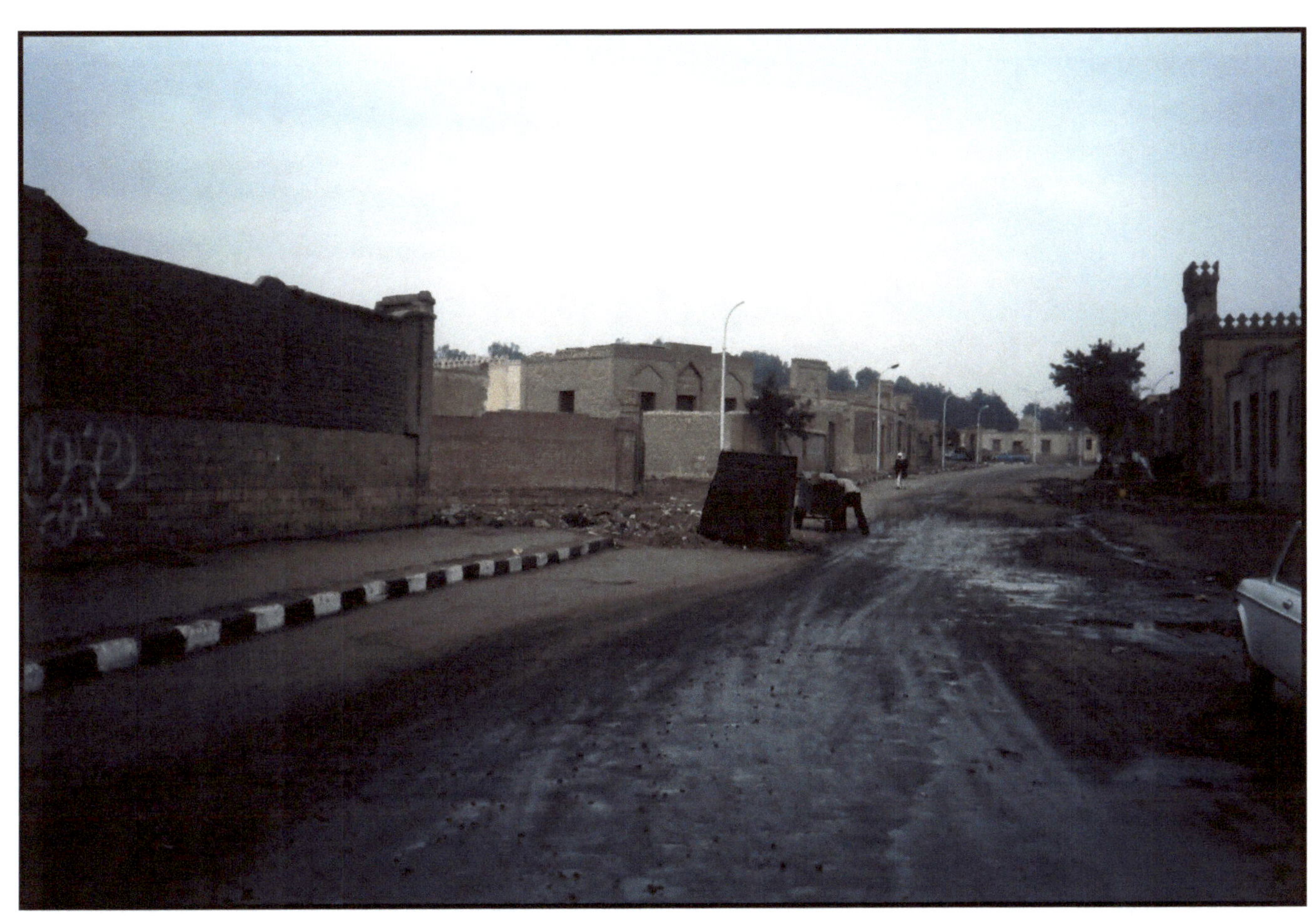

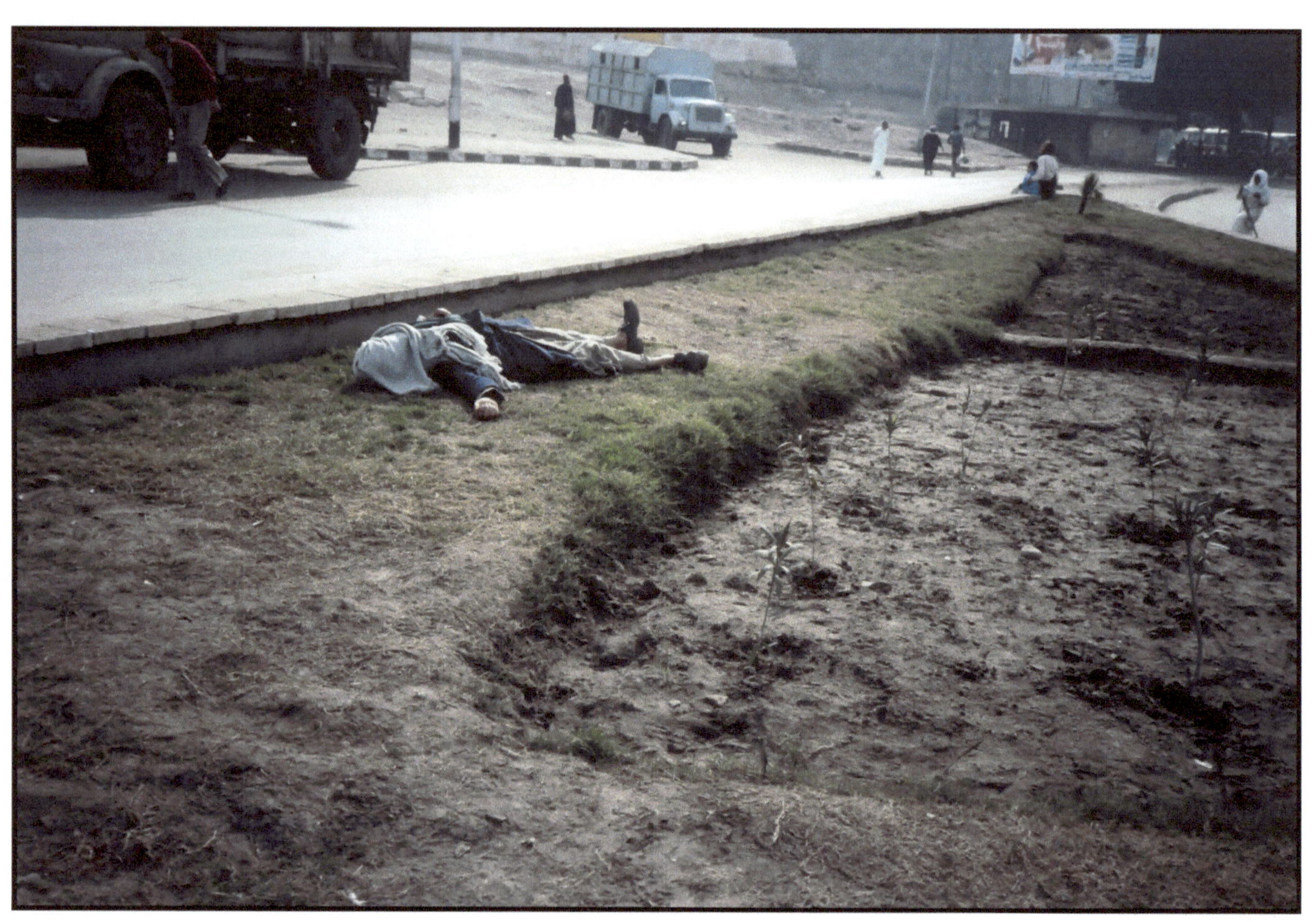

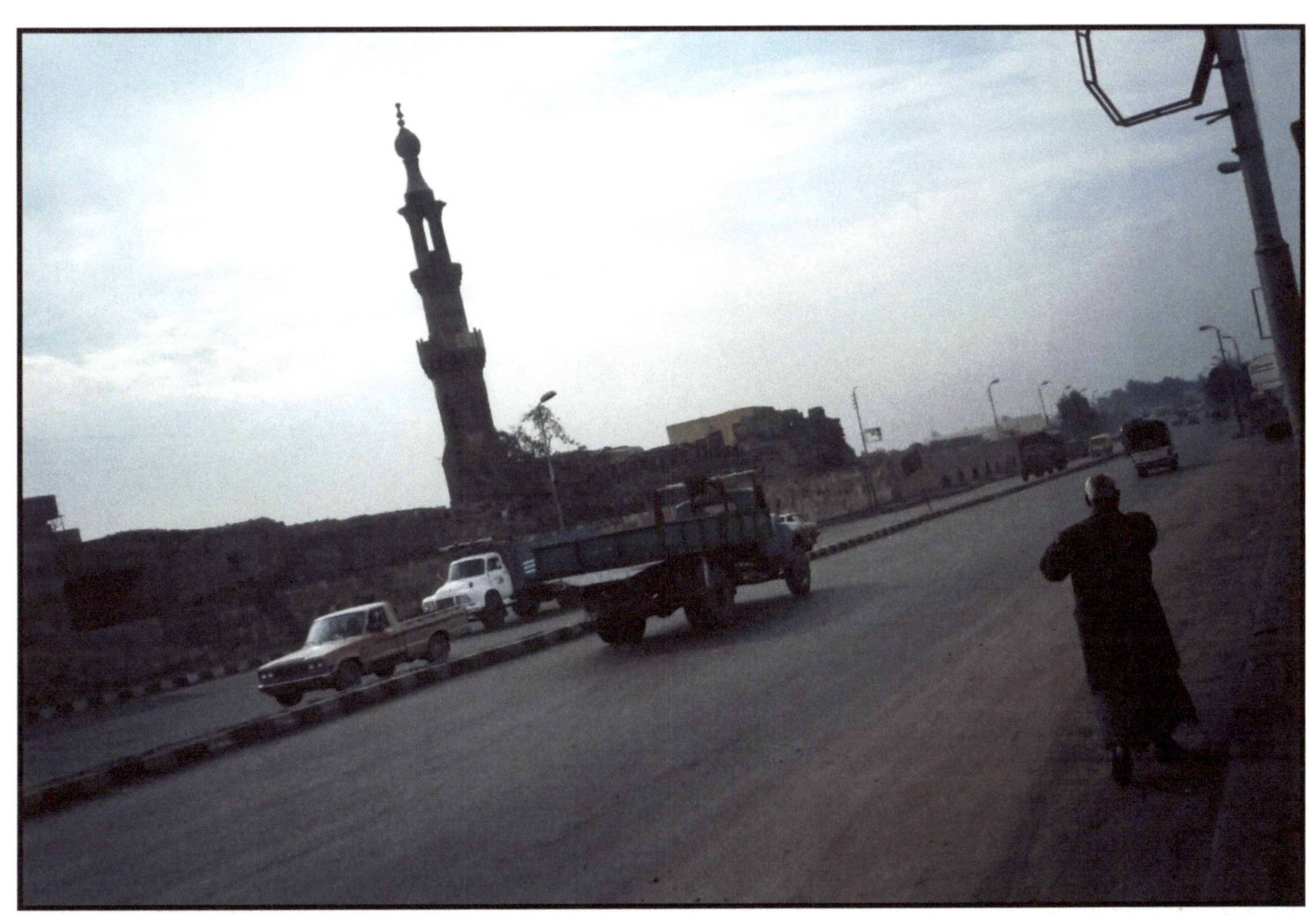

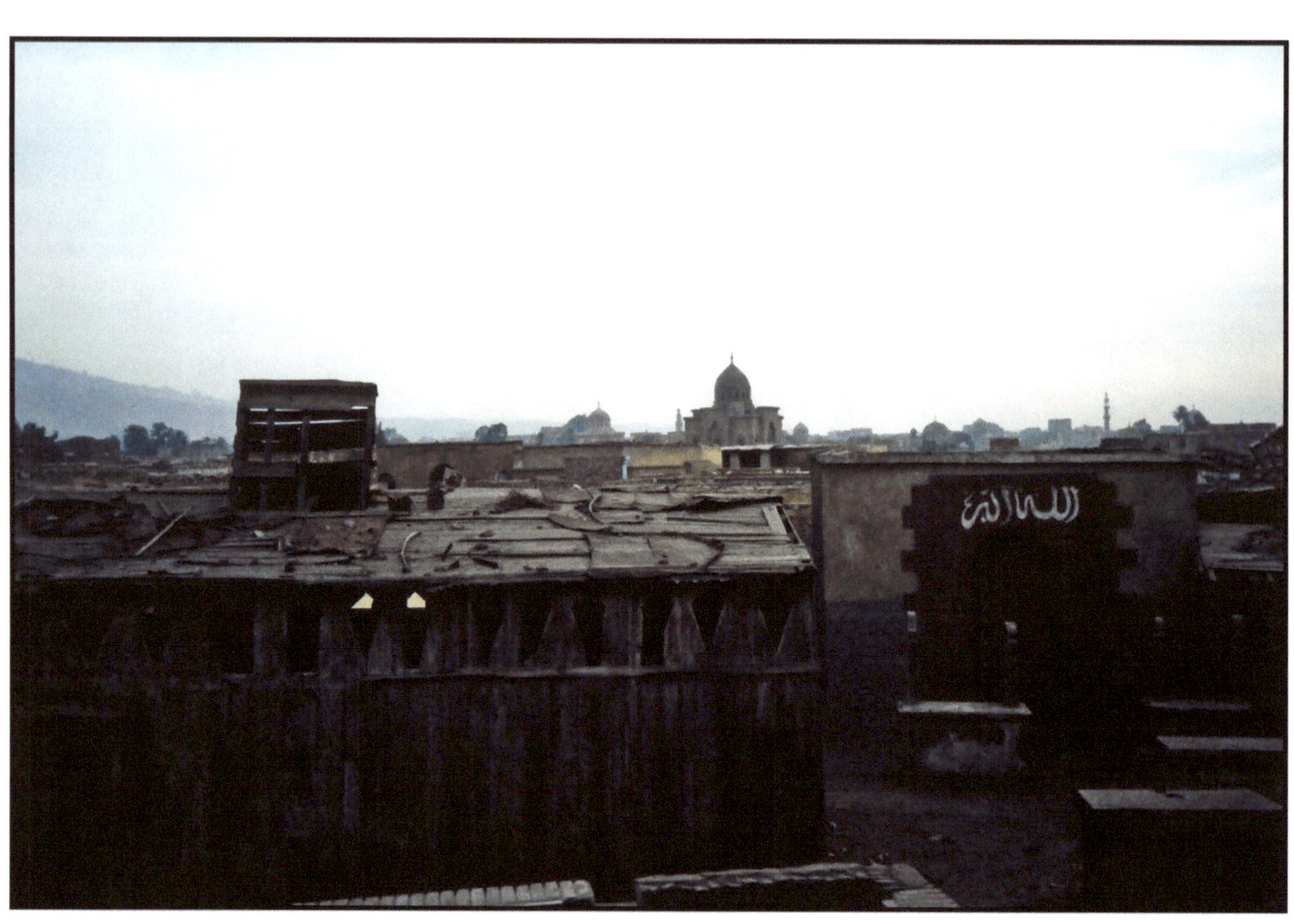

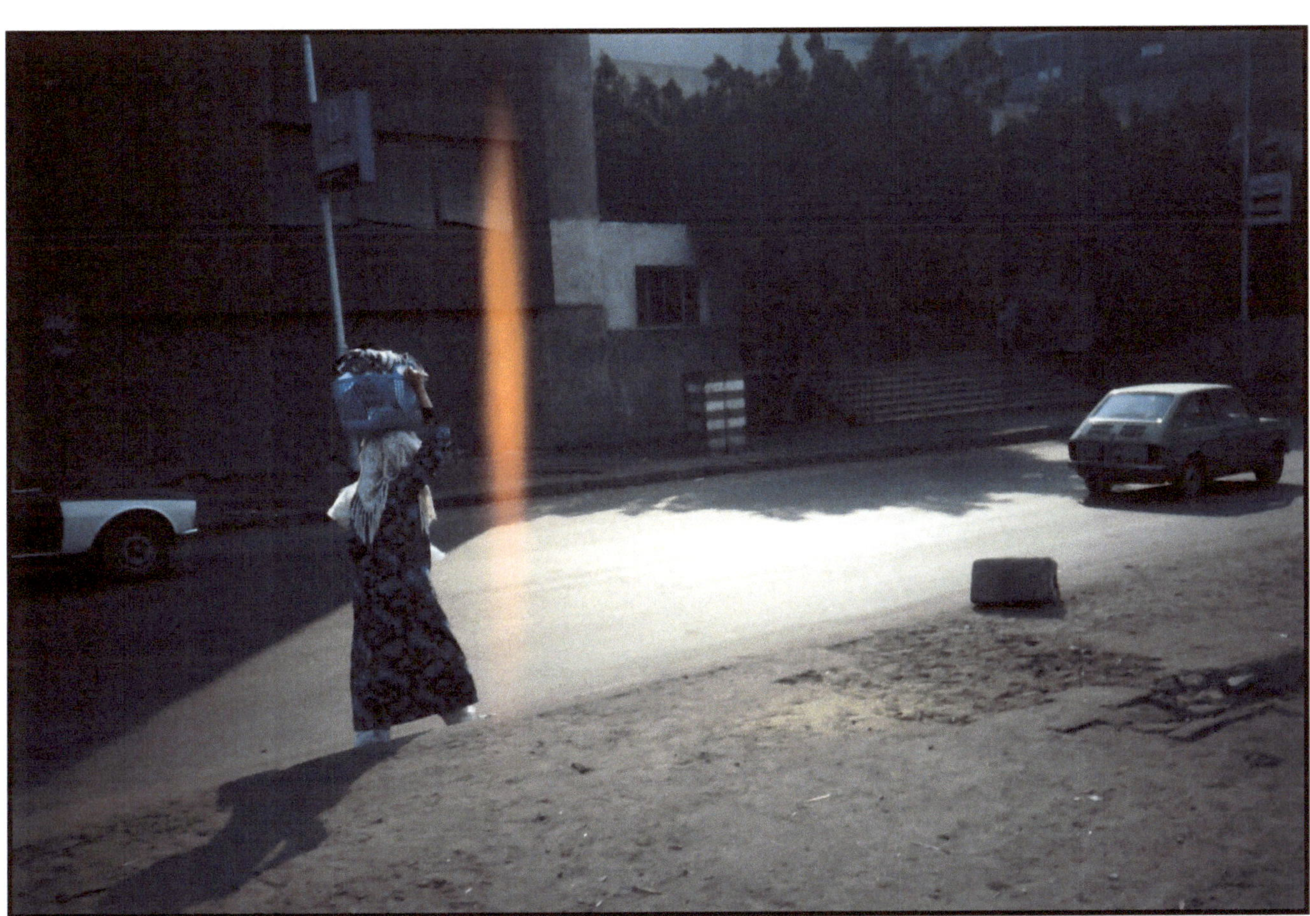

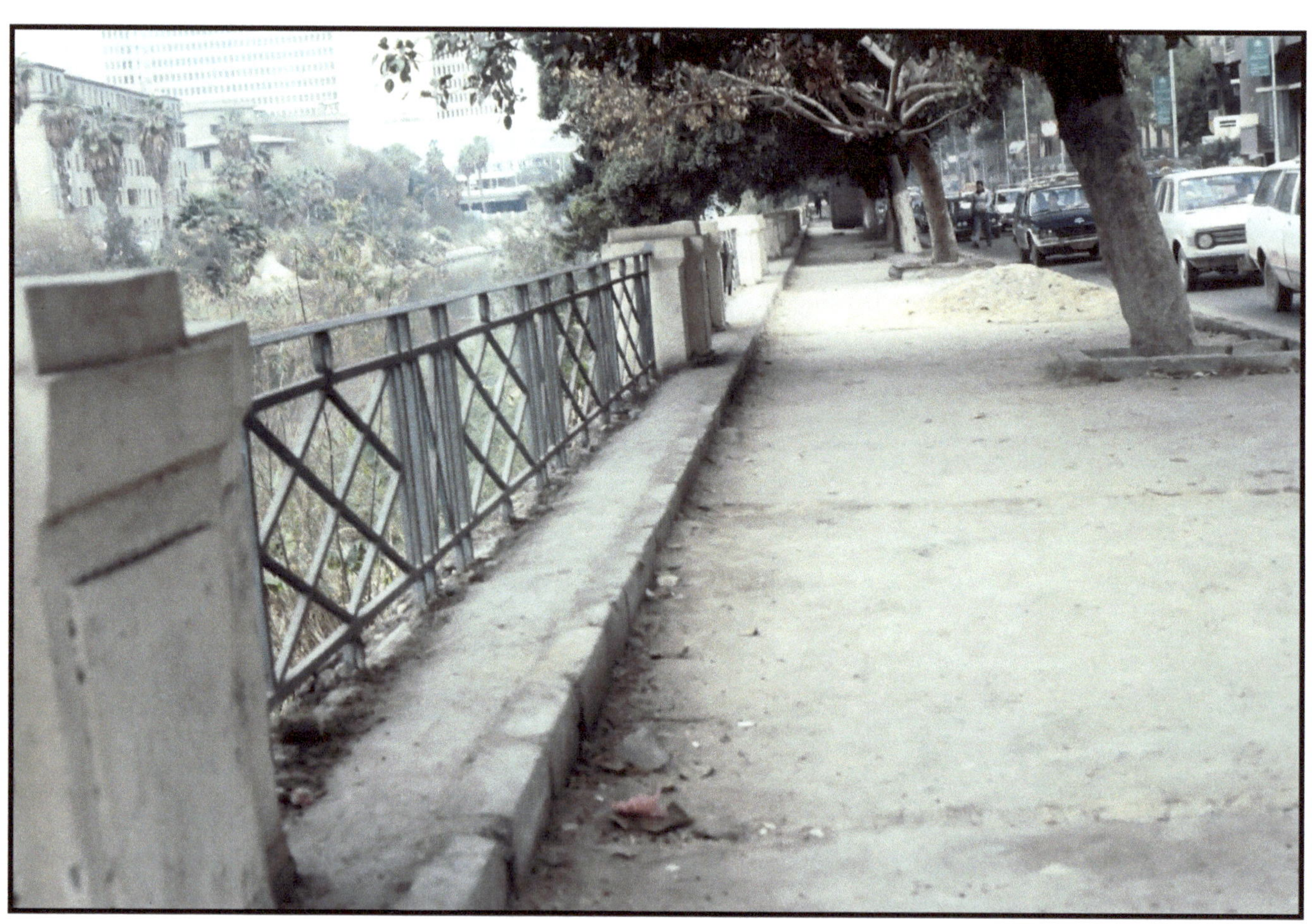

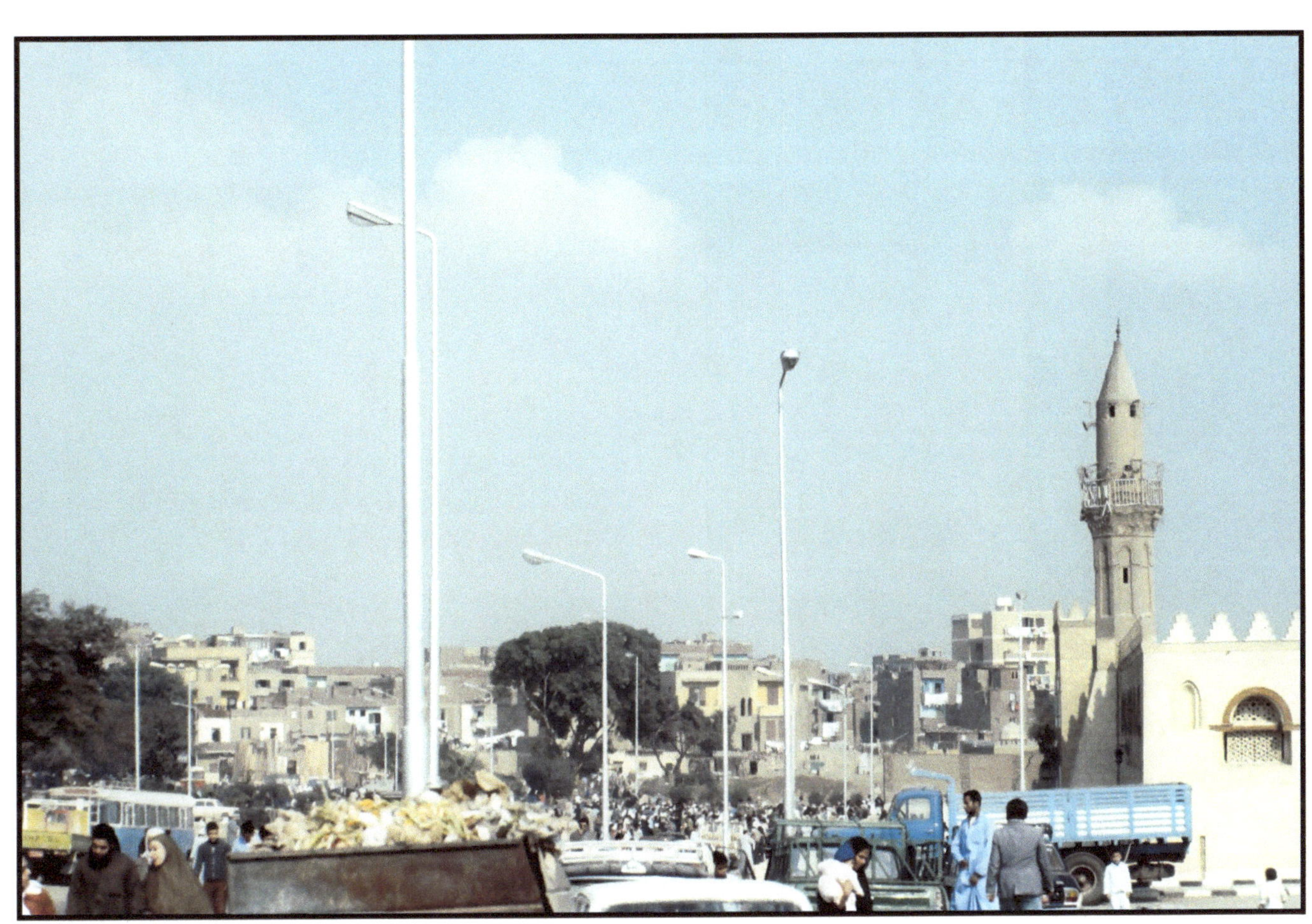

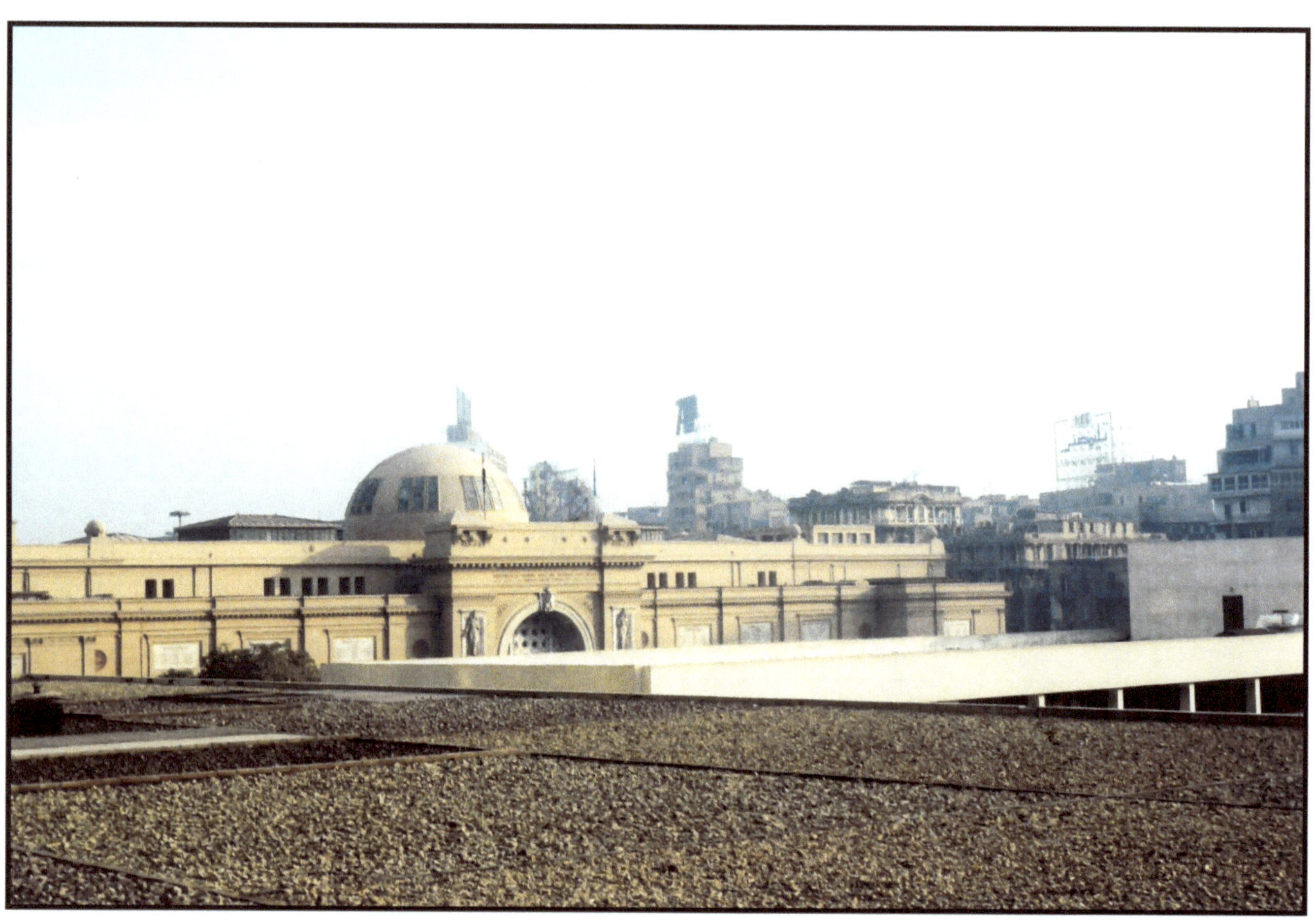

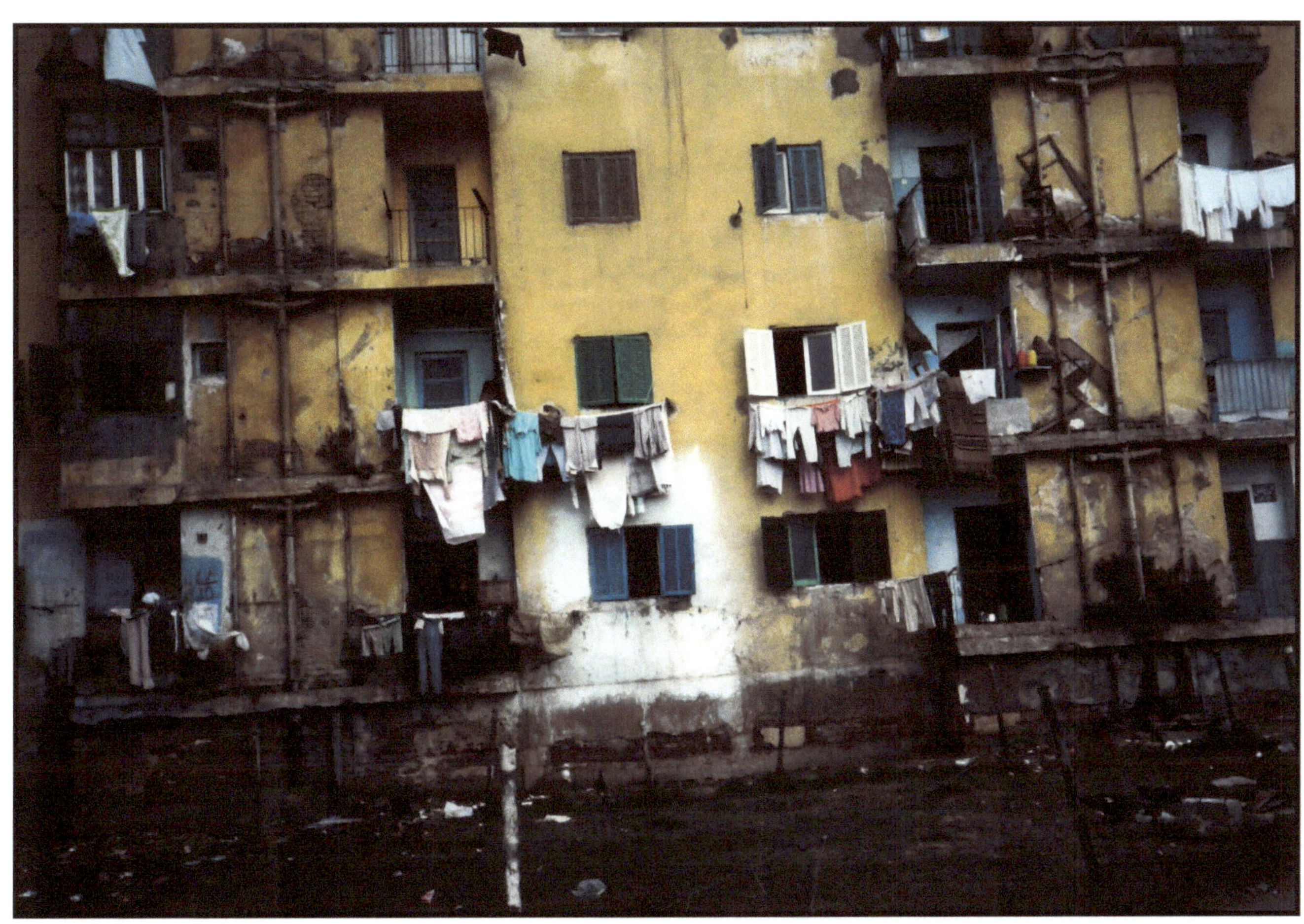

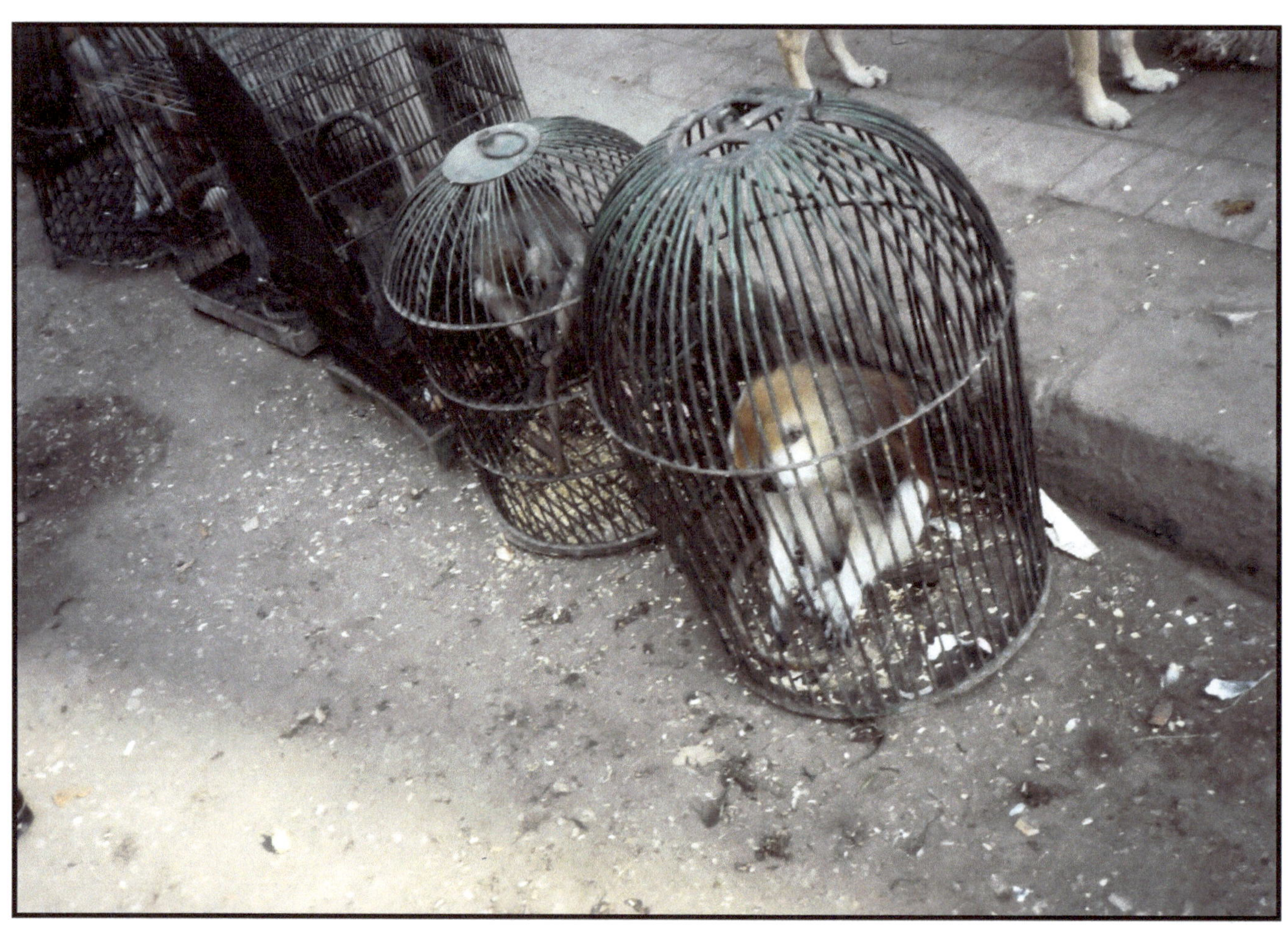

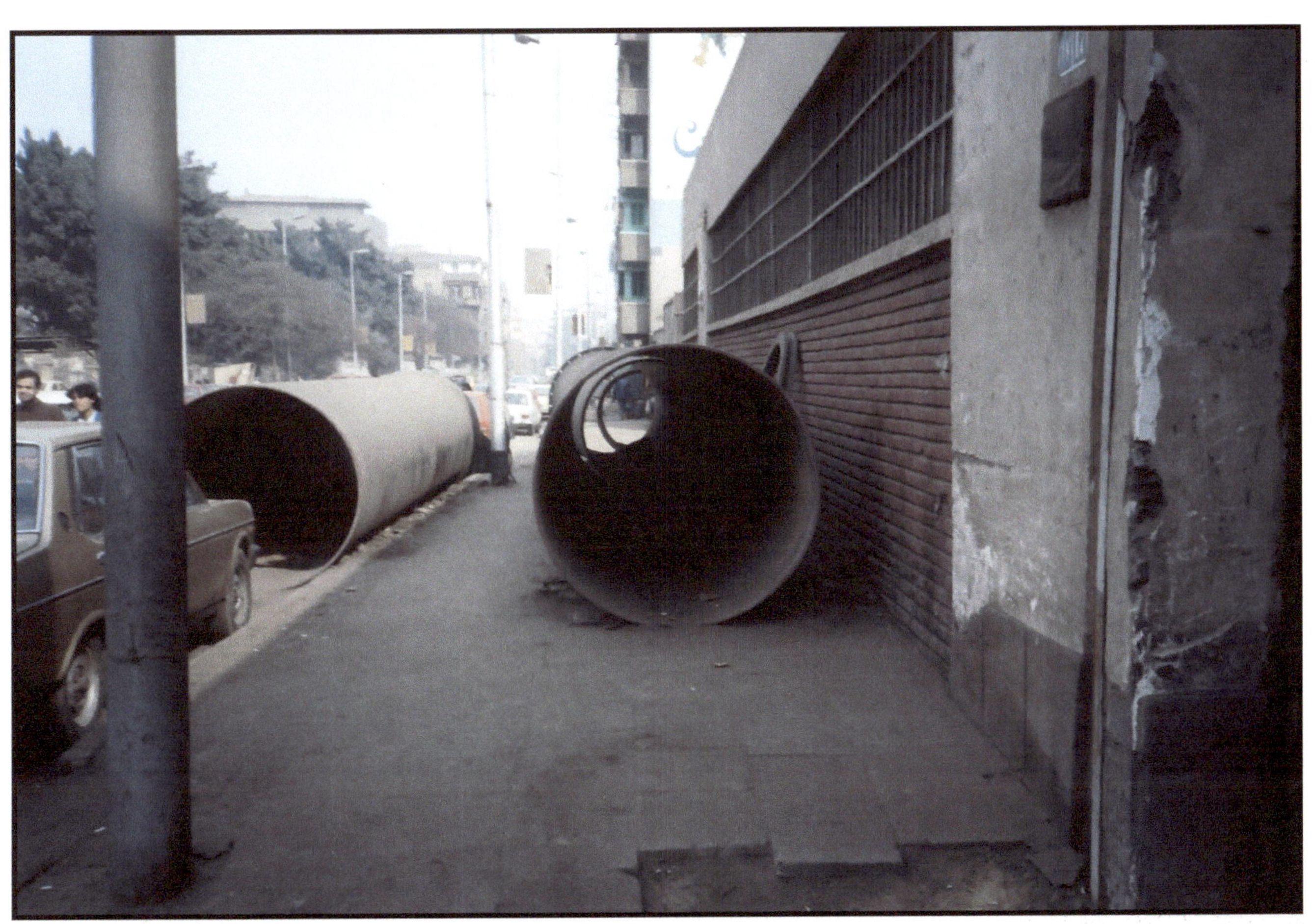

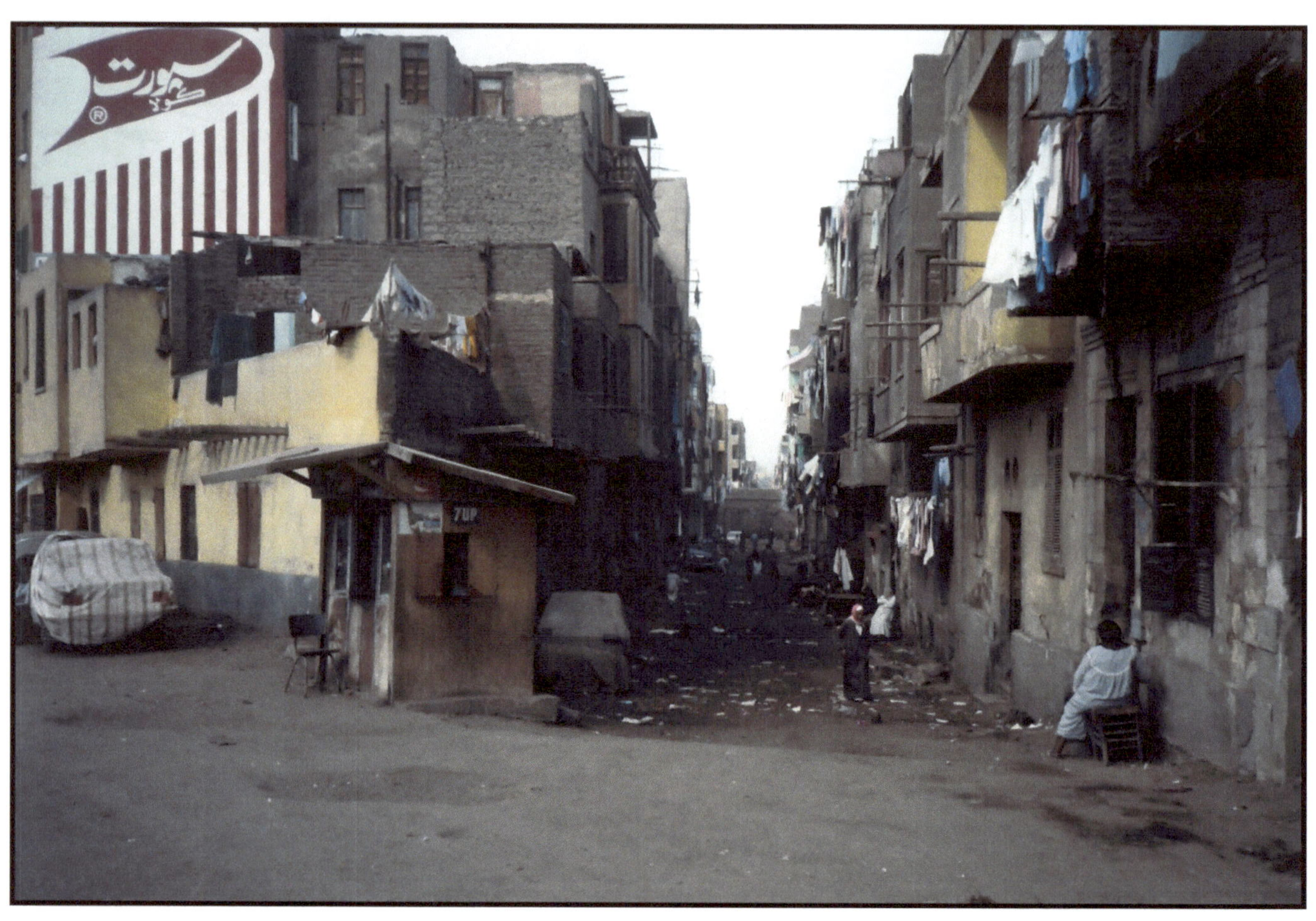
سبورت
كولا
7UP

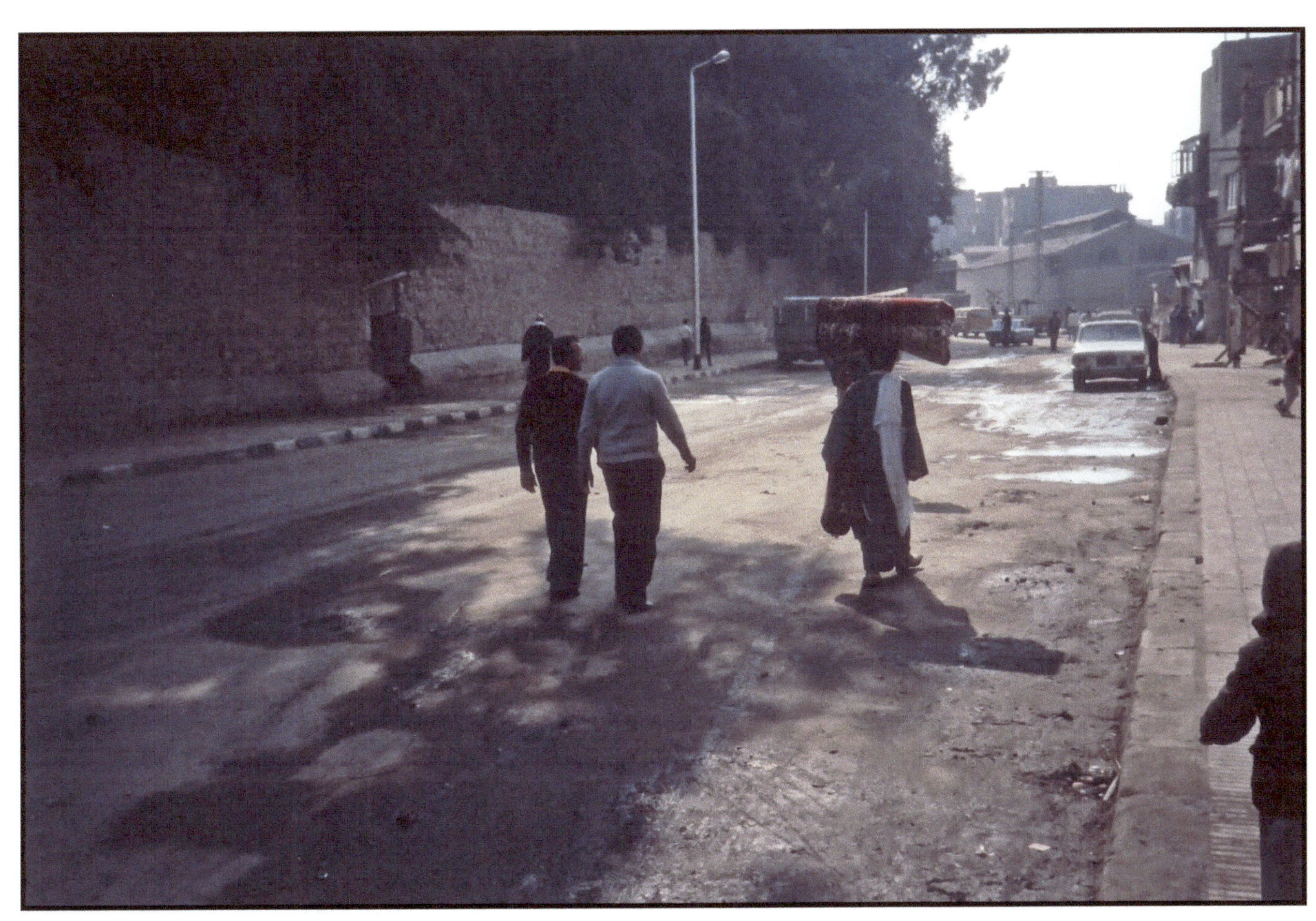

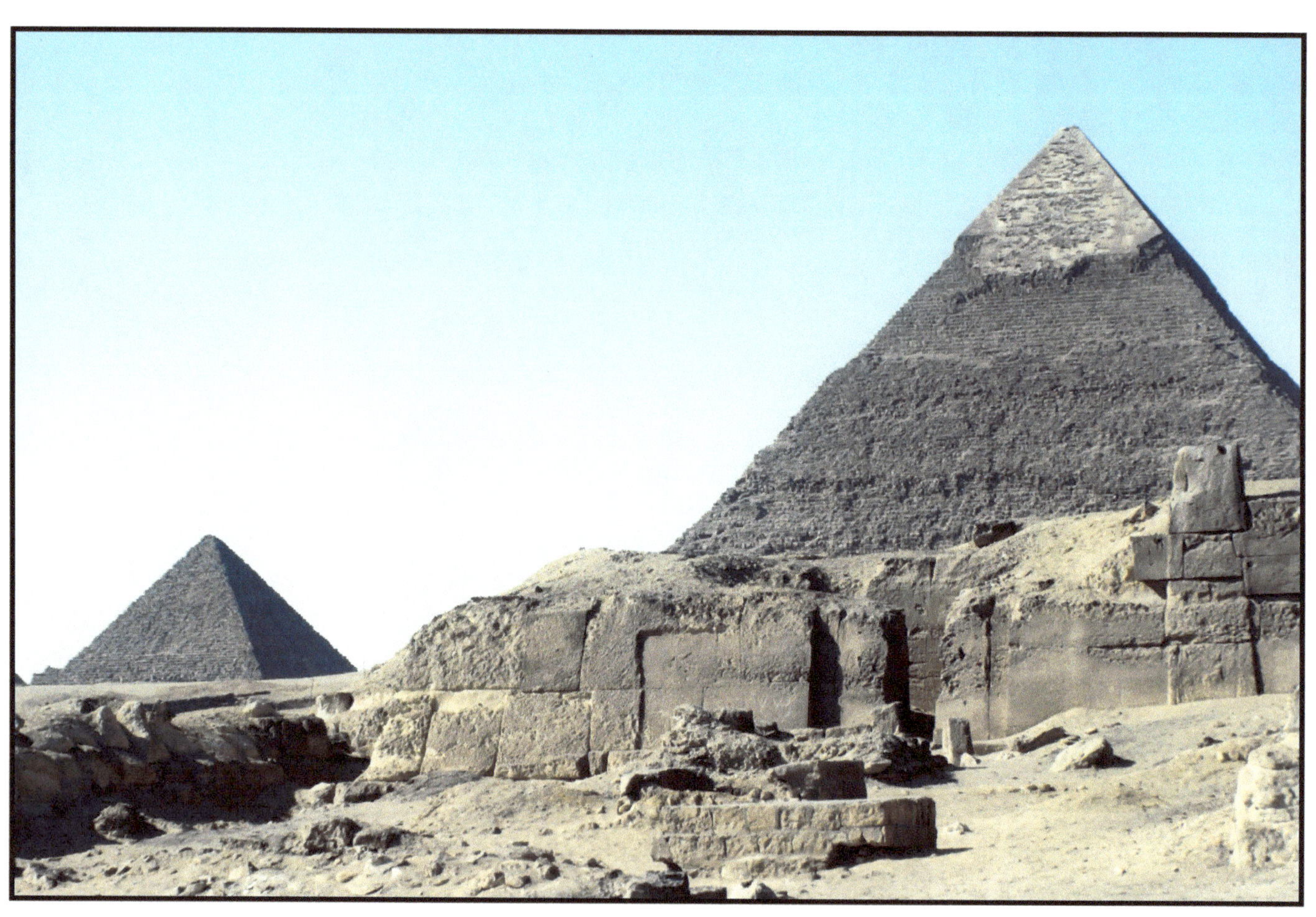

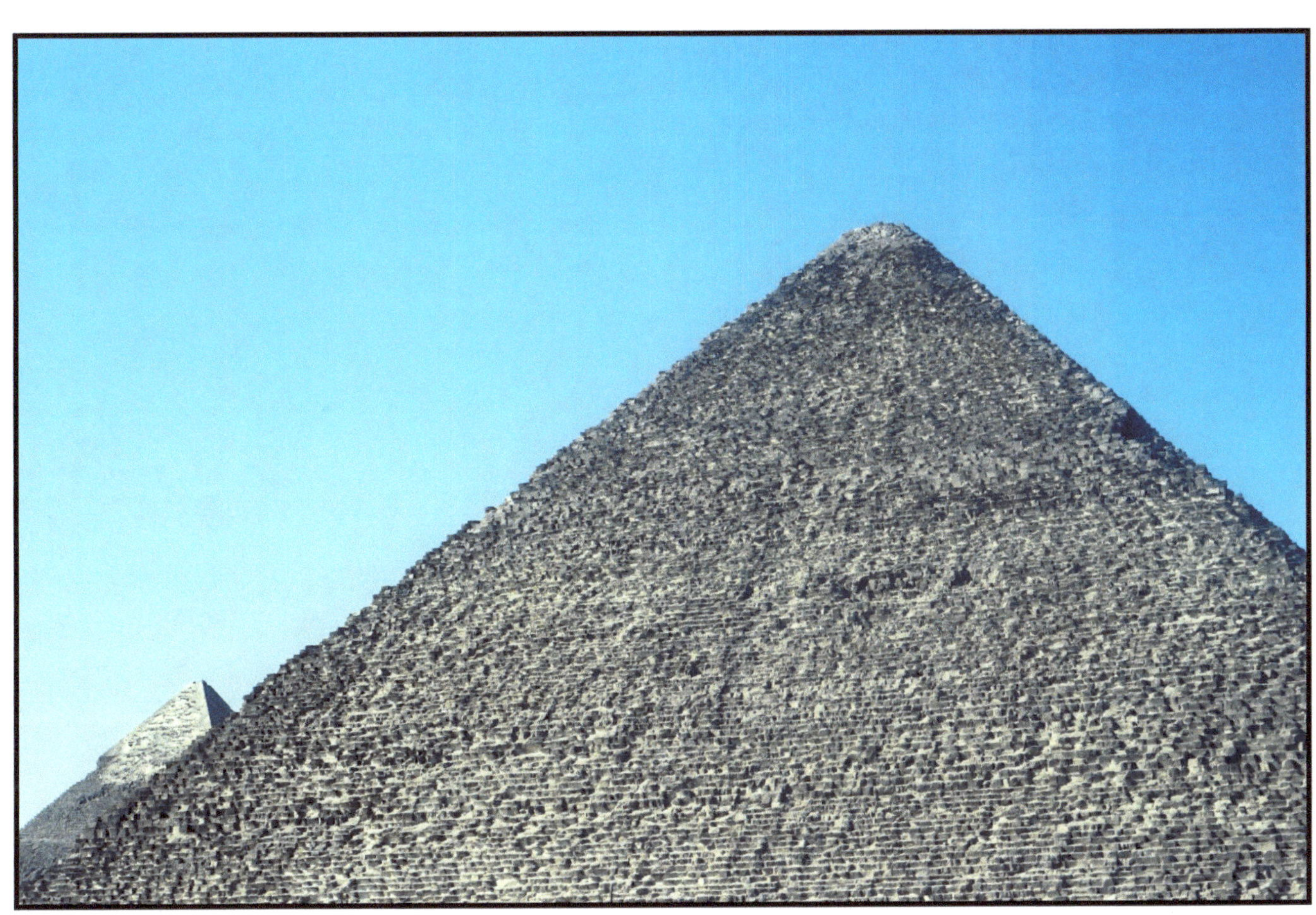

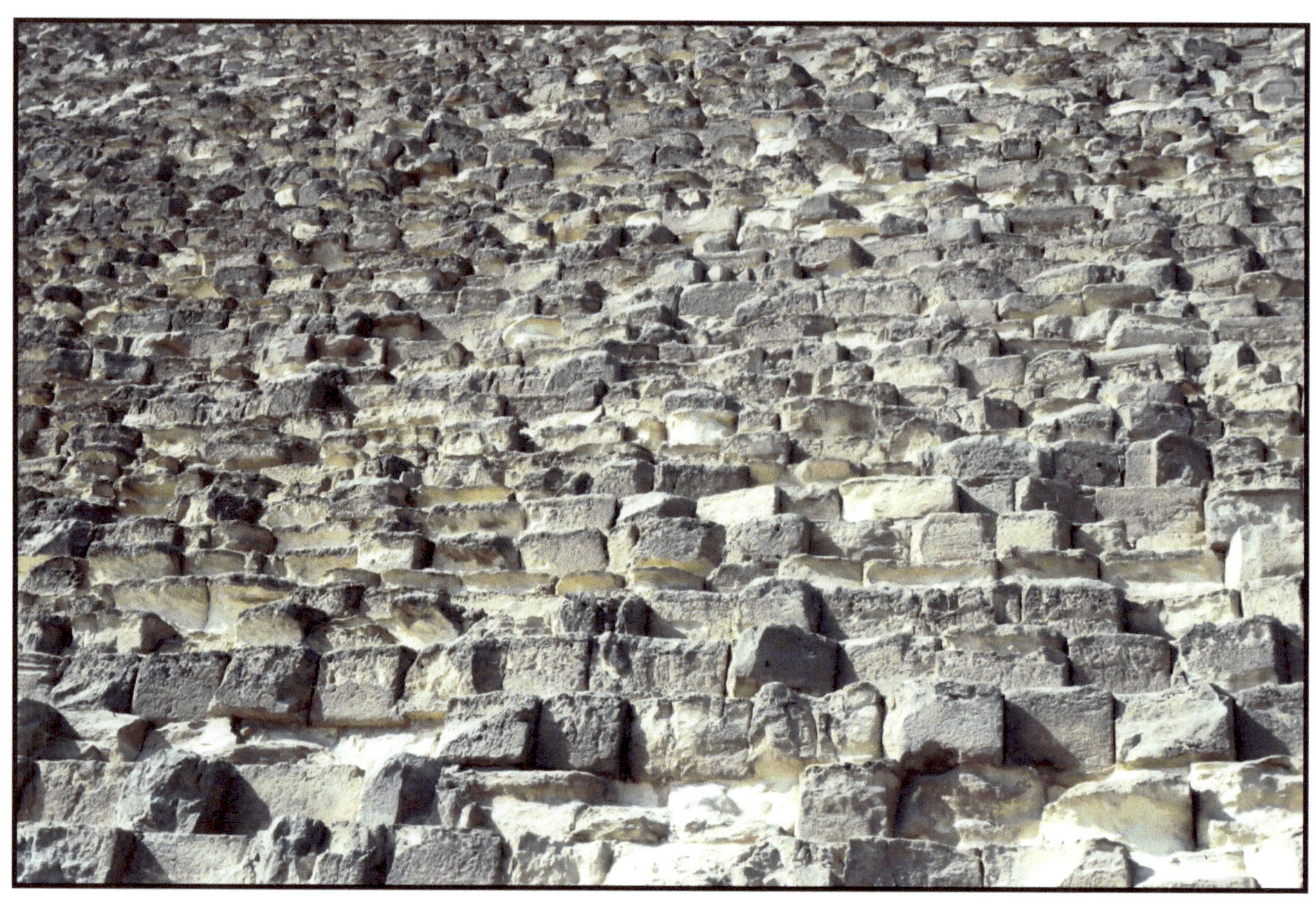

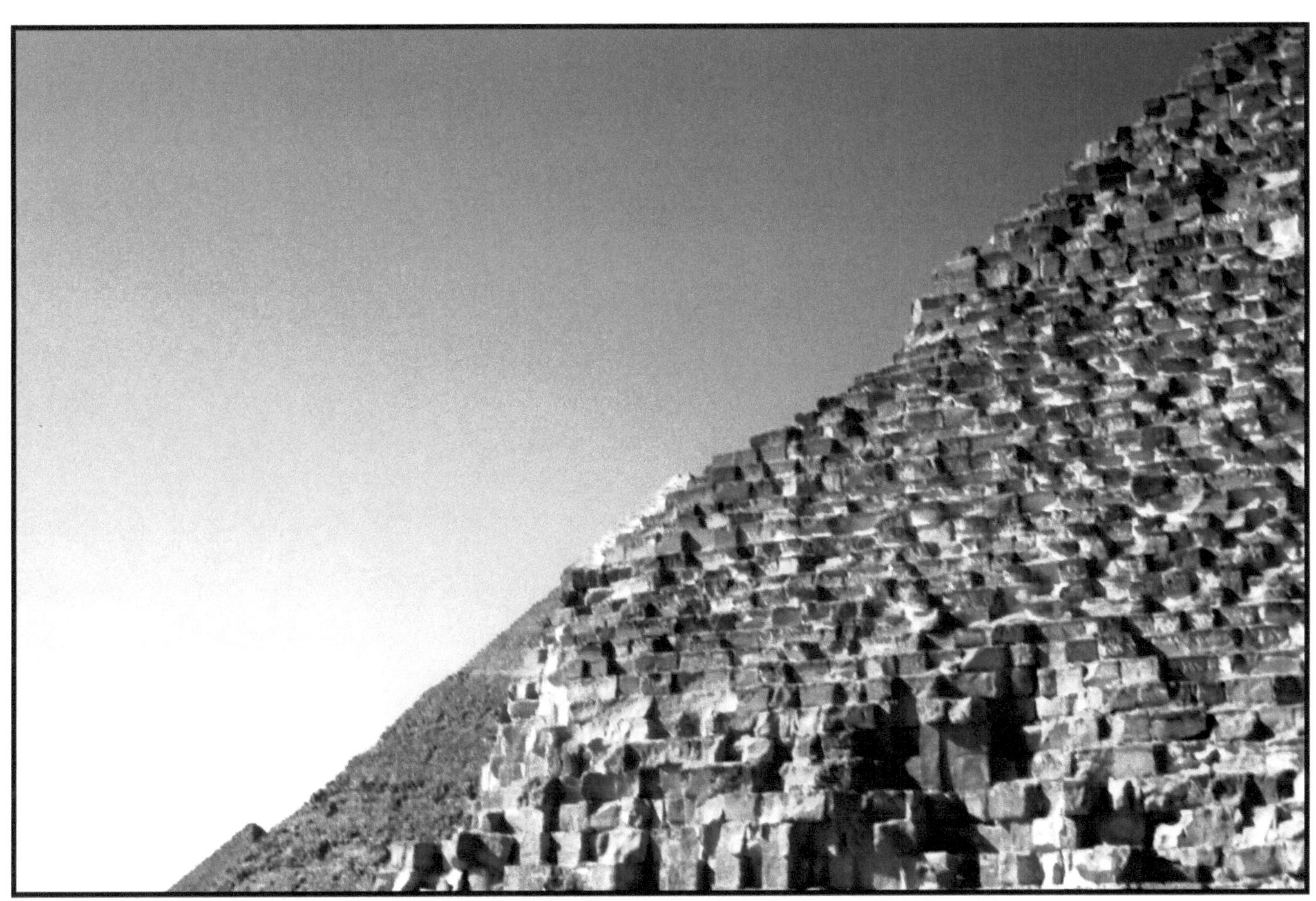

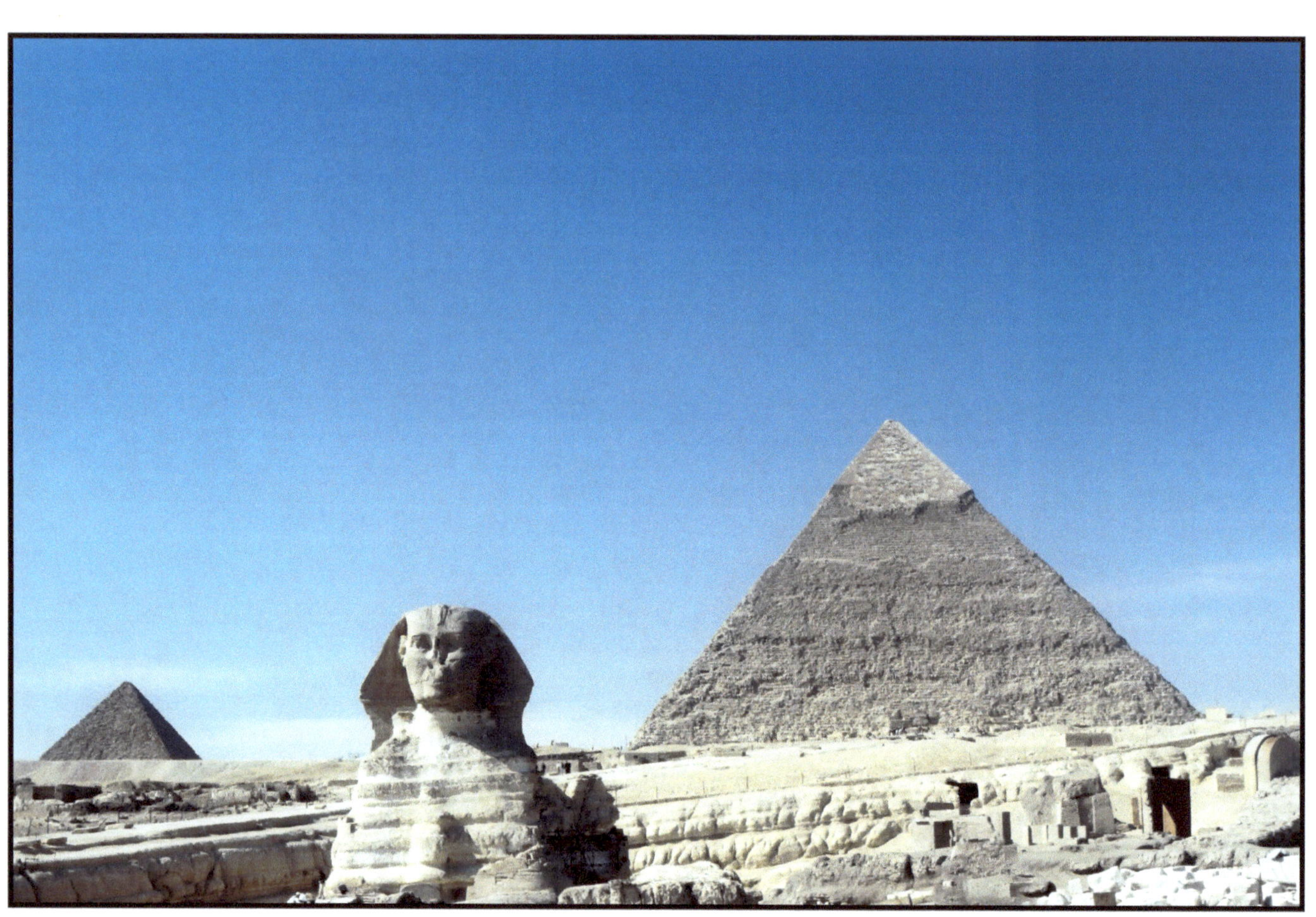

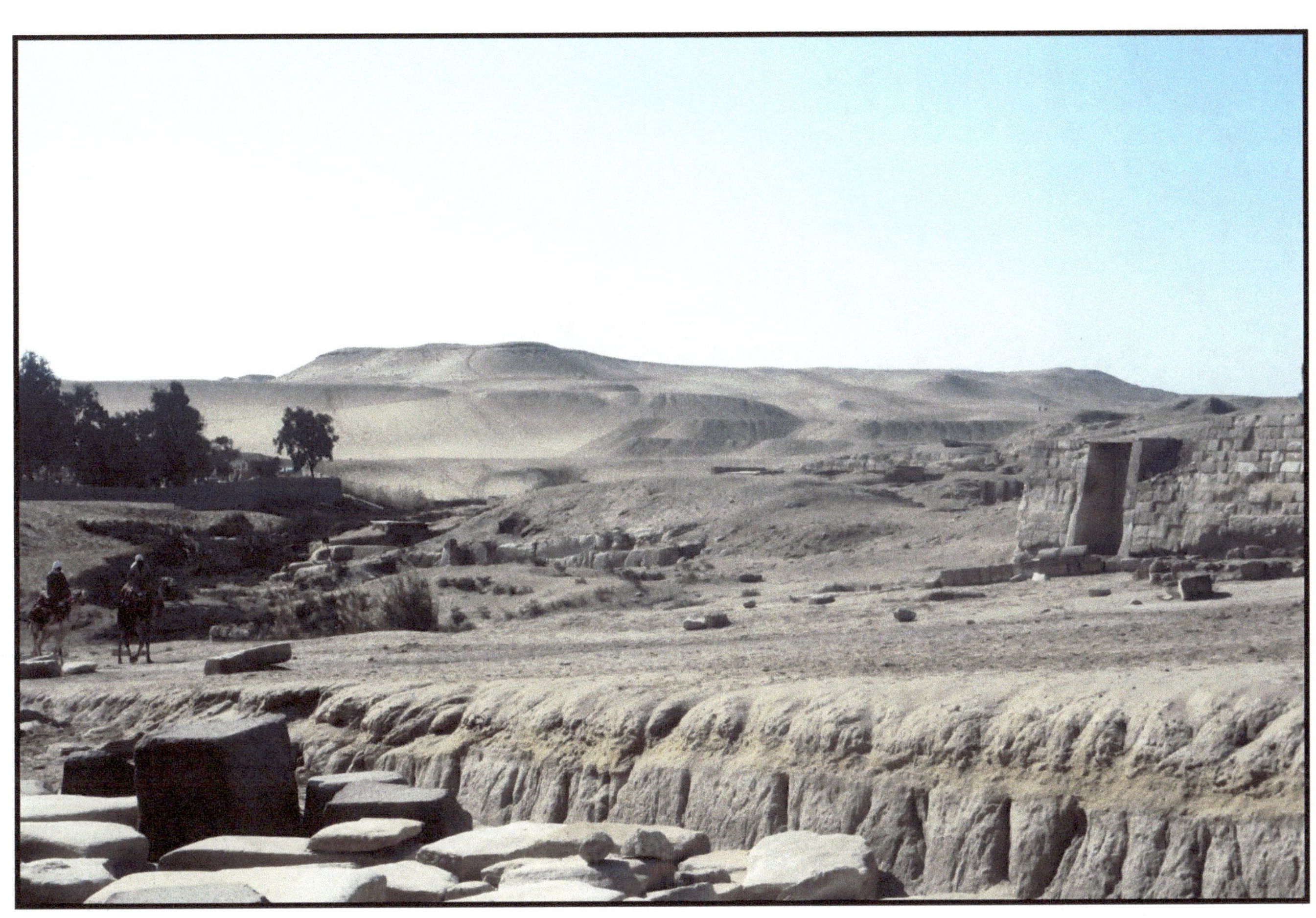

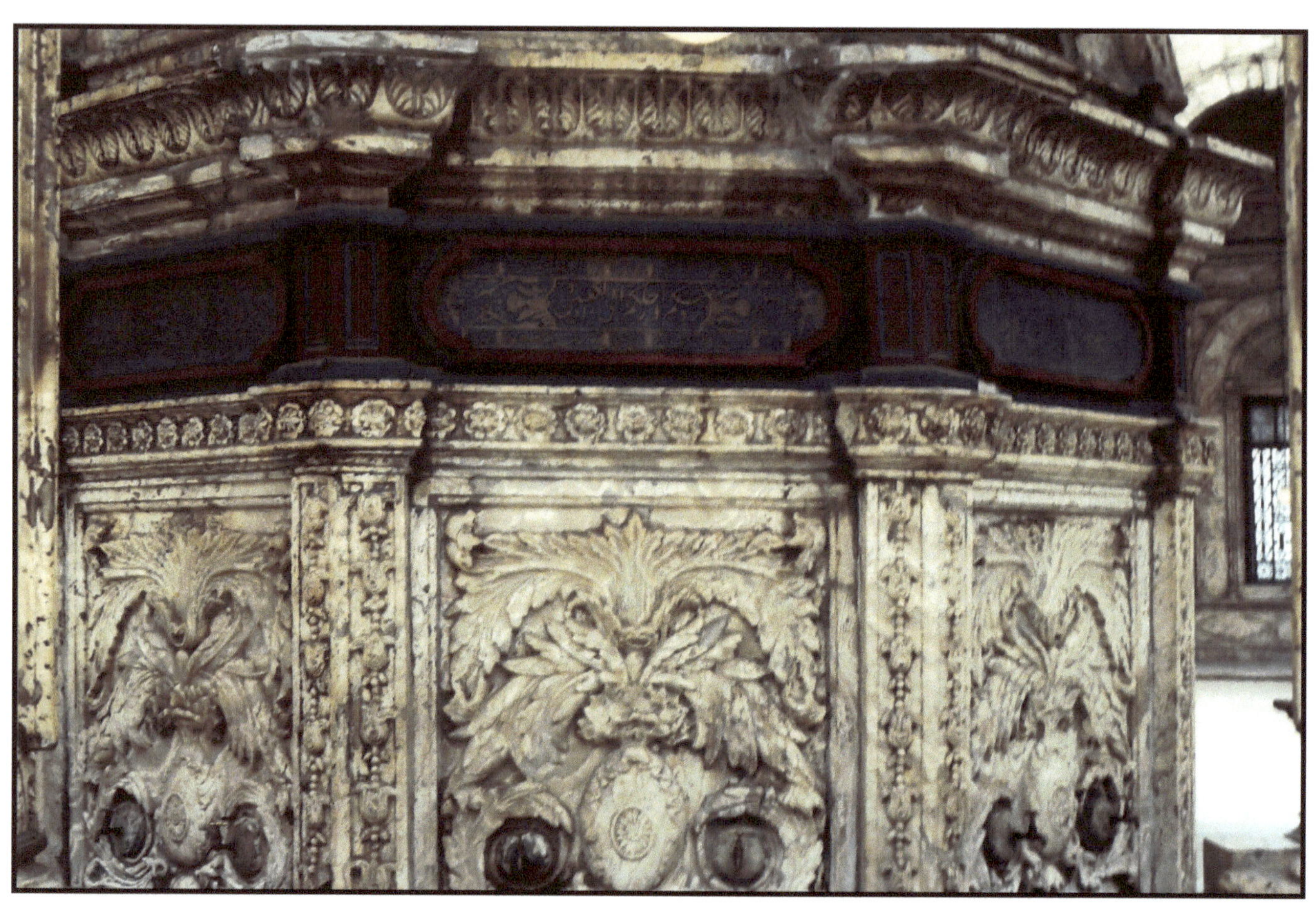

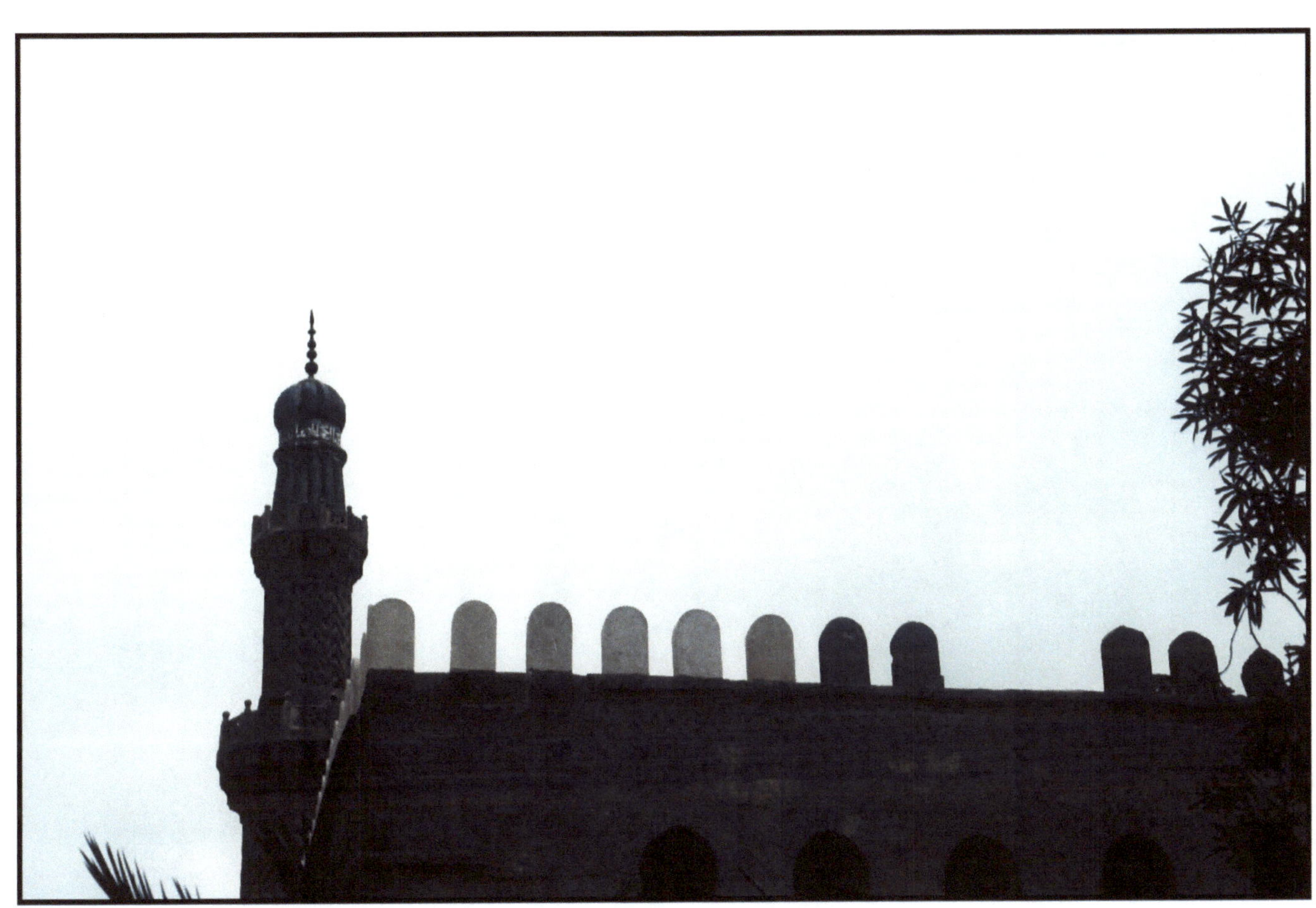

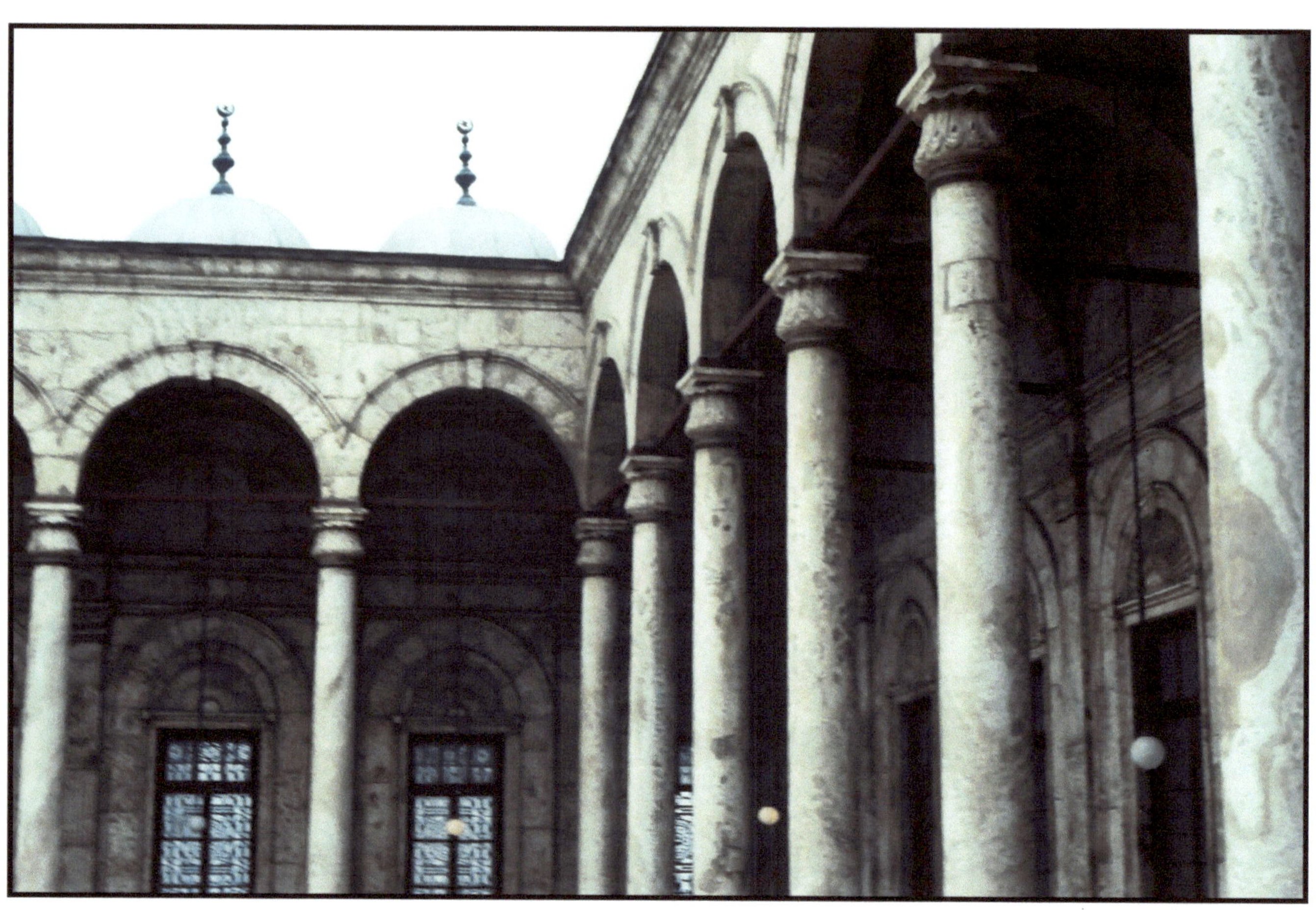

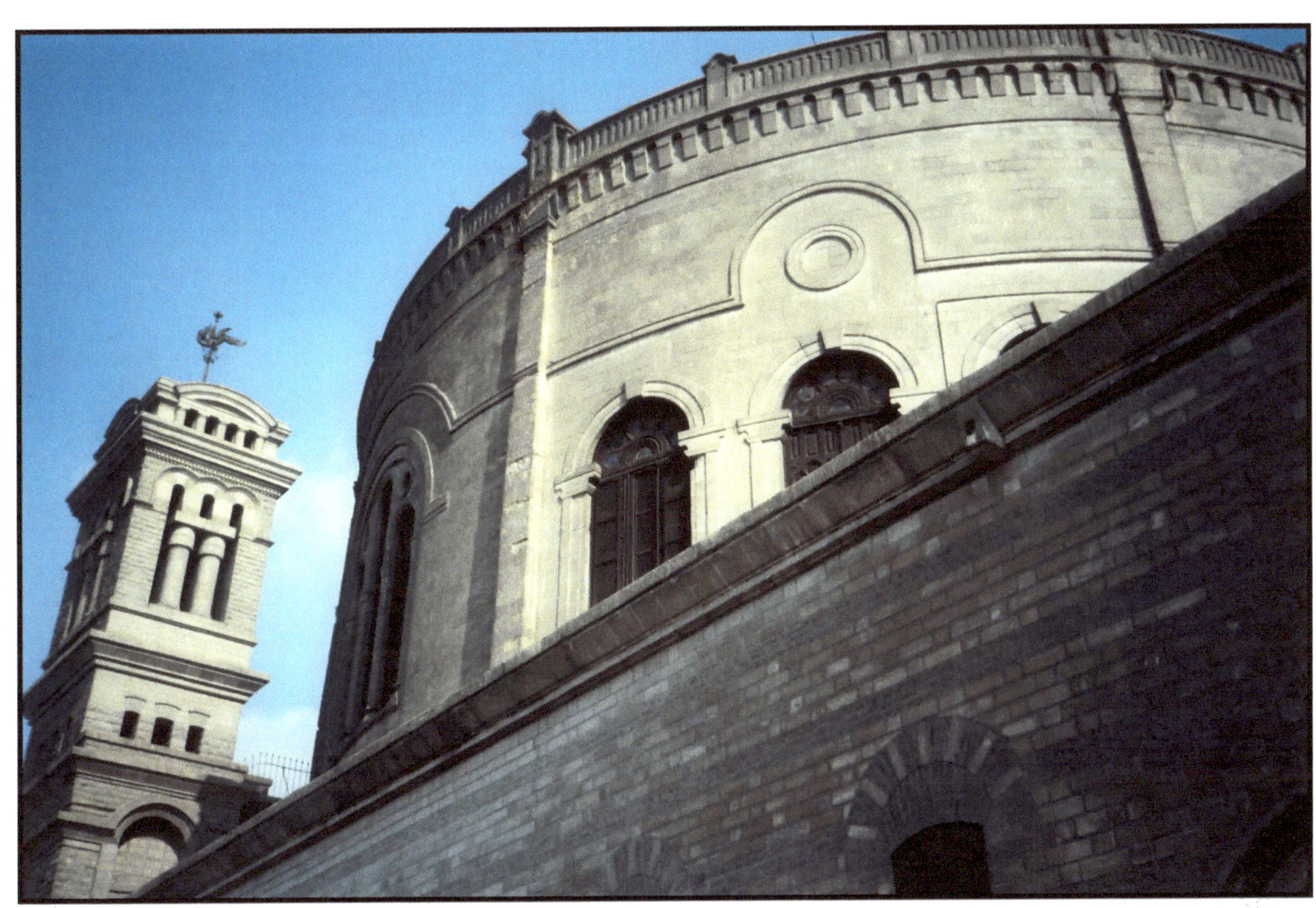

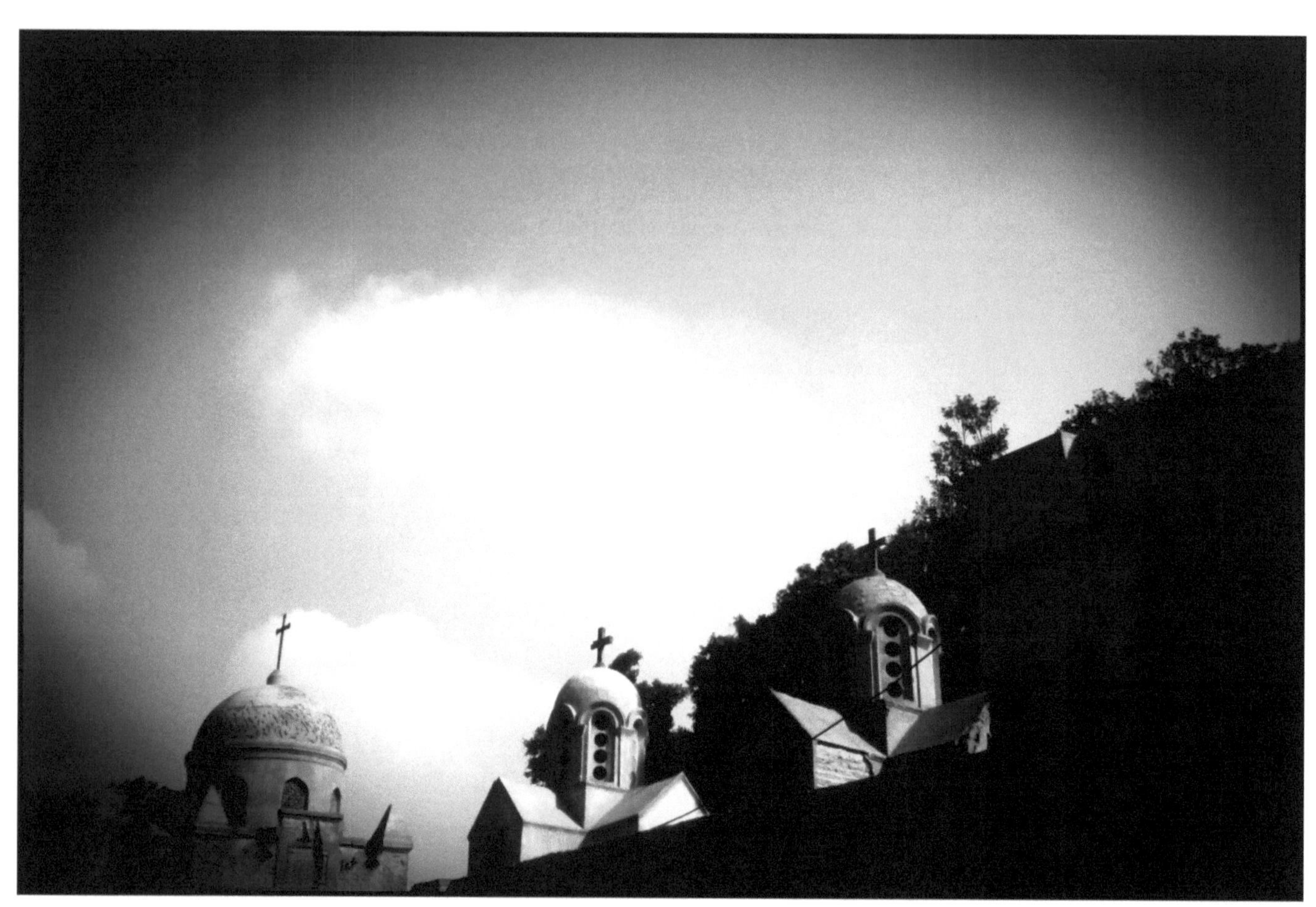

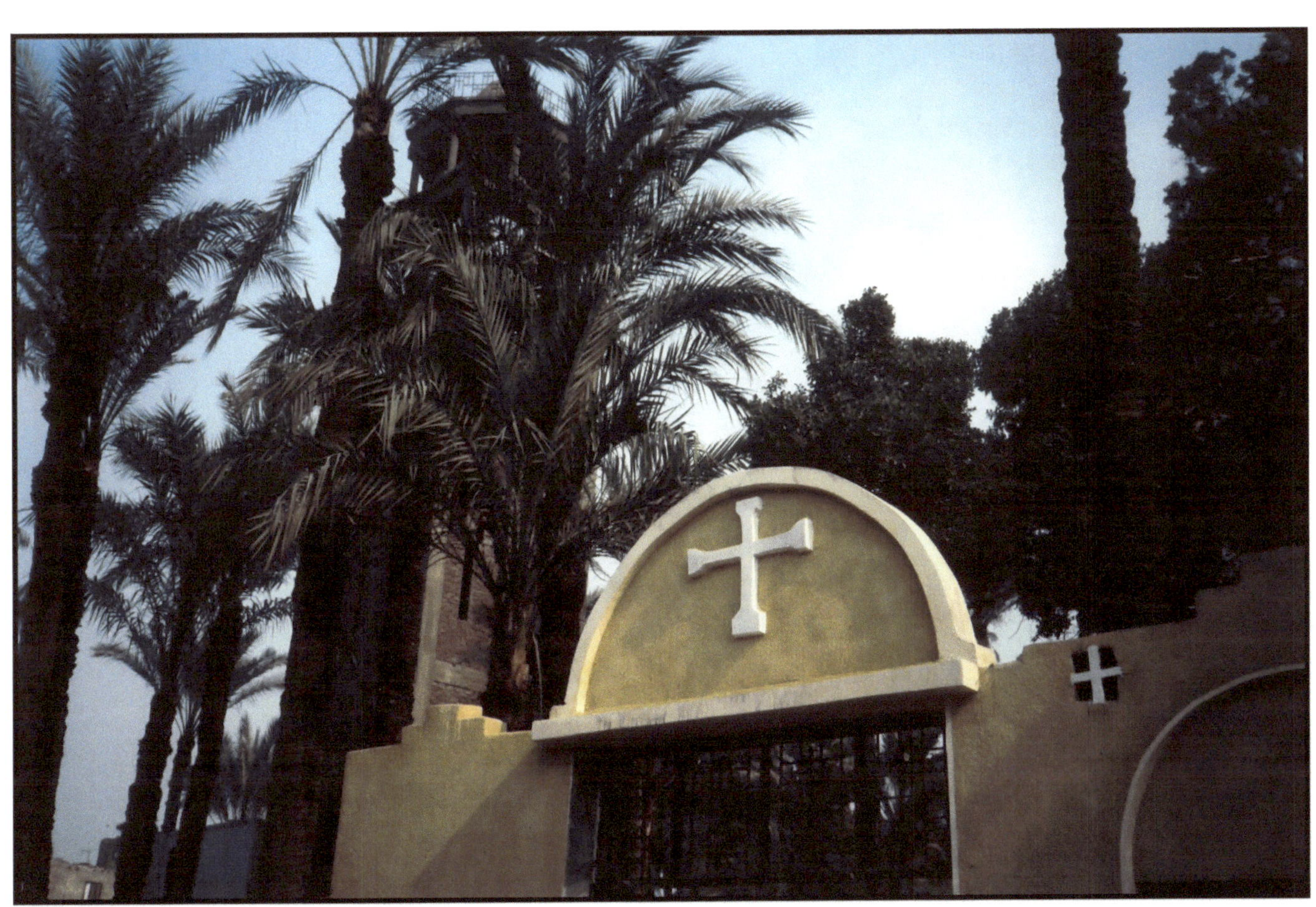

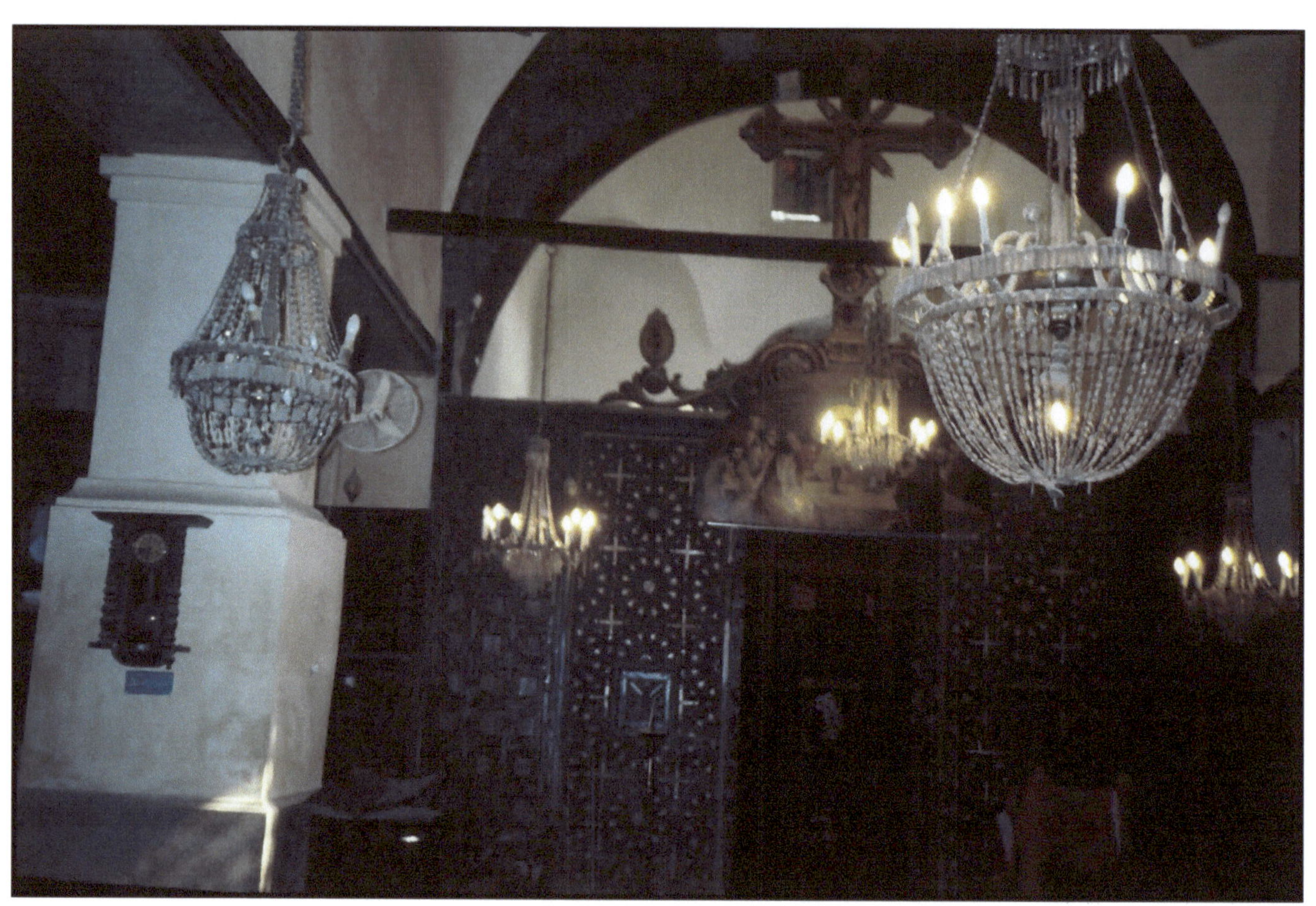

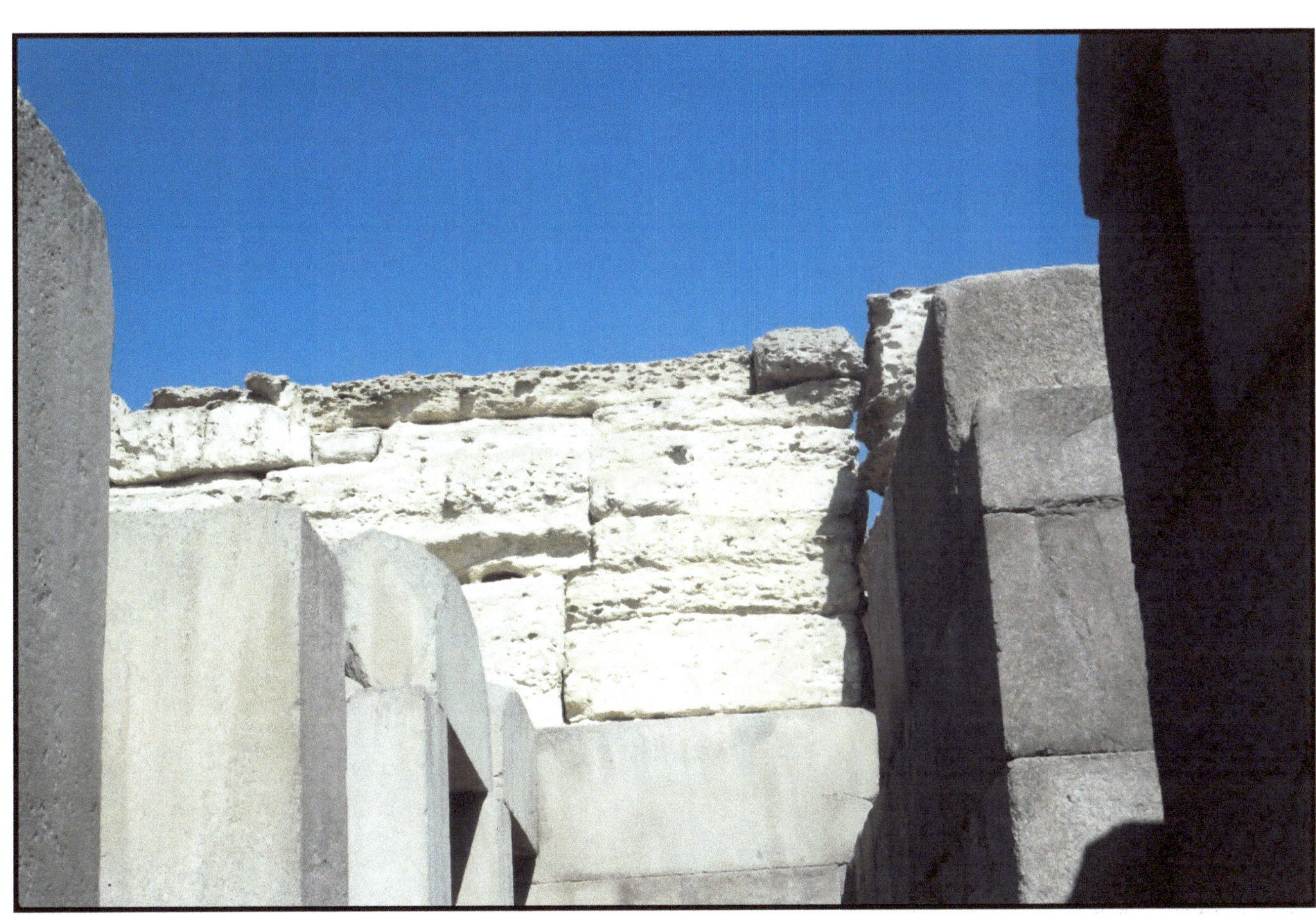

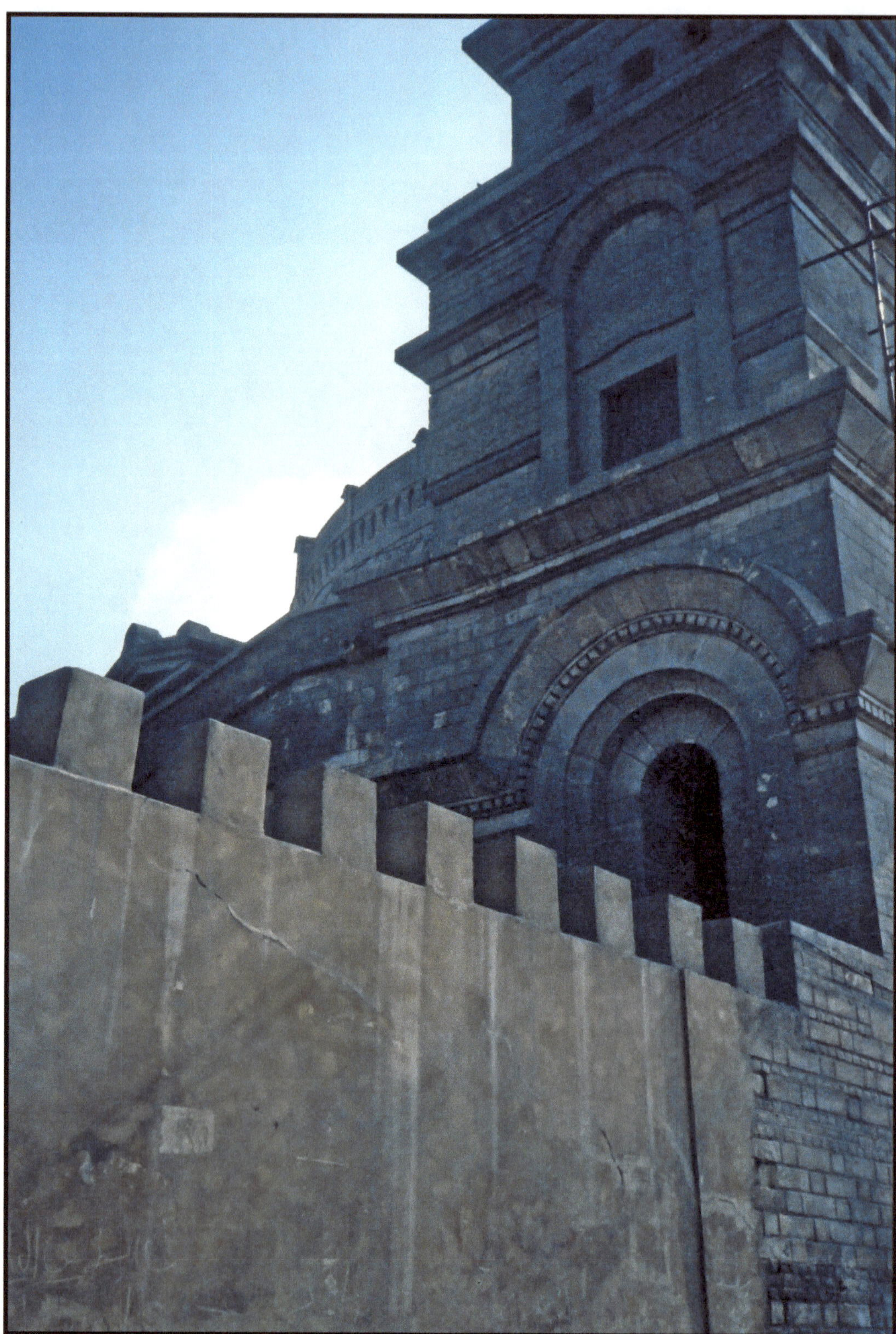

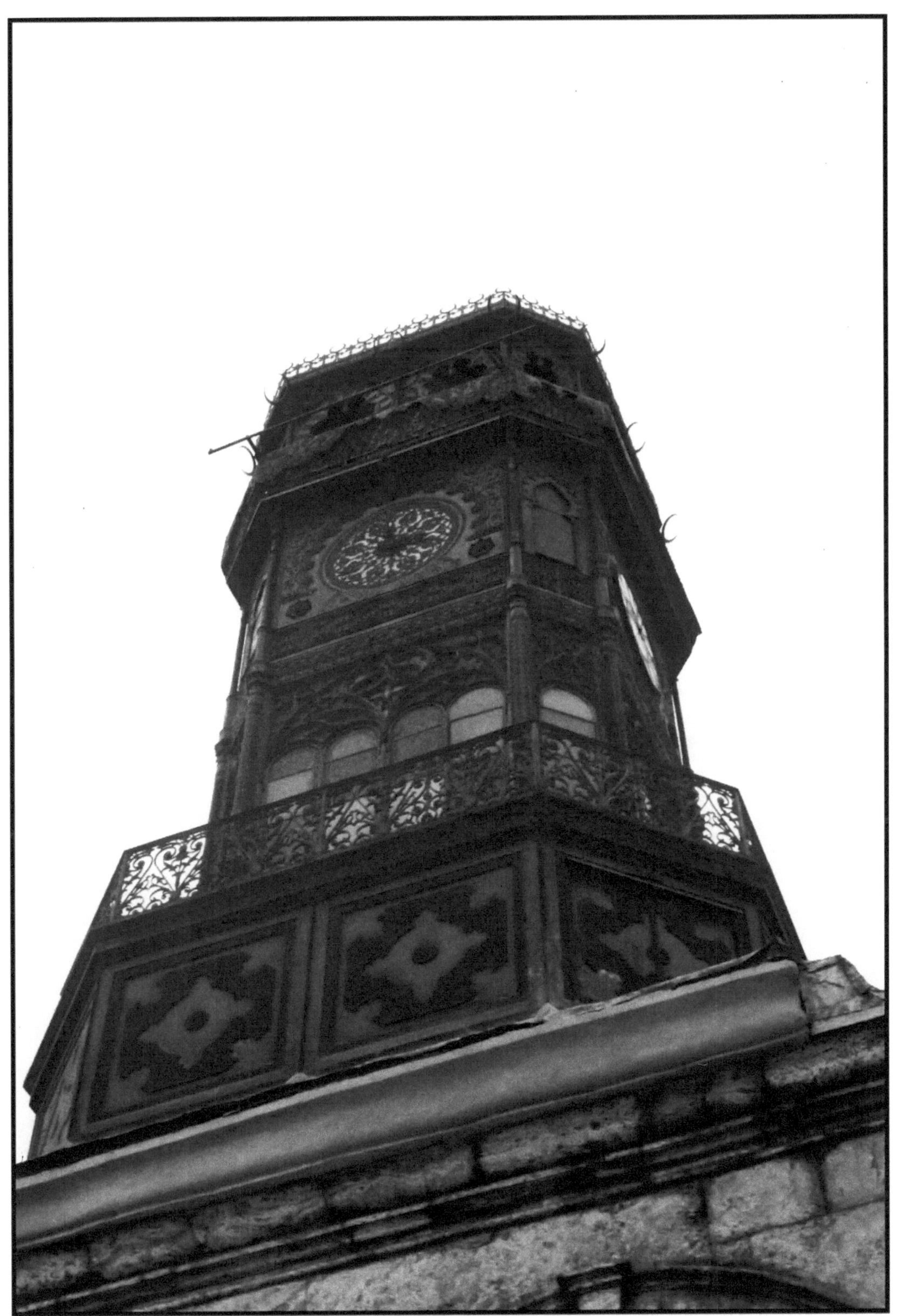

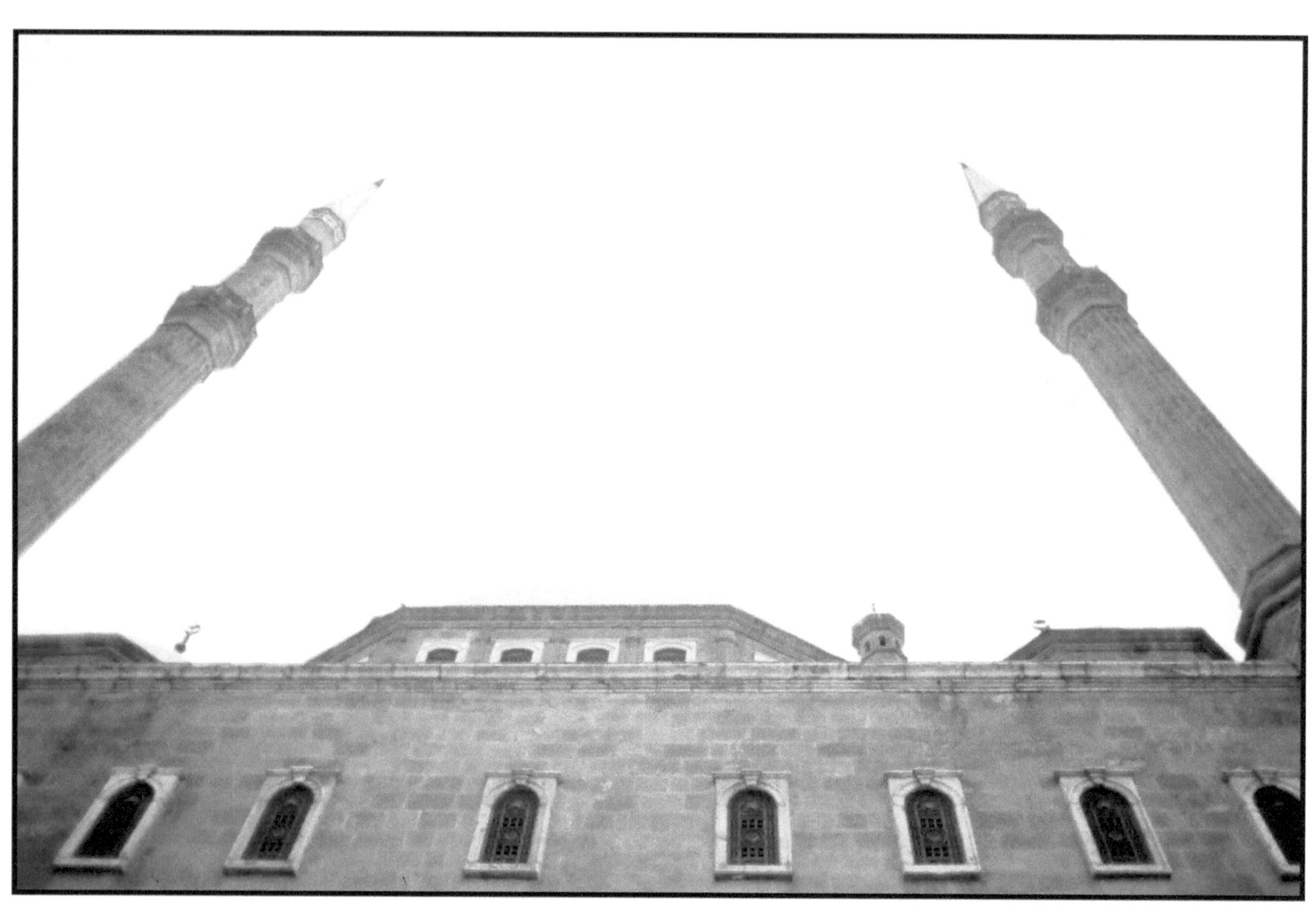

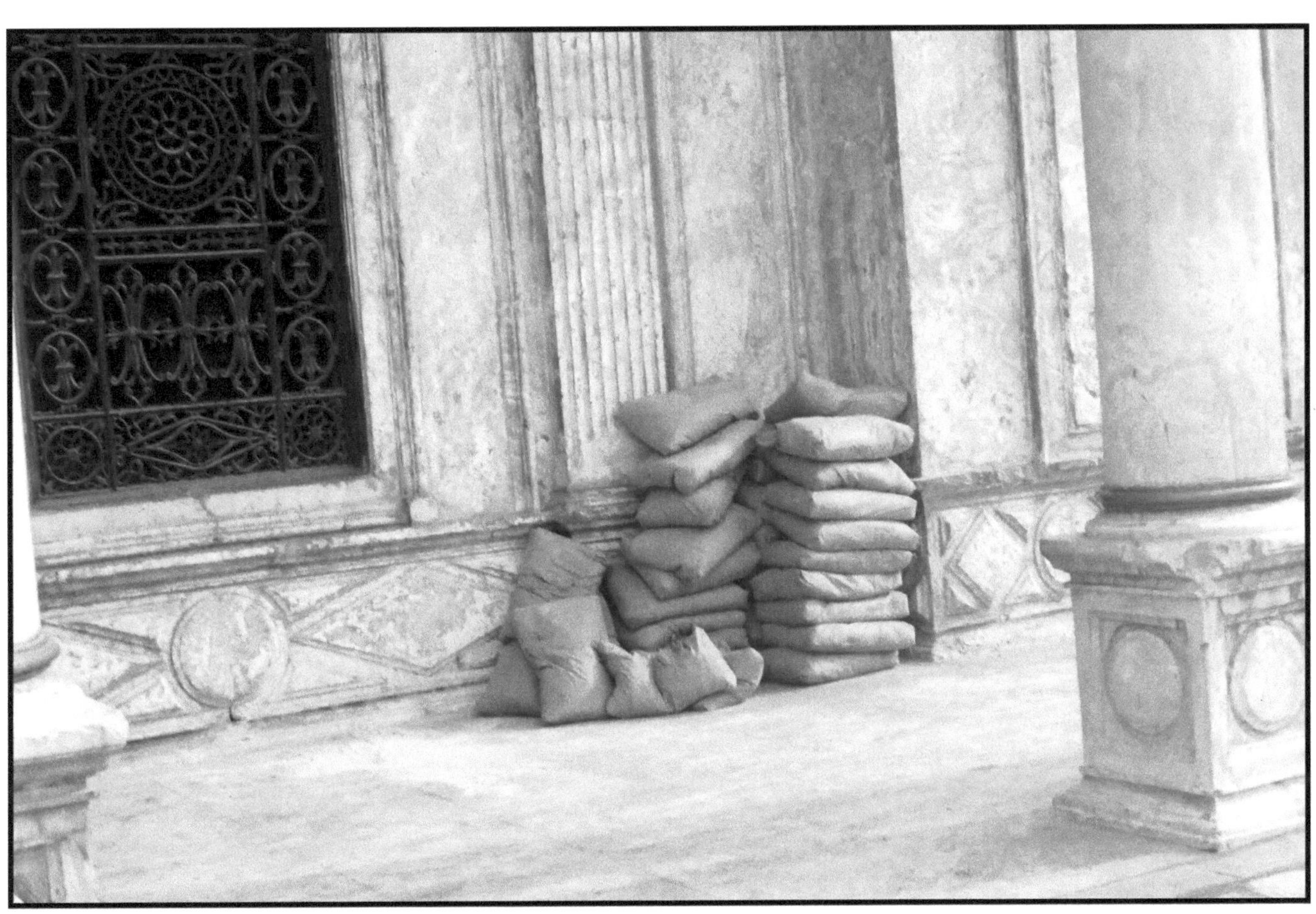

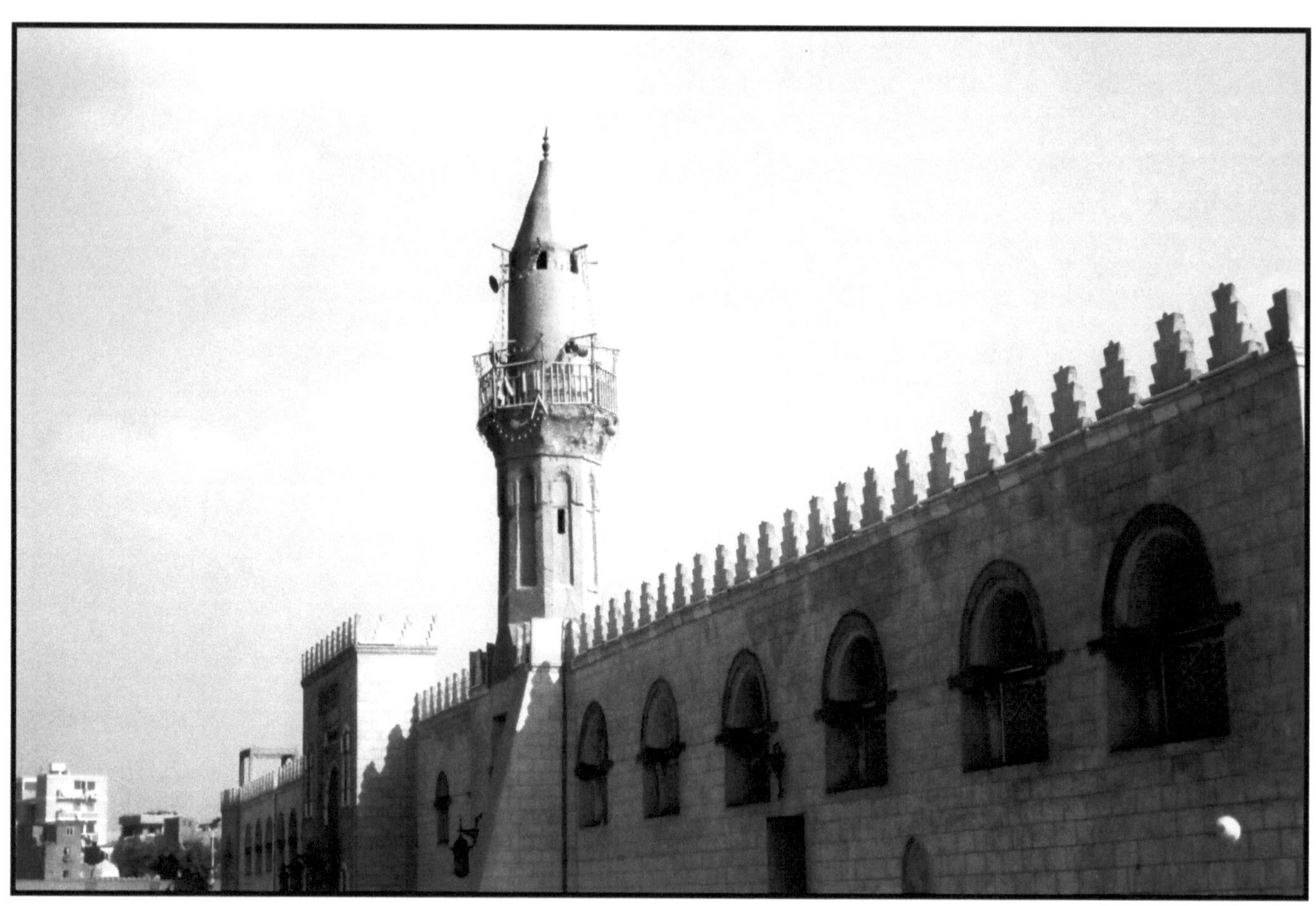

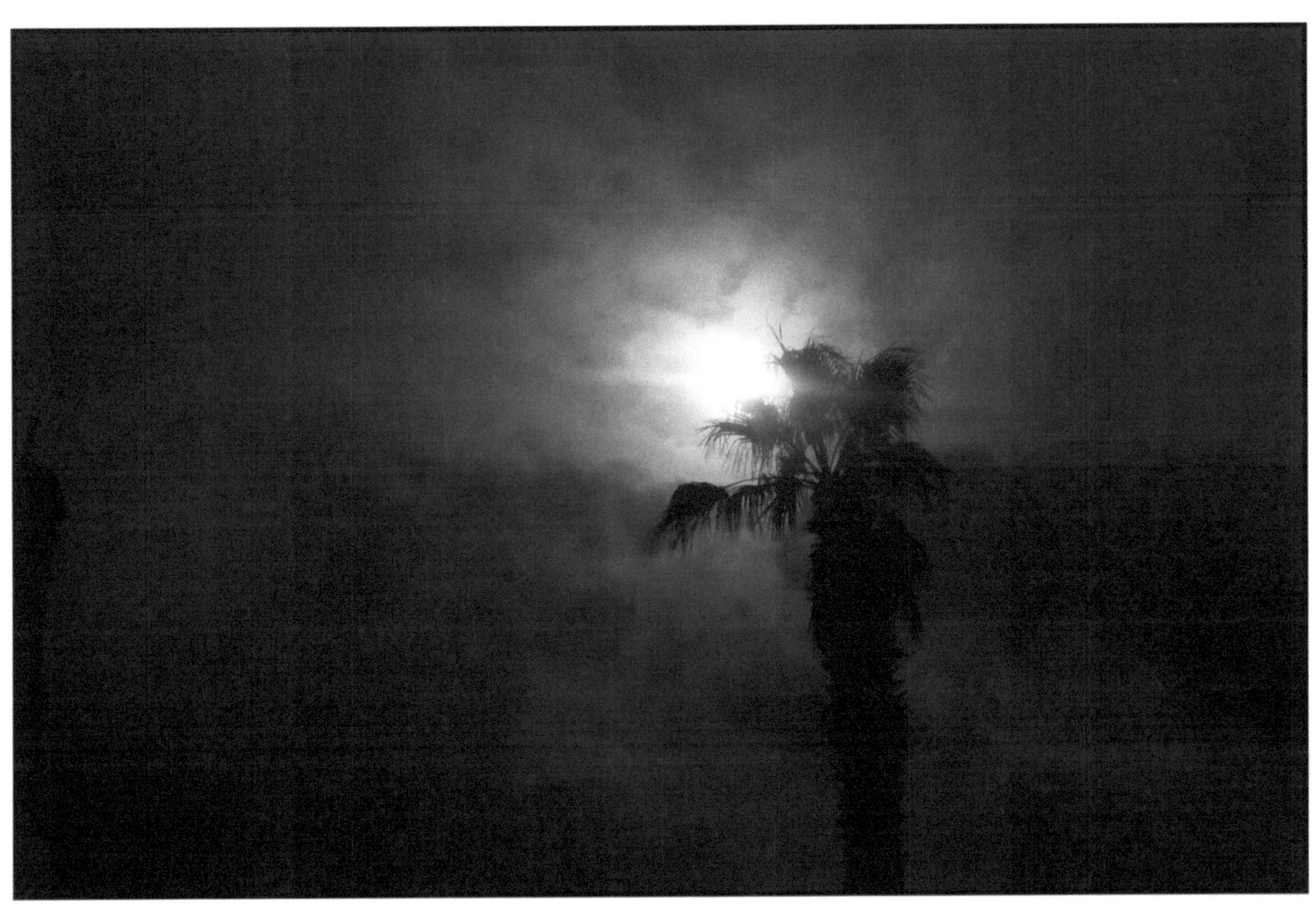

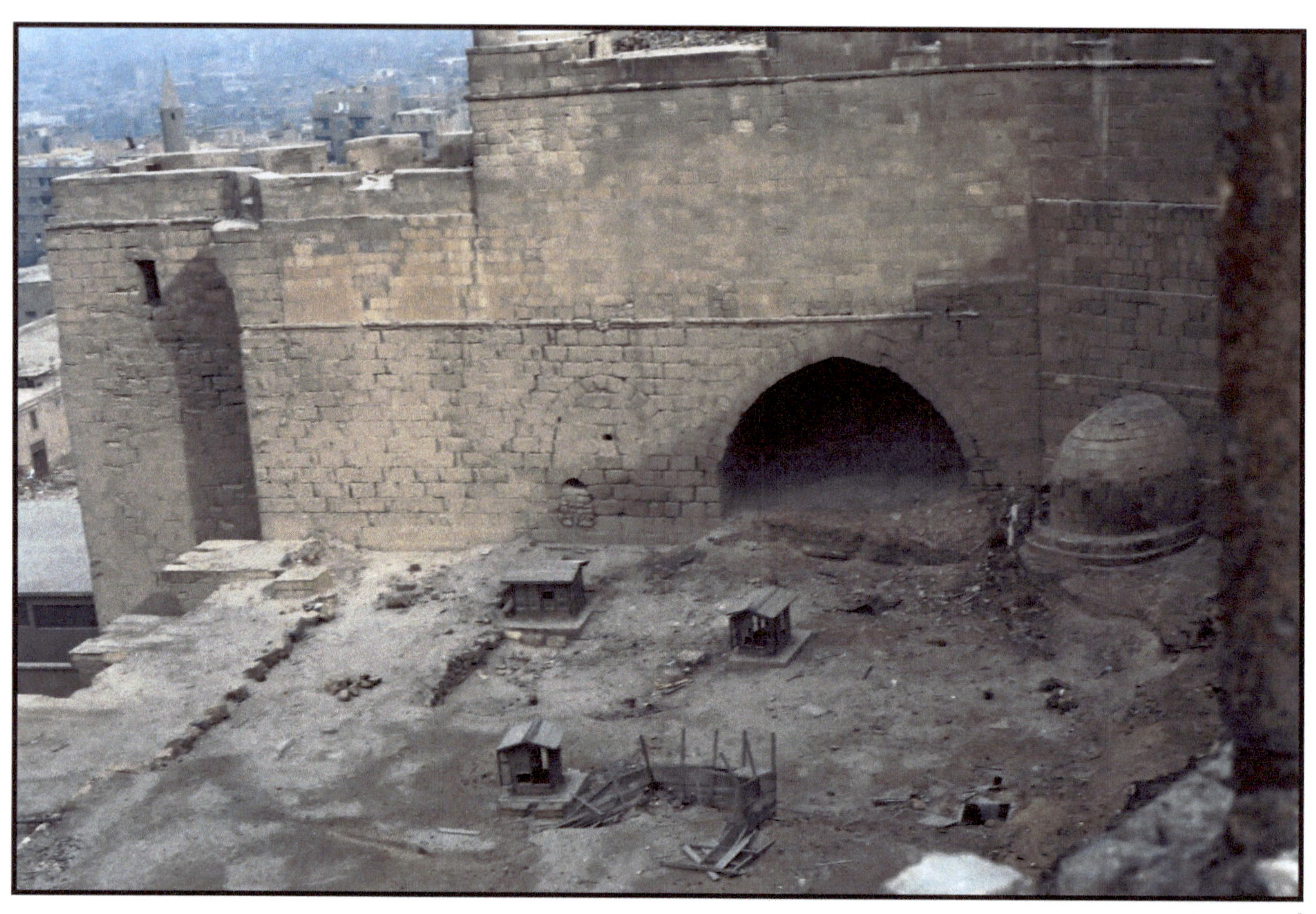

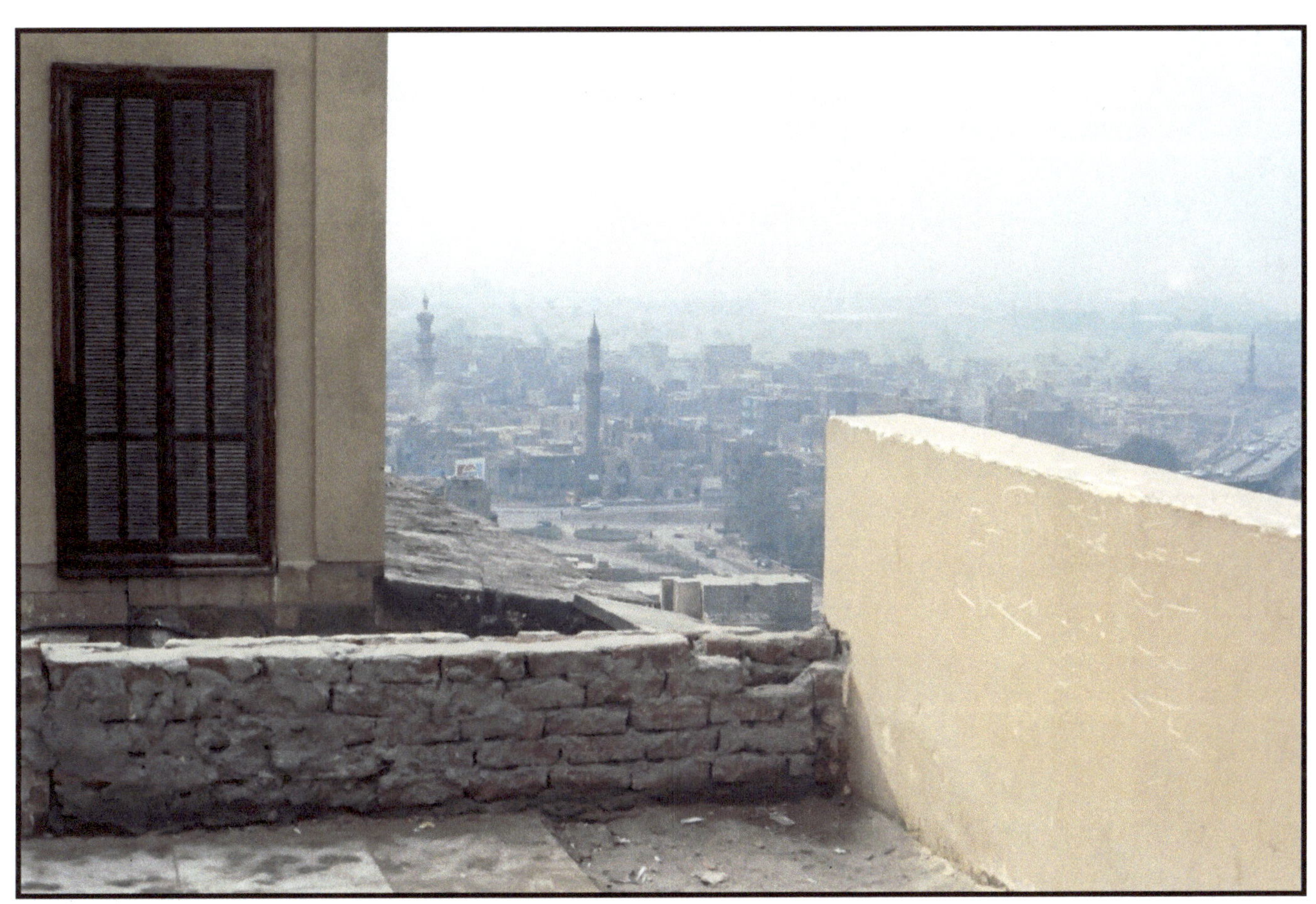

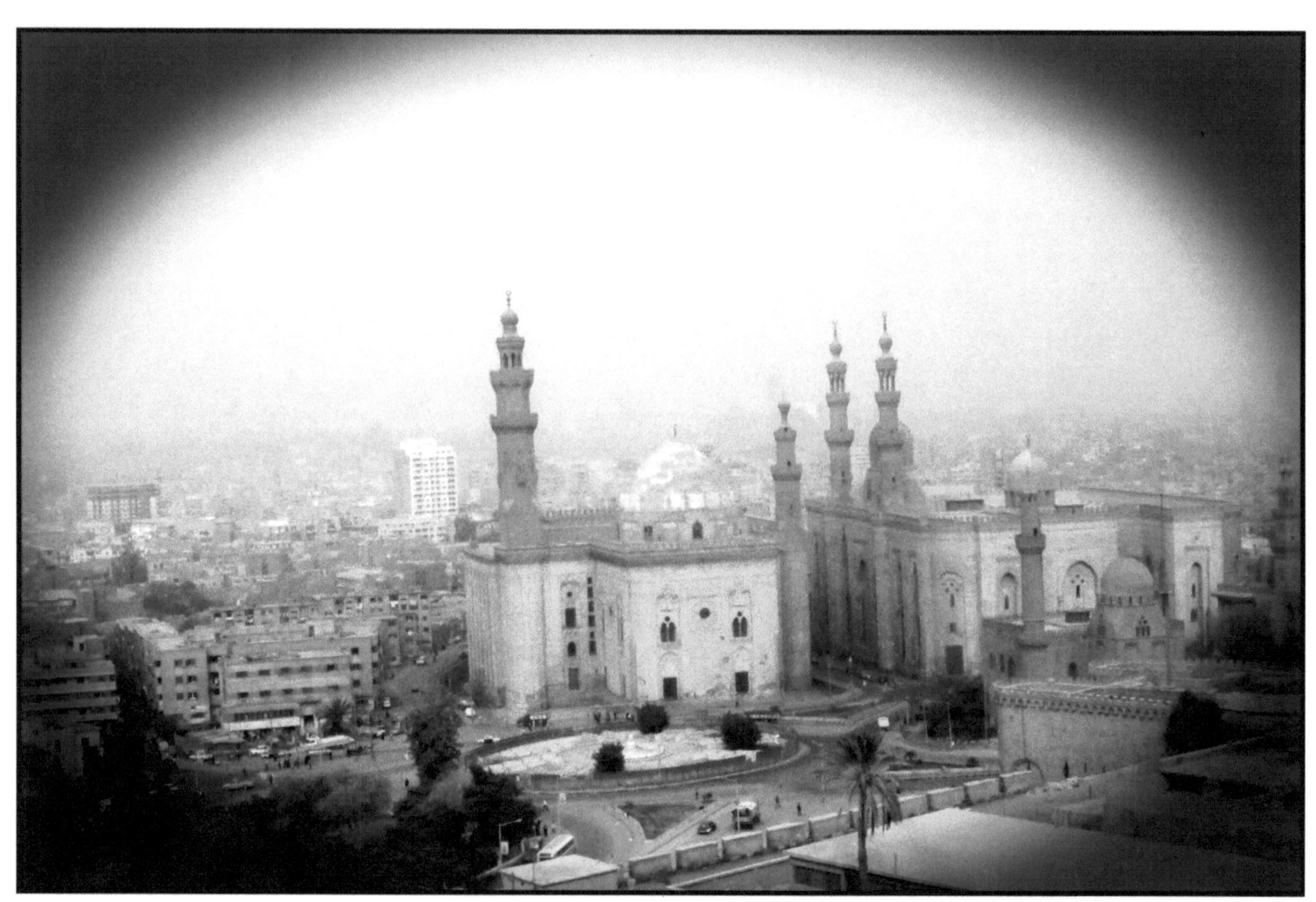

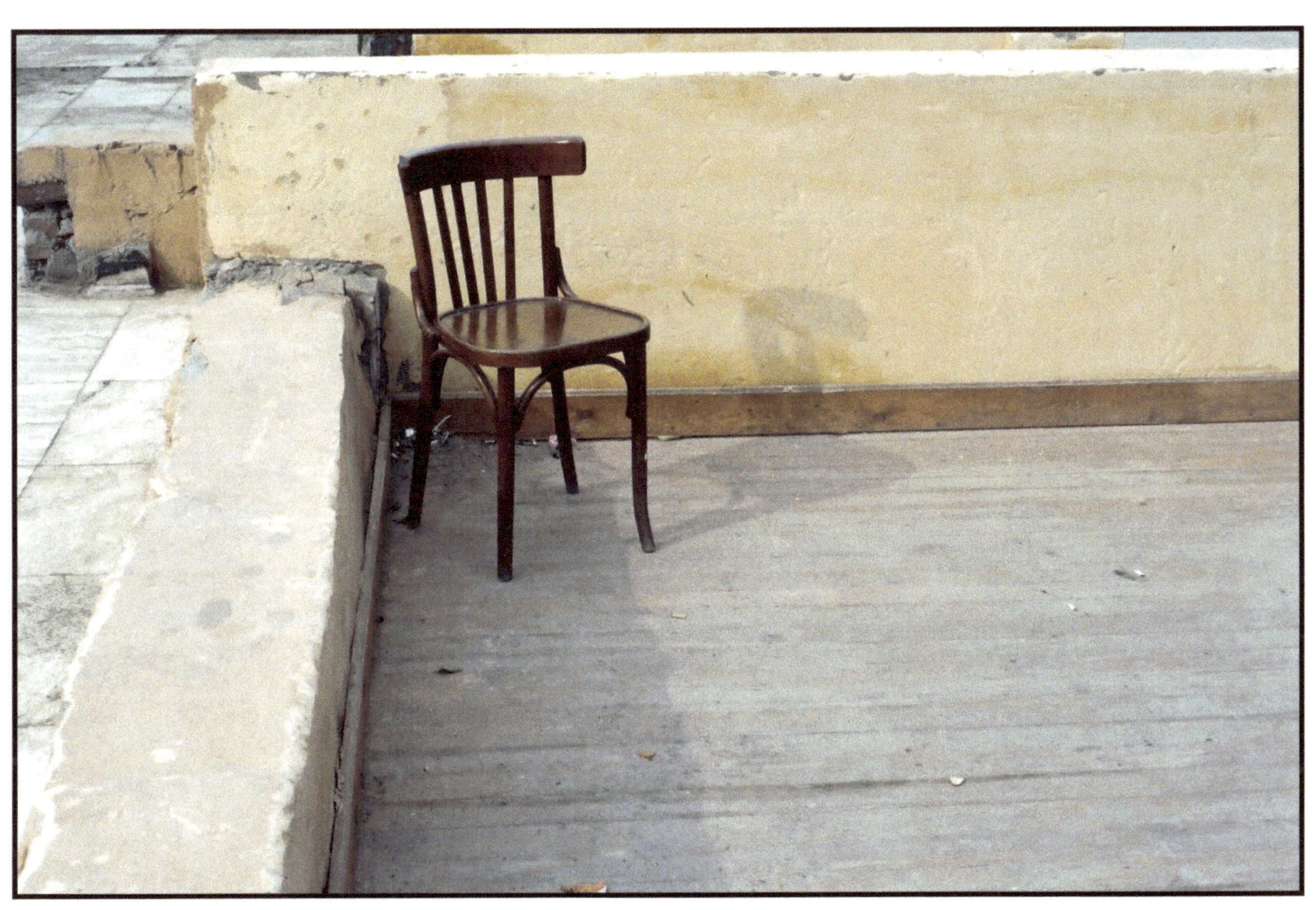

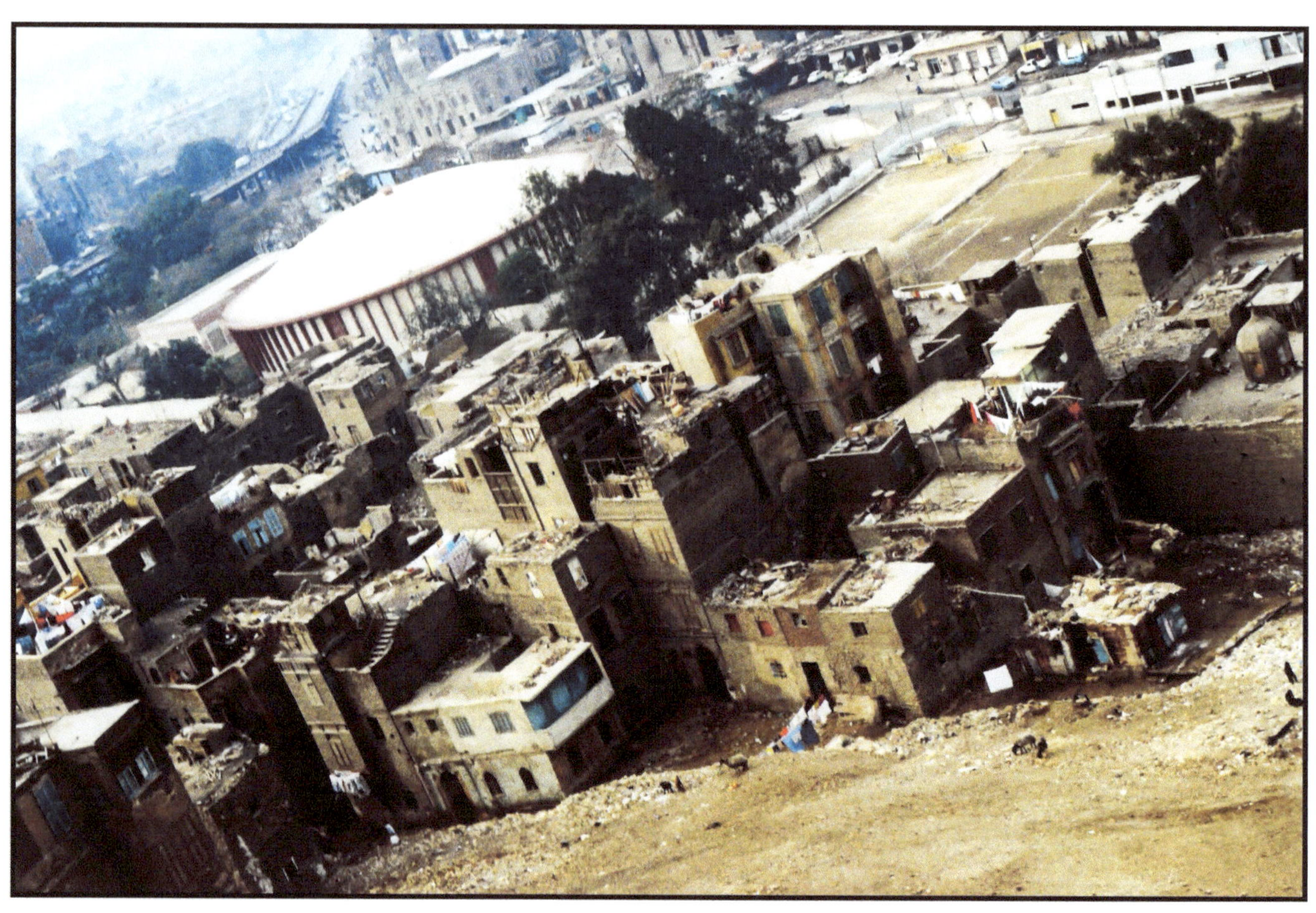

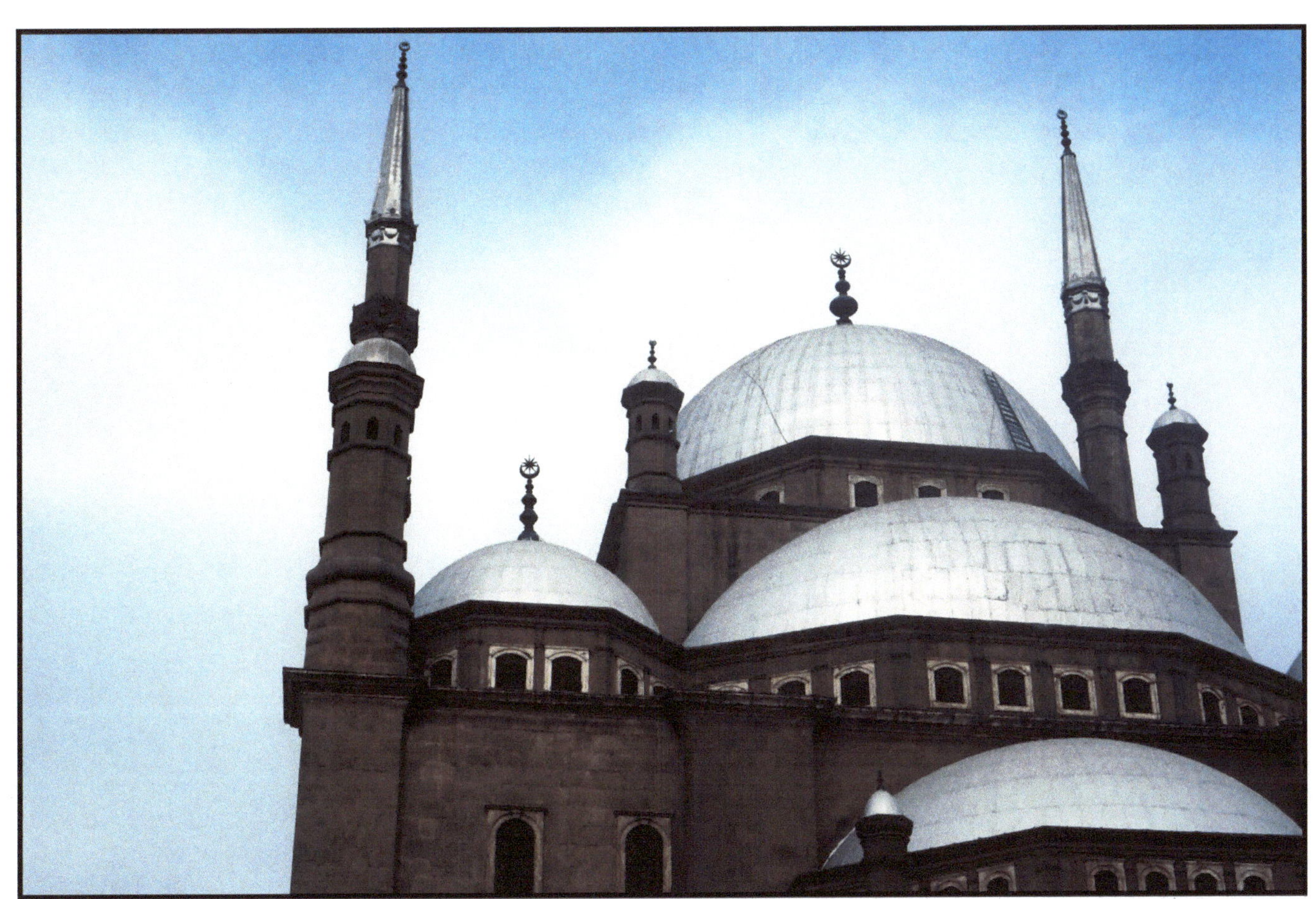

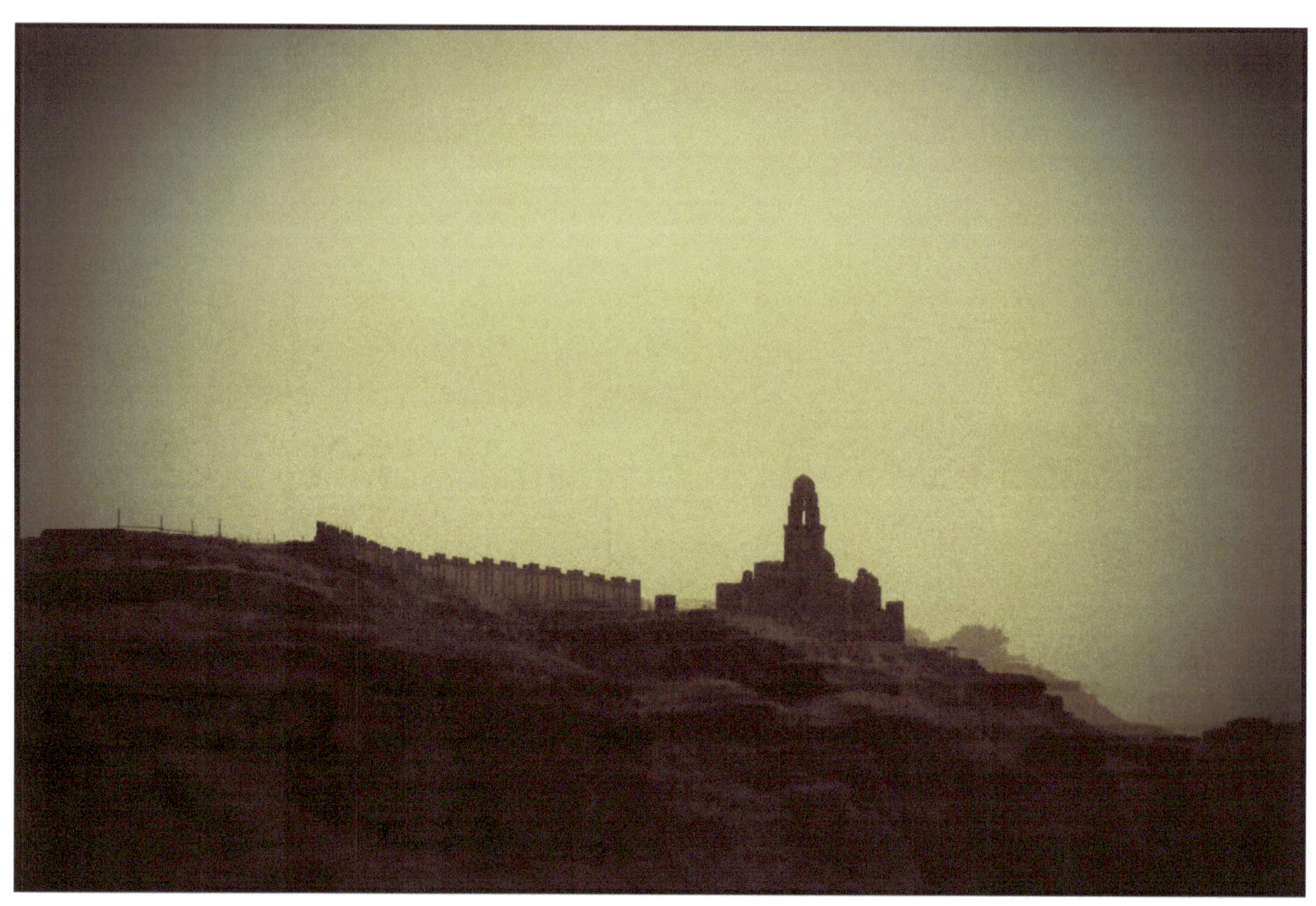

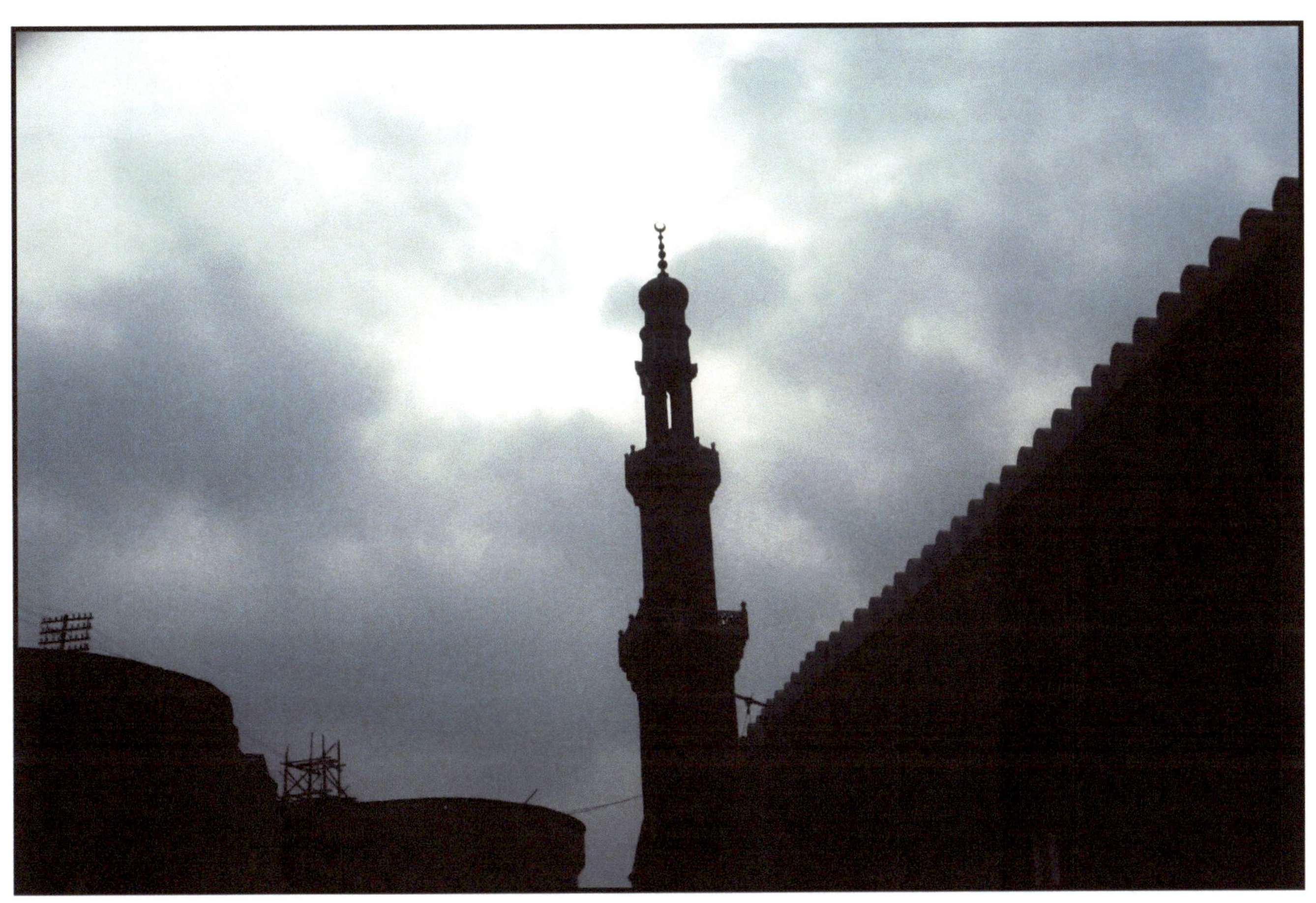

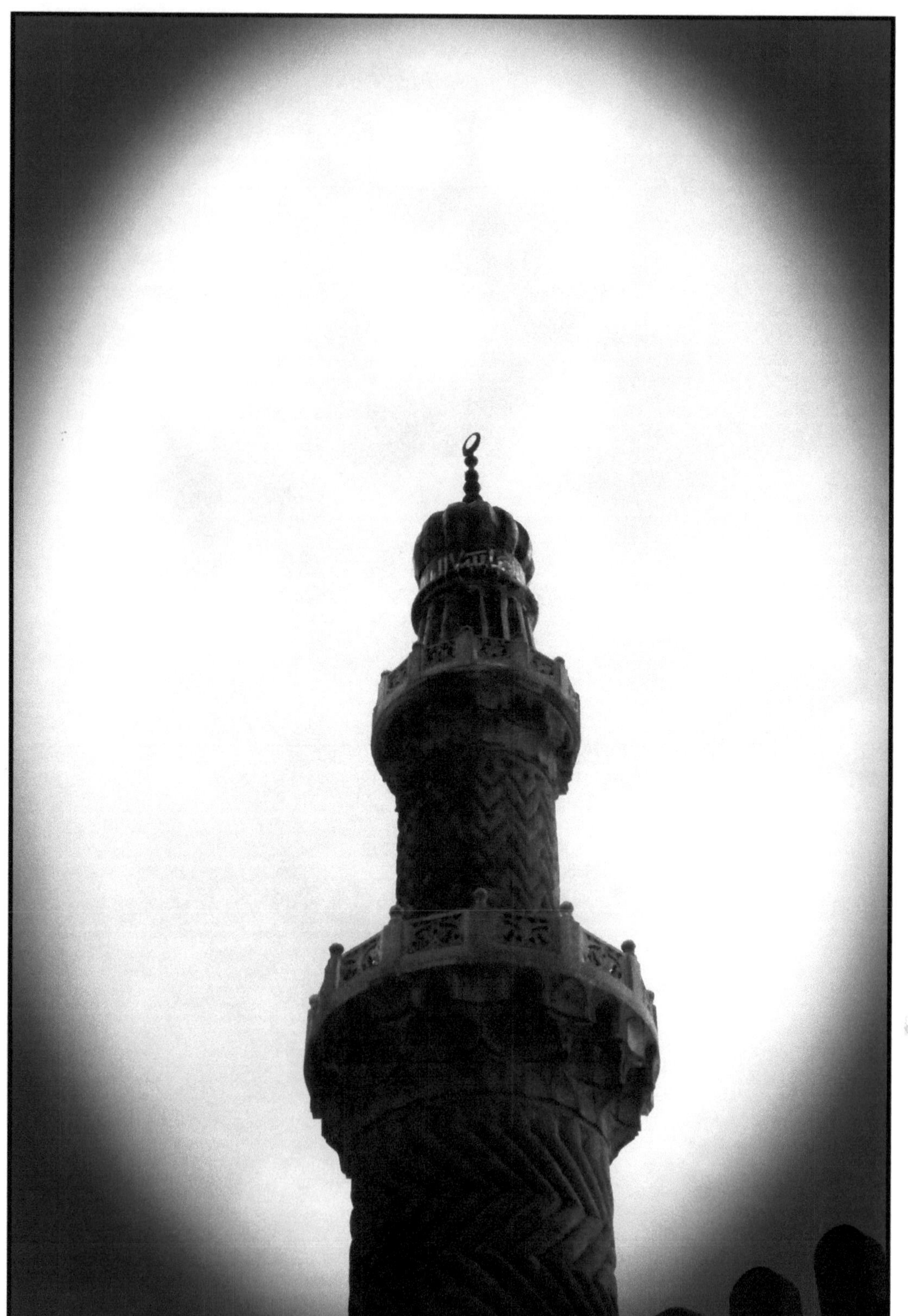

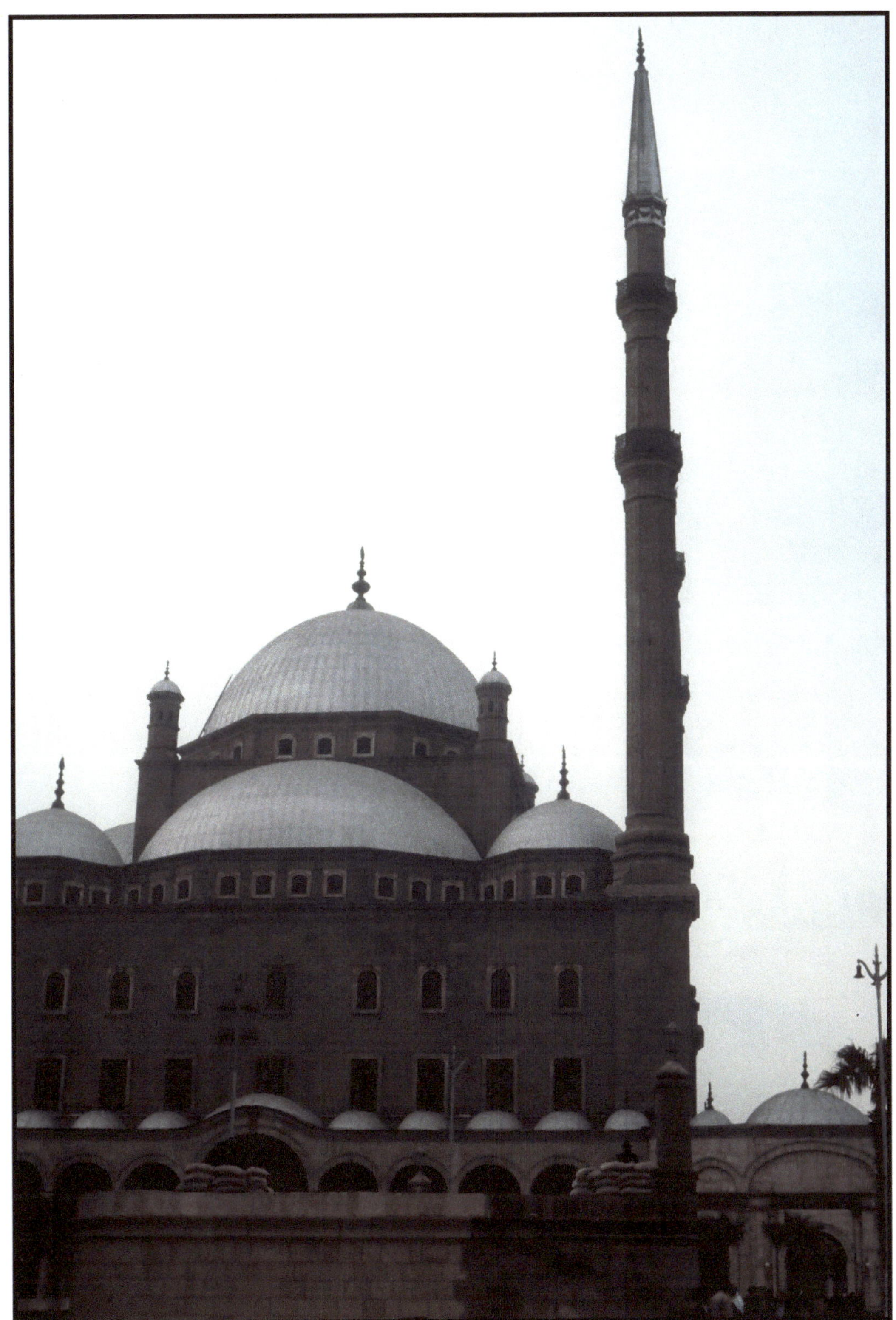

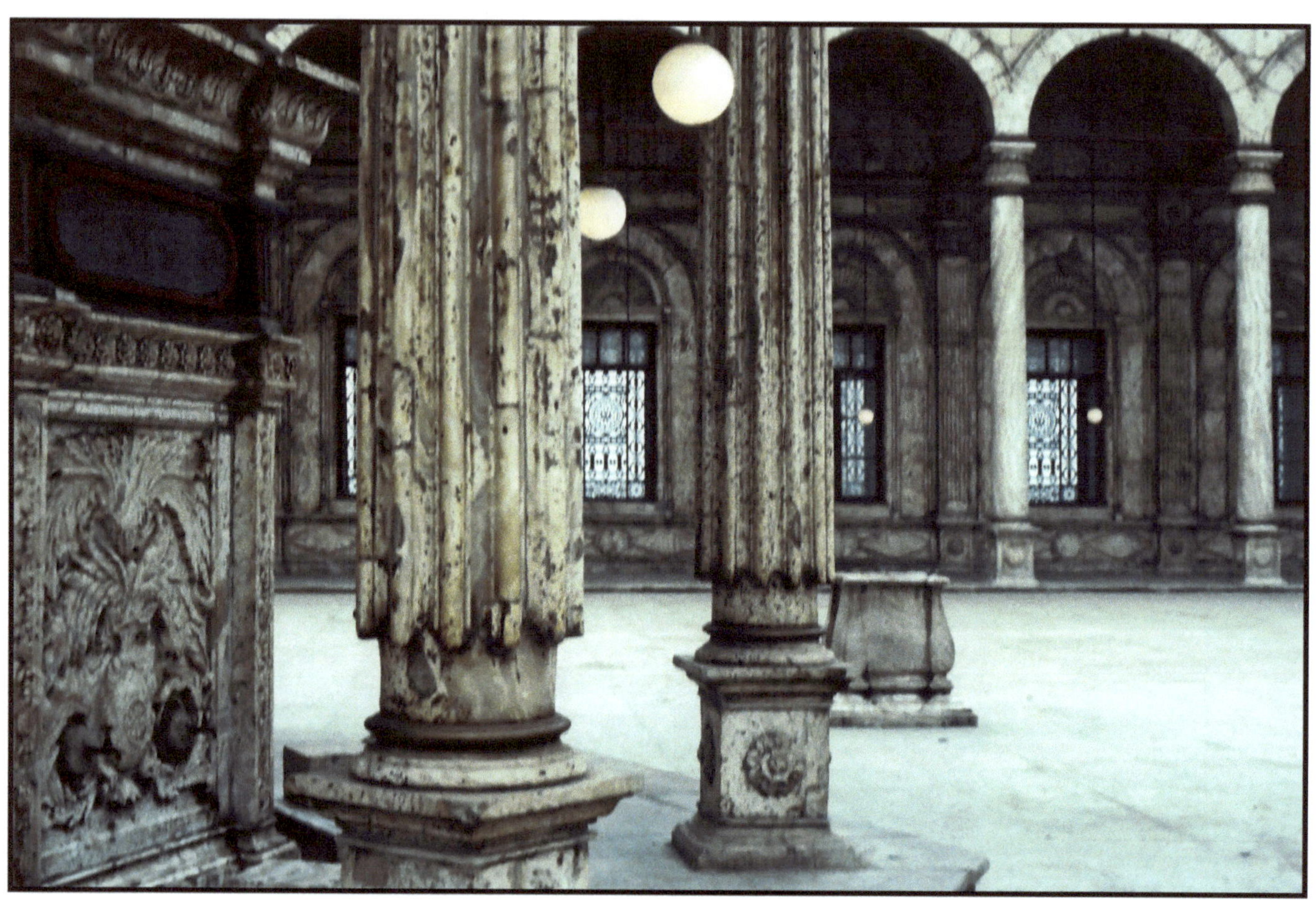

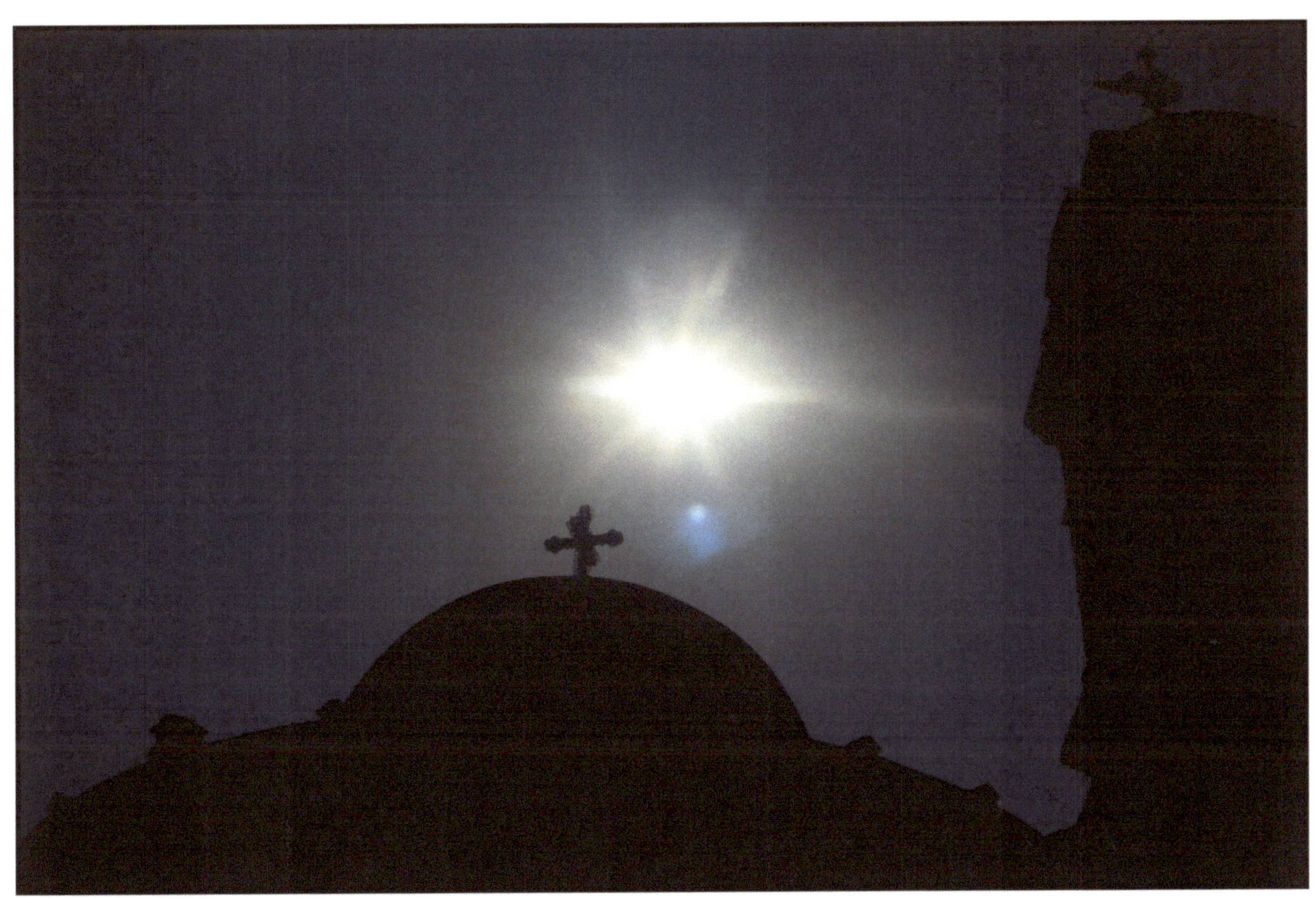

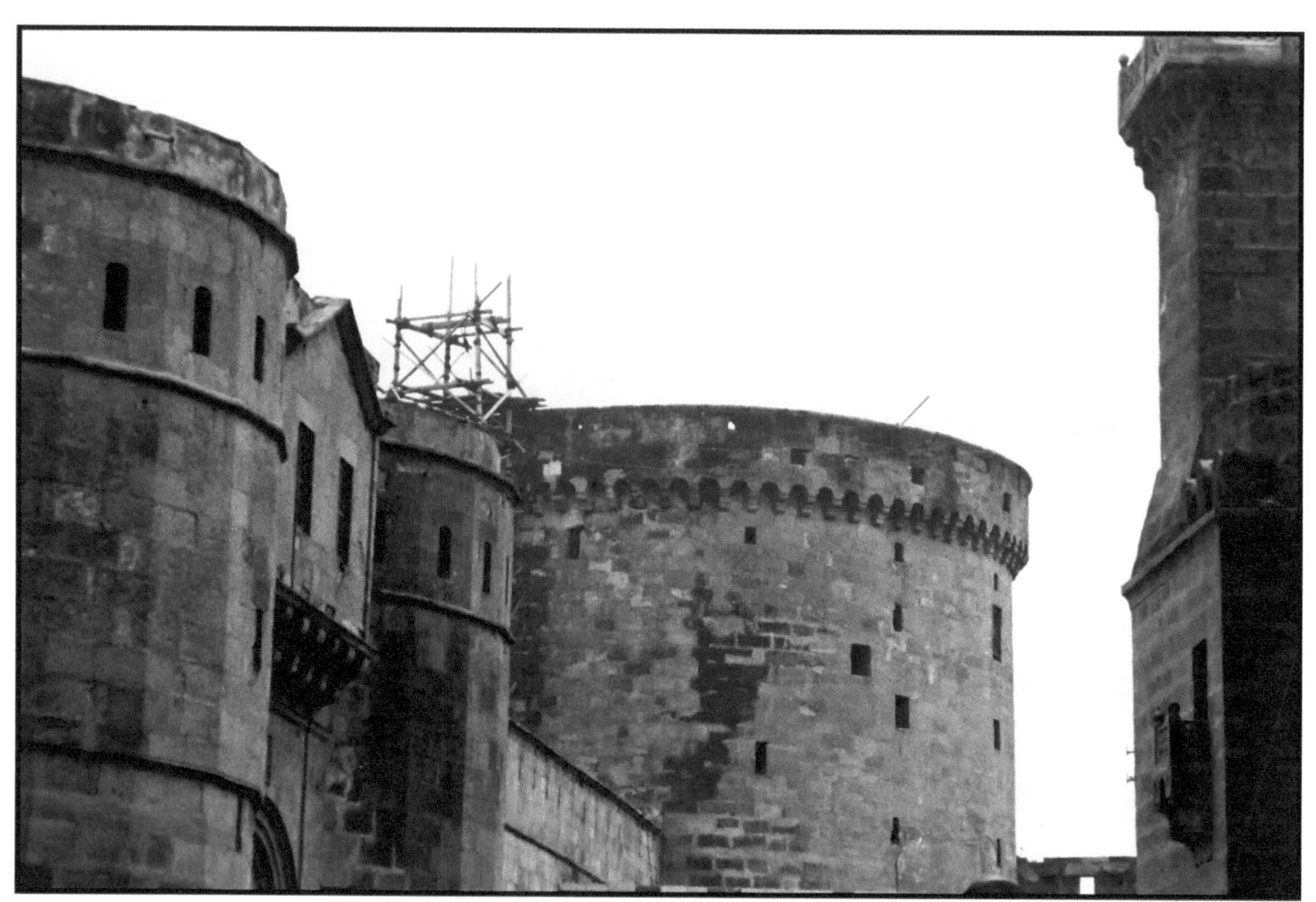

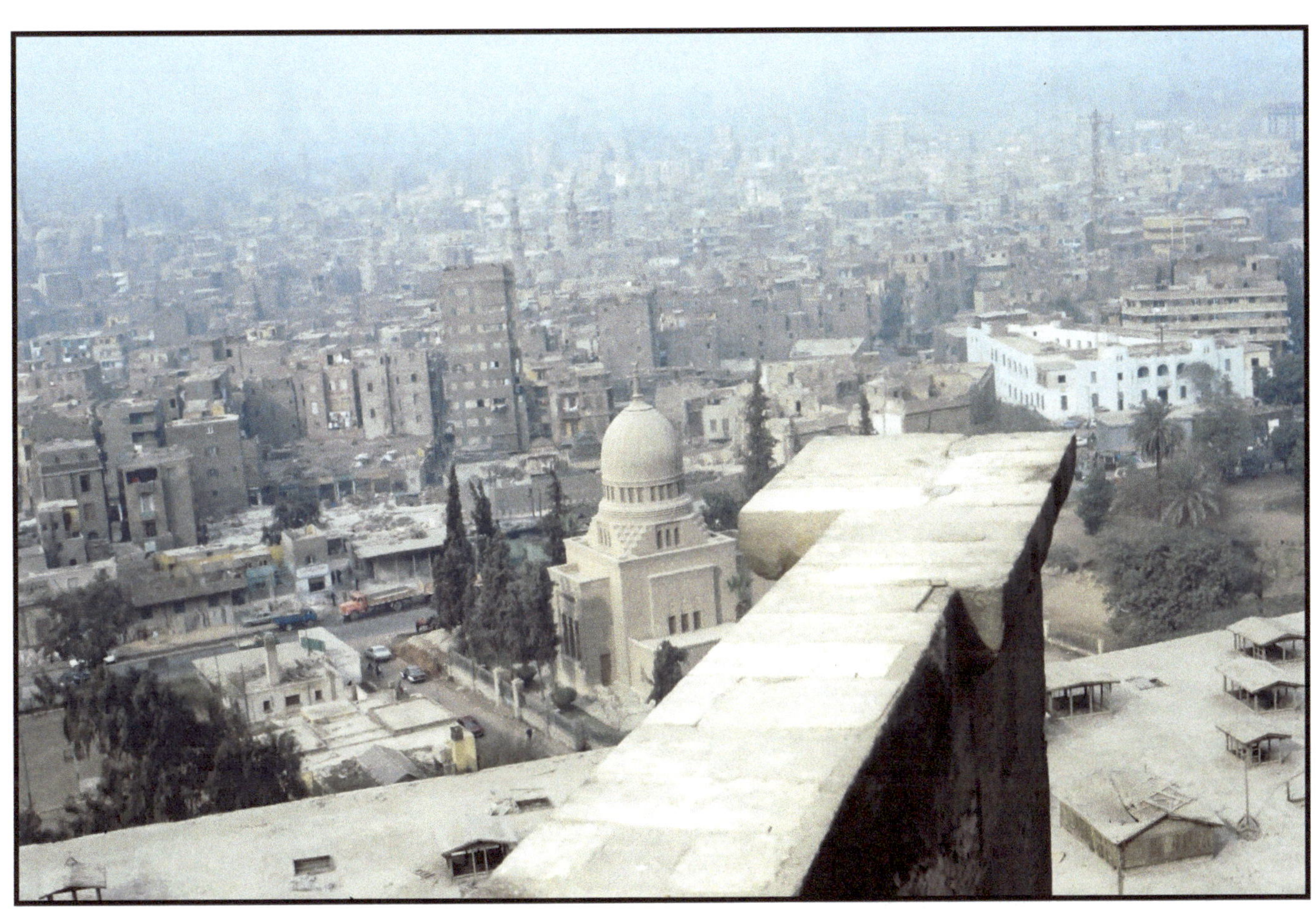

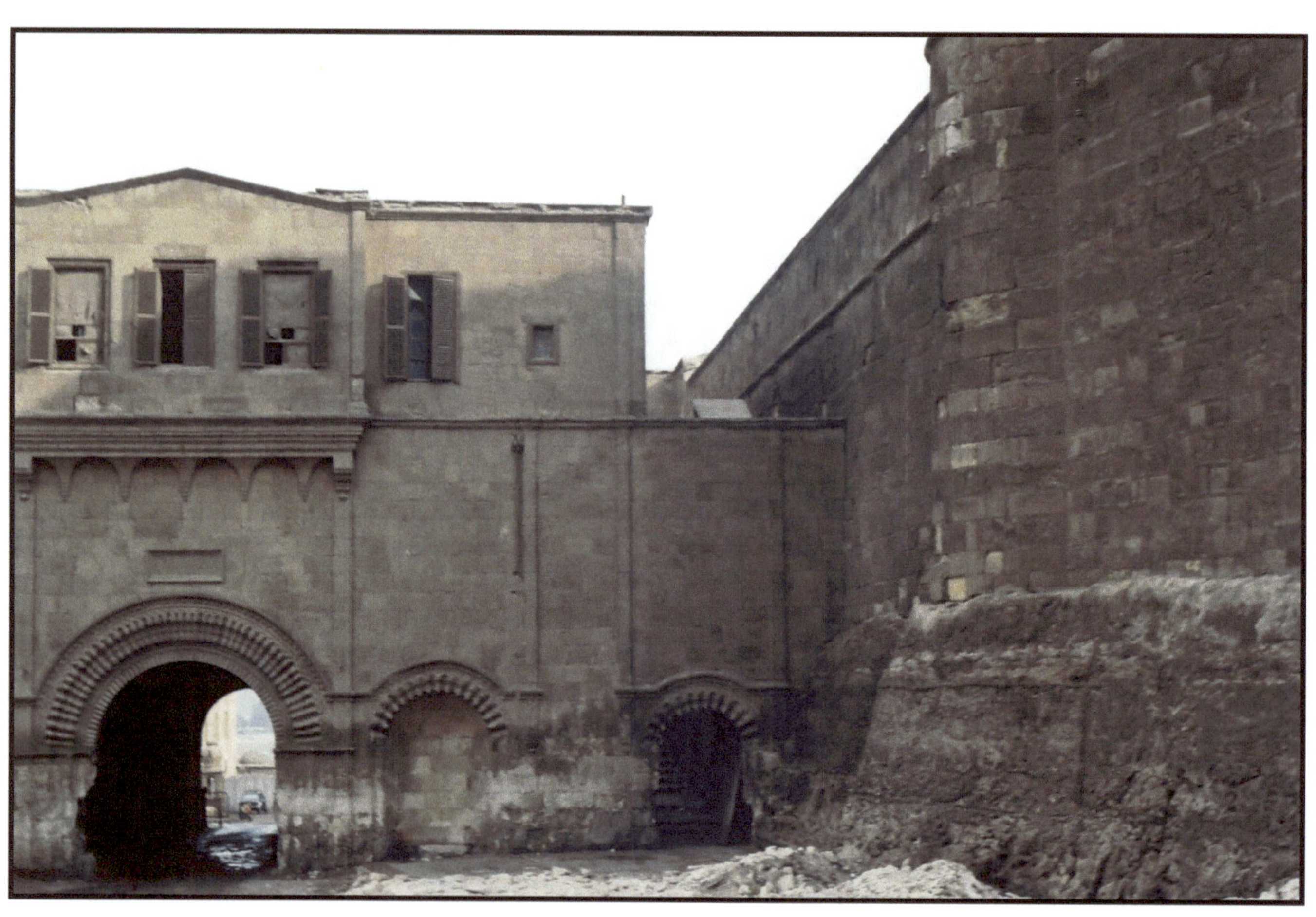

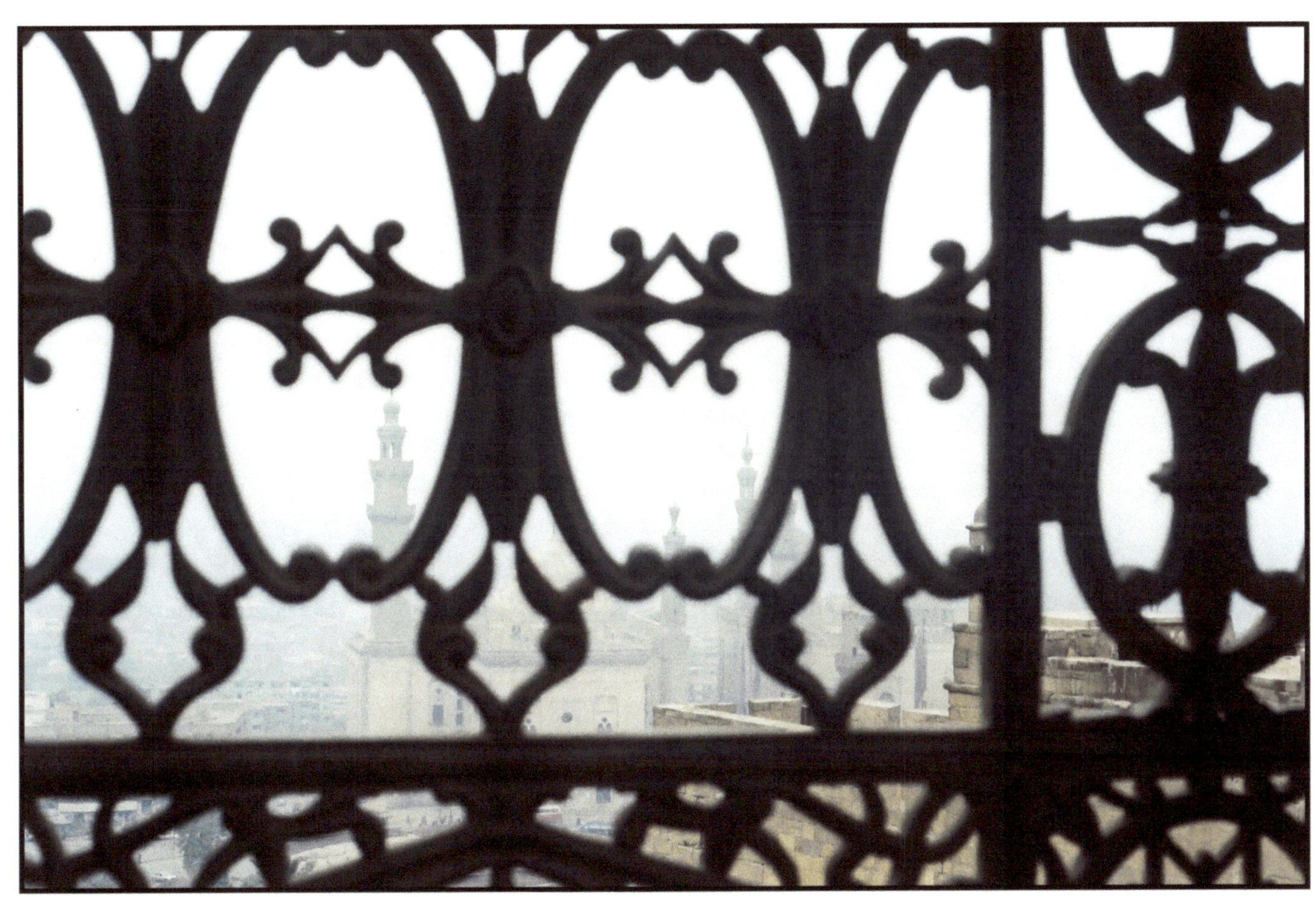

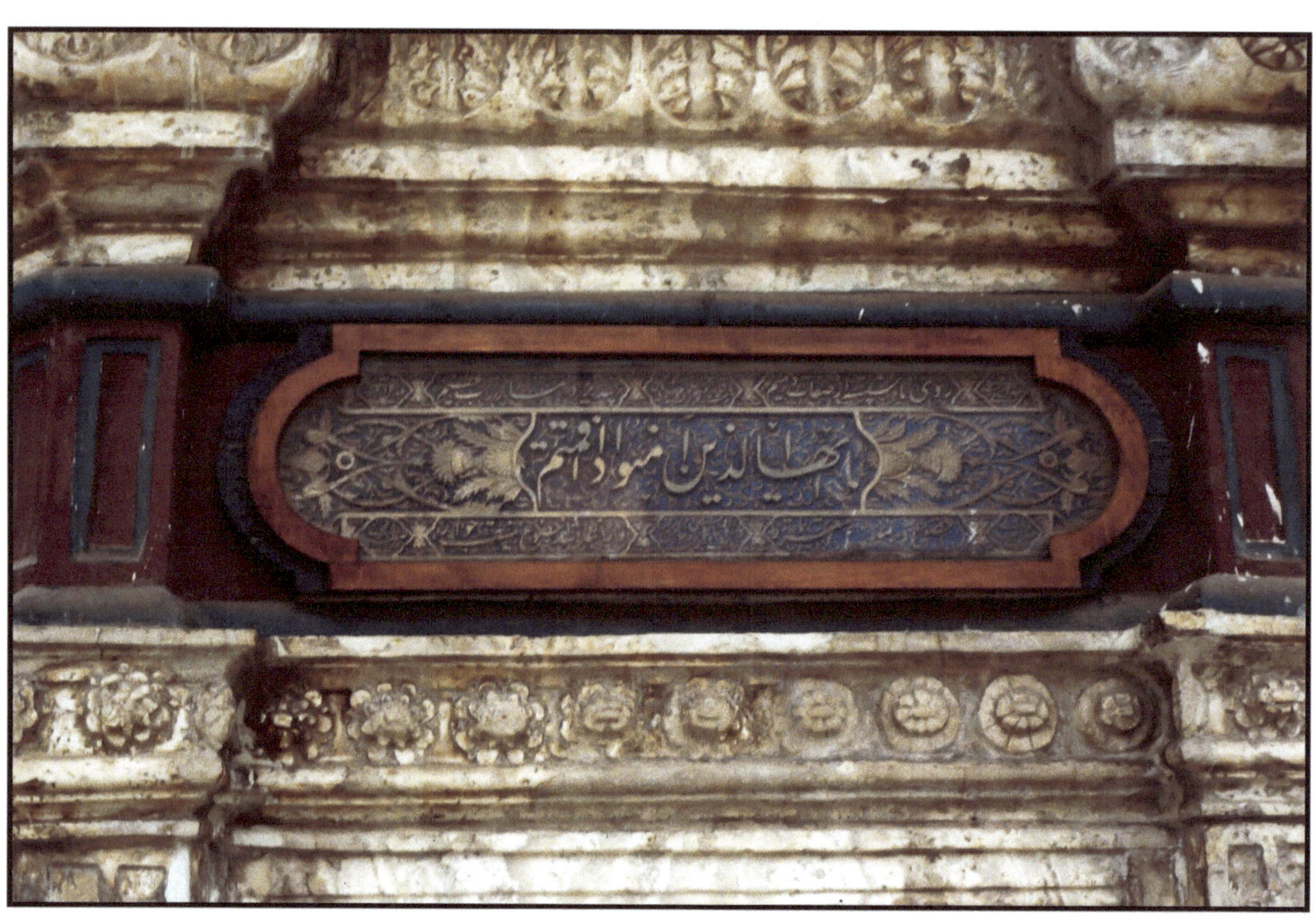
يا ايها الذين امنوا اذا قمتم

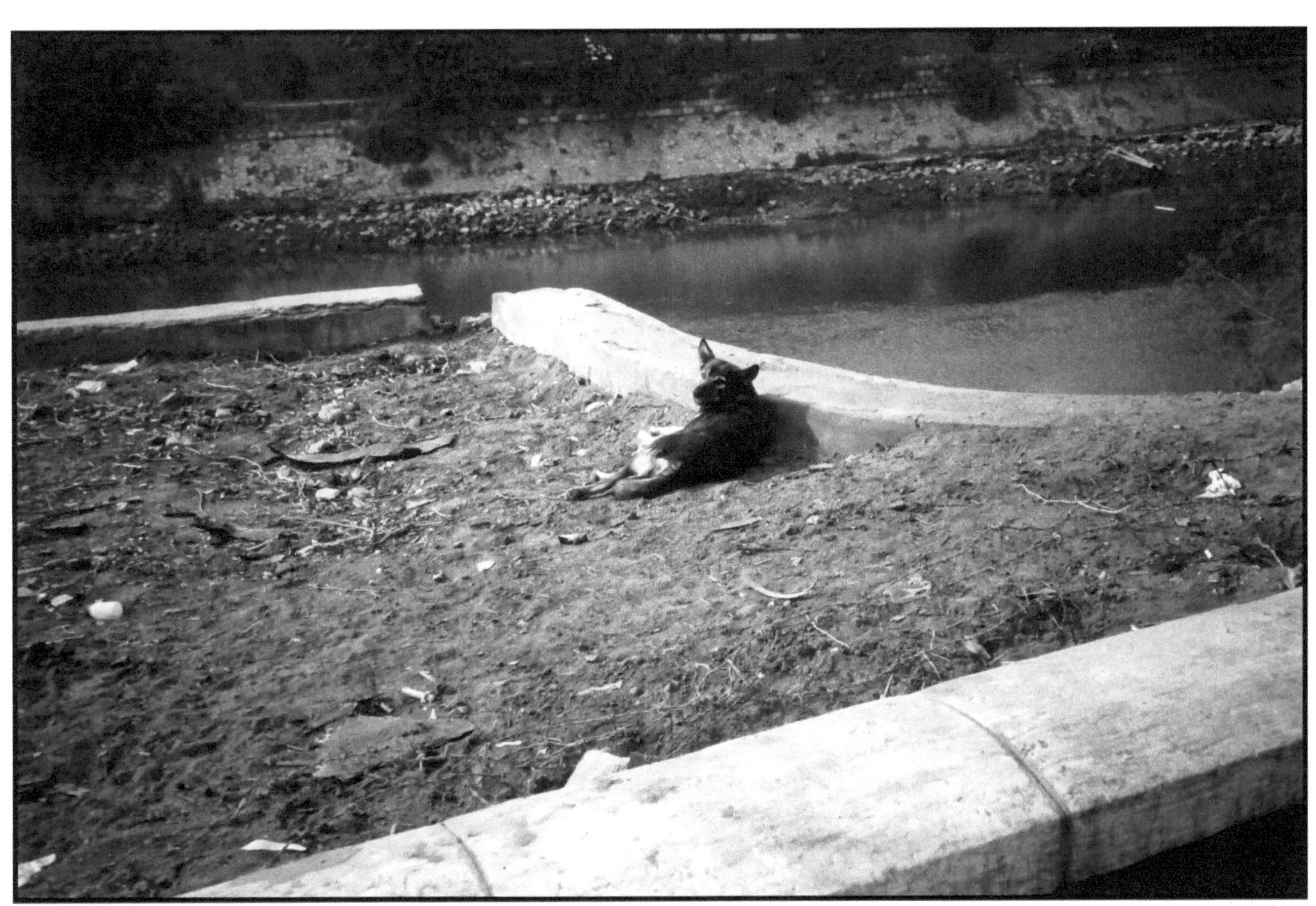

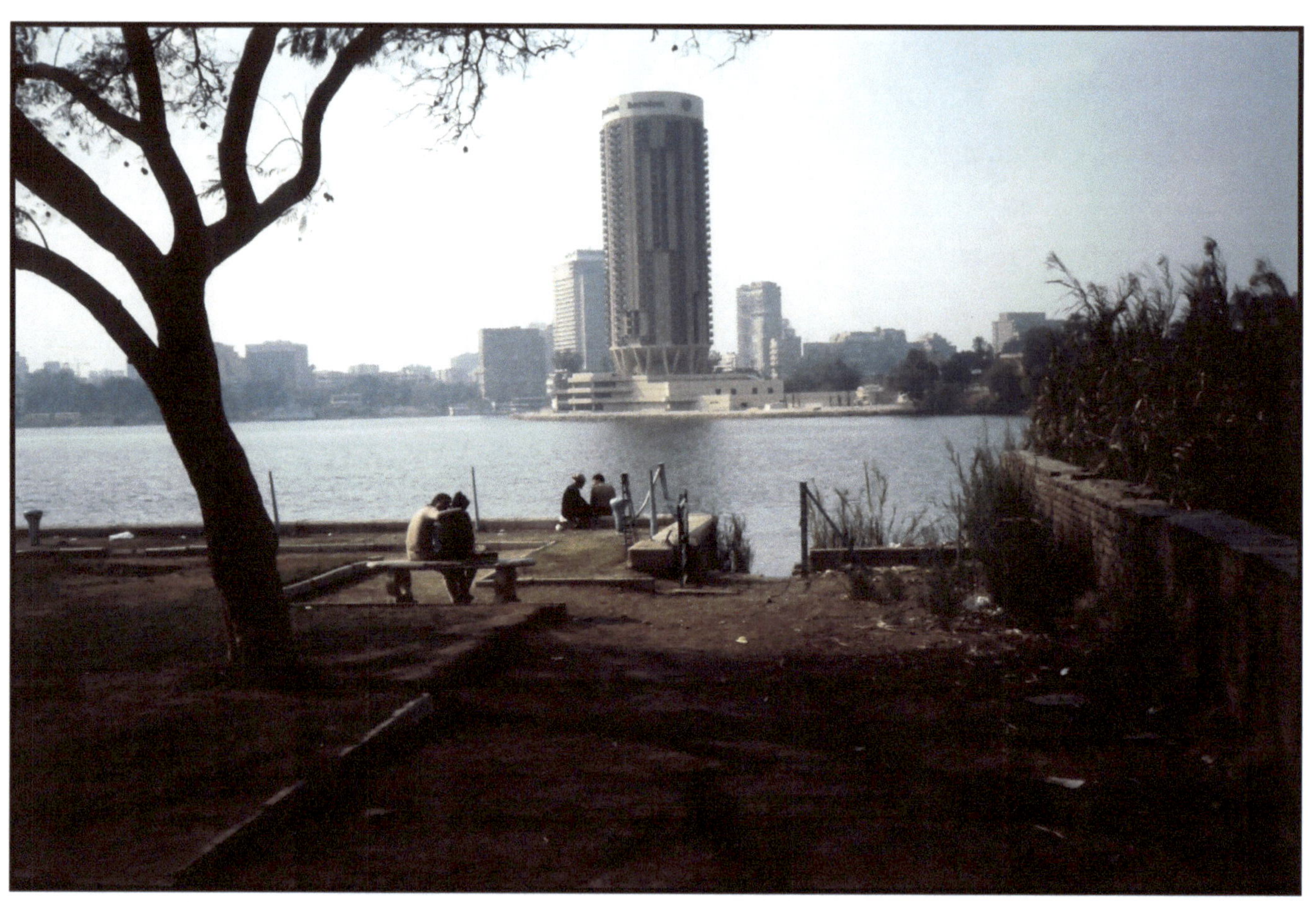

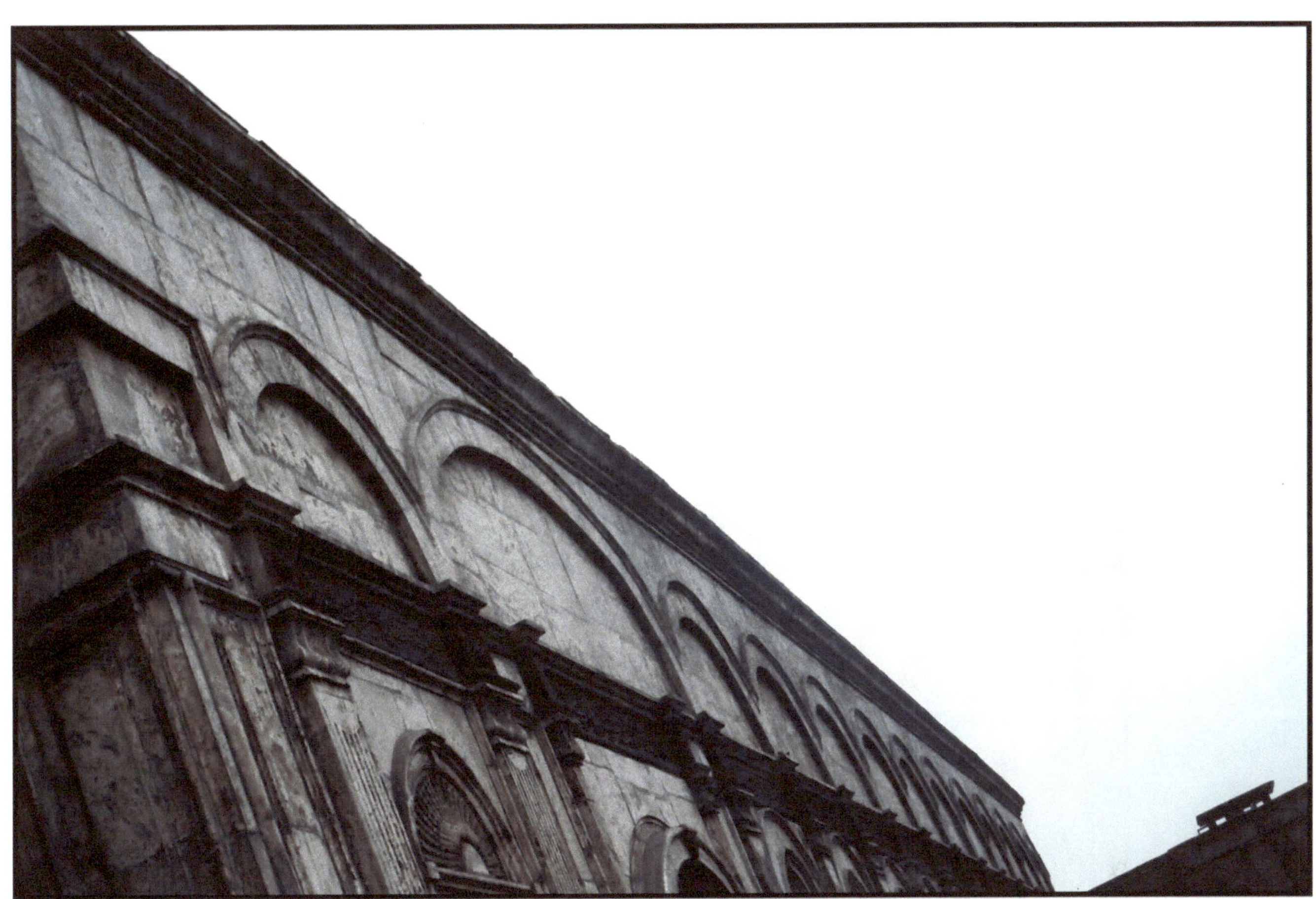

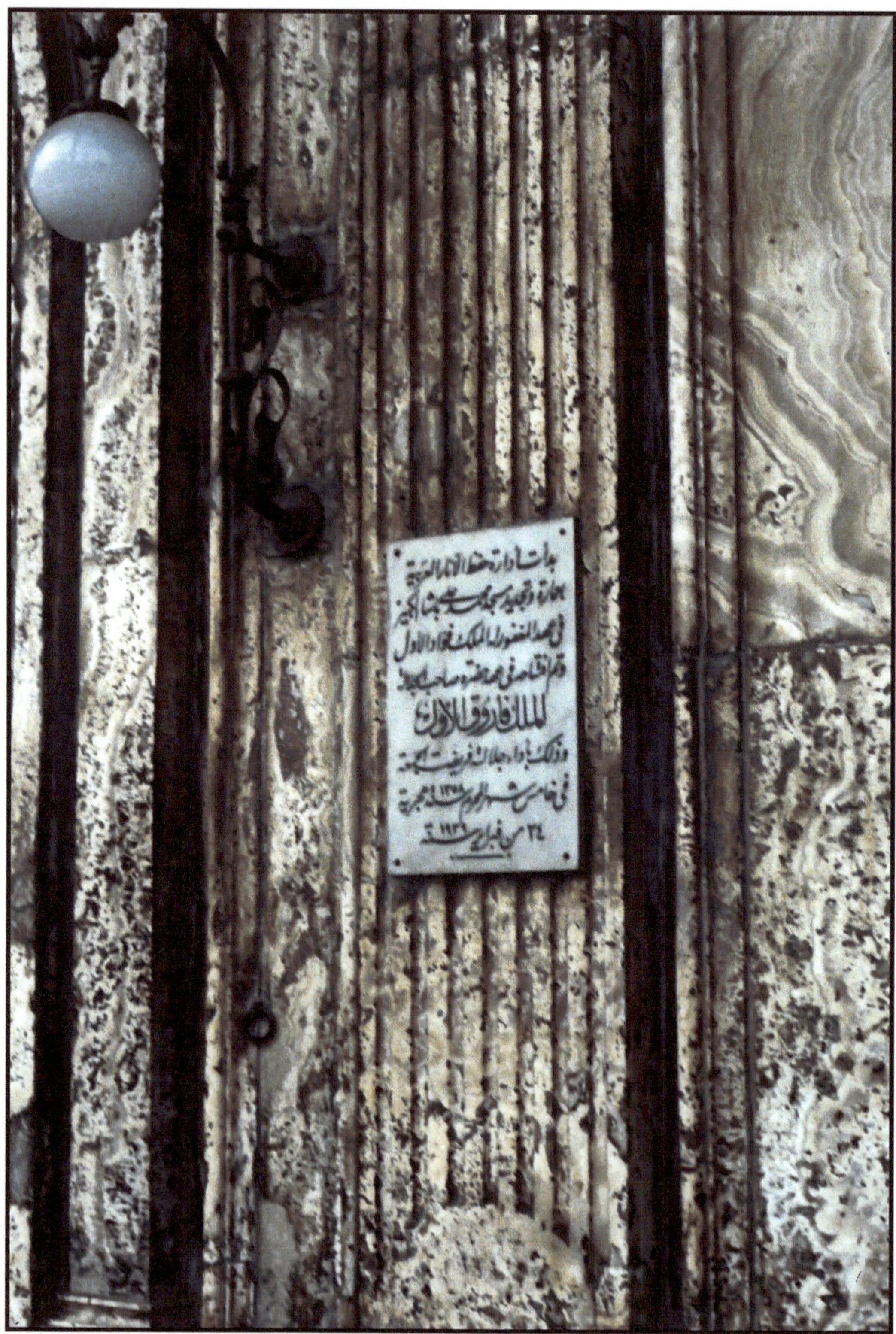
بدأت ادارة حفظ الآثار العربية
في عهد المغفور له الملك فؤاد الاول
للملك فاروق الاول
وذلك بأداء جلالته فريضة الجمعة
٢٤ من فبراير سنة ١٩٣٦

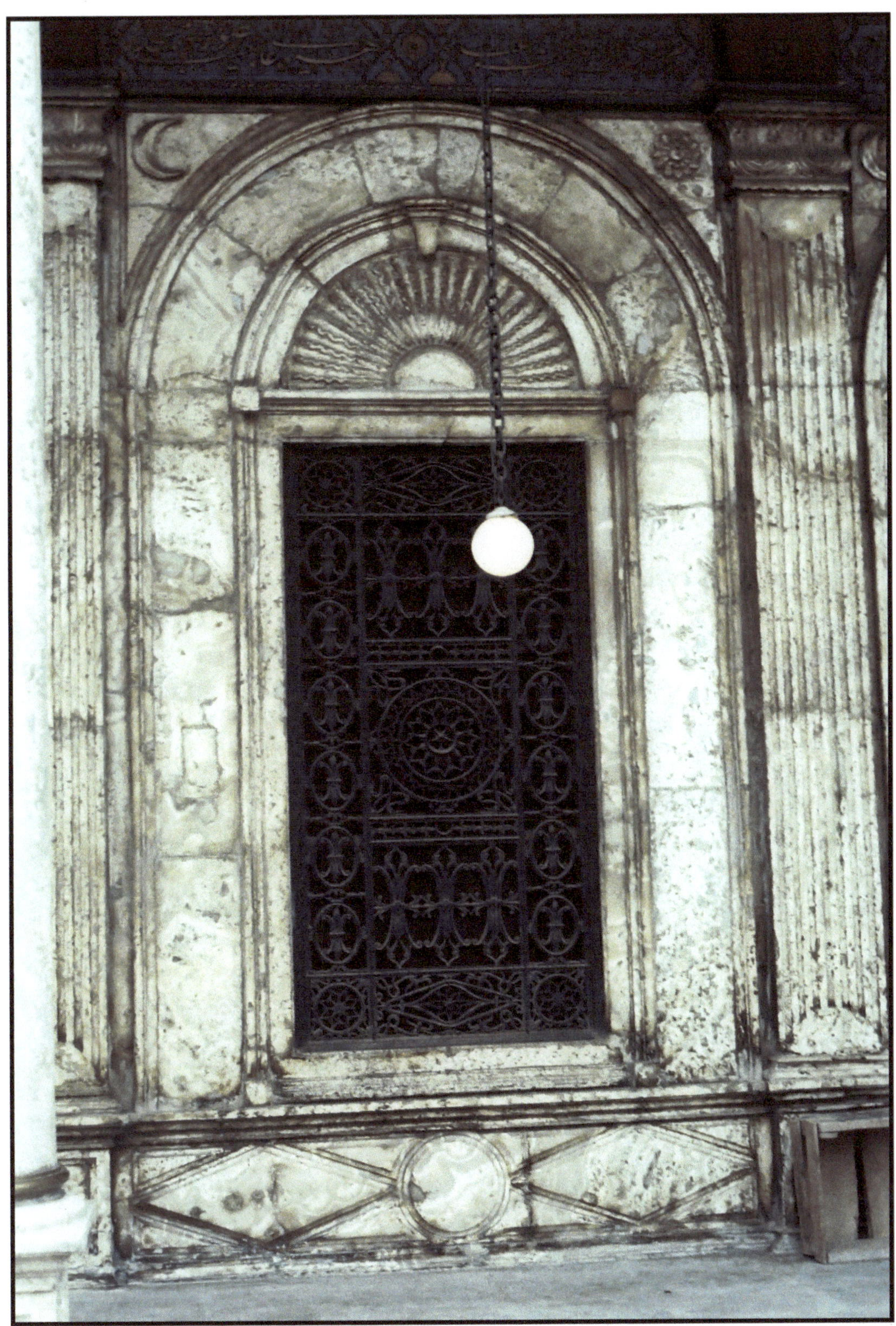

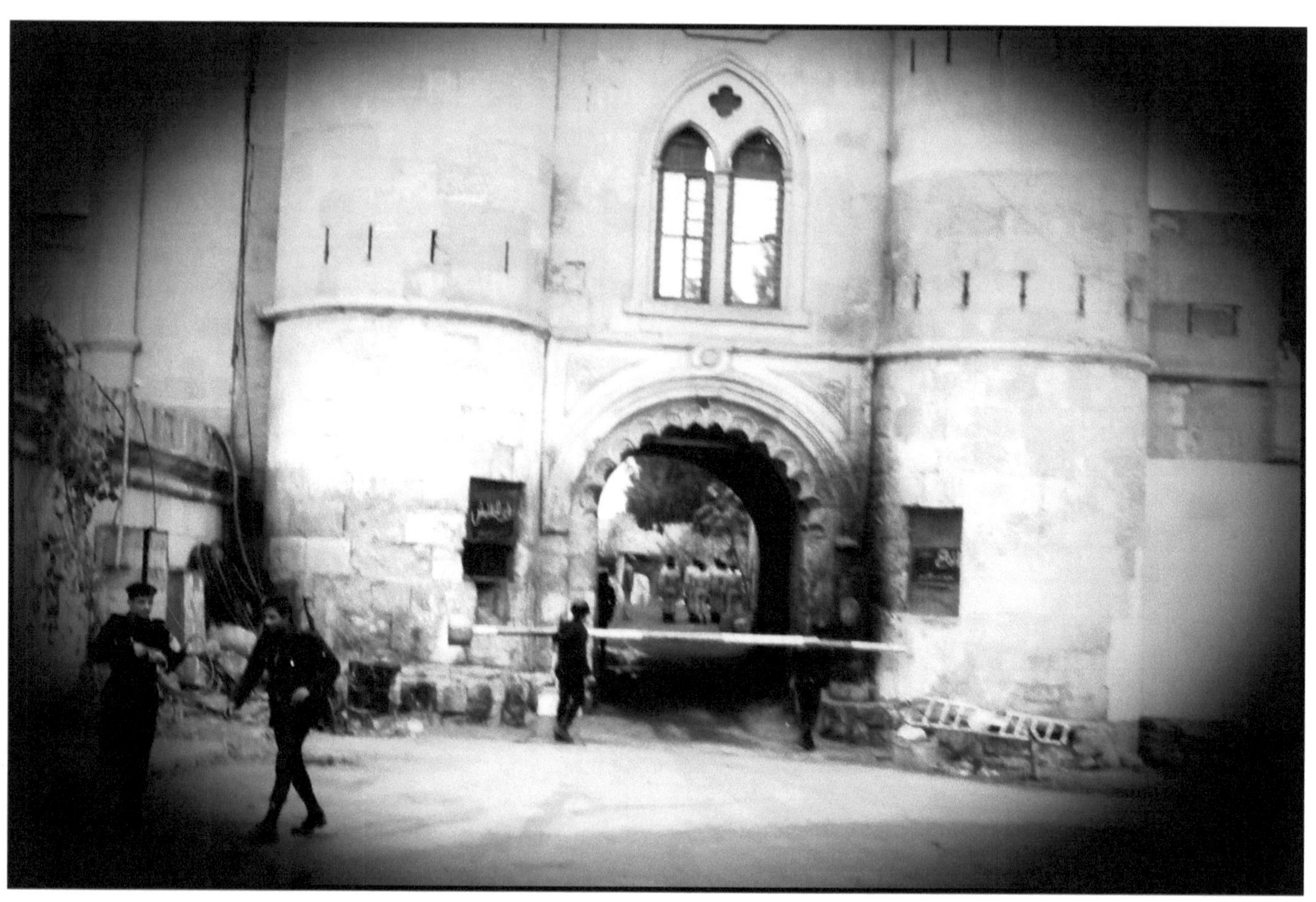

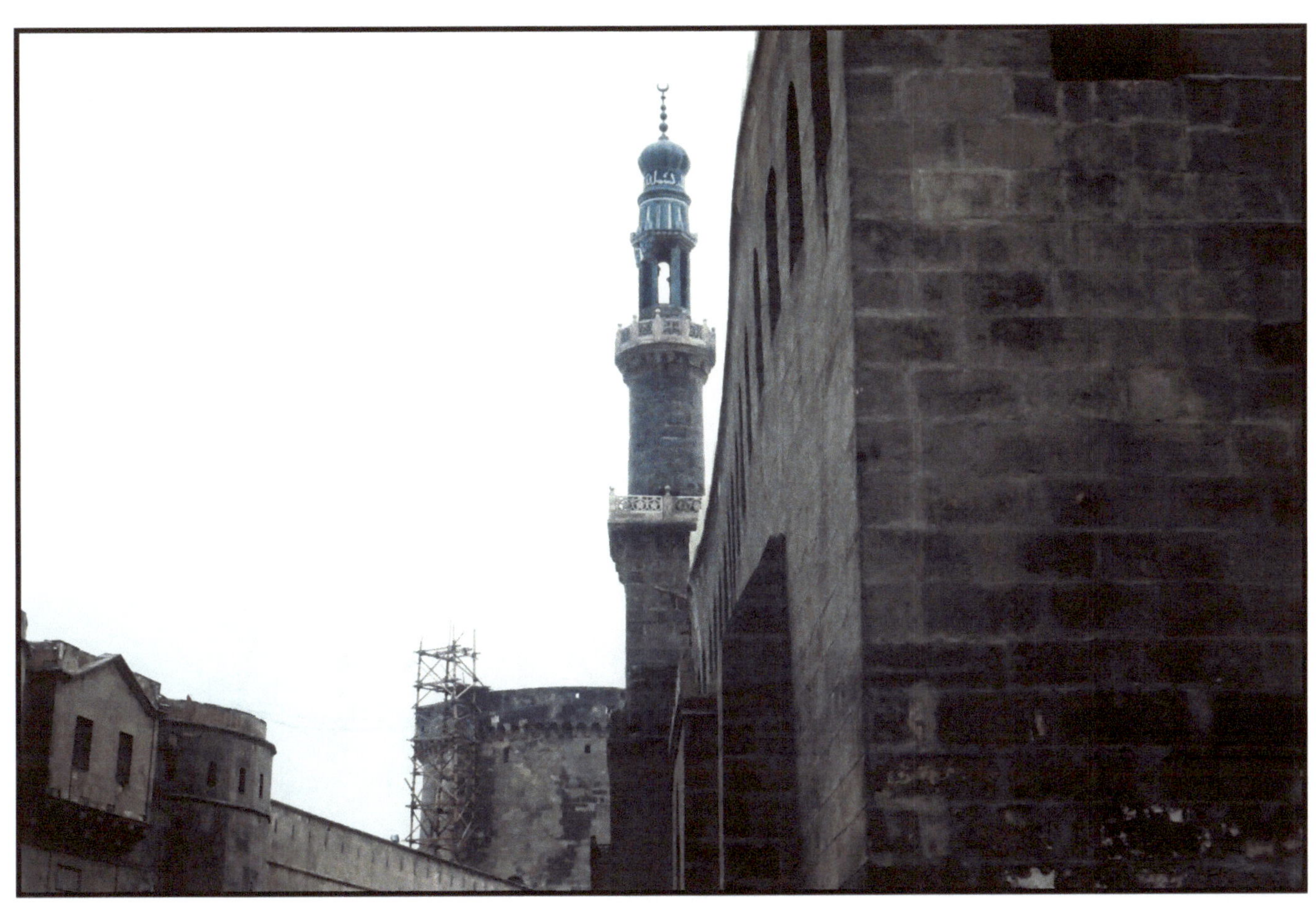

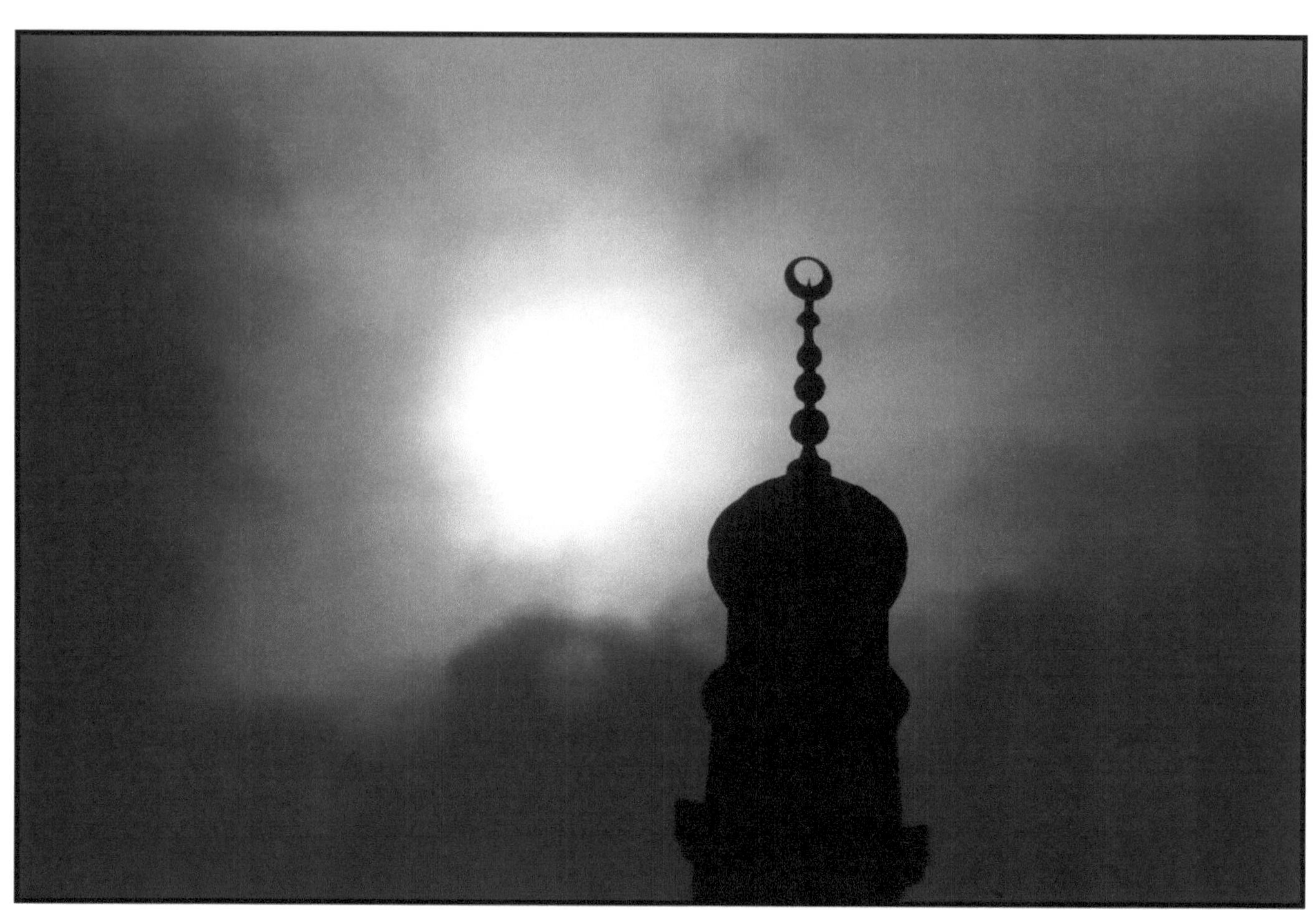

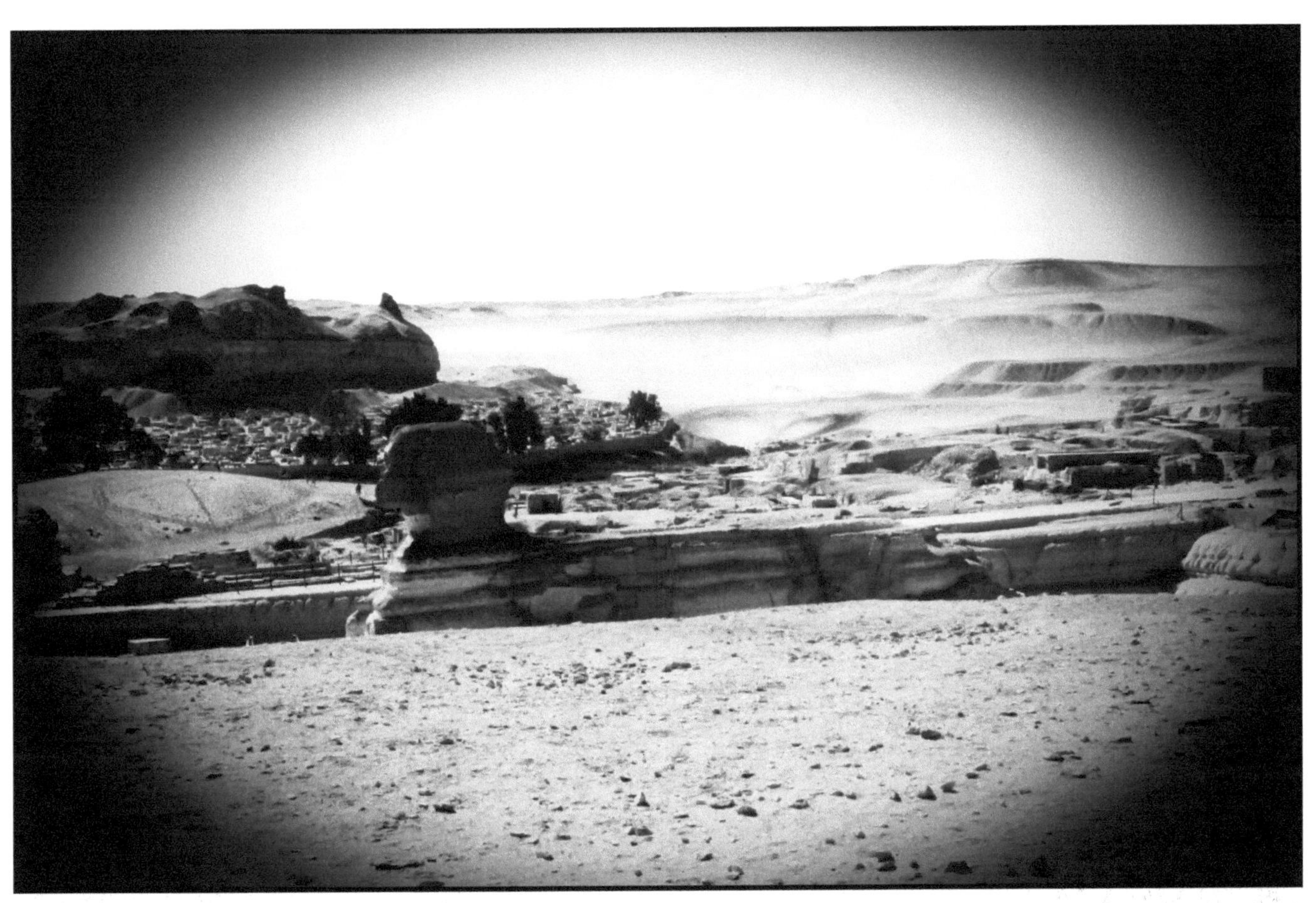

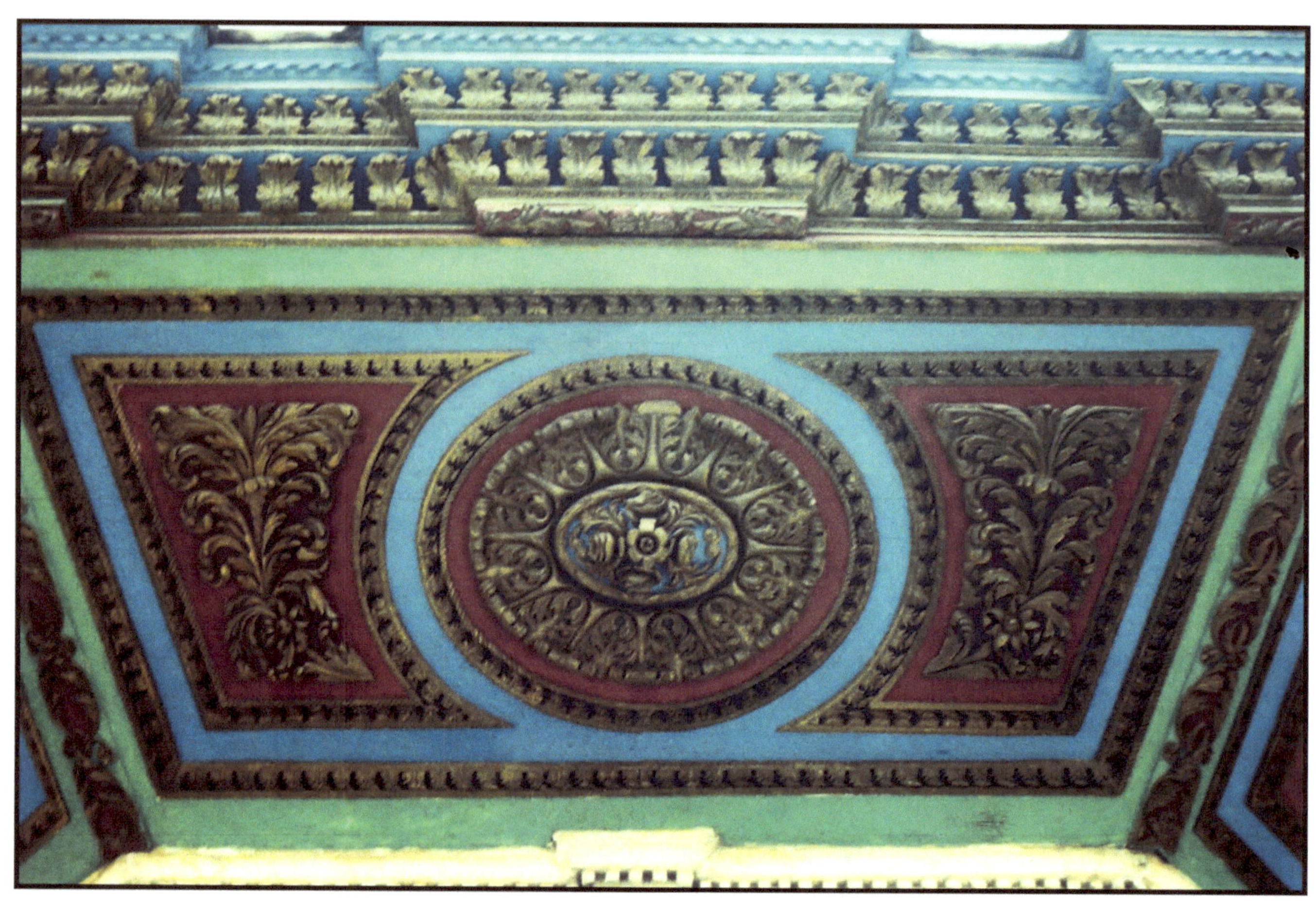

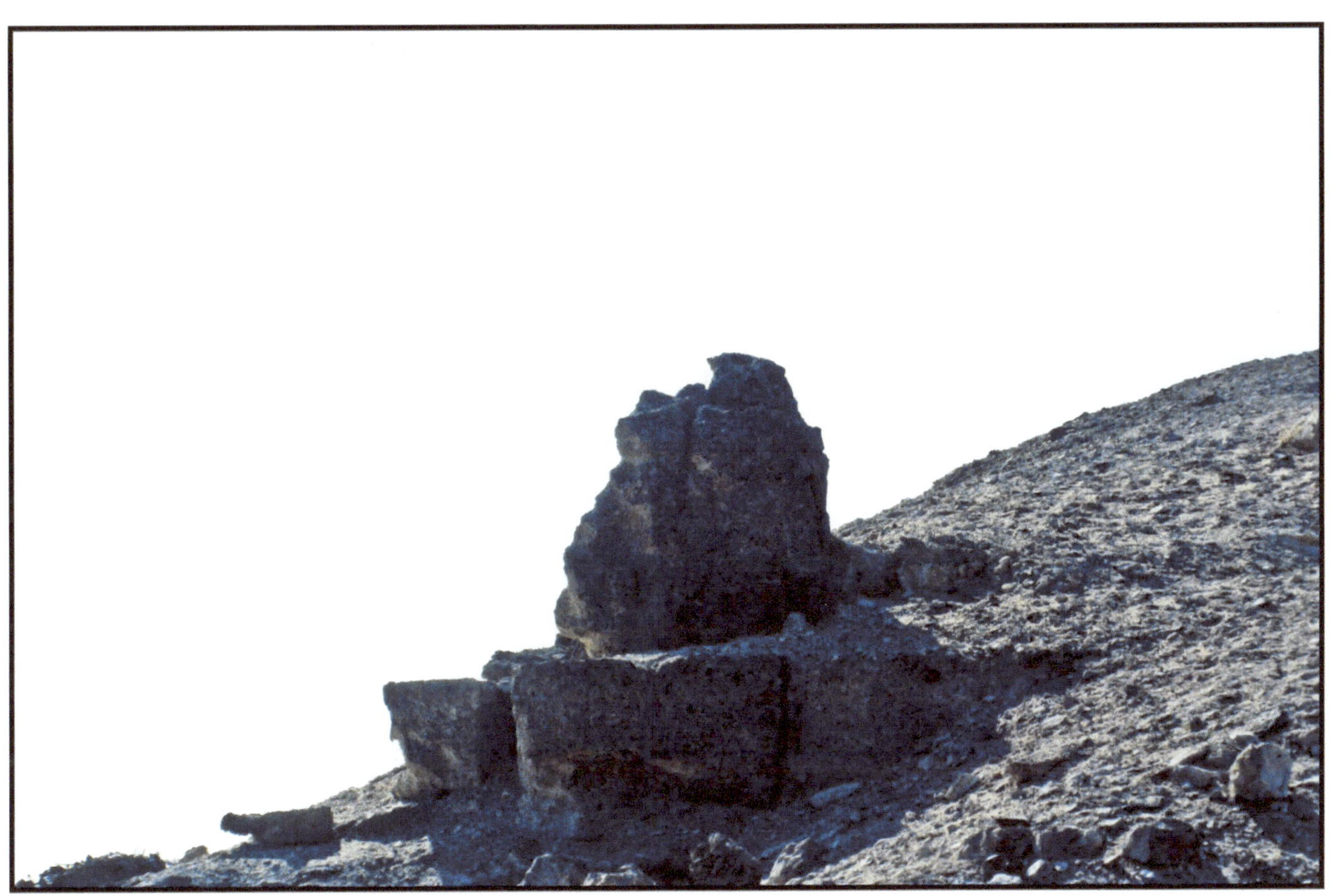

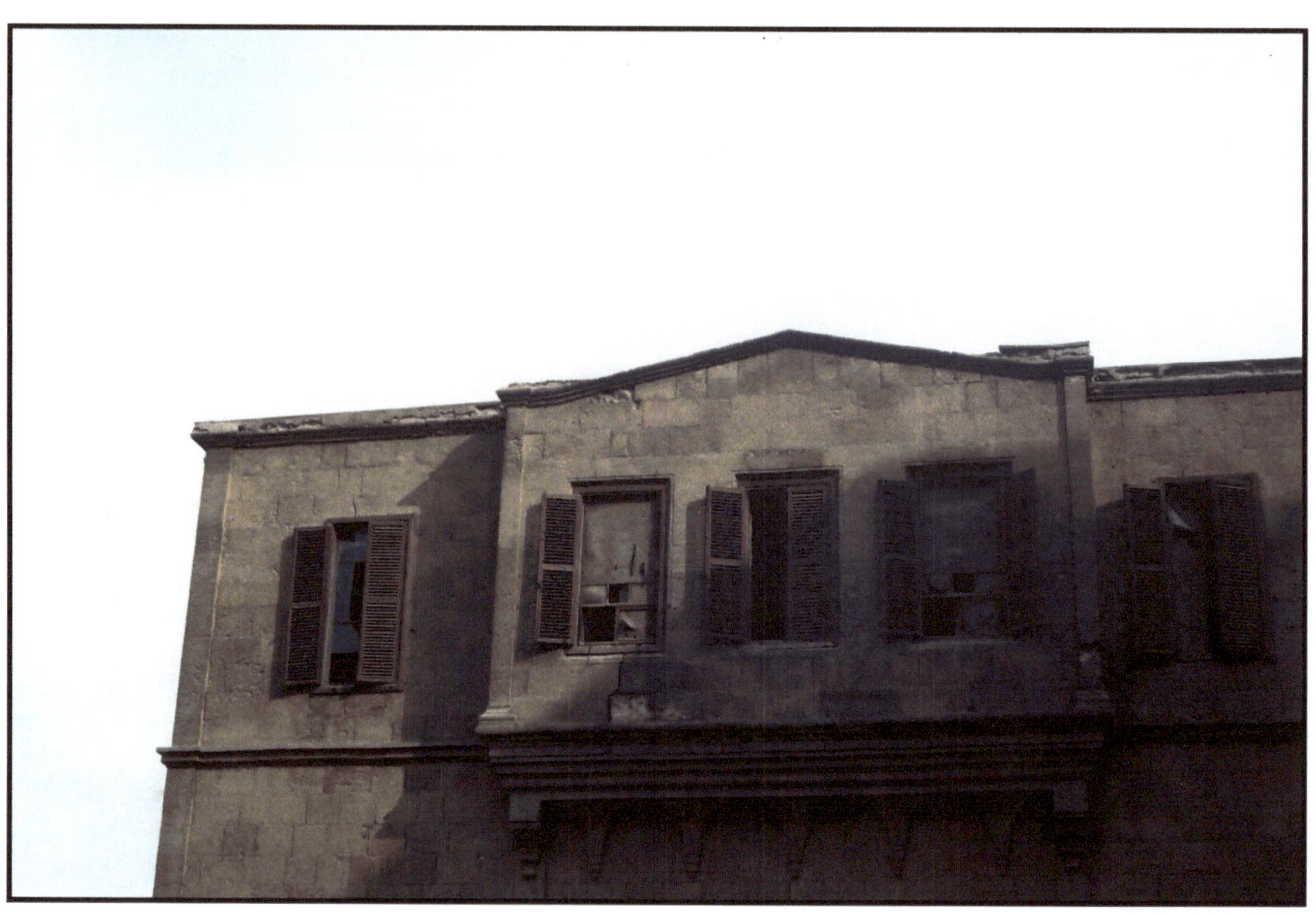

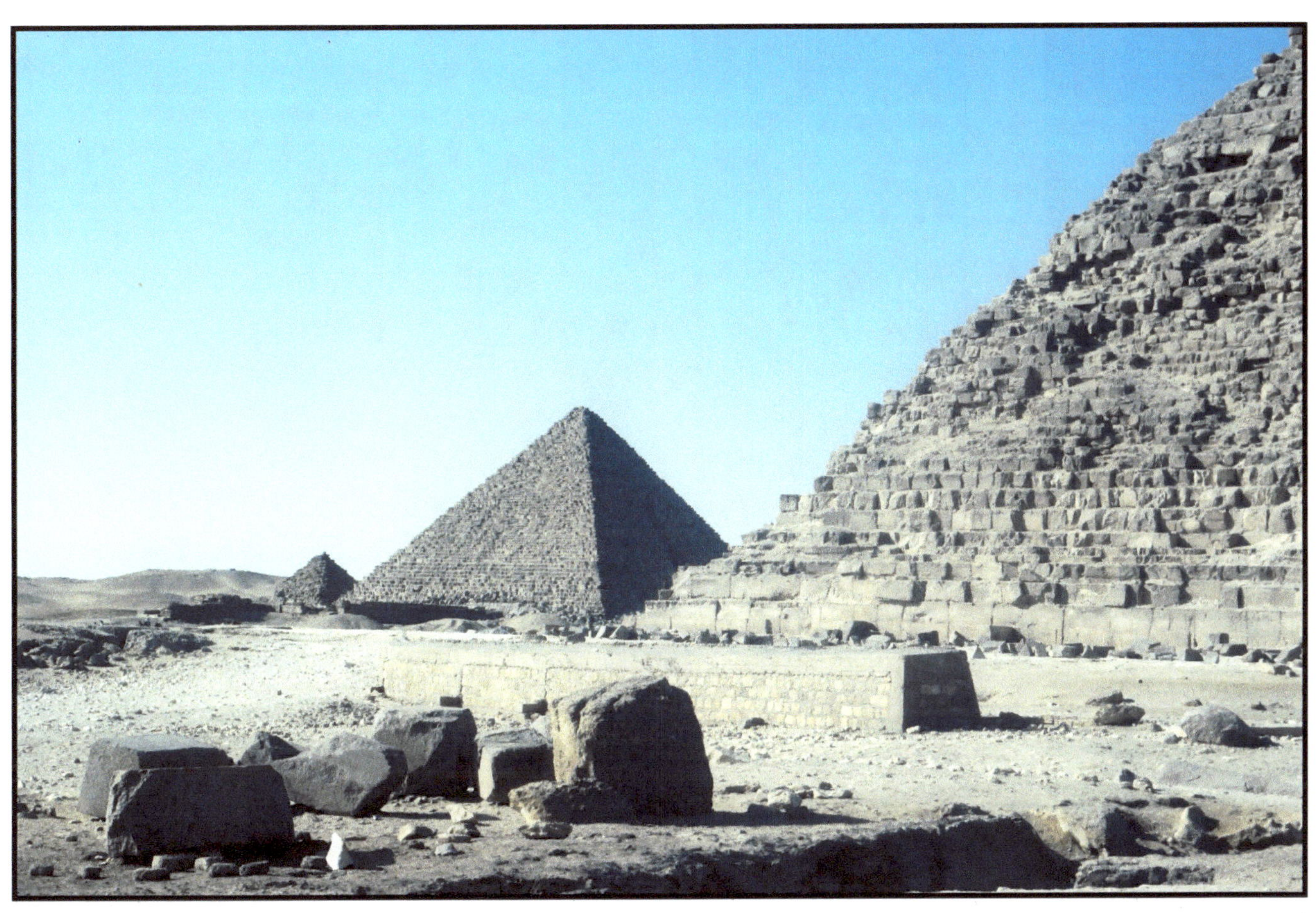

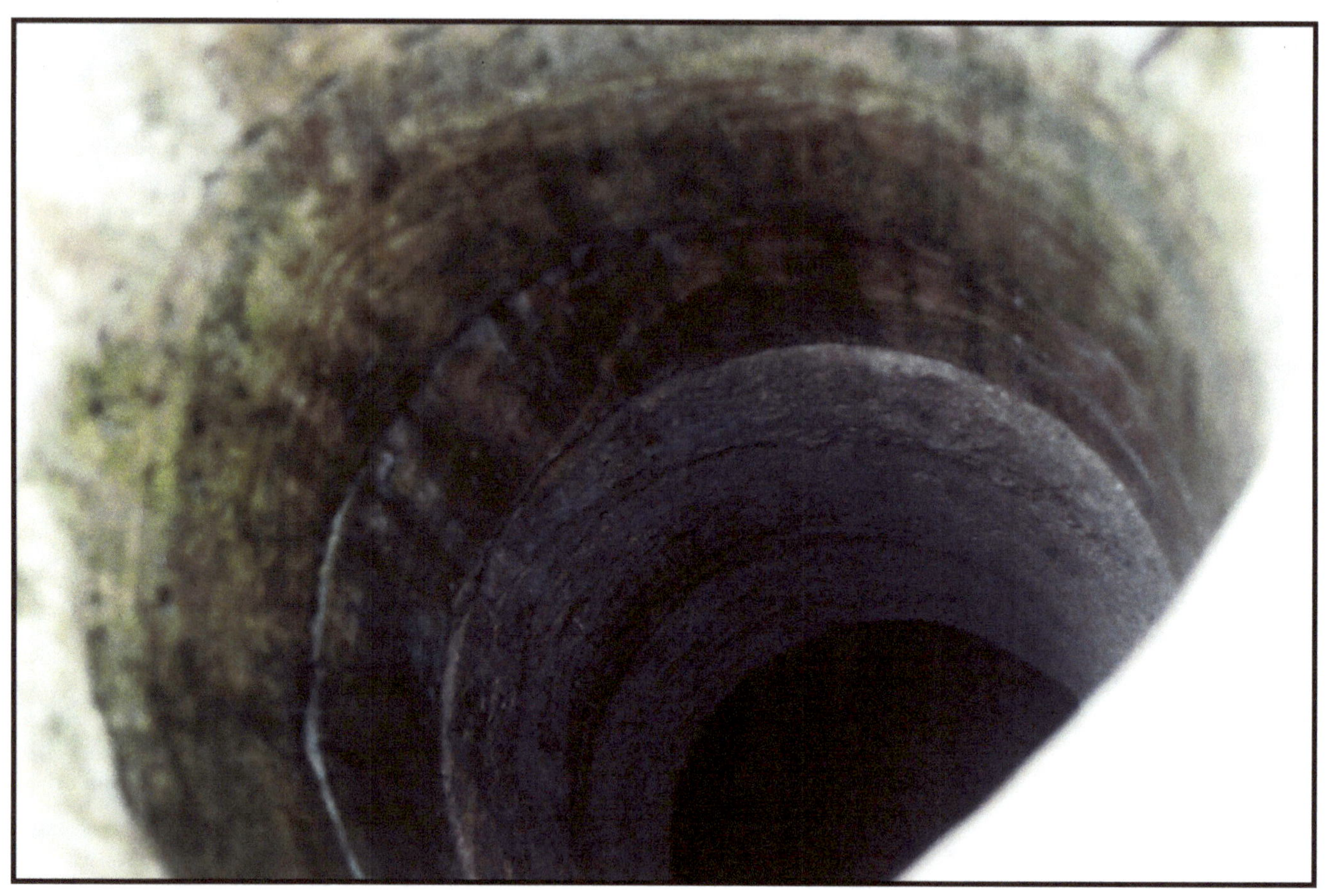

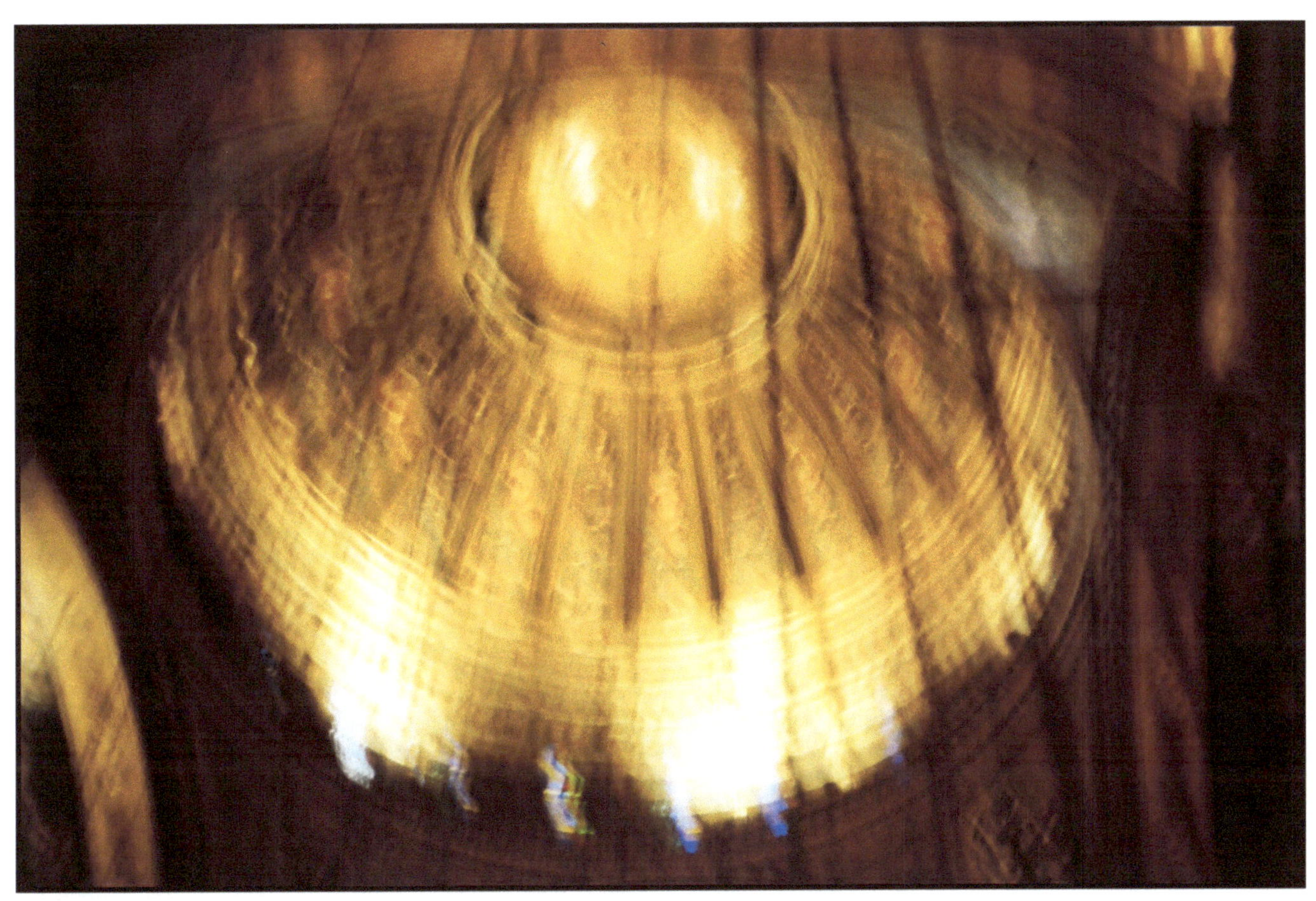

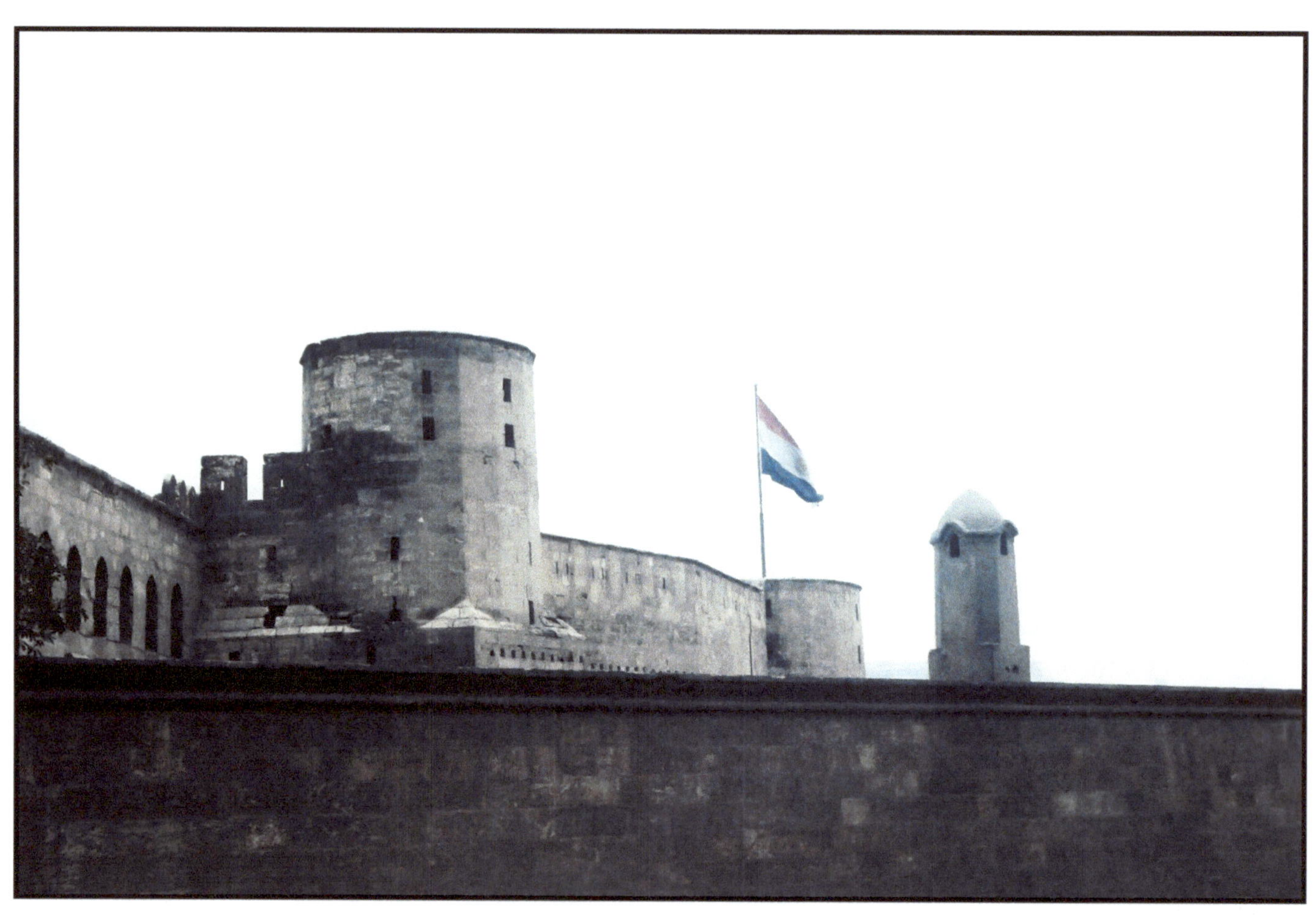

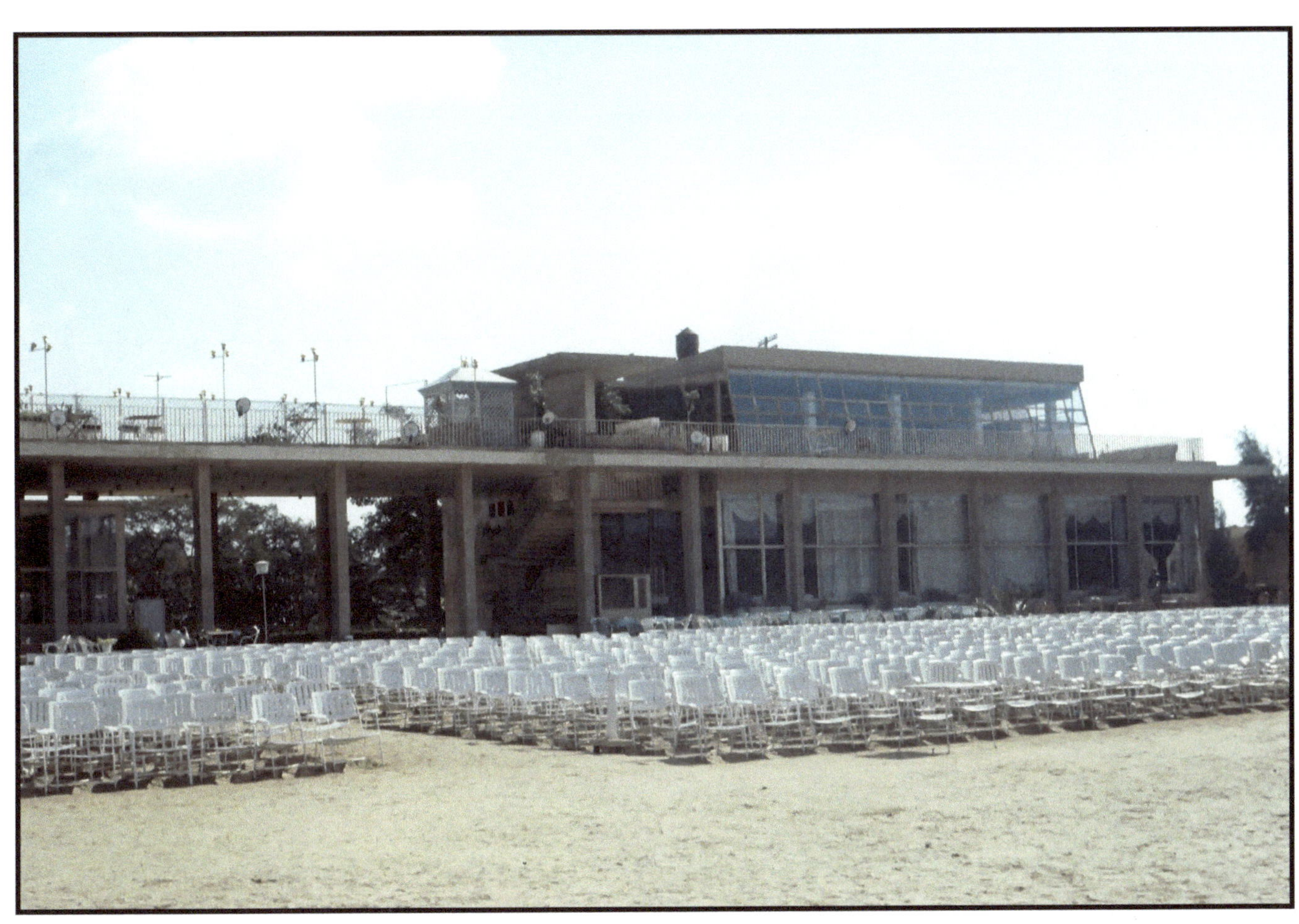

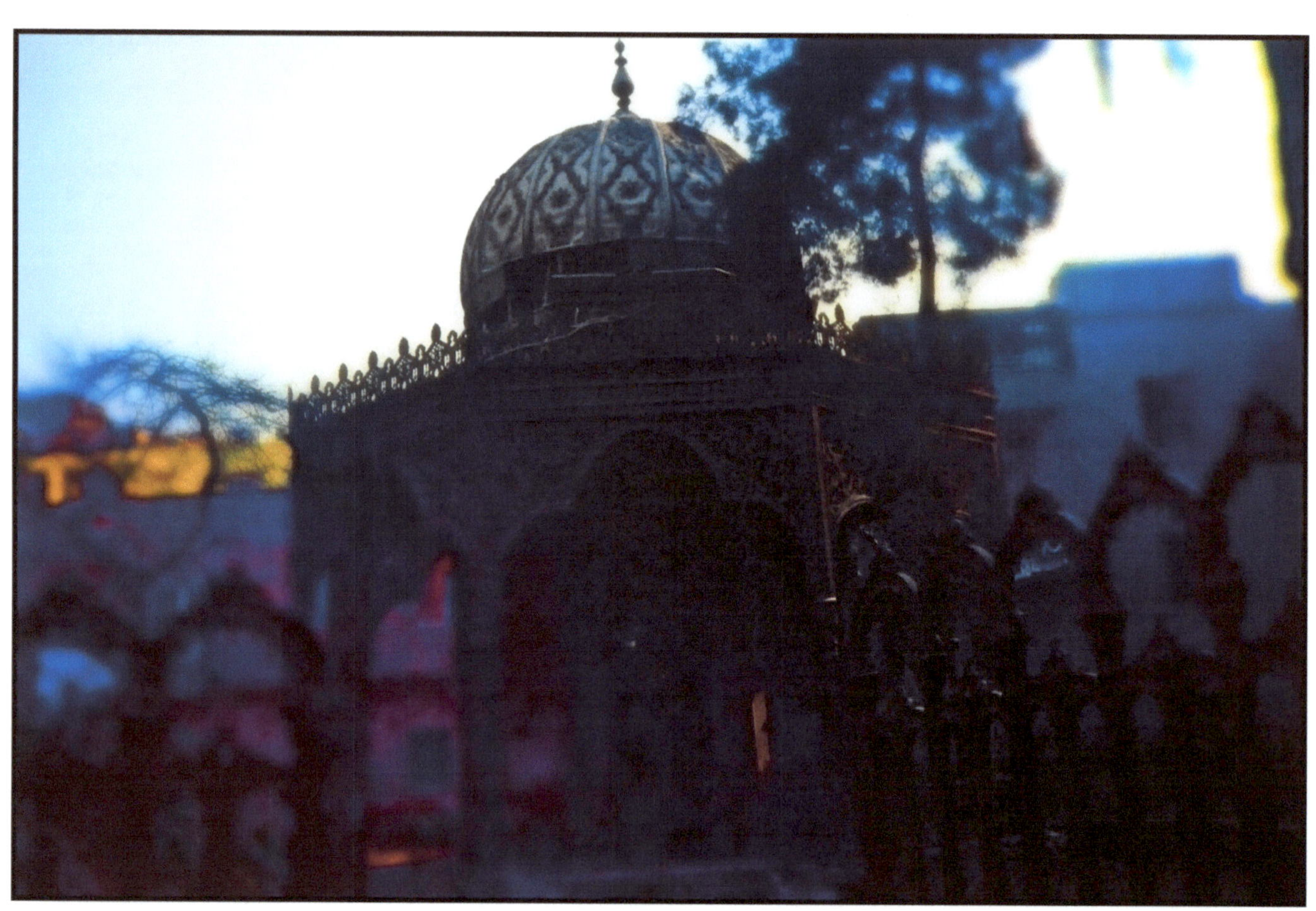

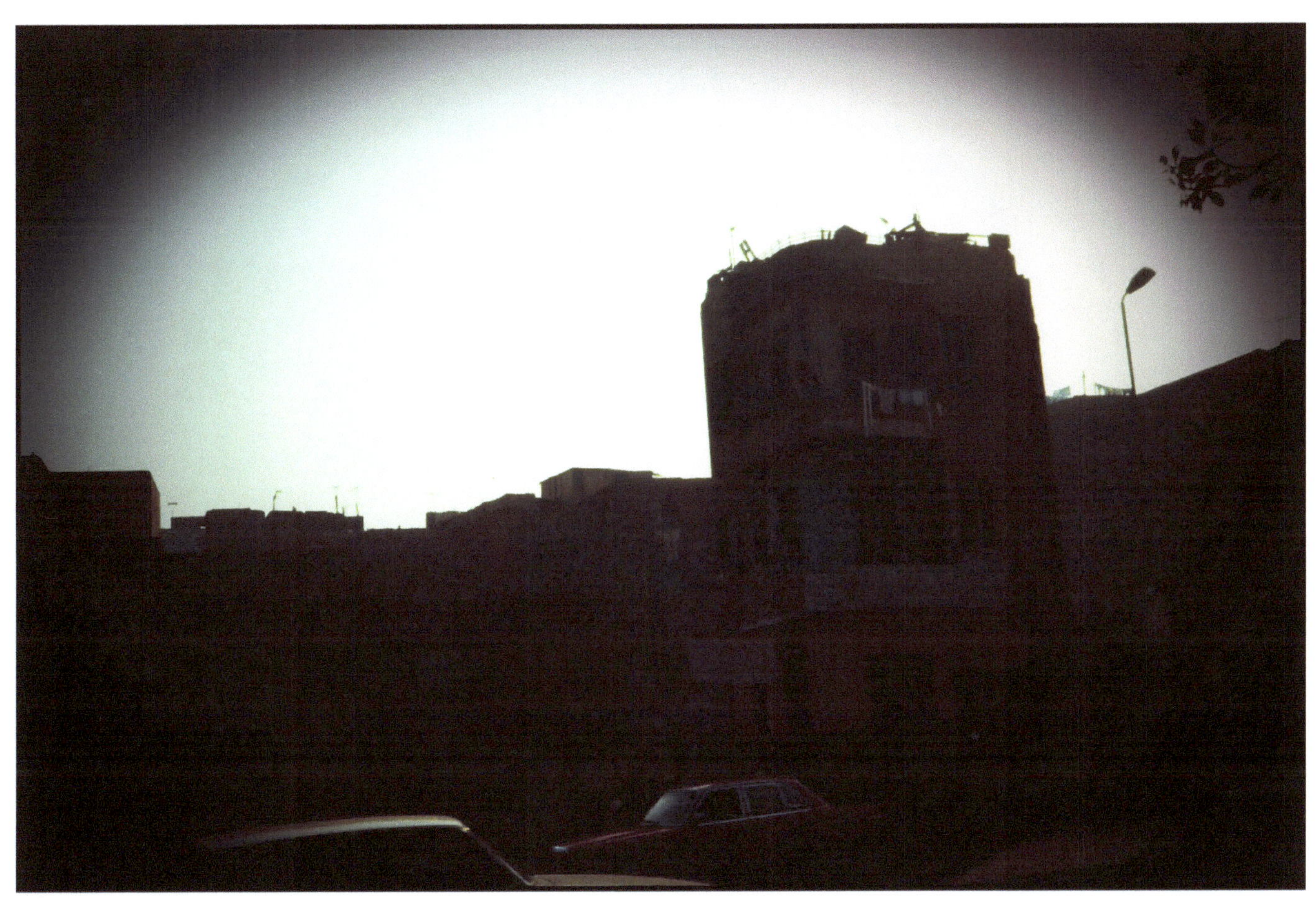

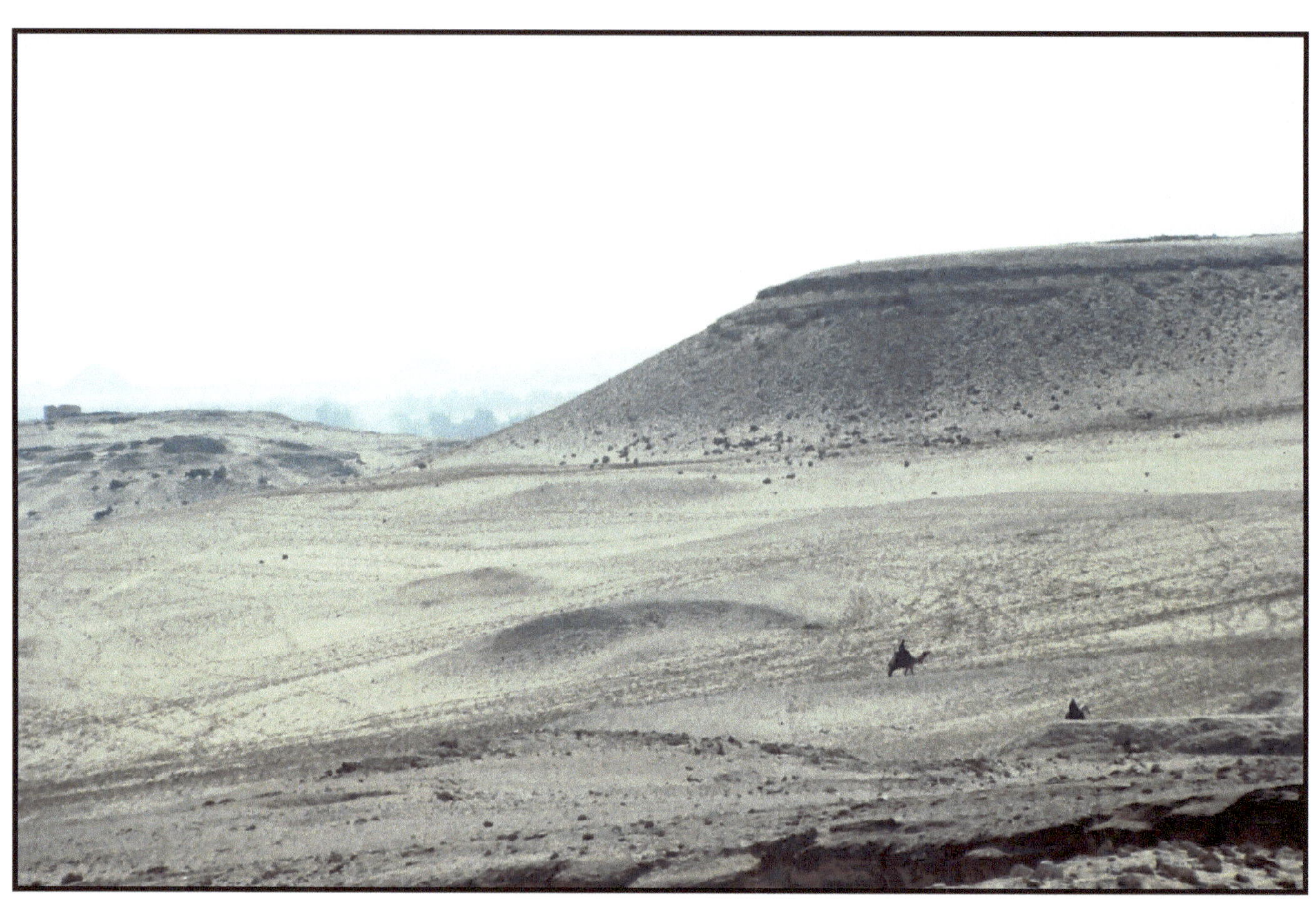

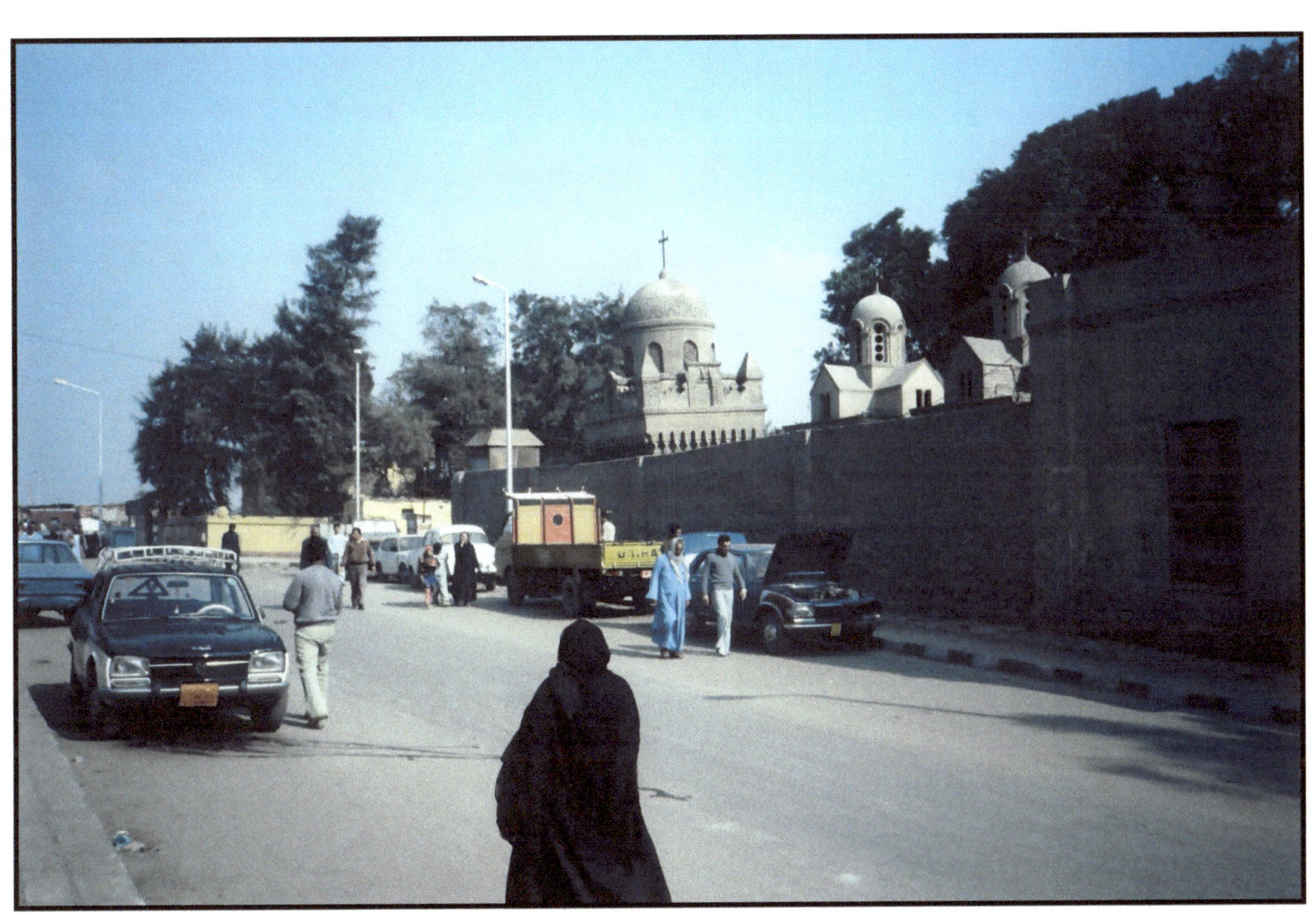

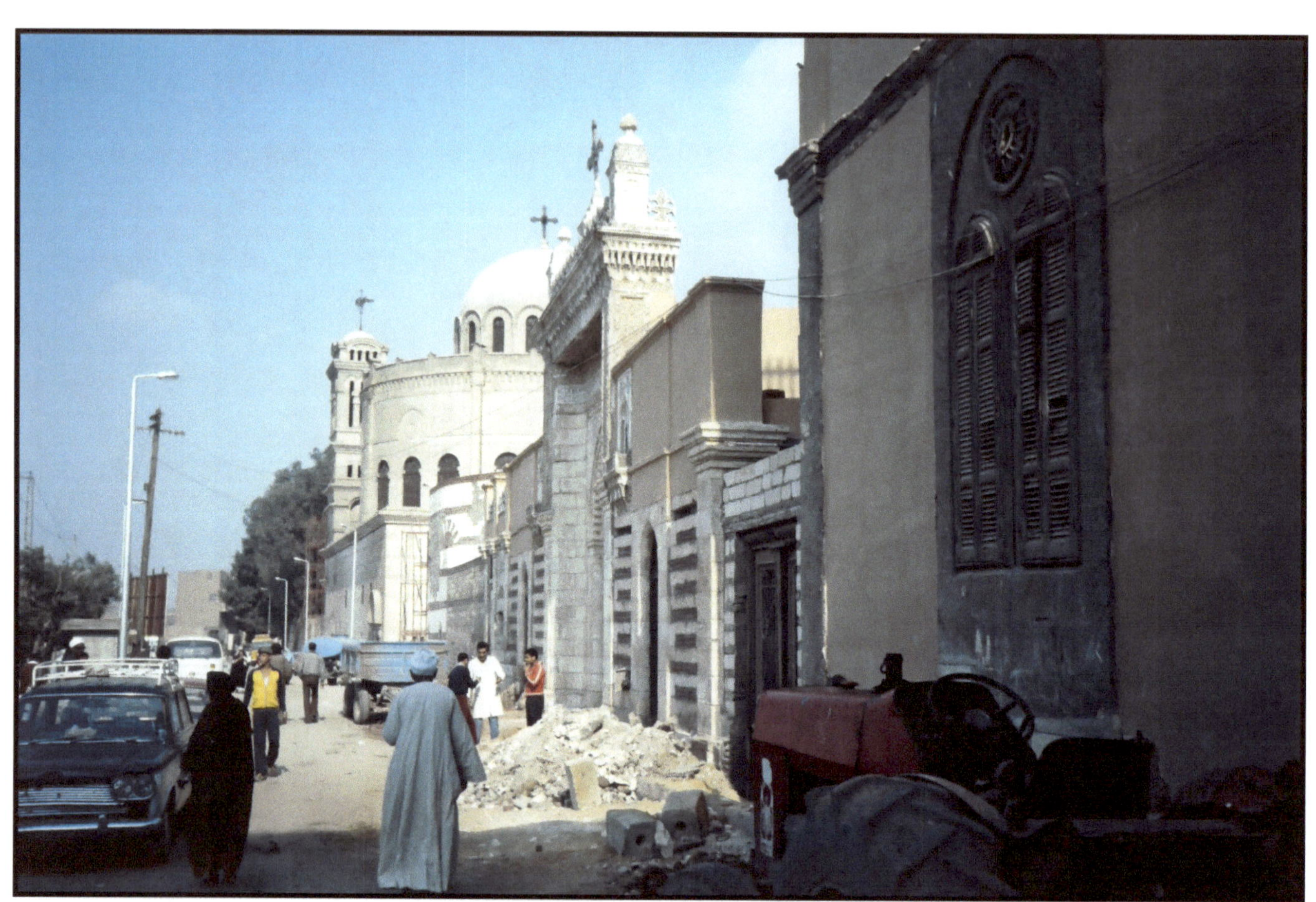

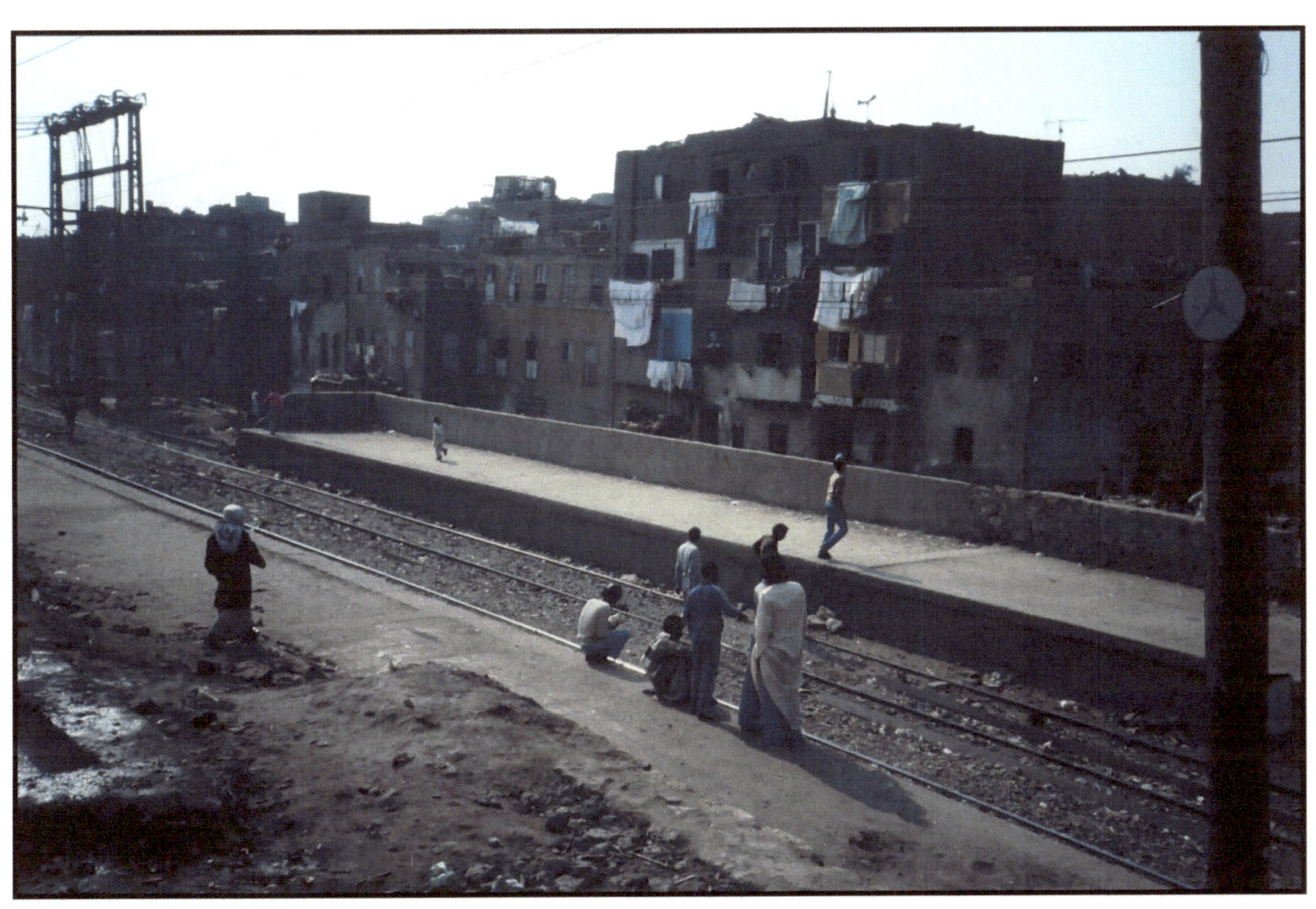

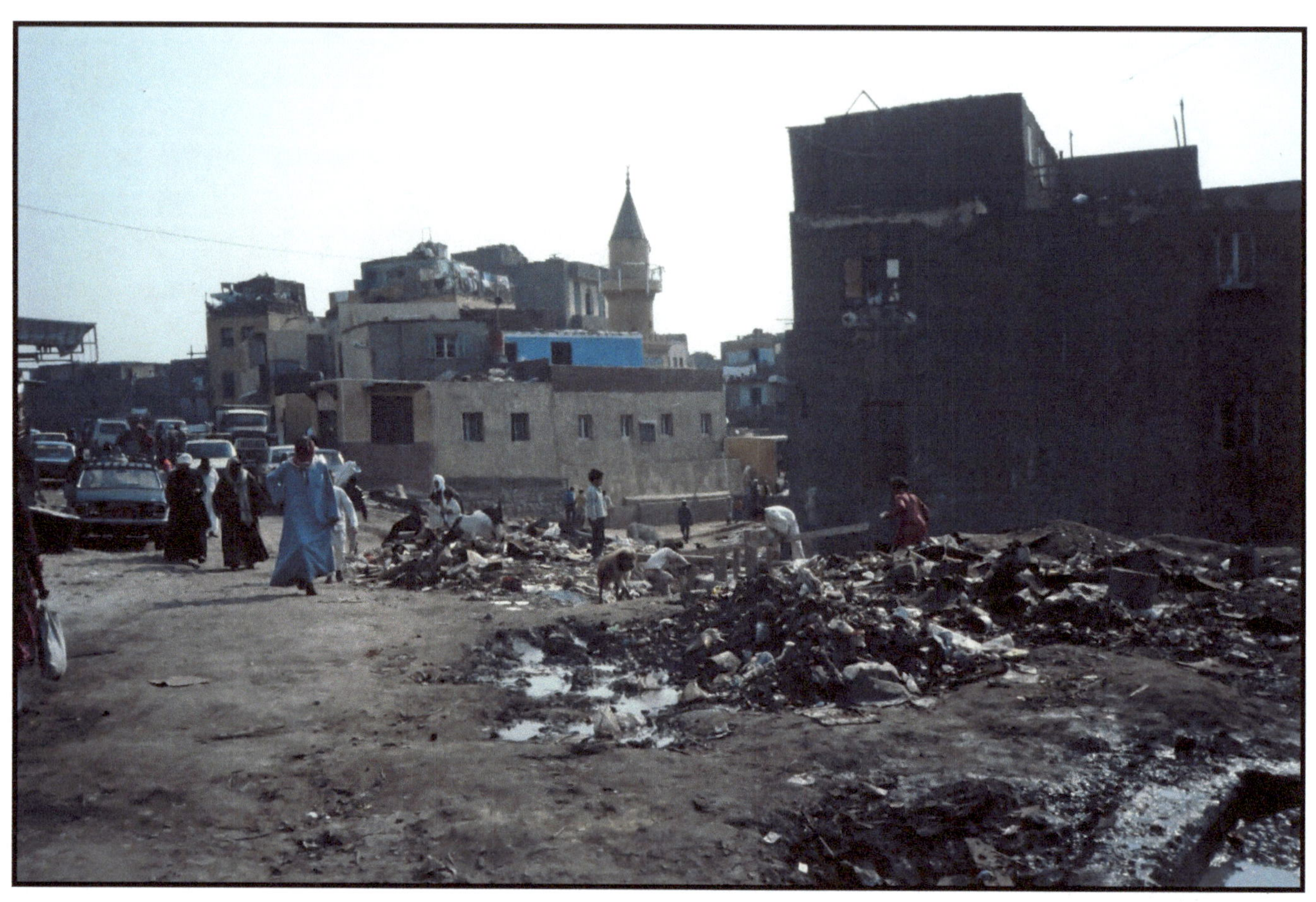

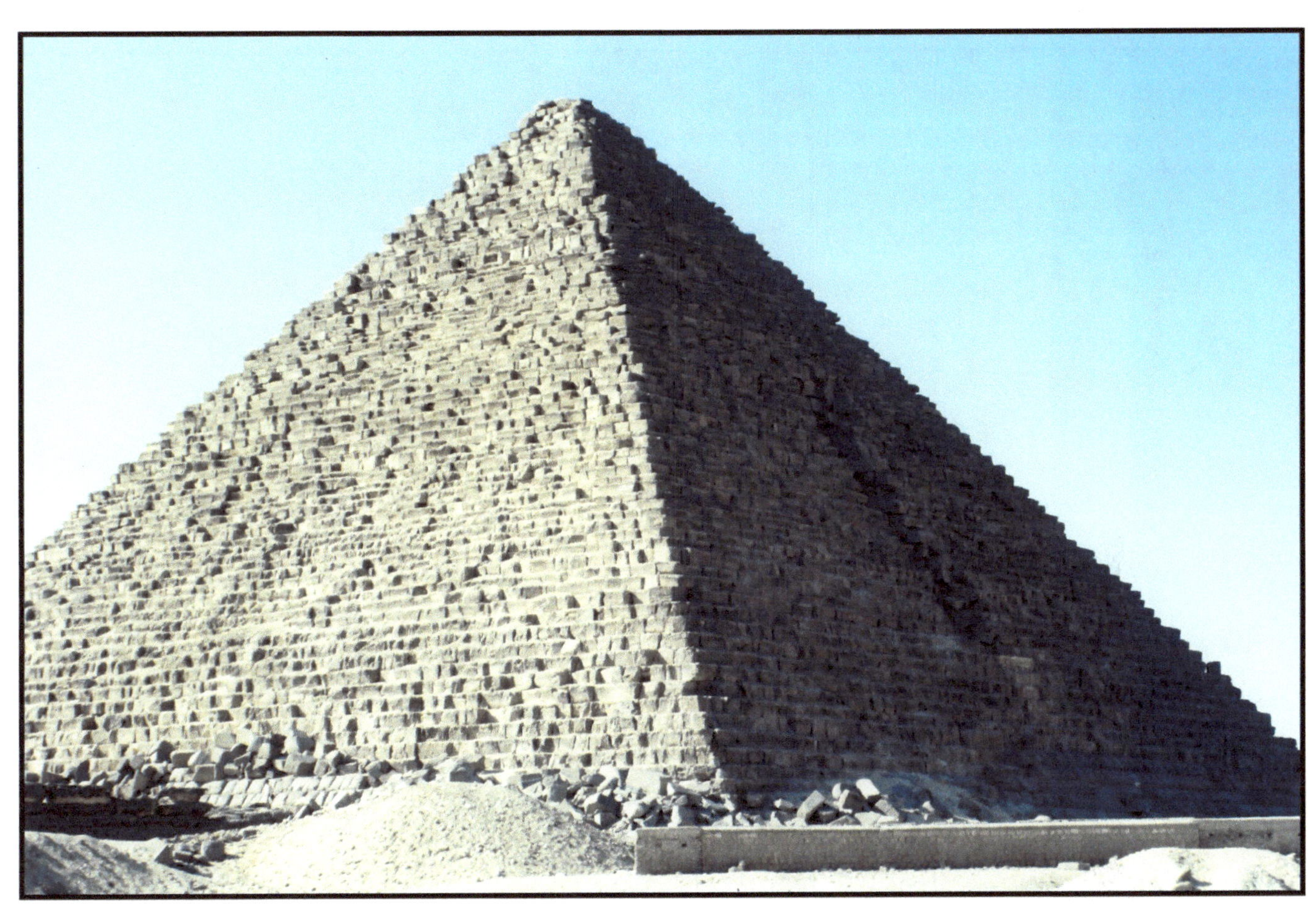

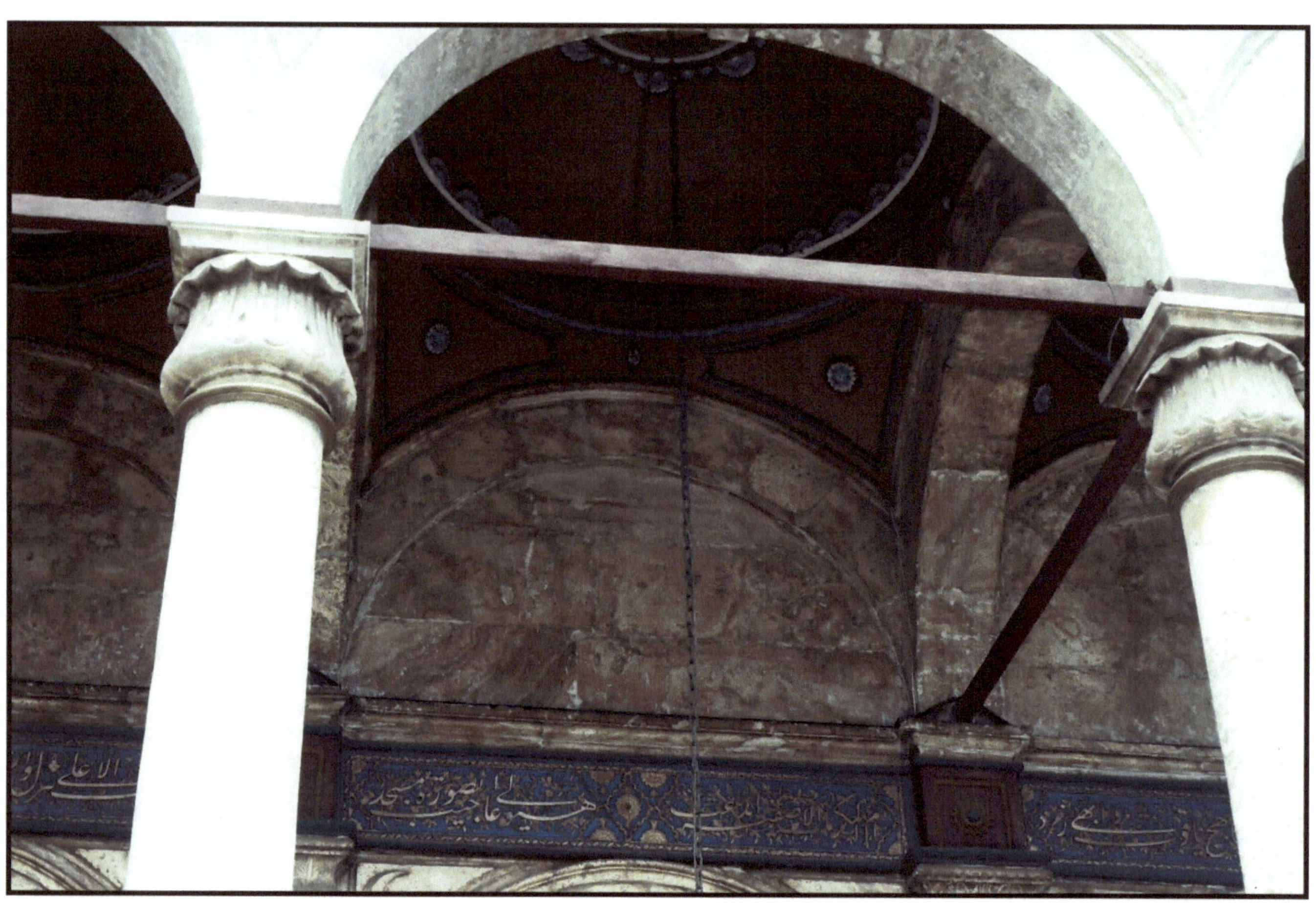

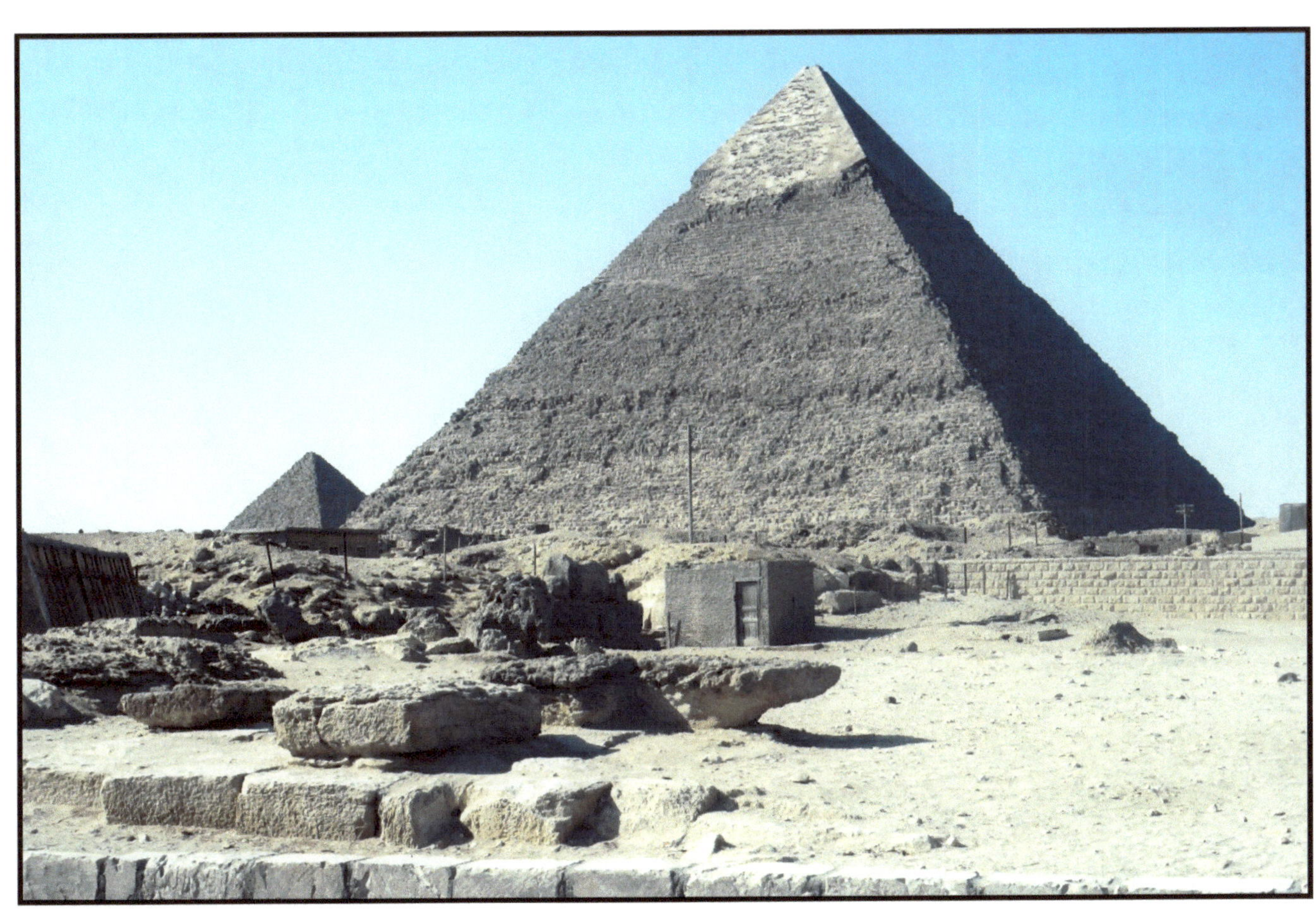

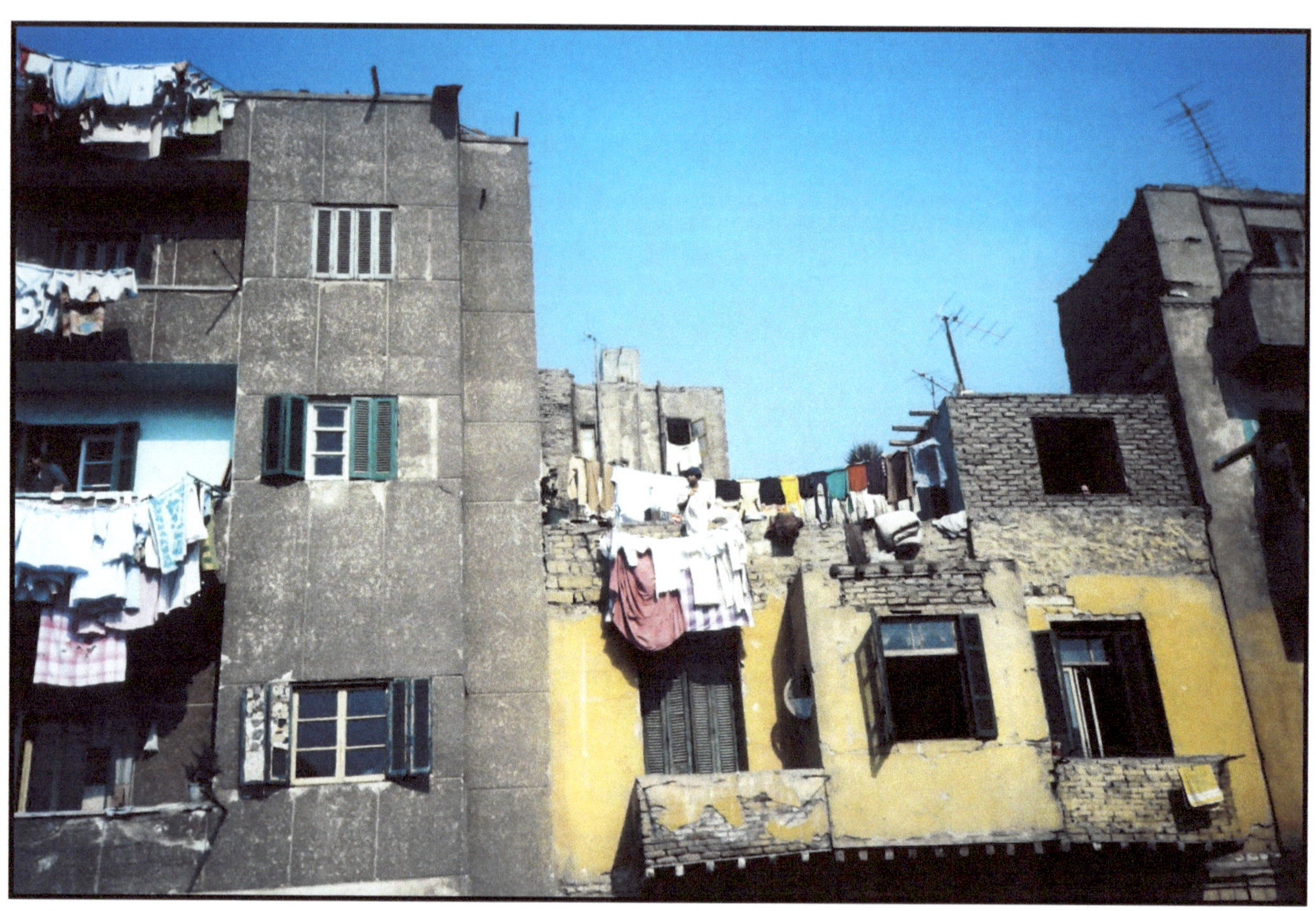

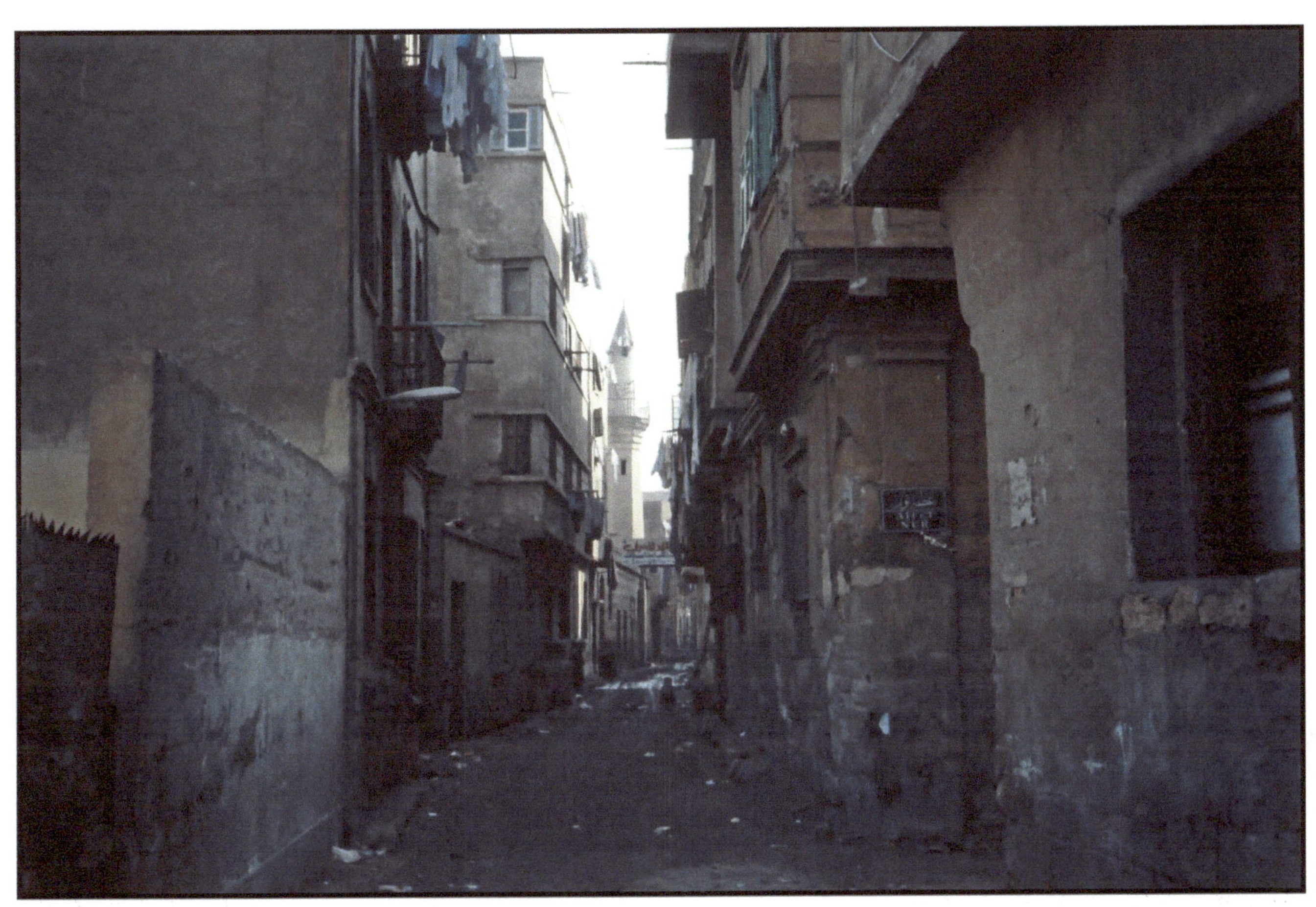

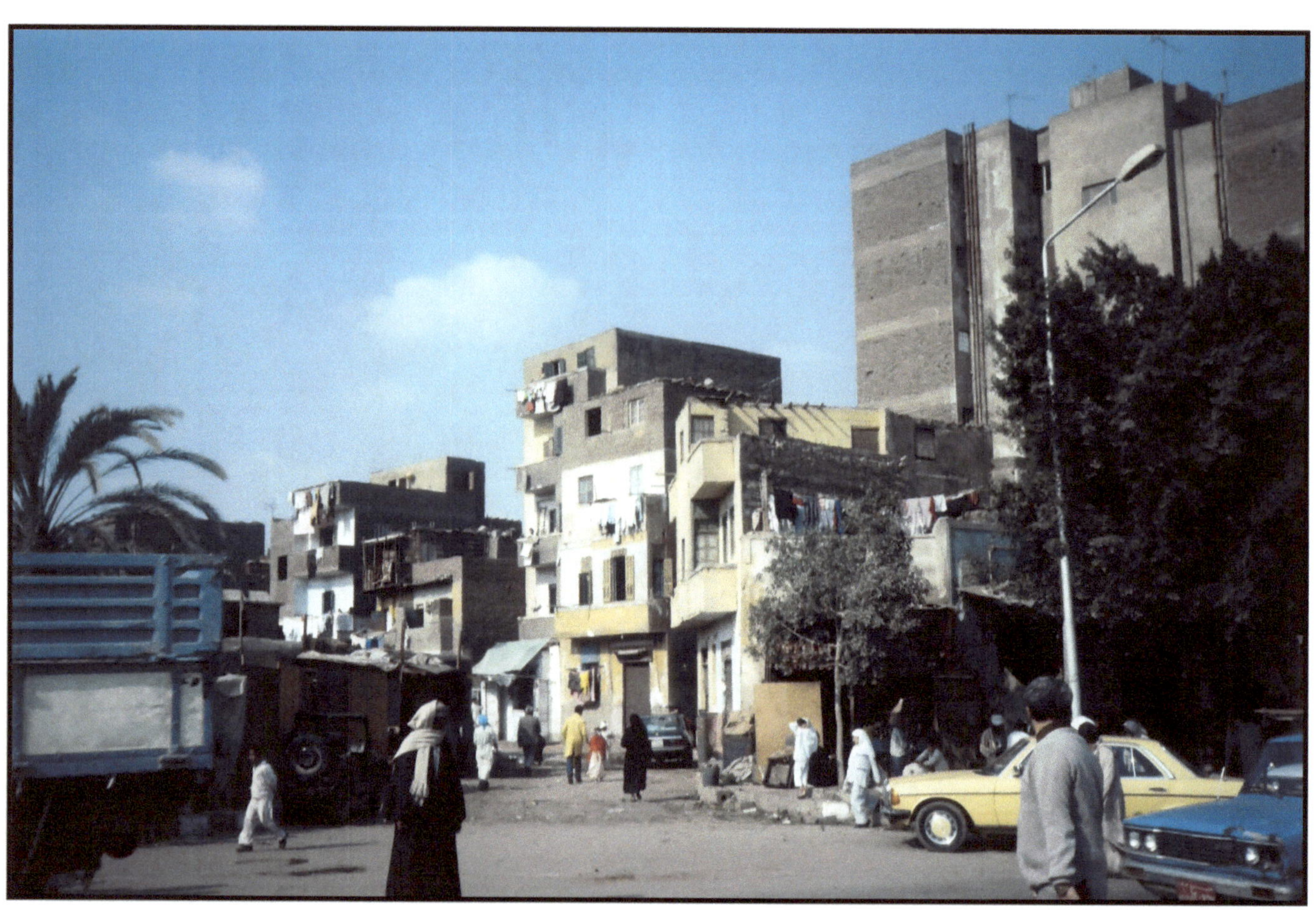

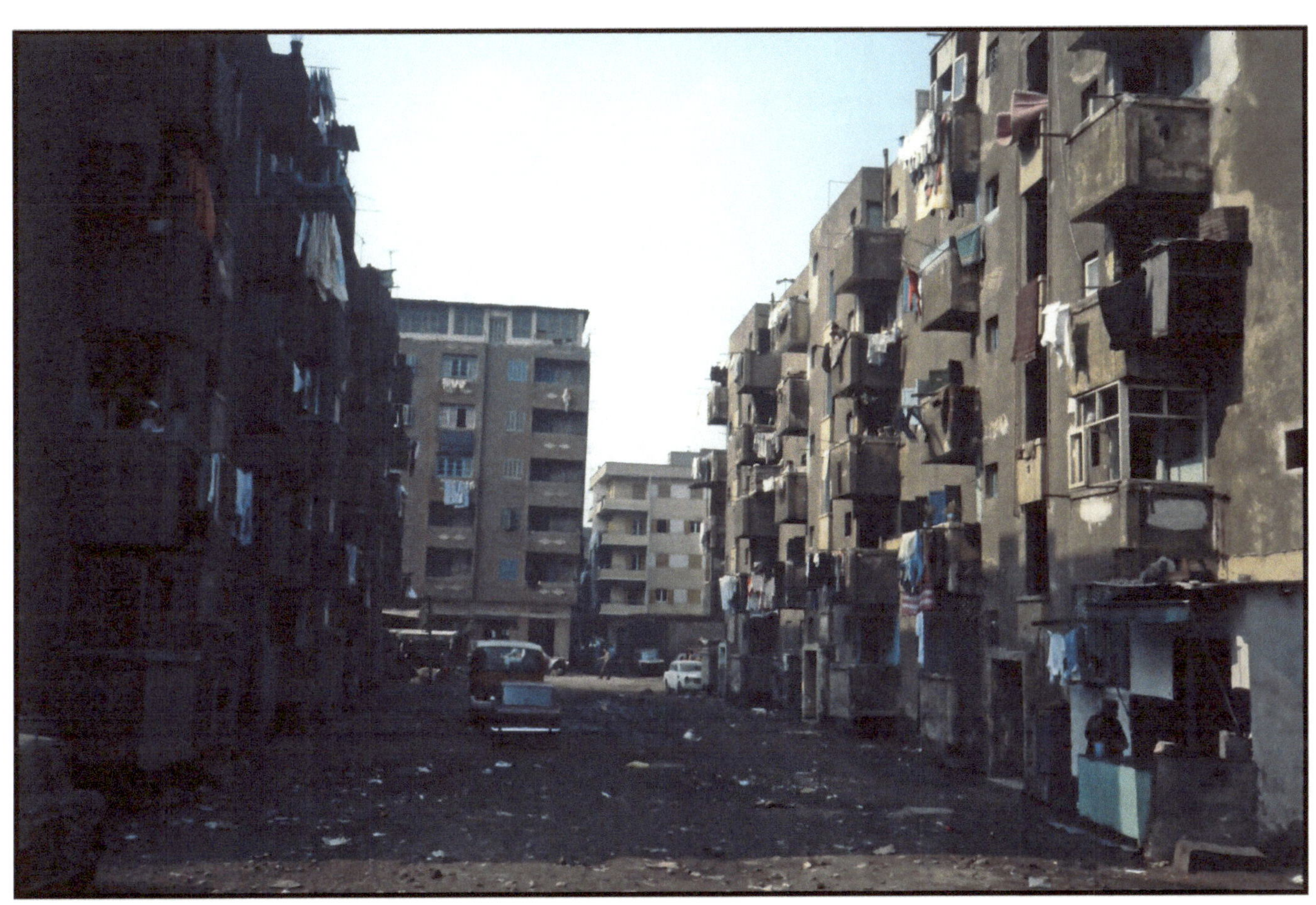

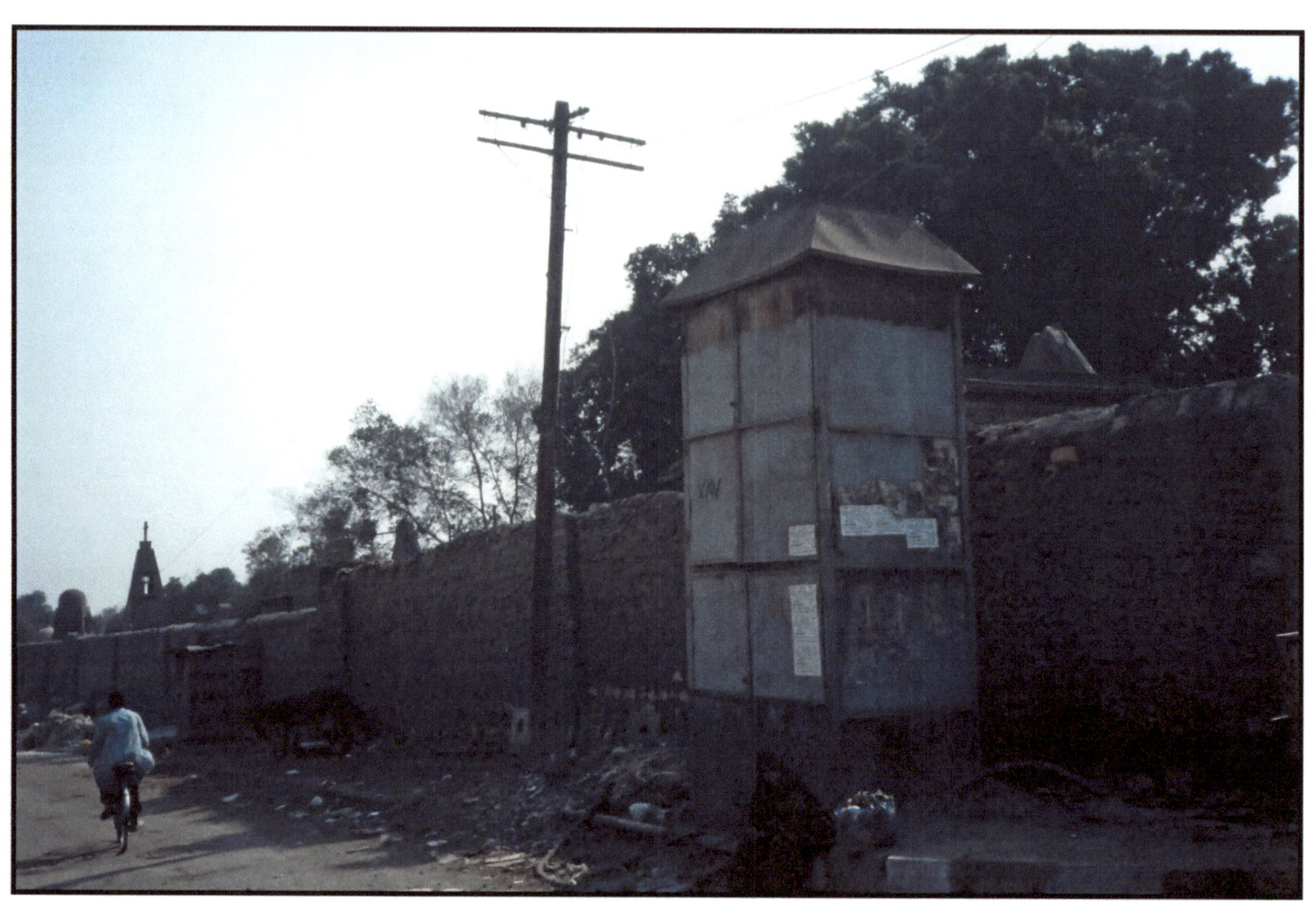

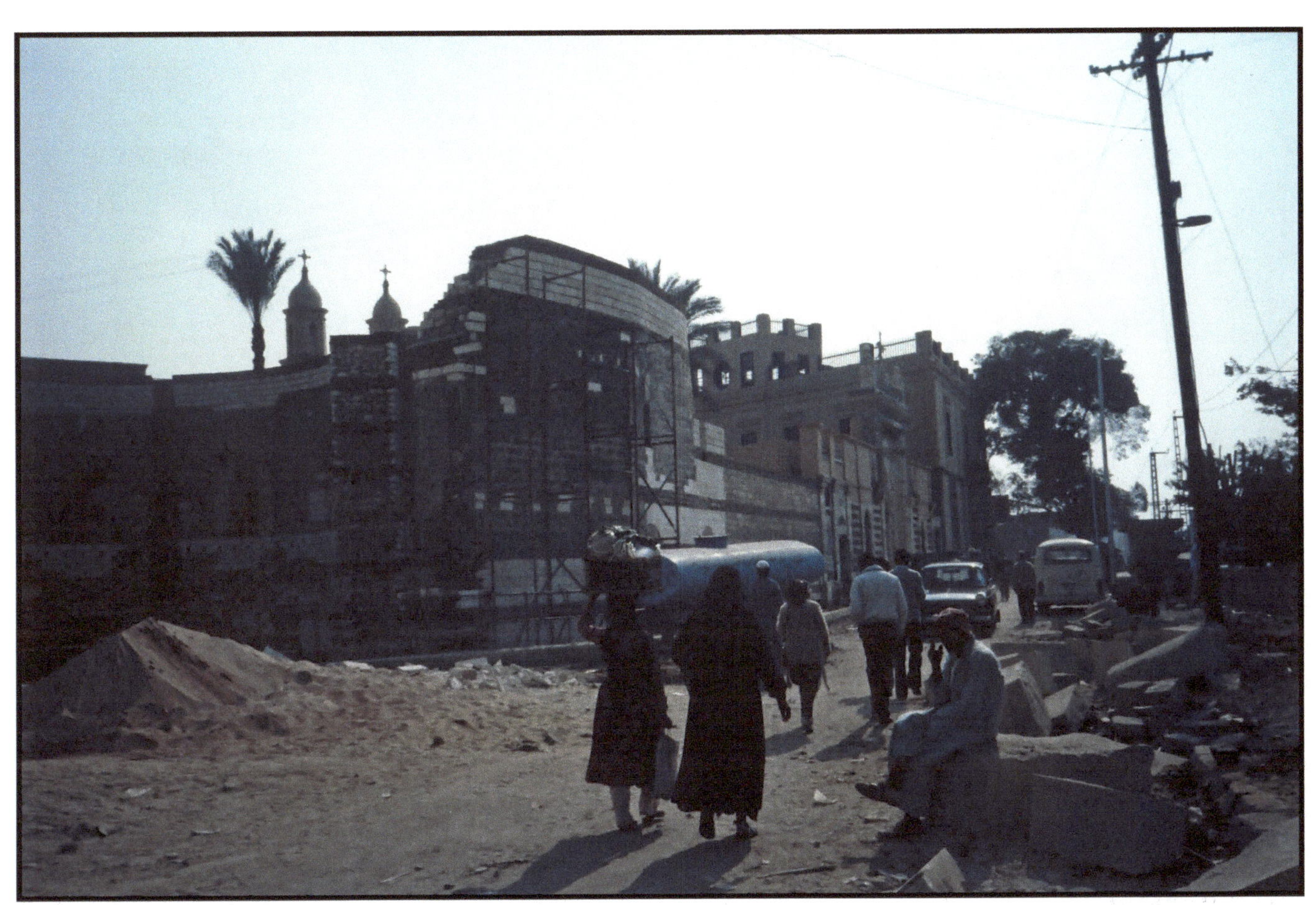

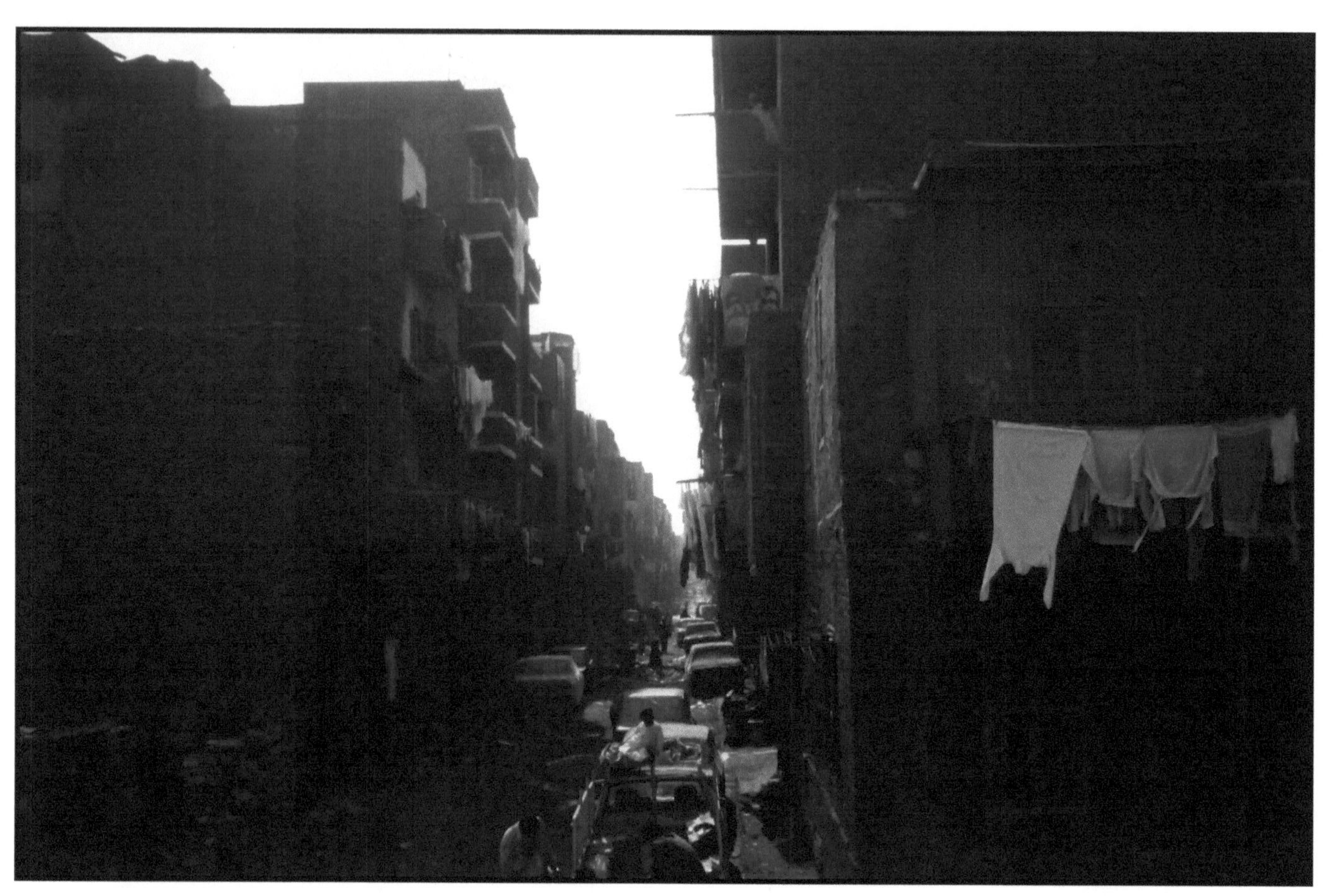

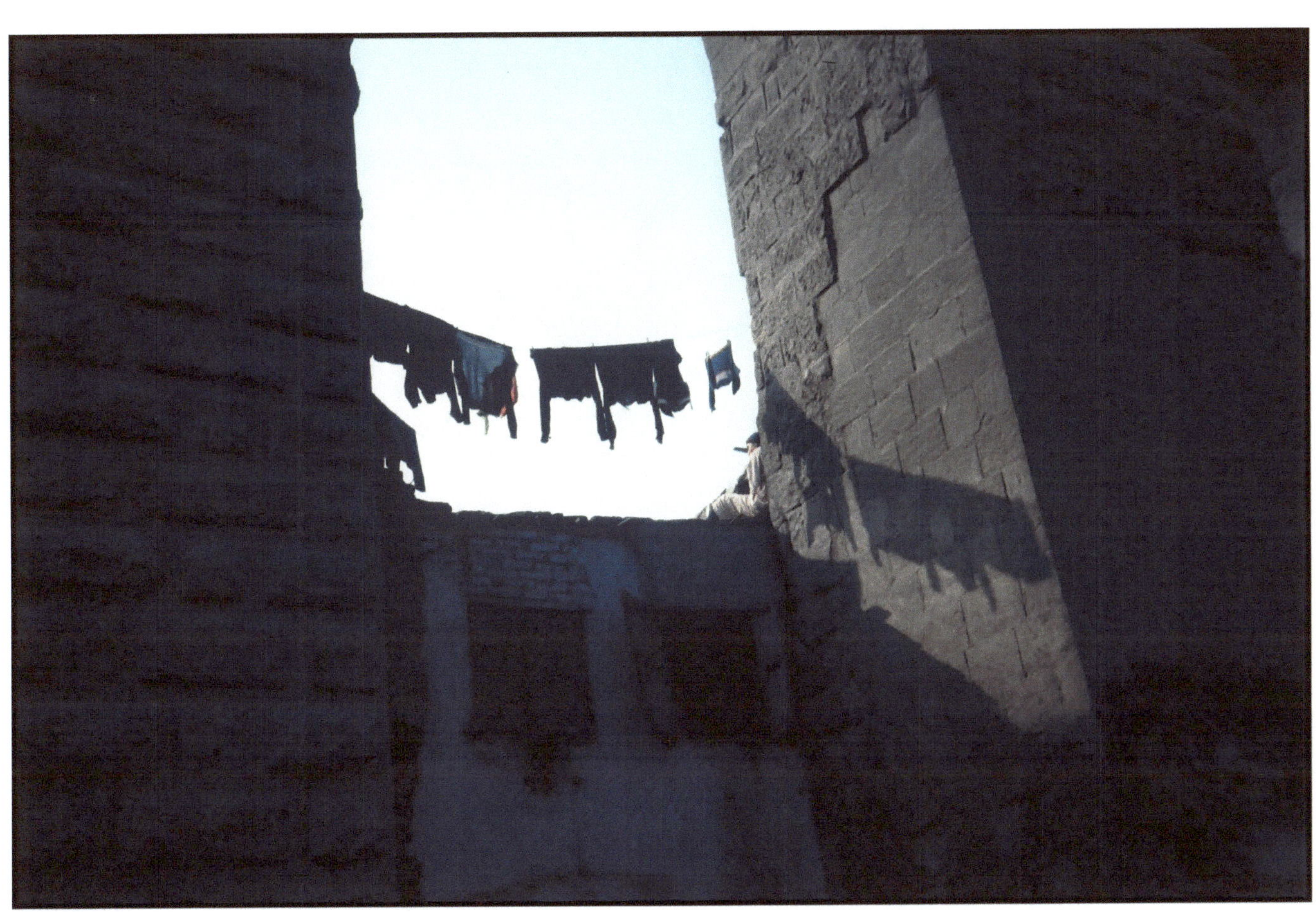

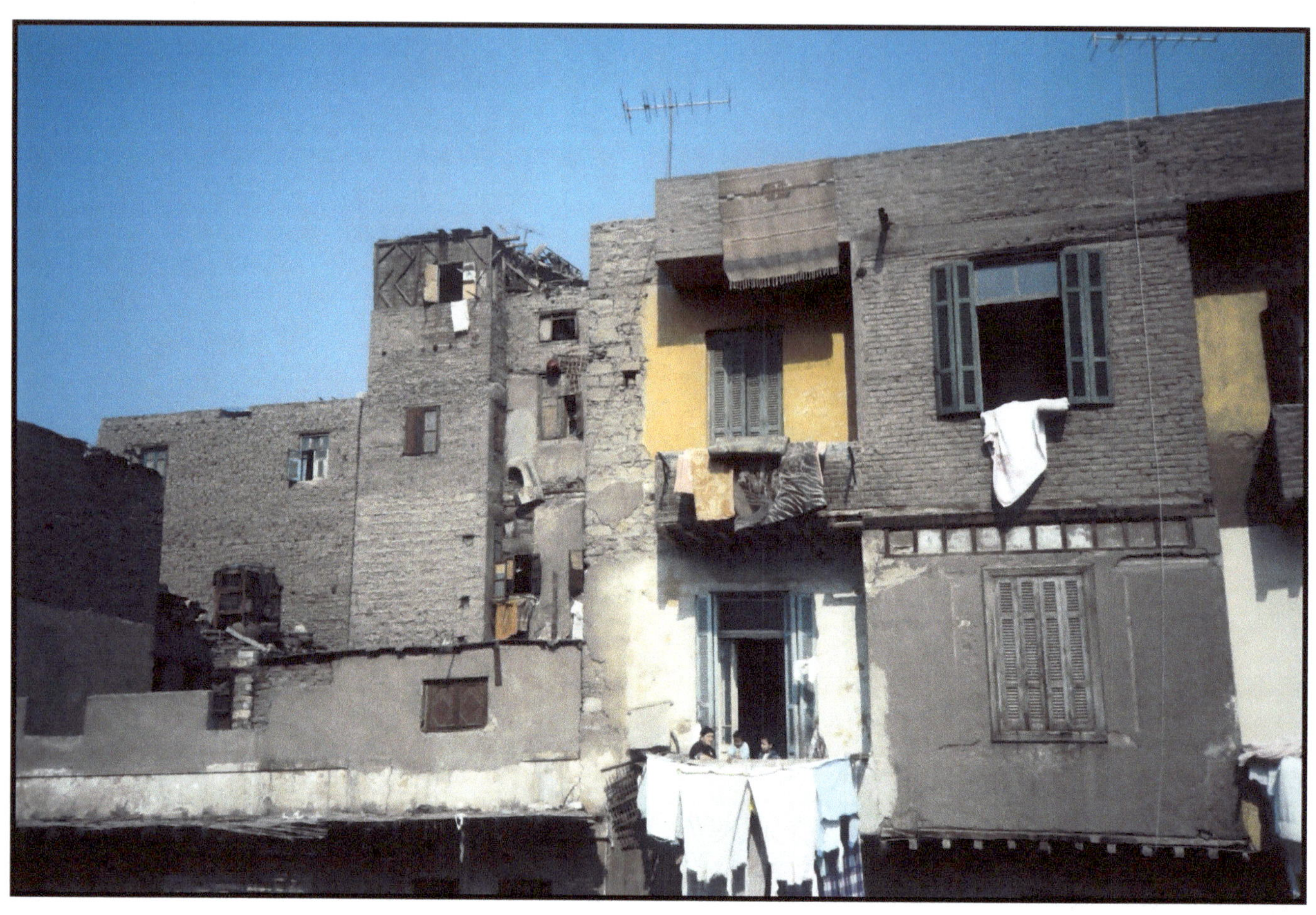

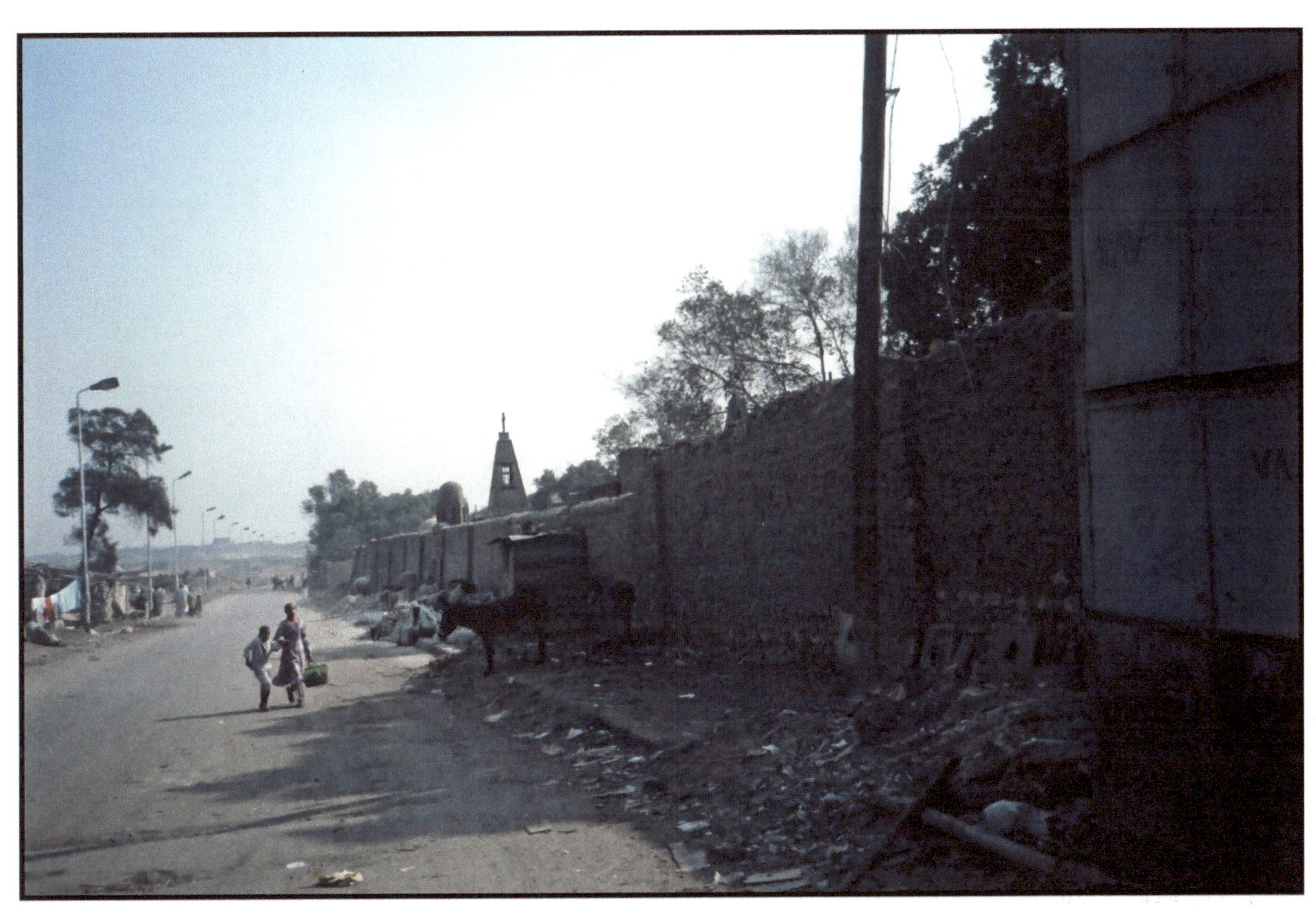

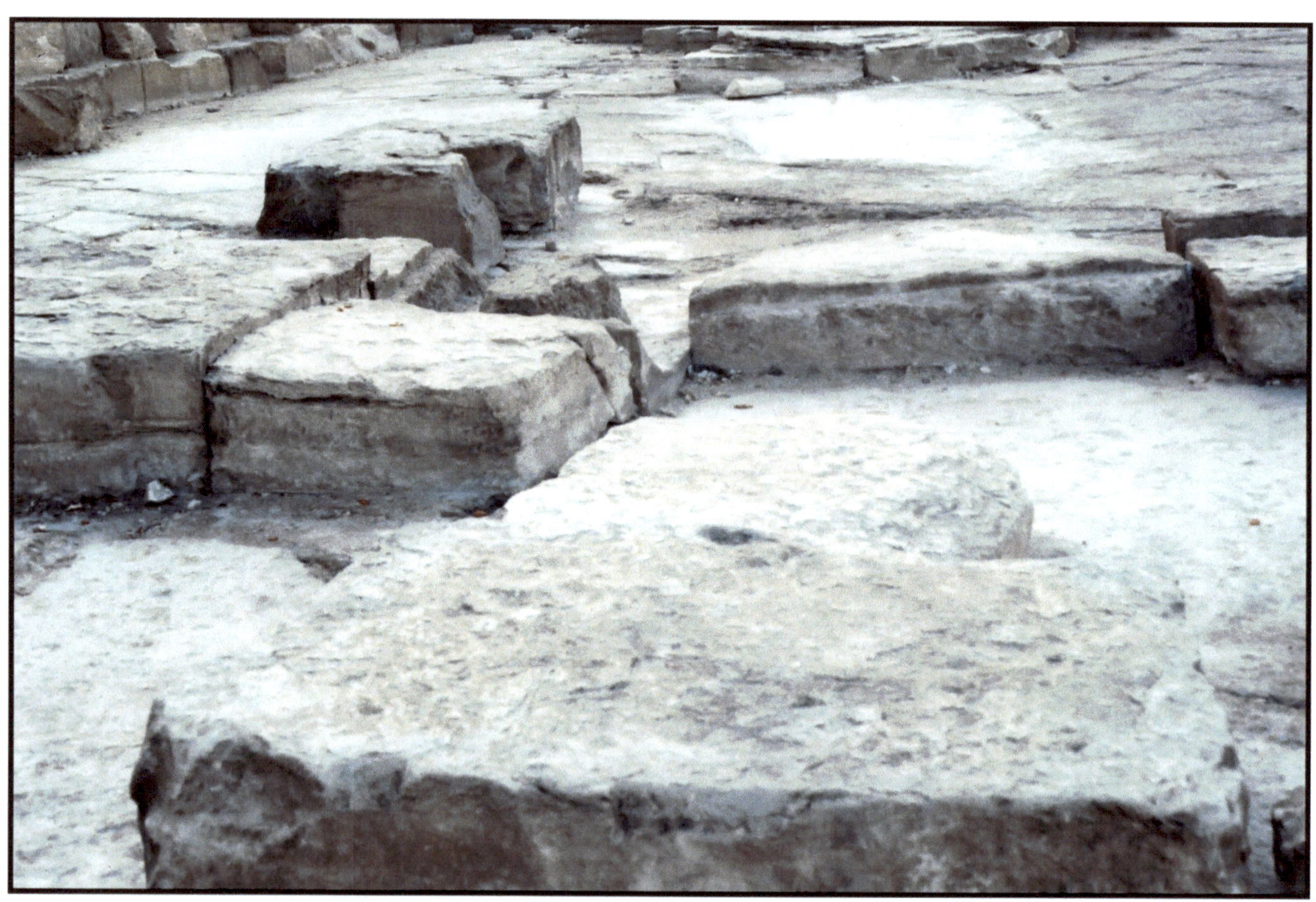

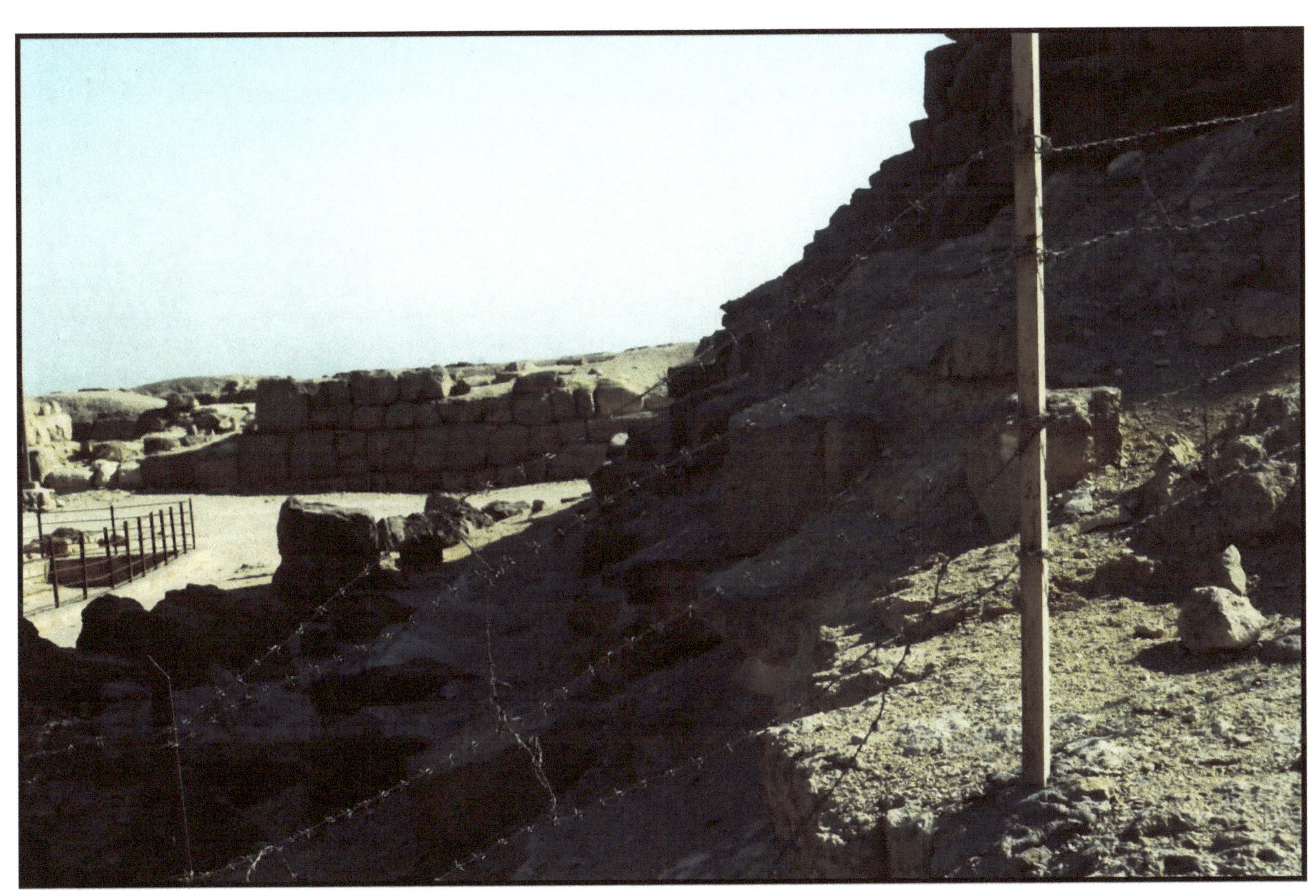

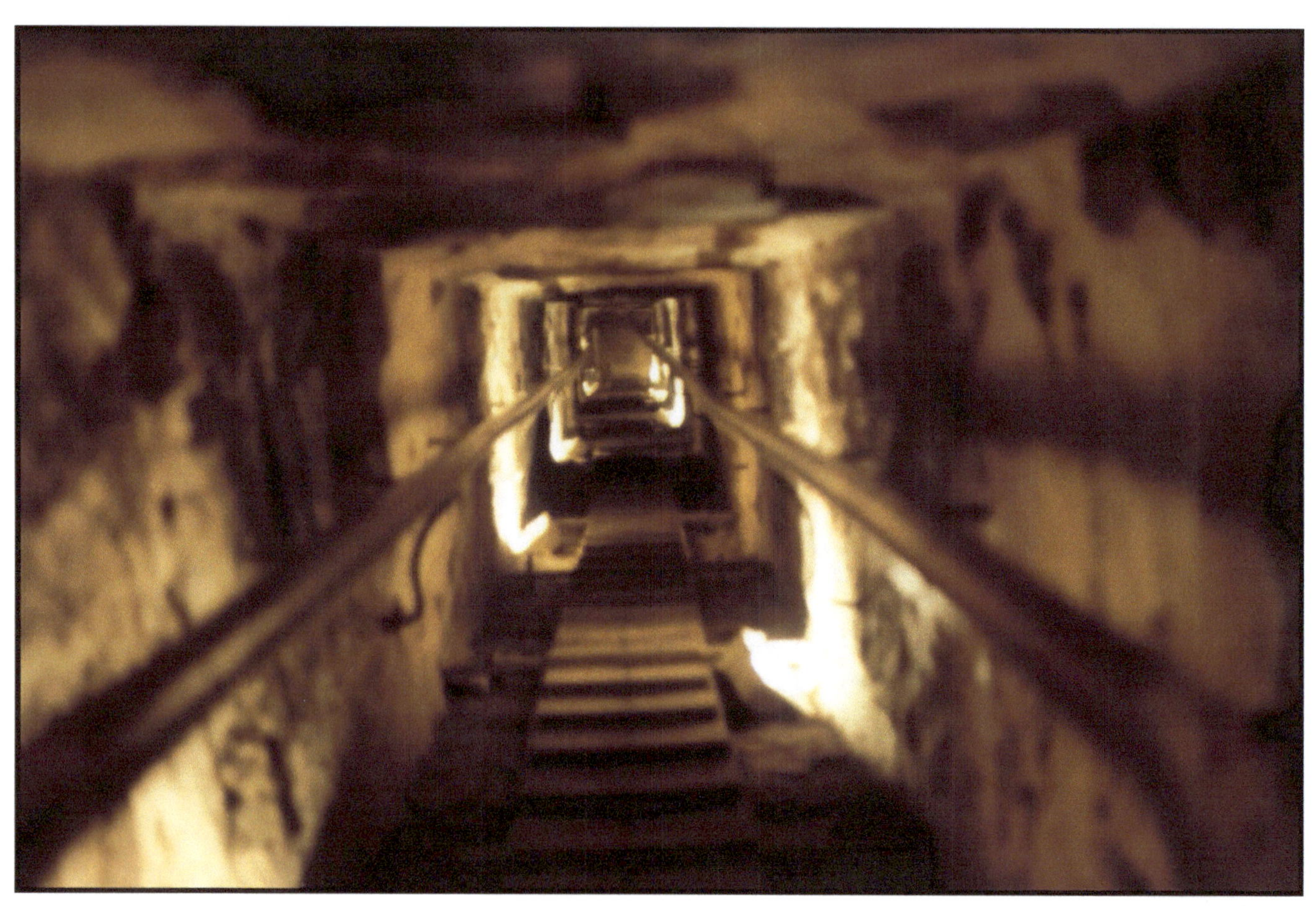

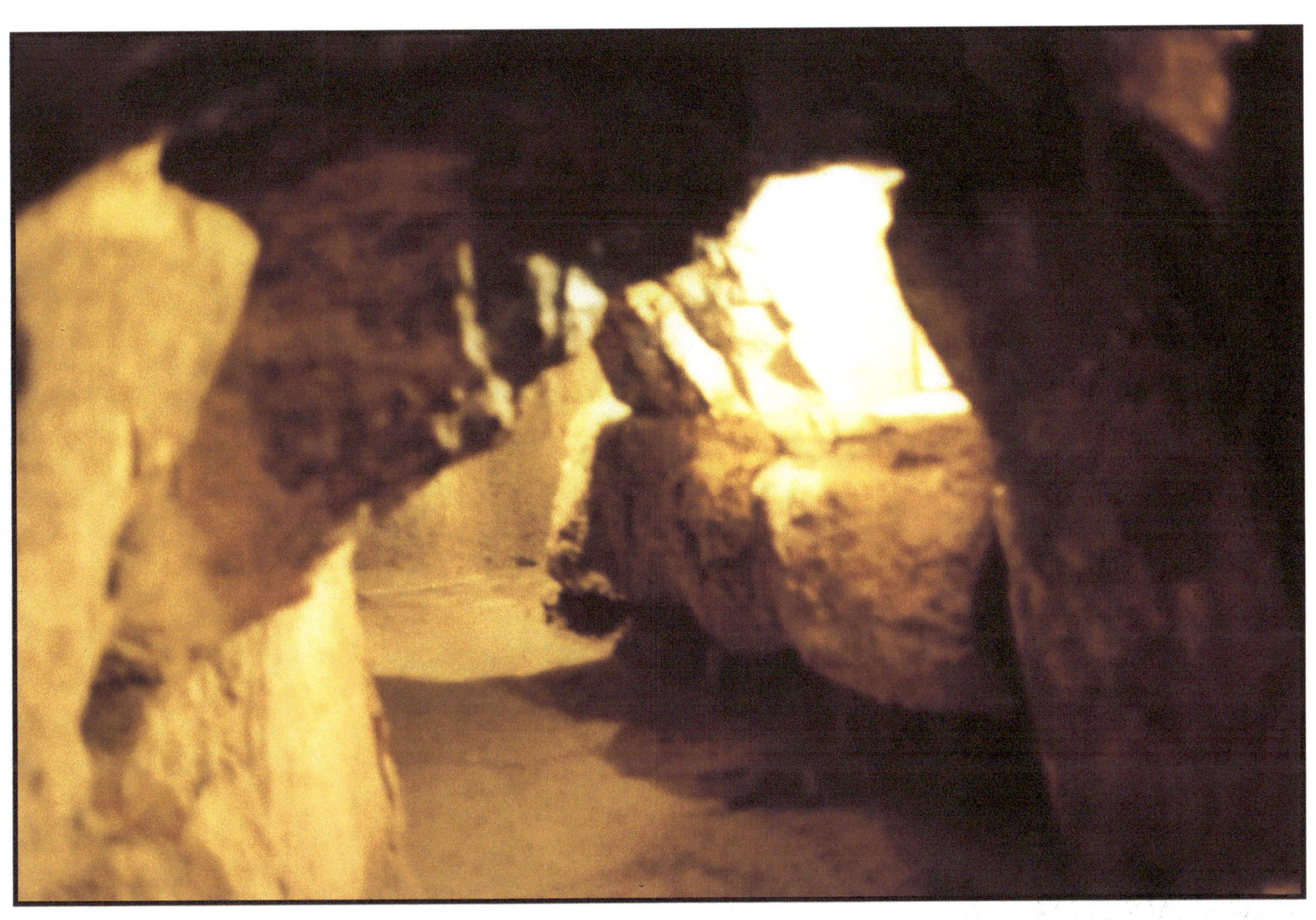

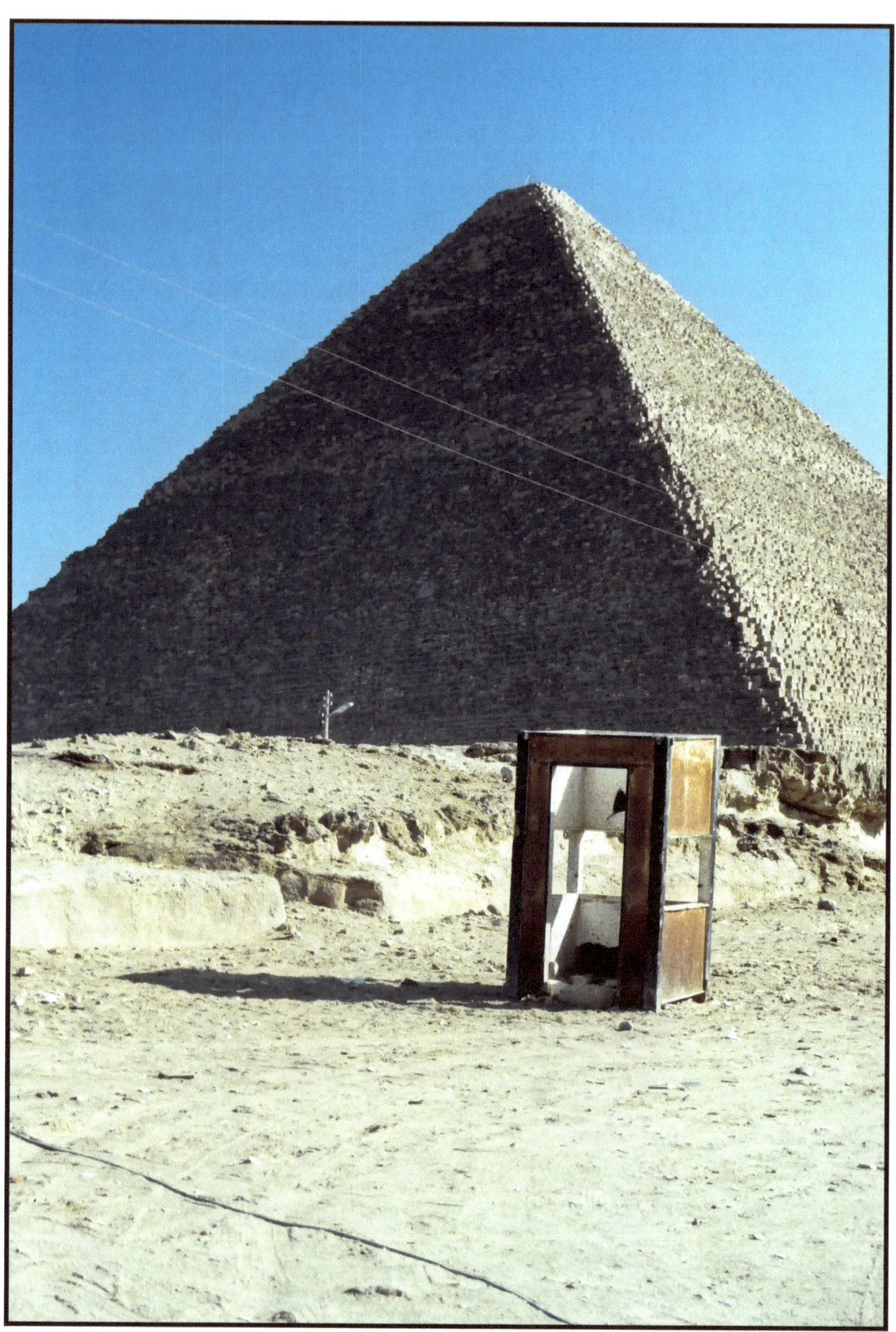

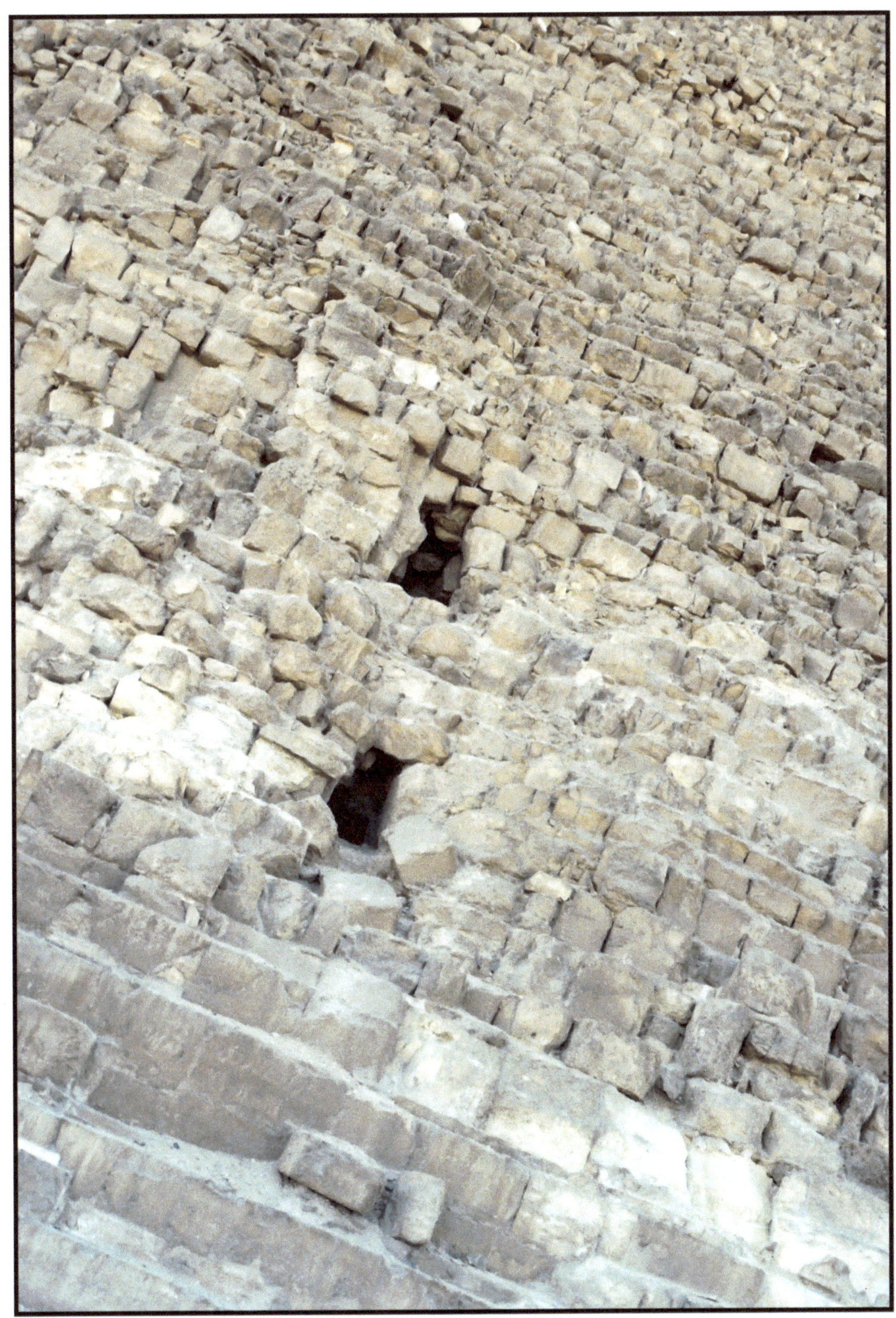

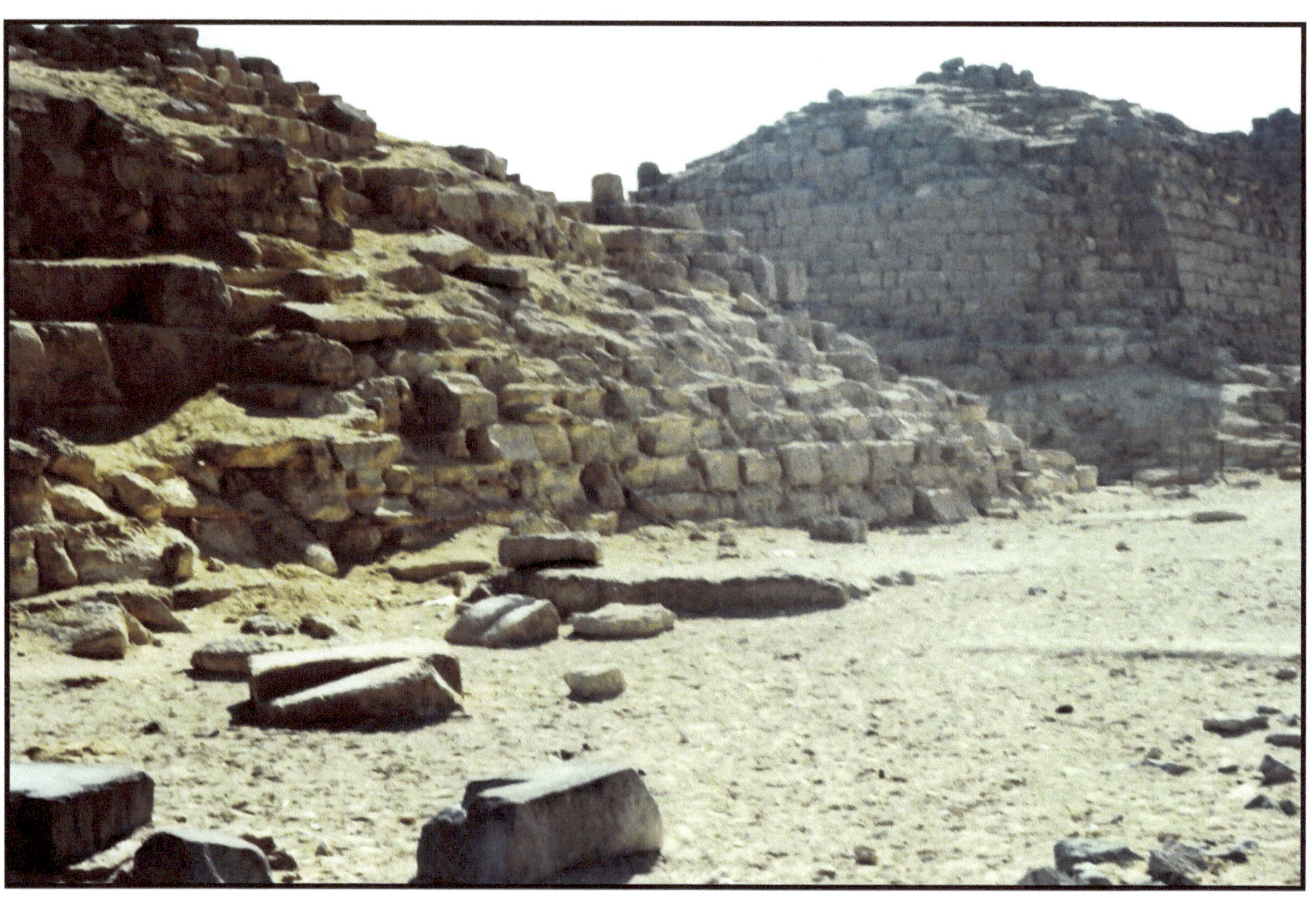

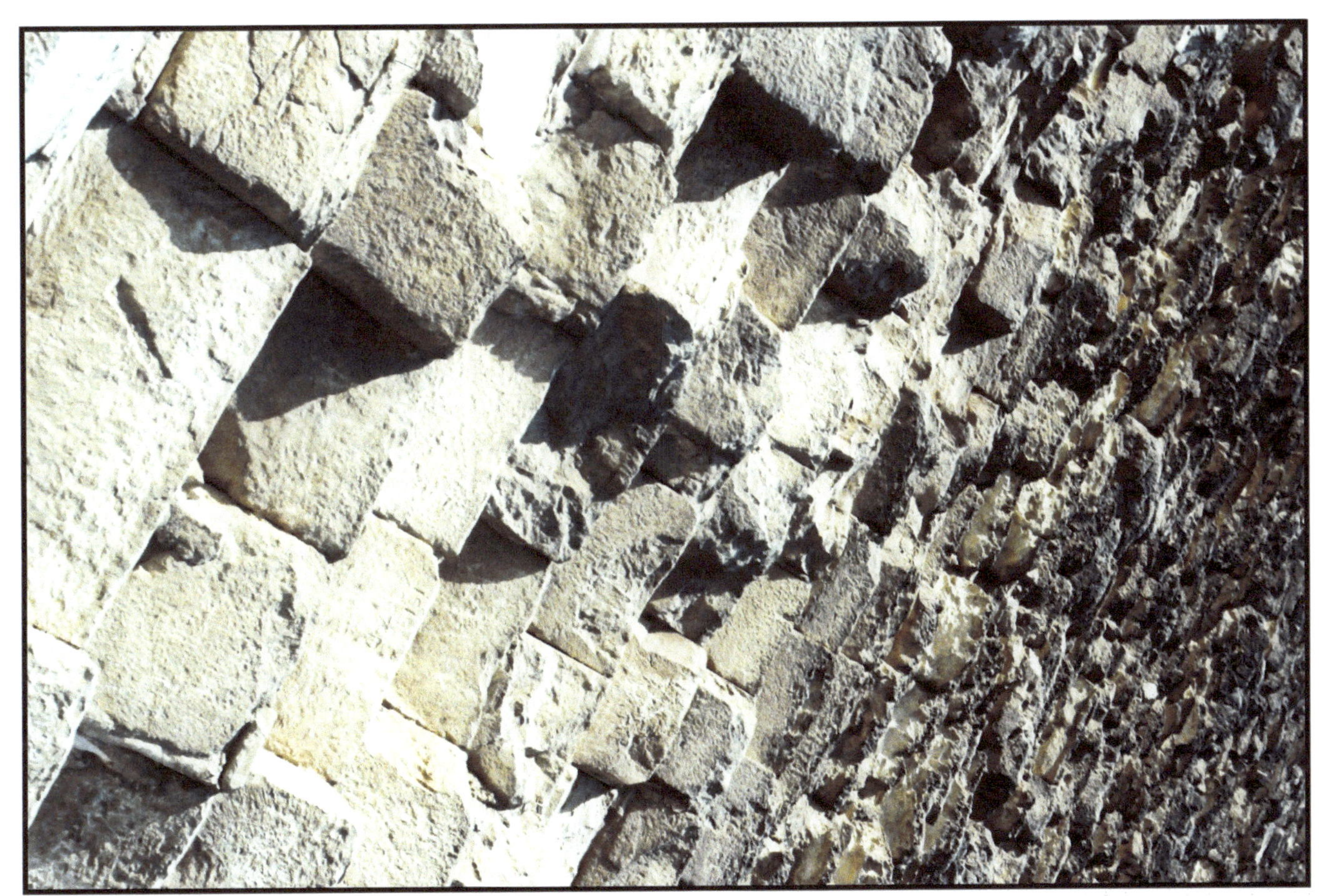

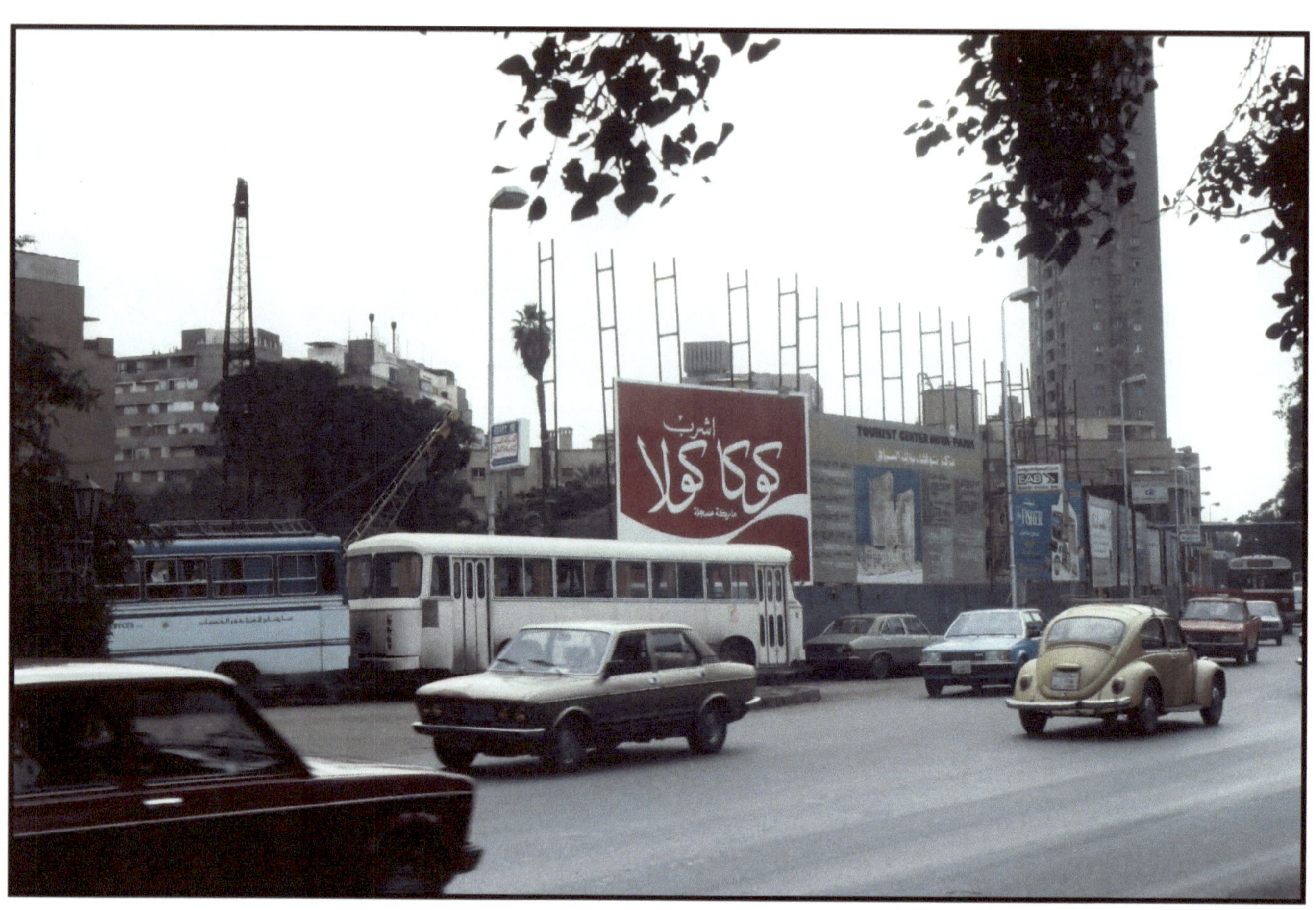
اشرب
كوكا كولا
ماركة مسجلة
TOURIST CENTER

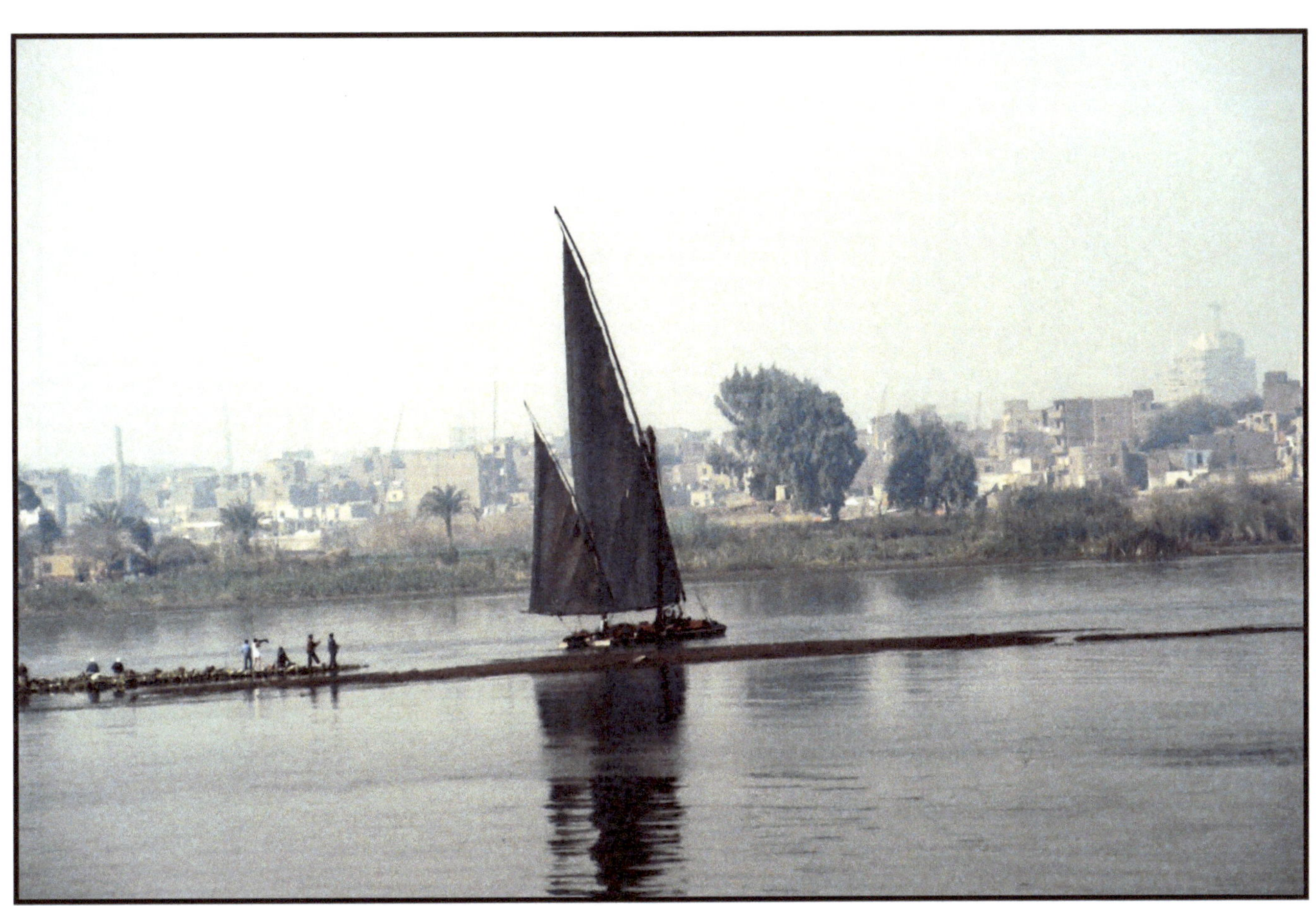

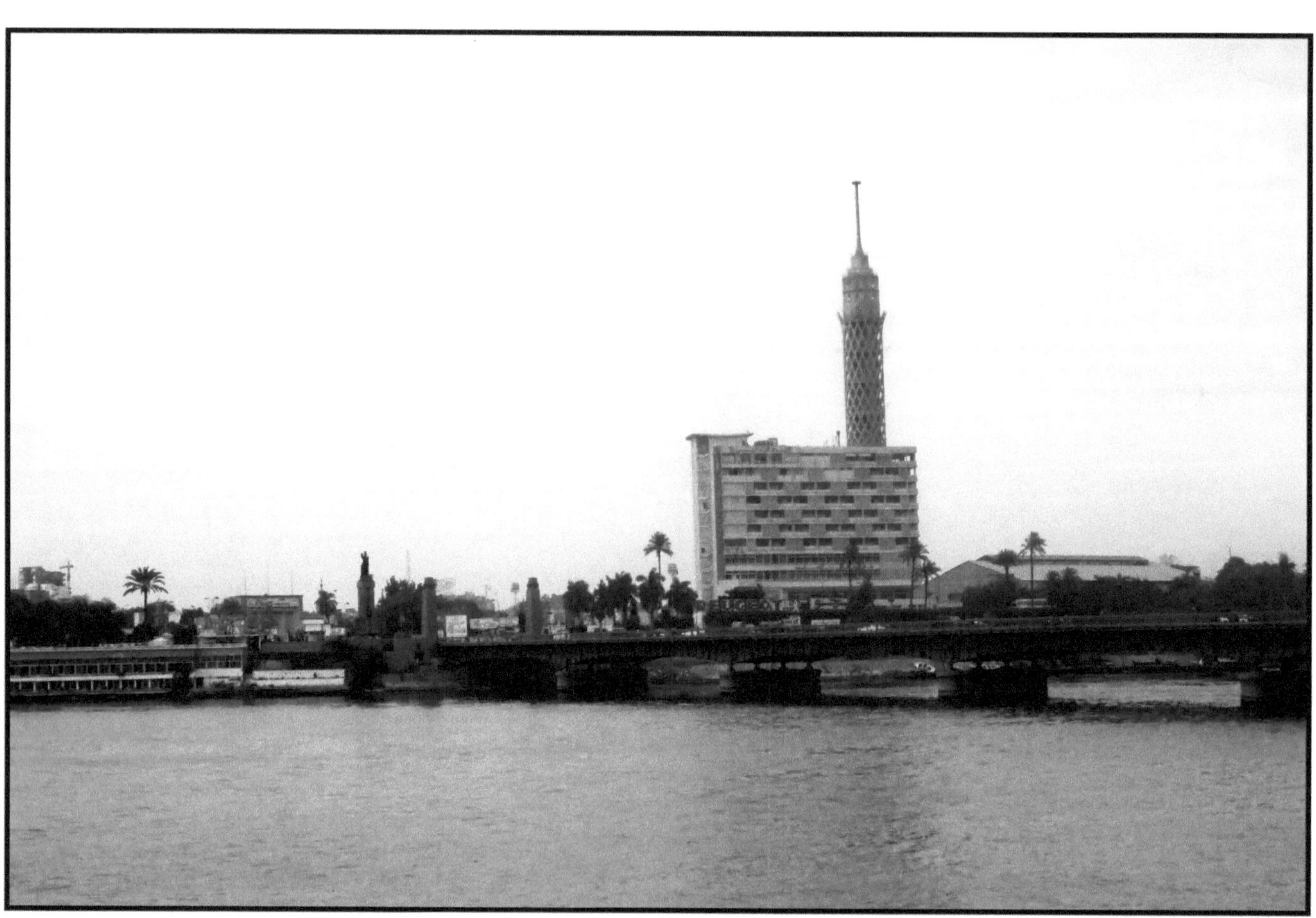

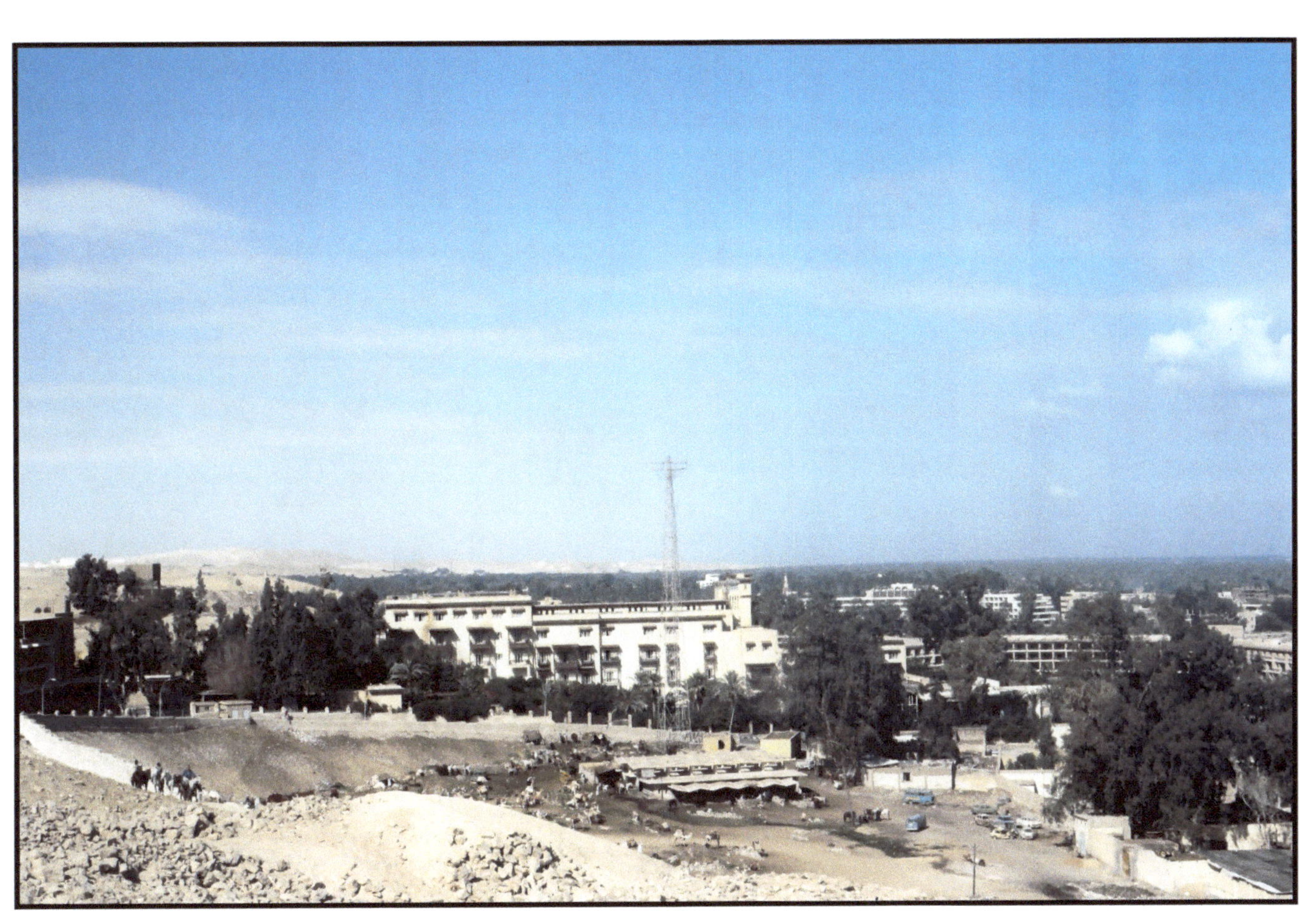

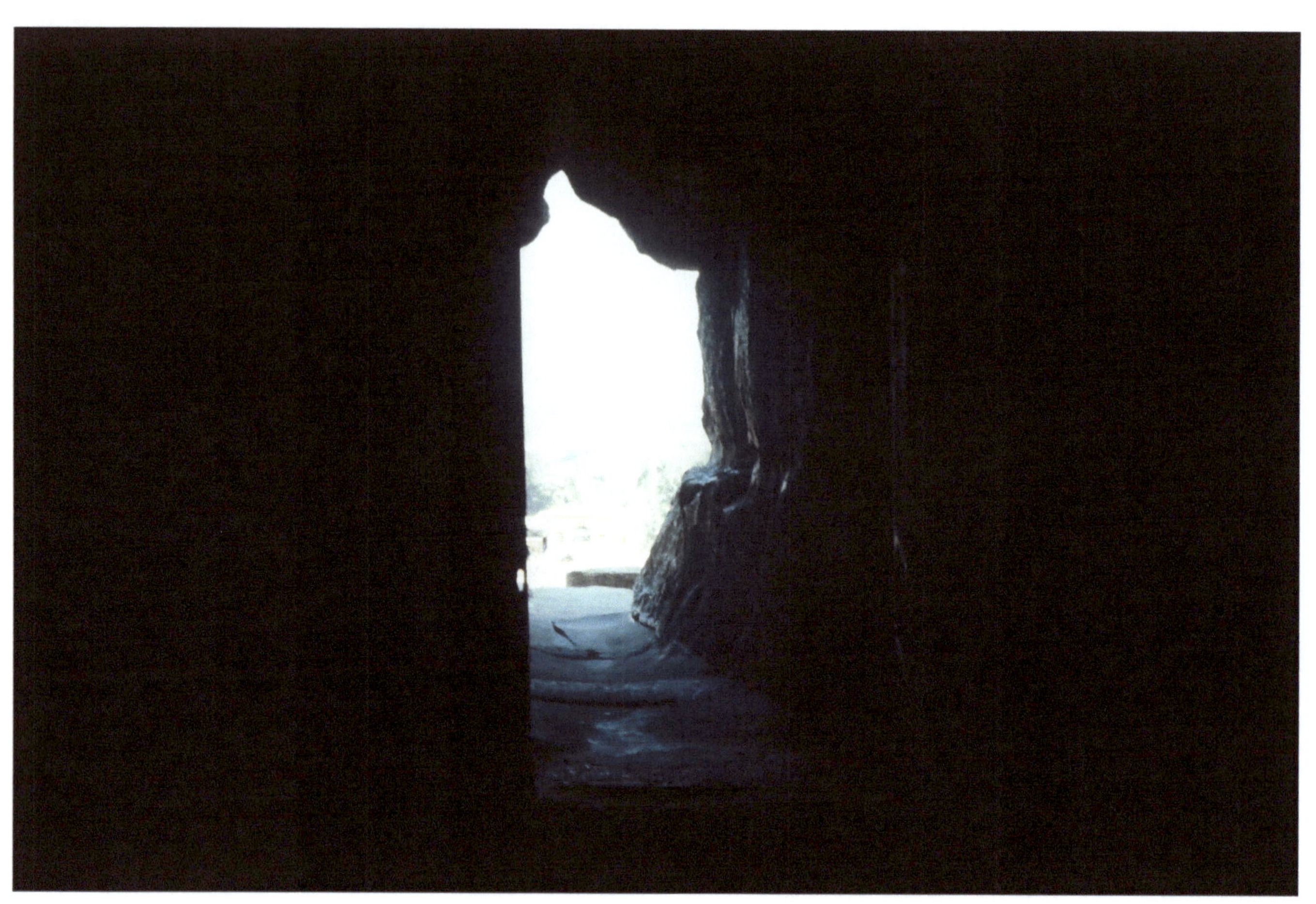

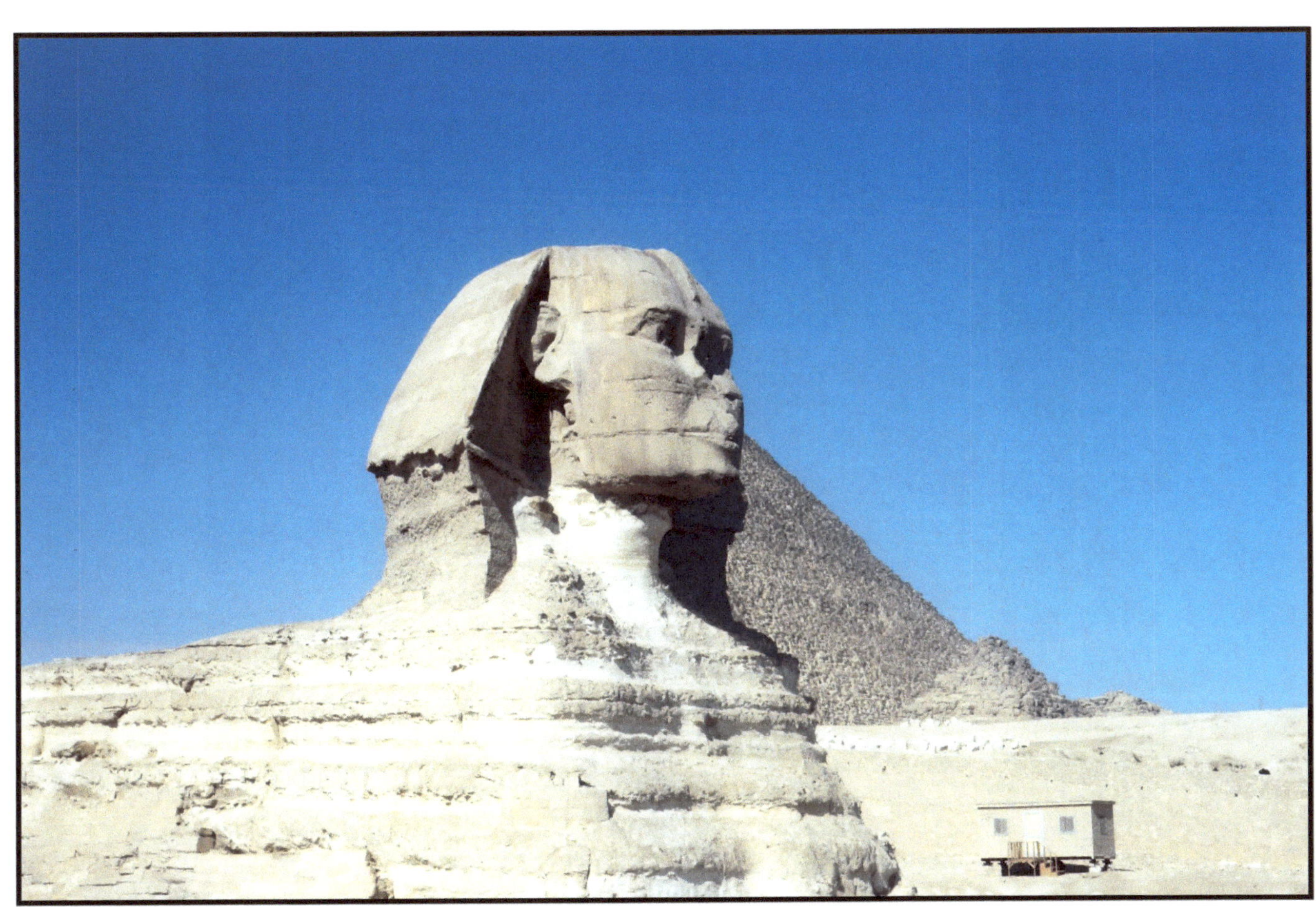

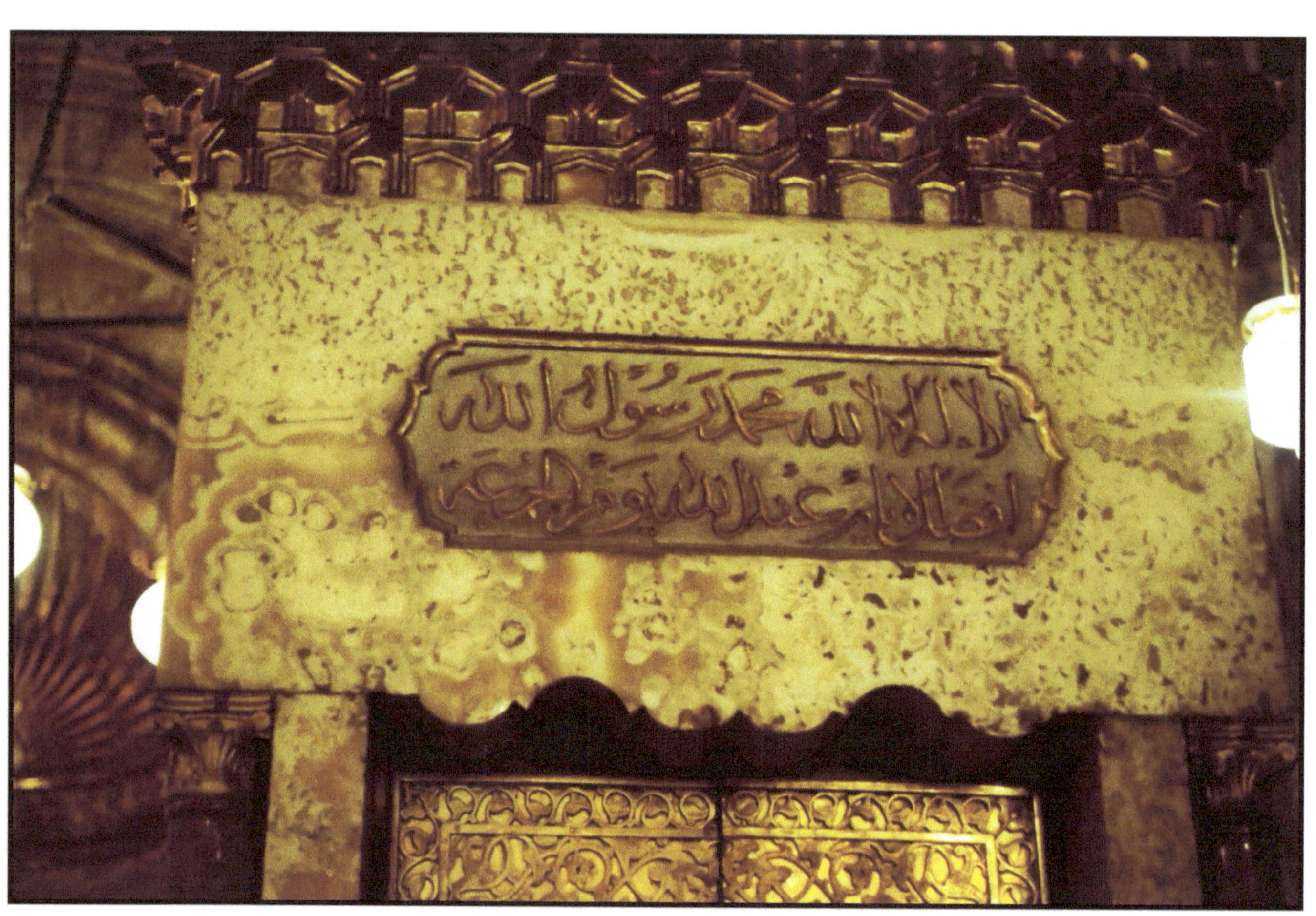
لا اله الا الله محمد رسول الله
افضل الايام عند الله يوم الجمعة

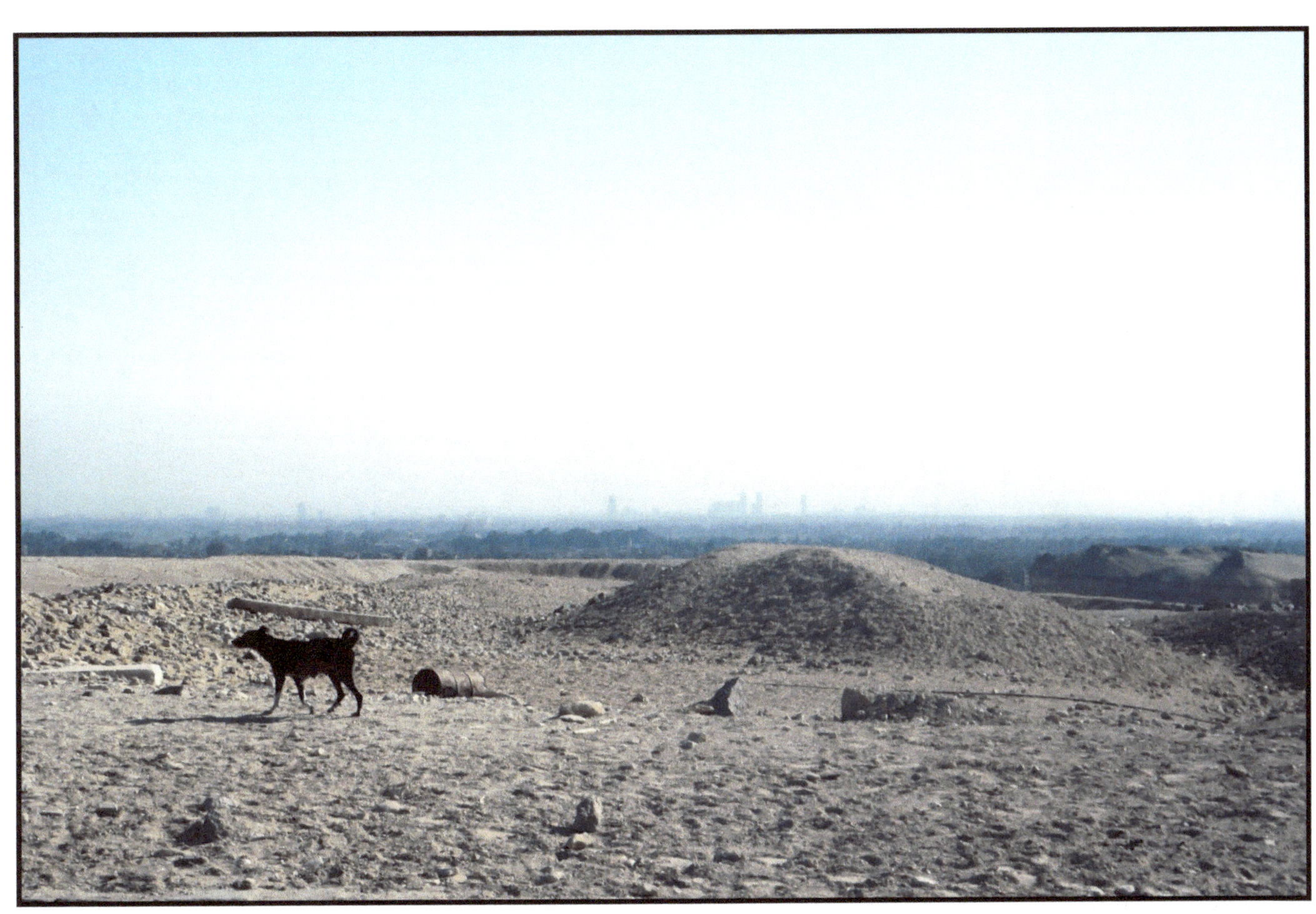

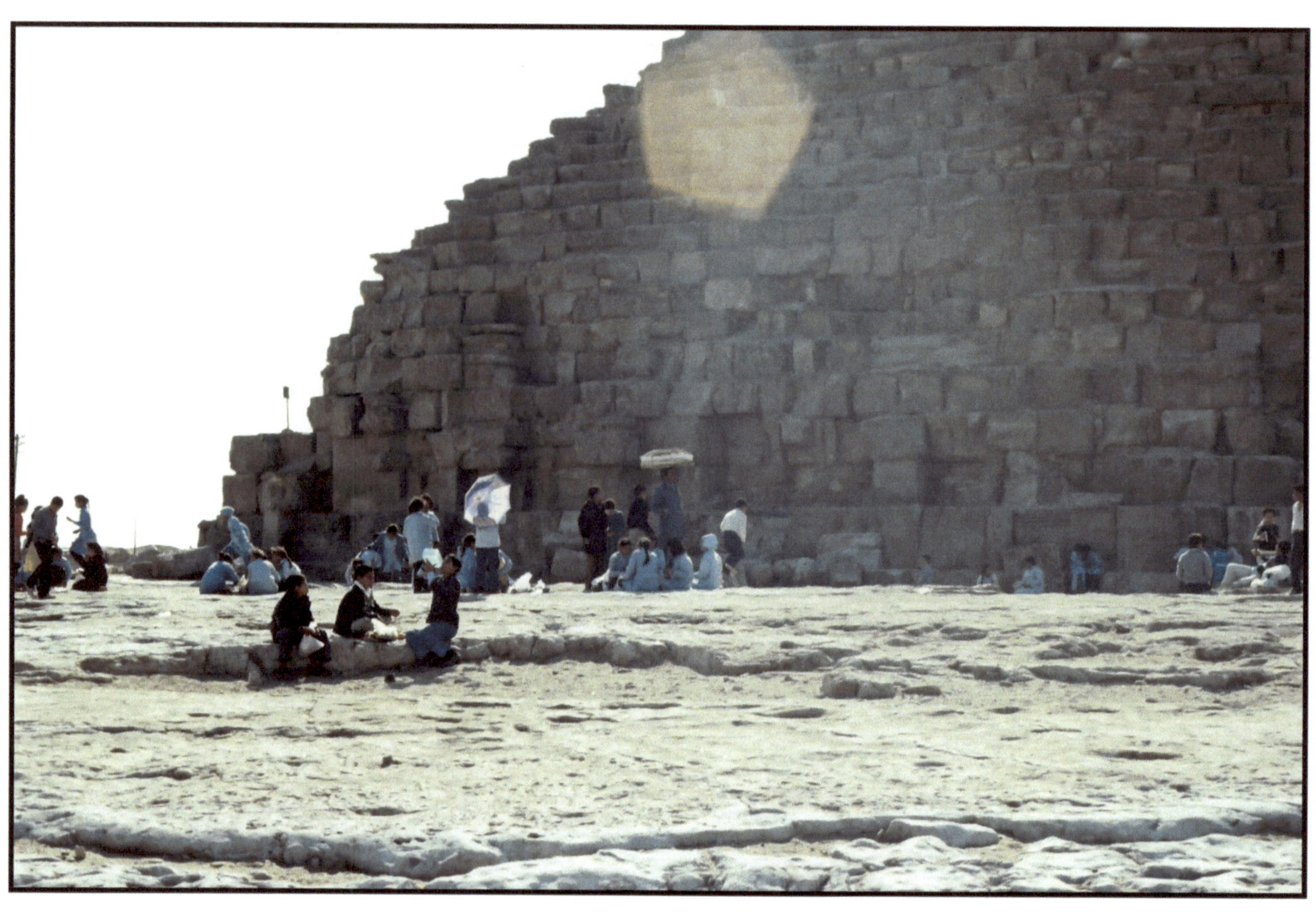

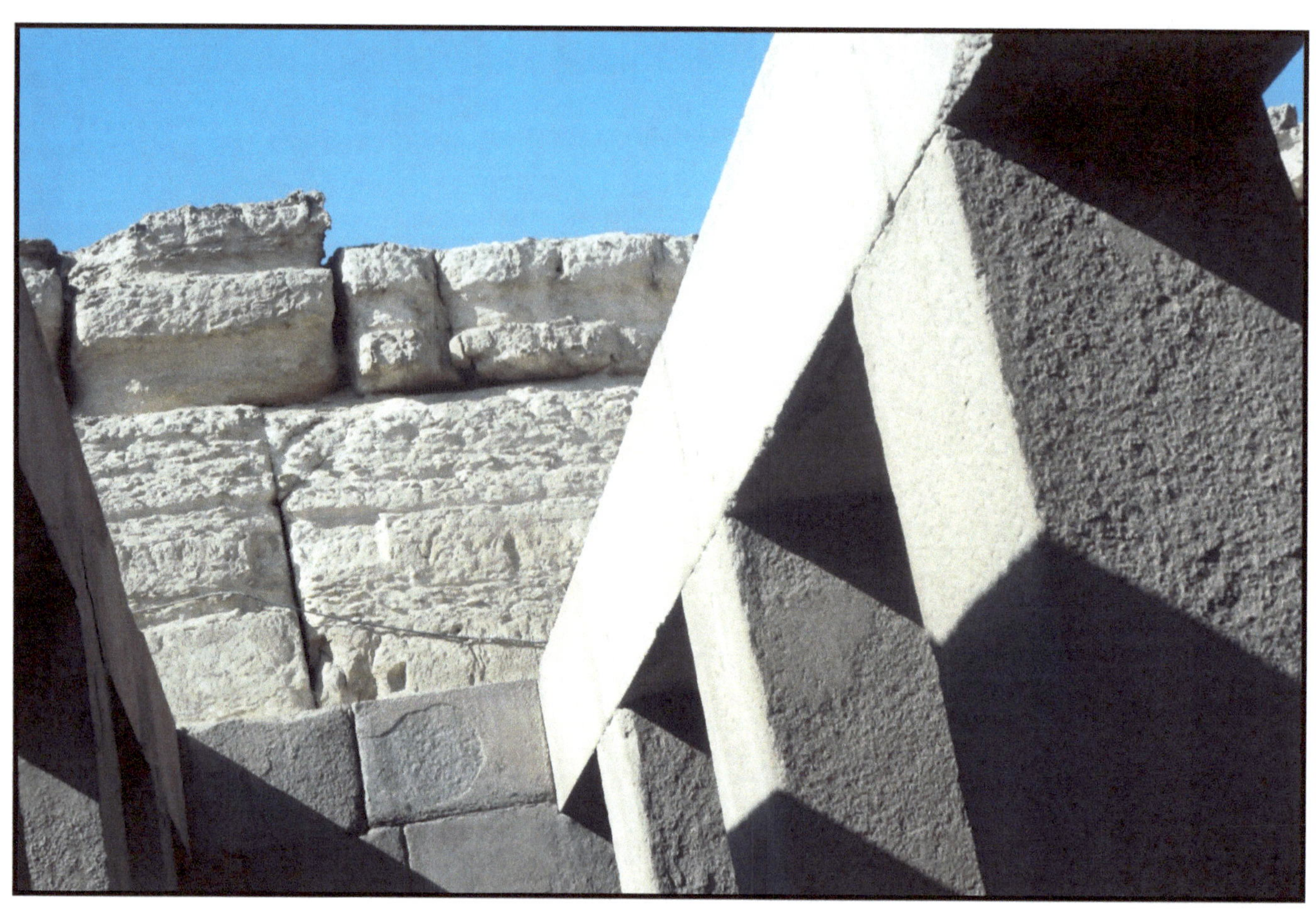

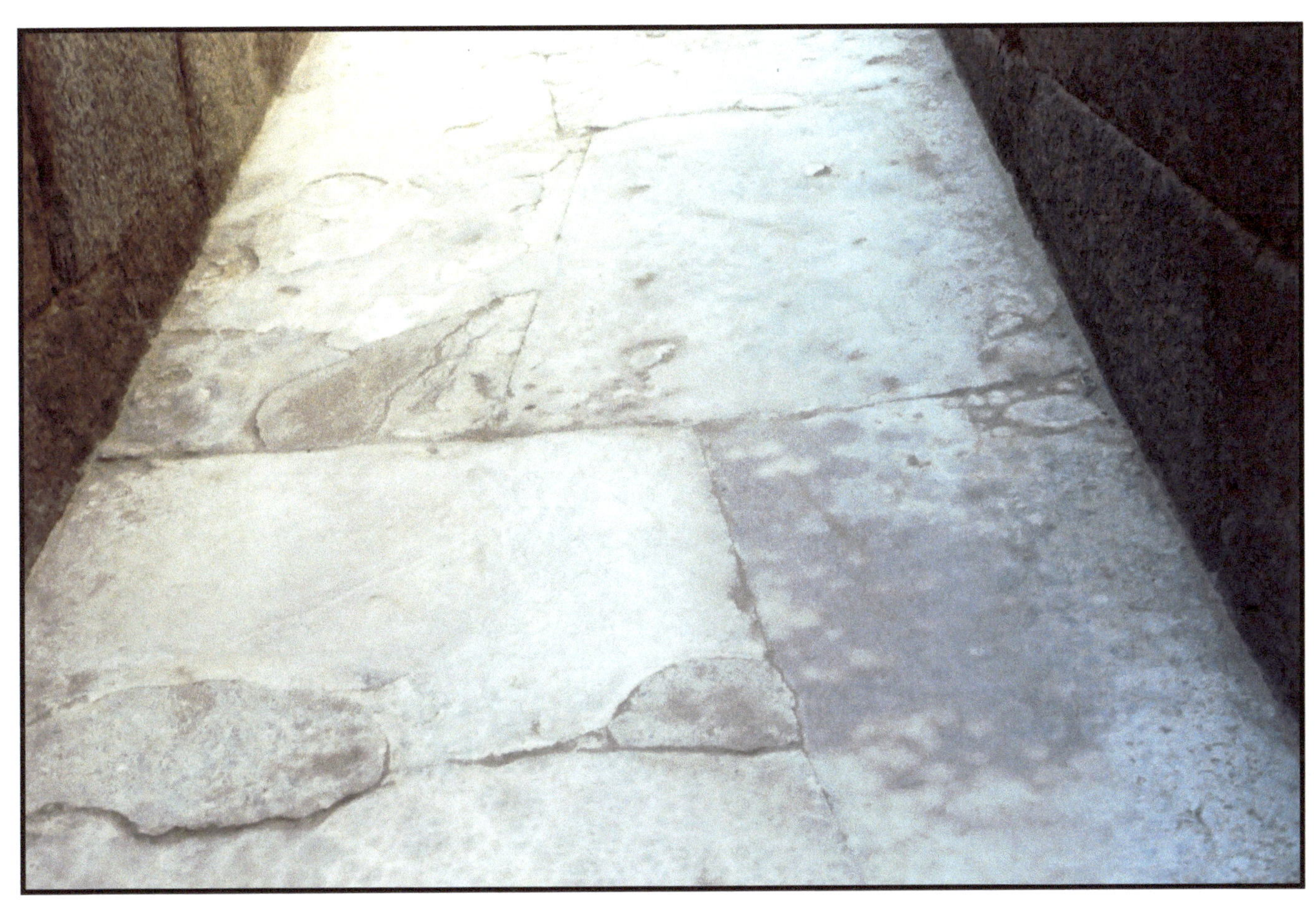

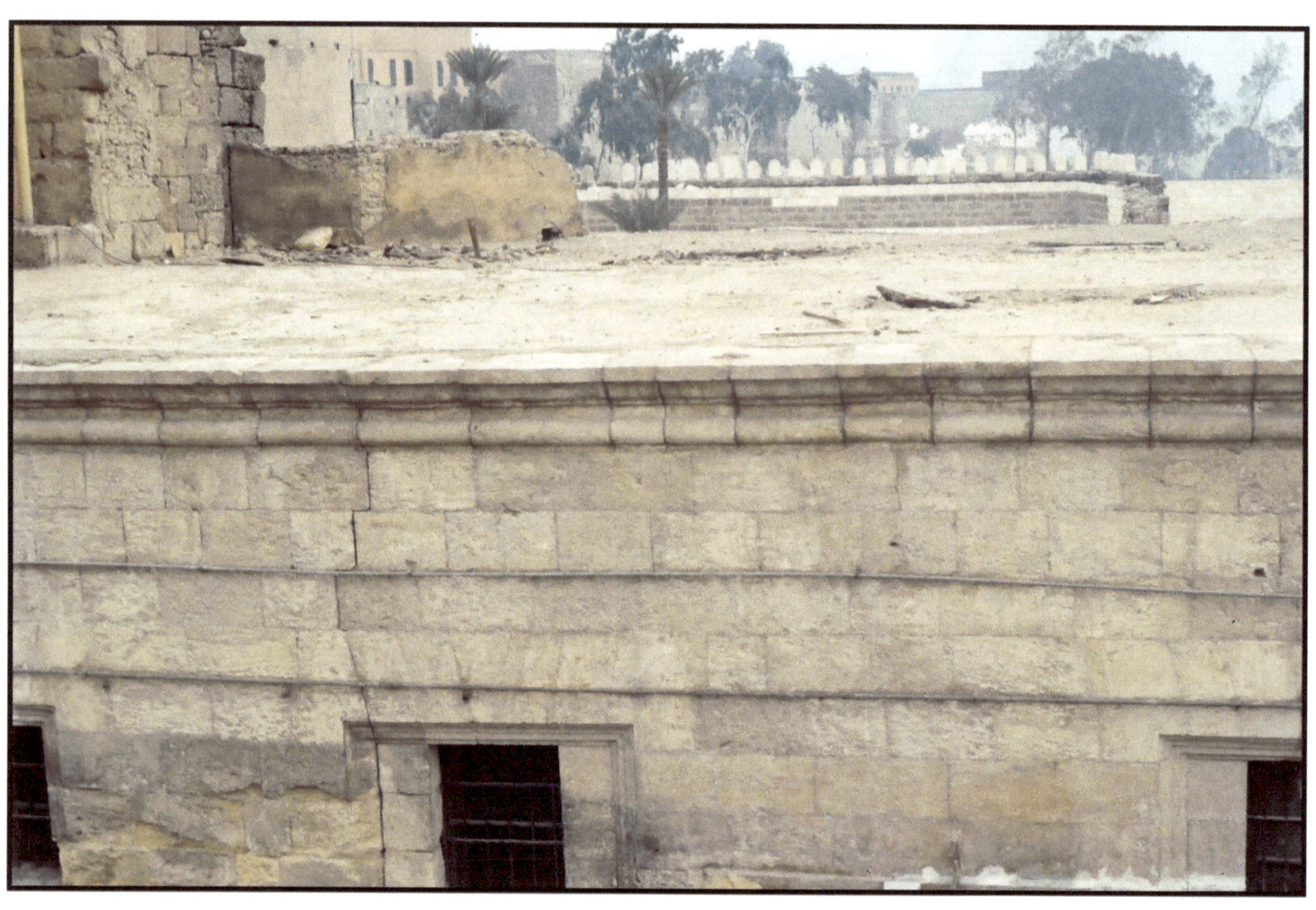

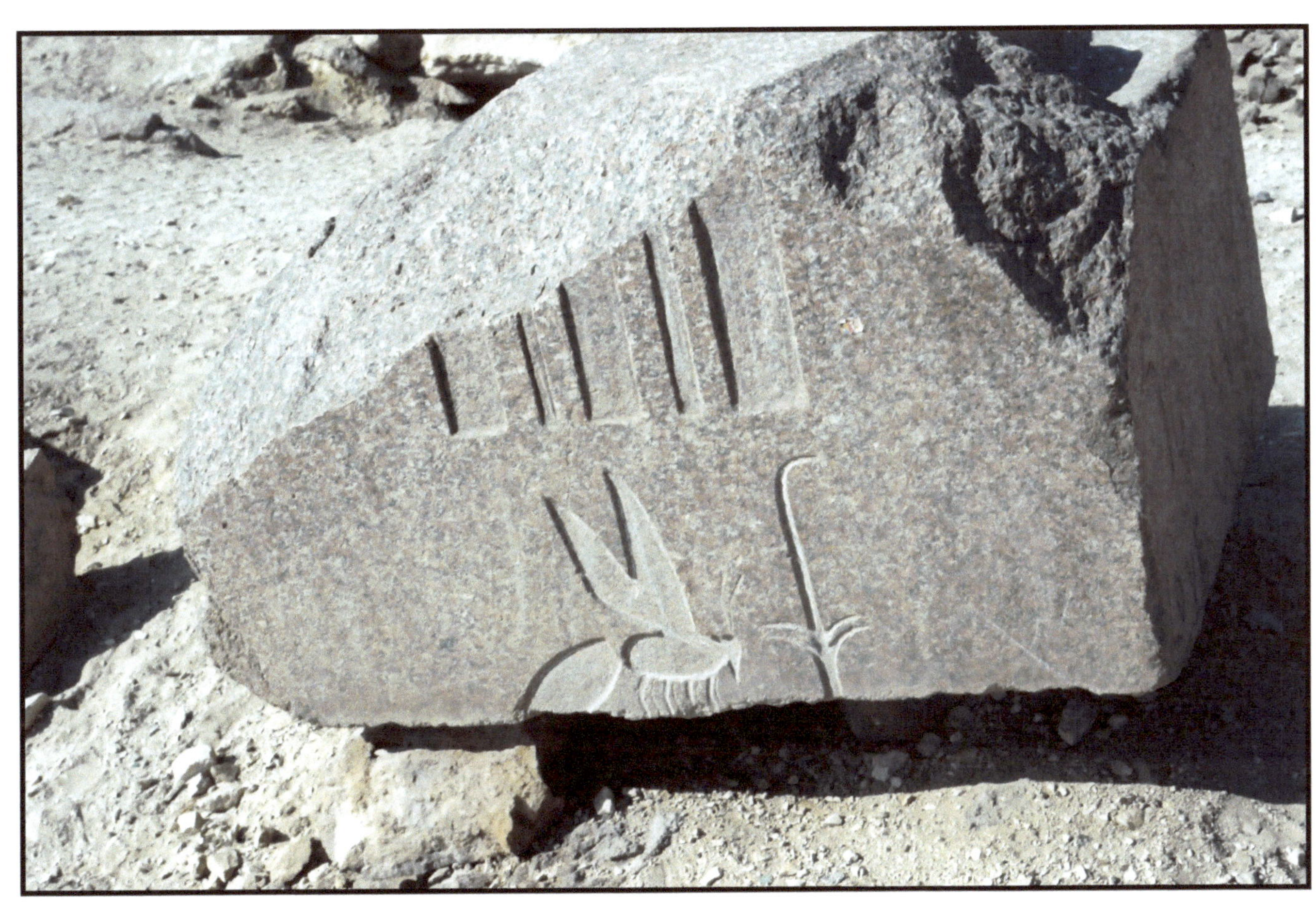

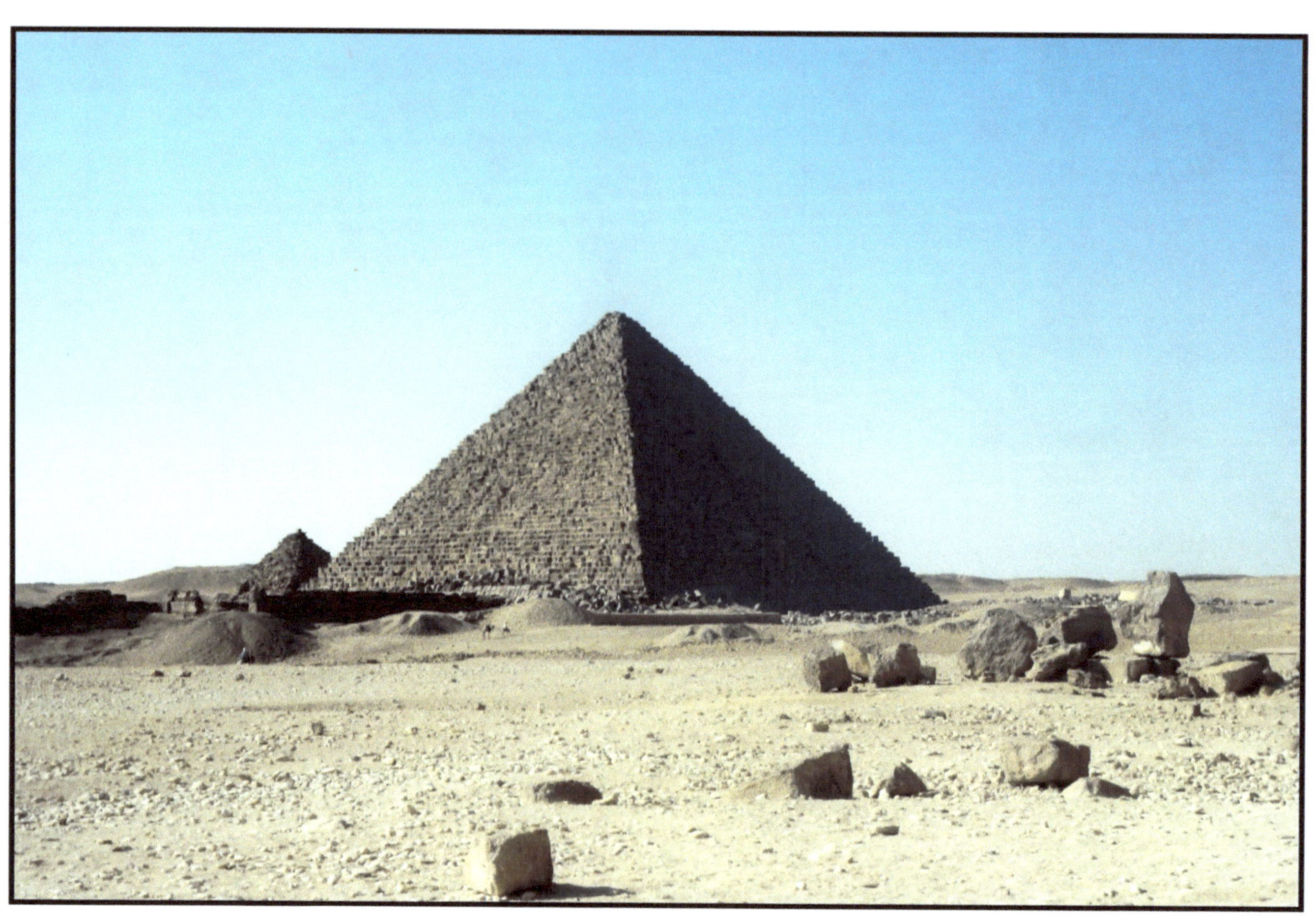

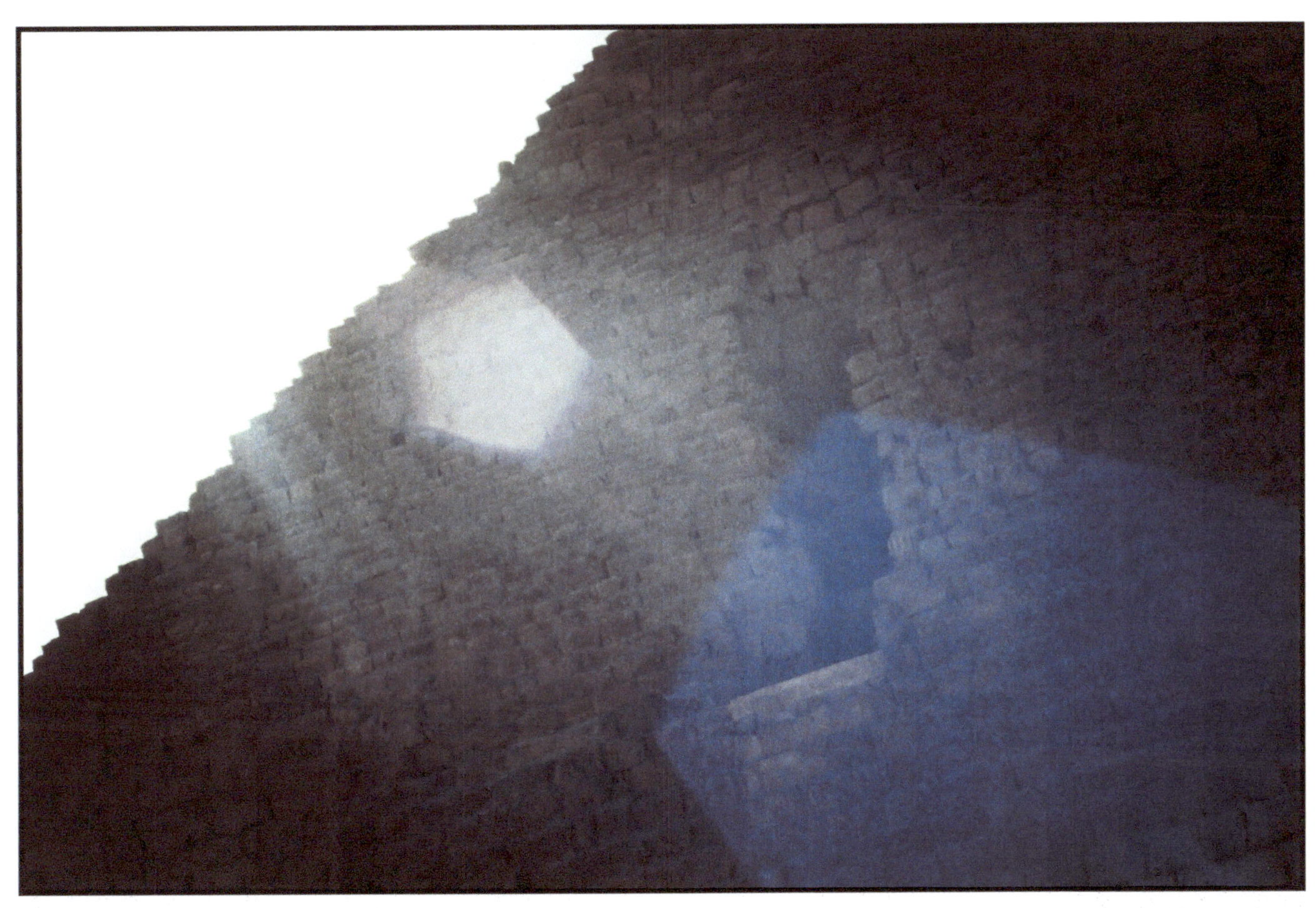

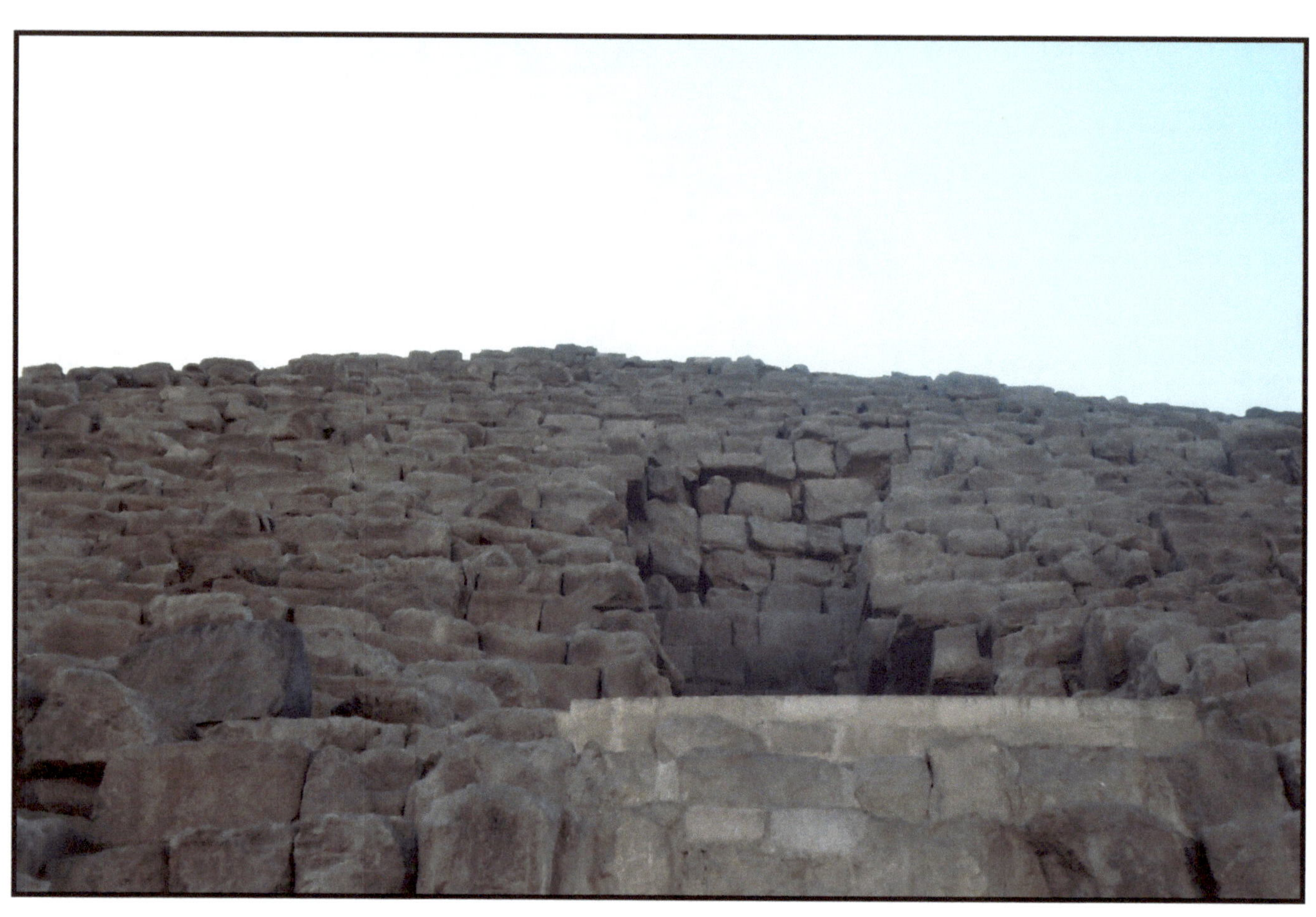

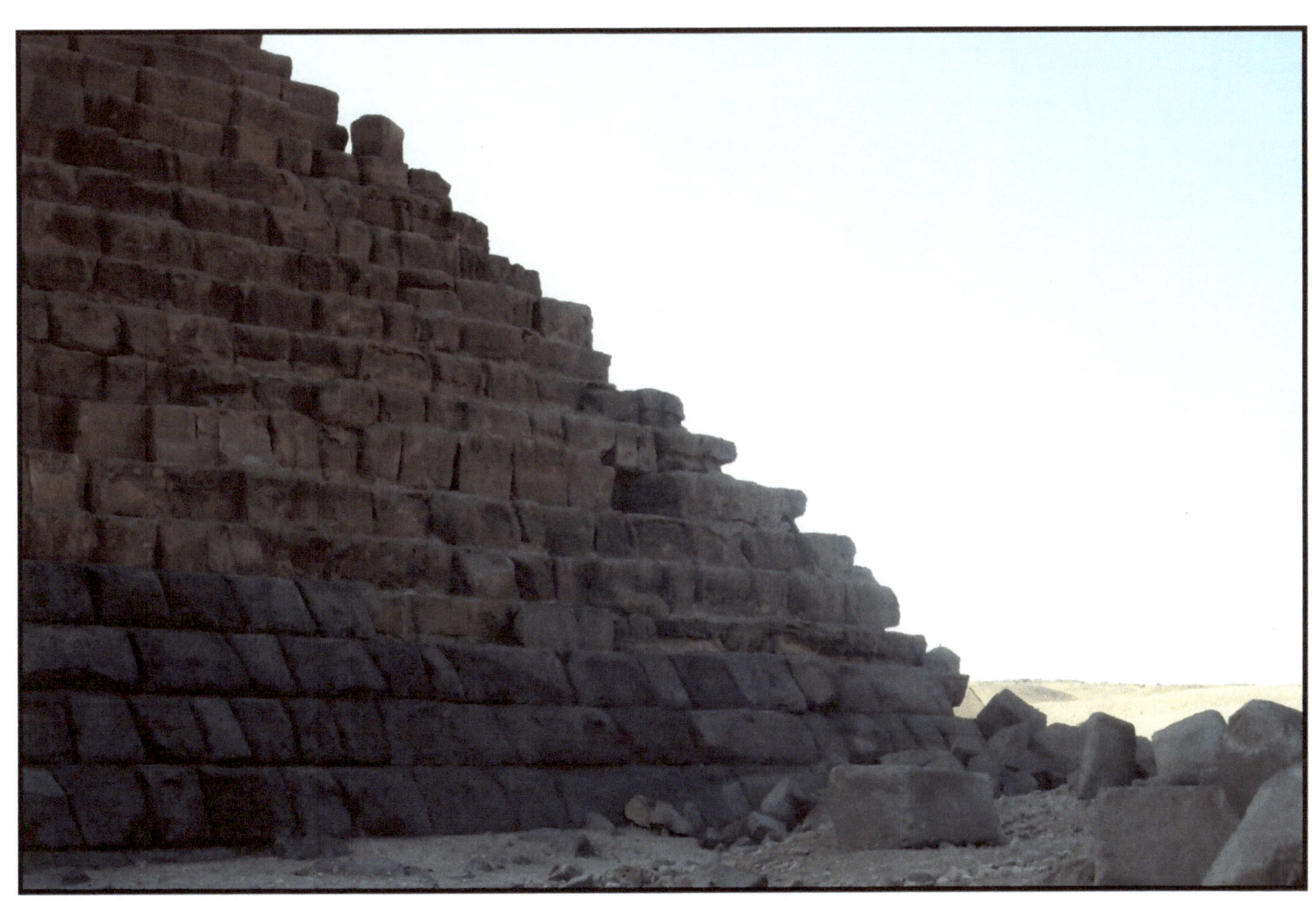

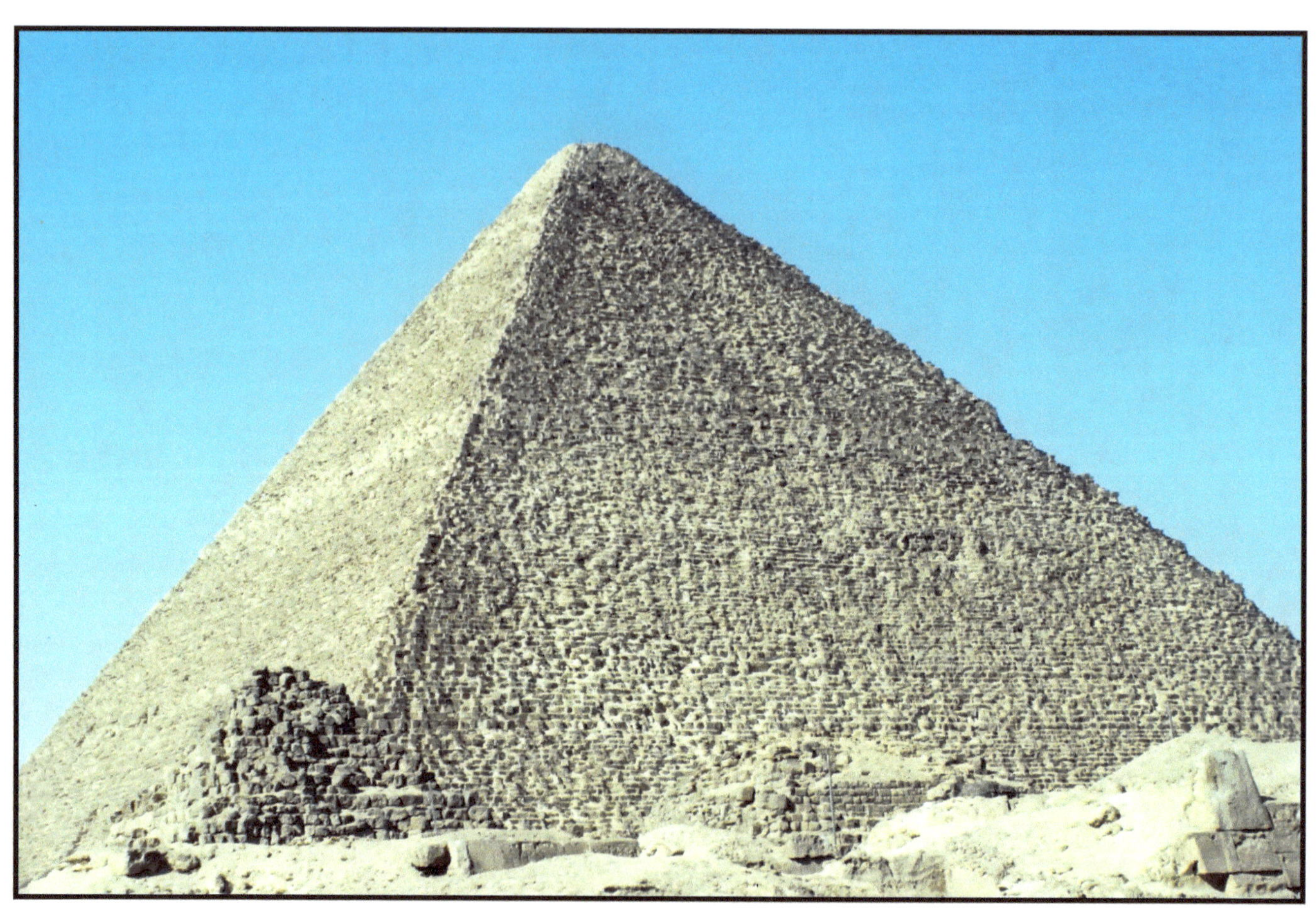

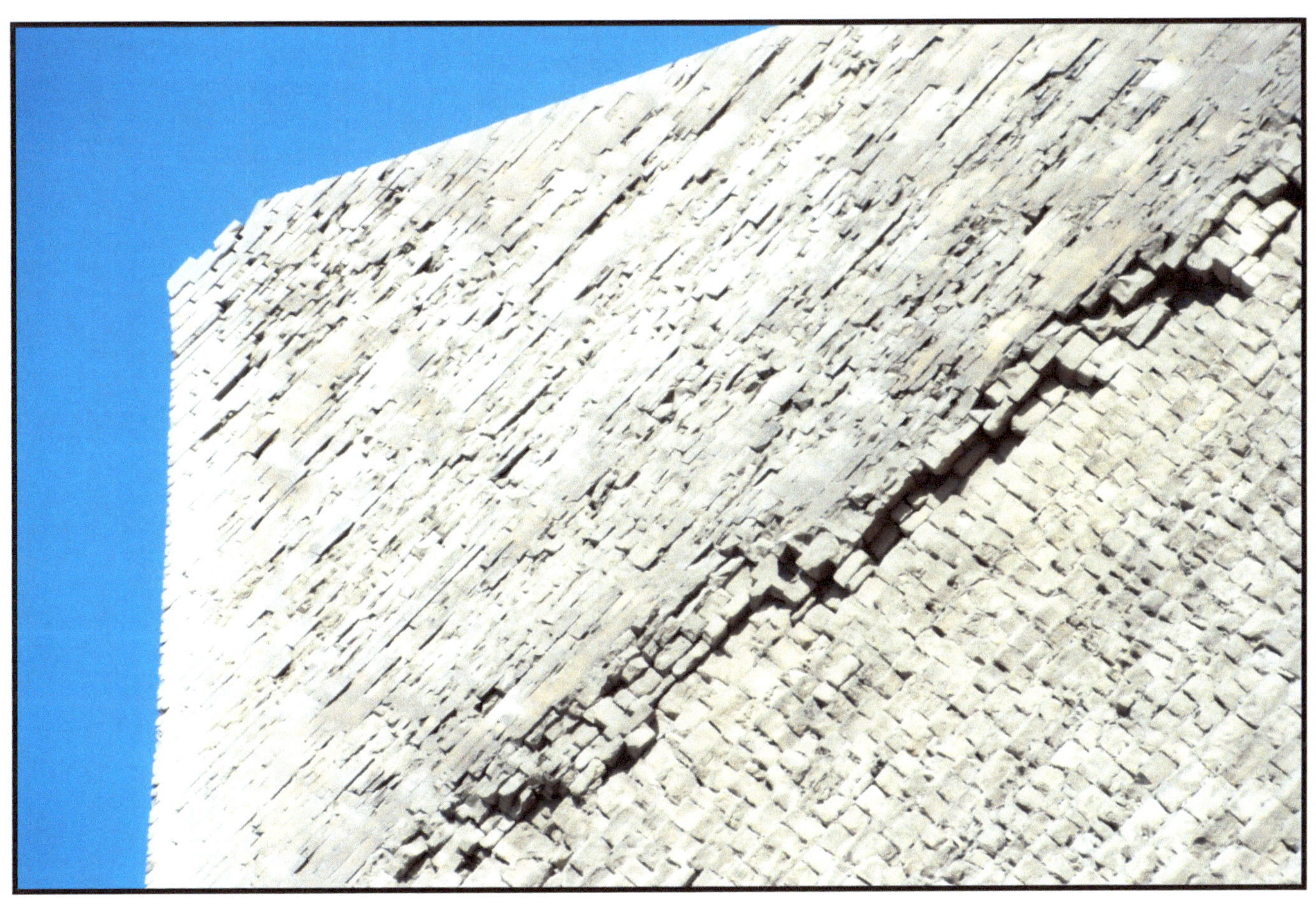

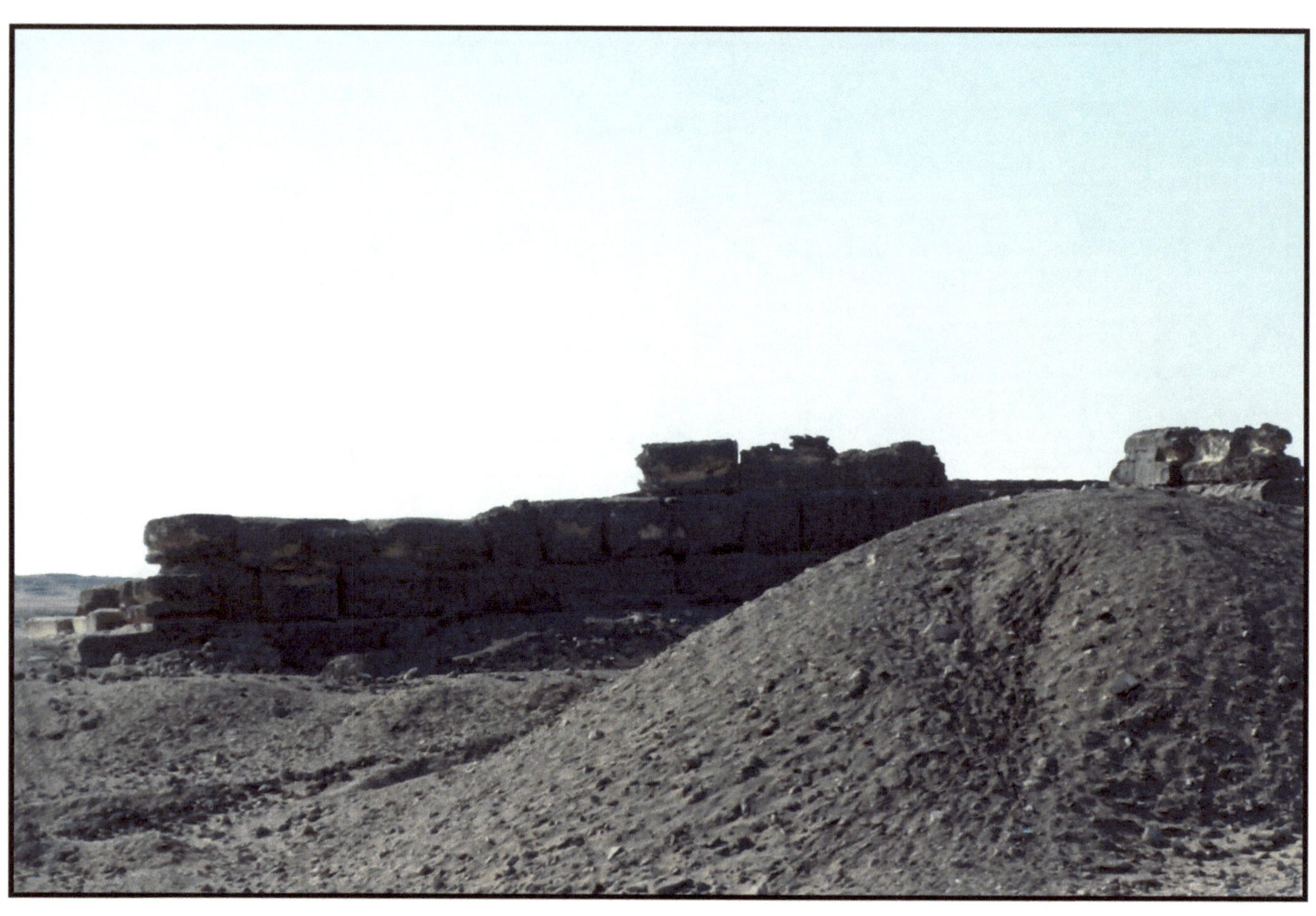

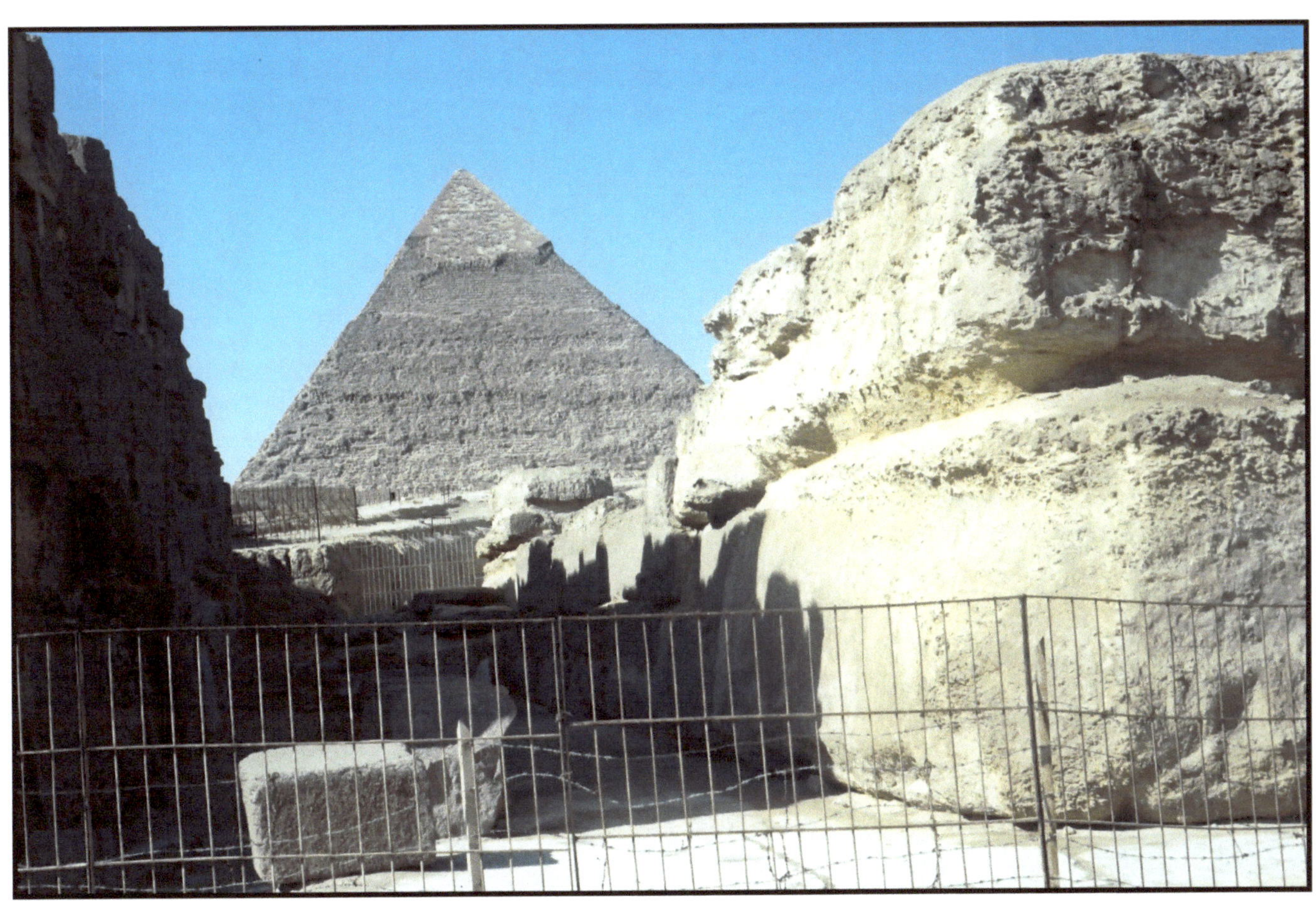

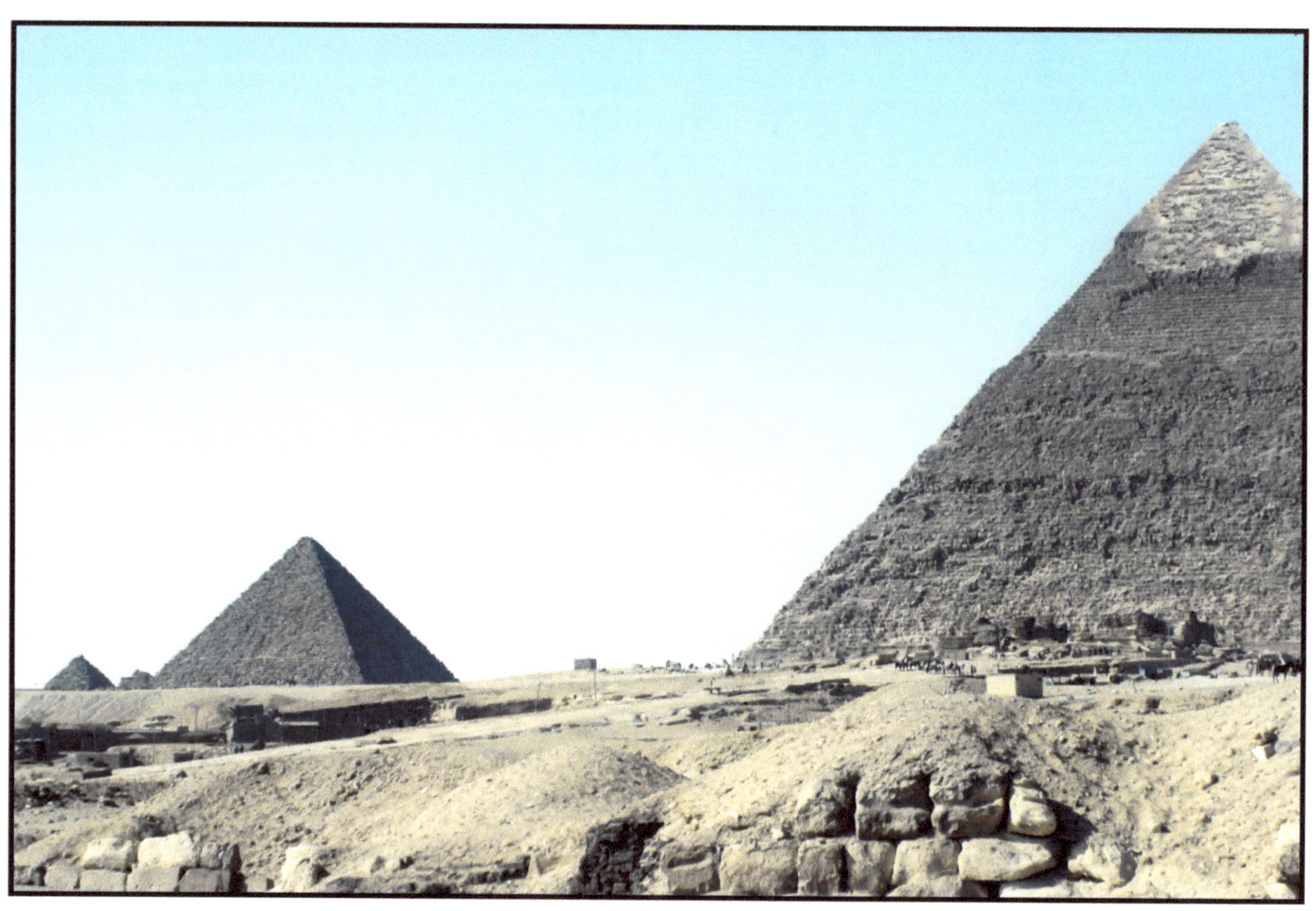

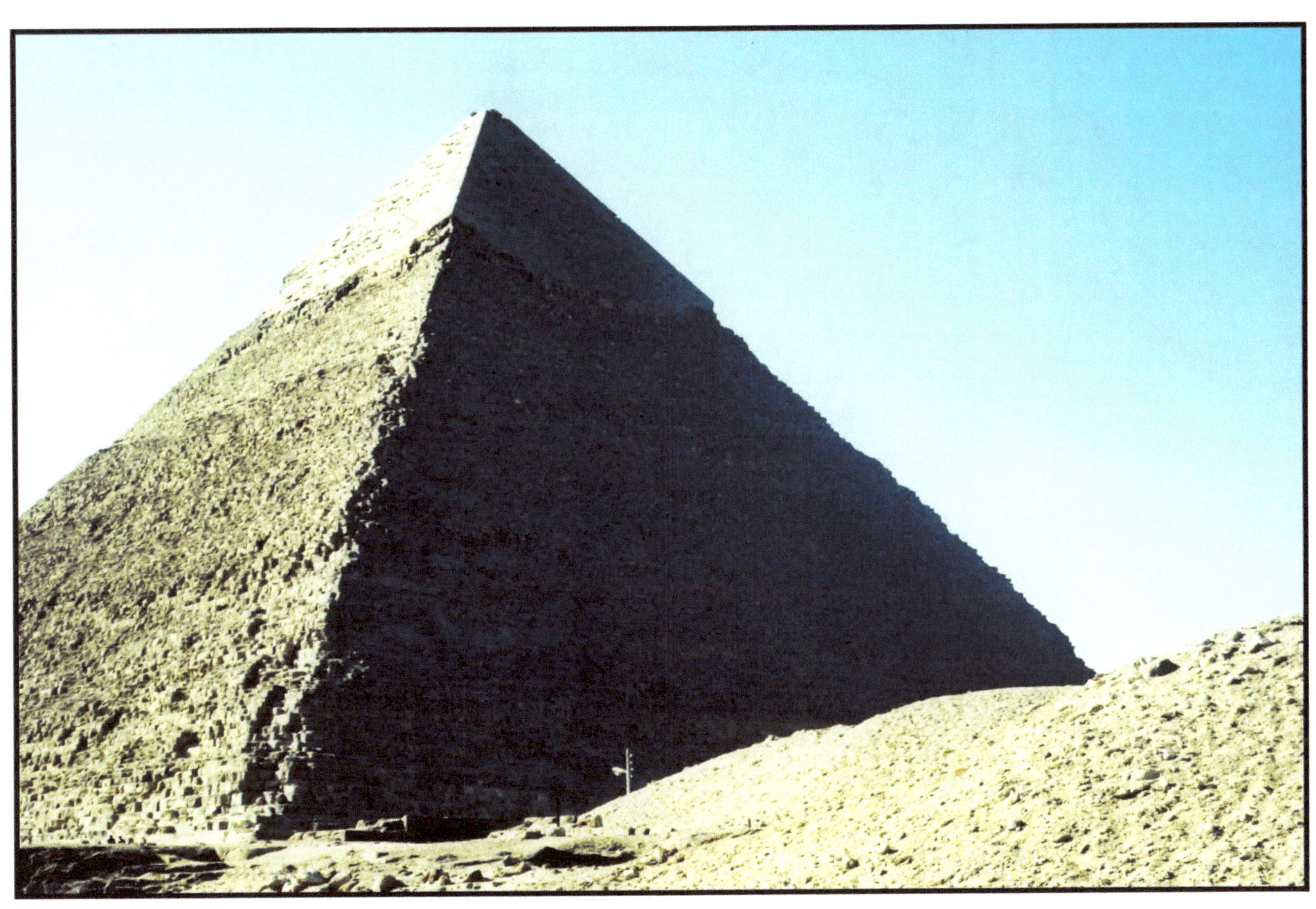

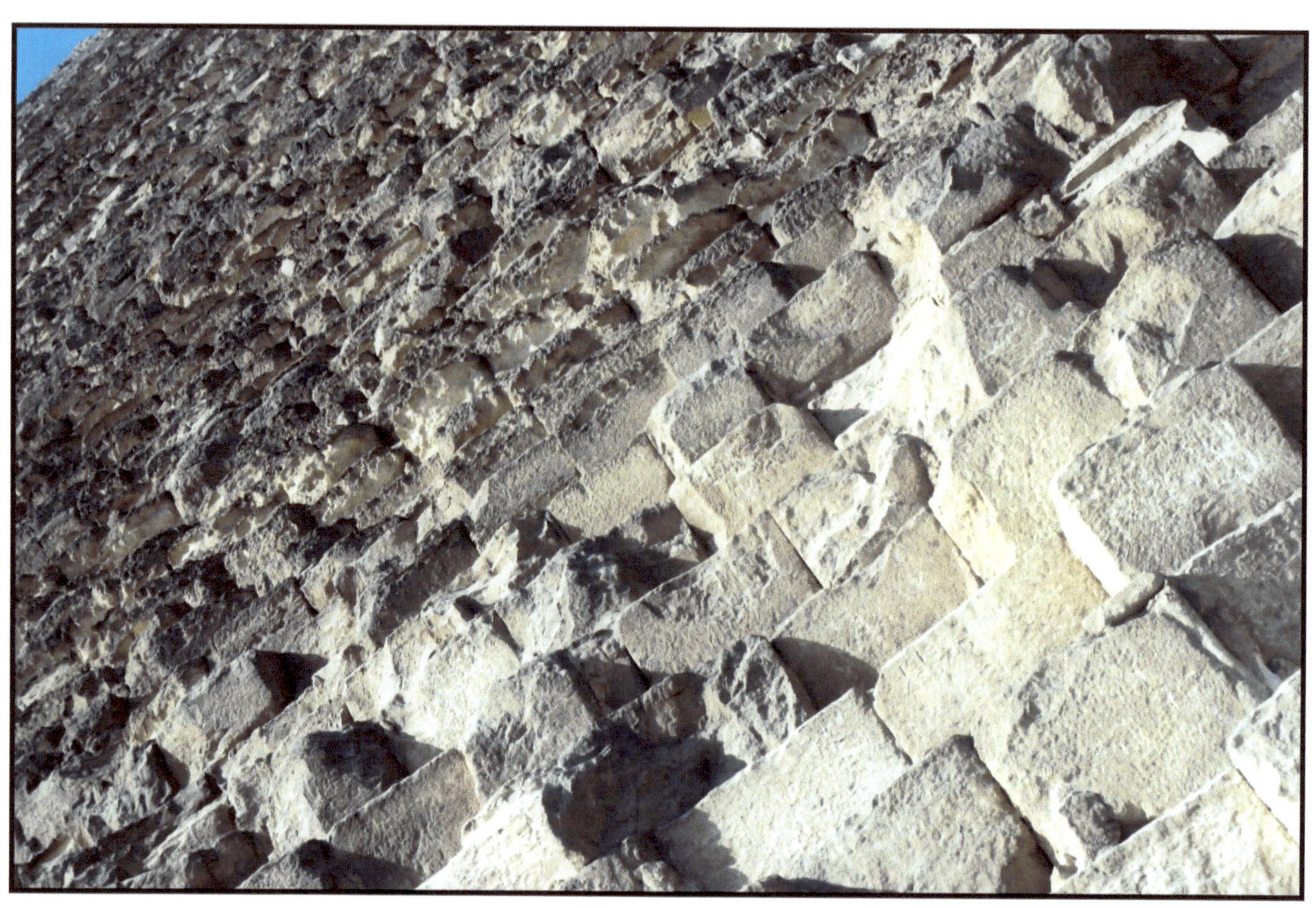

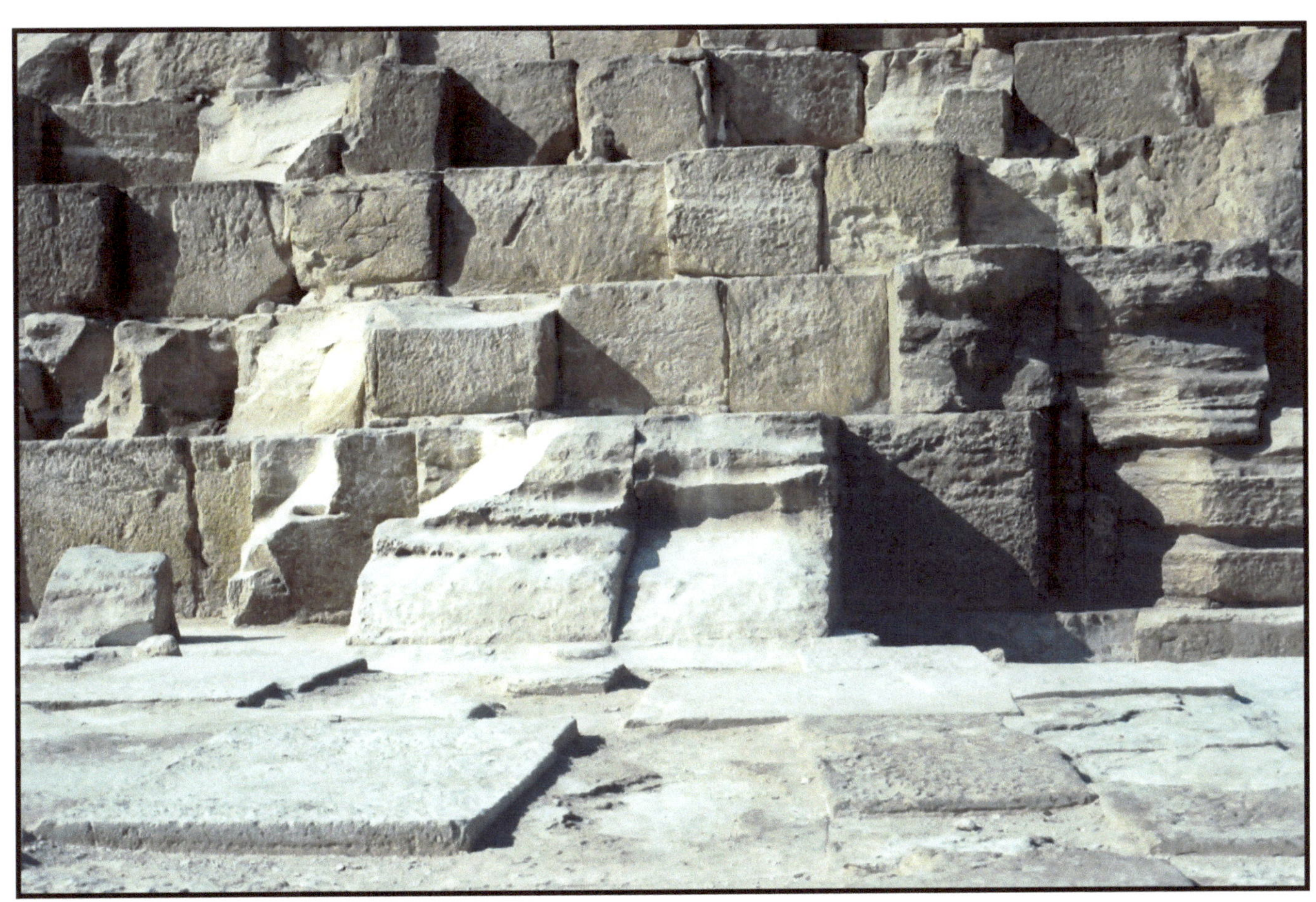

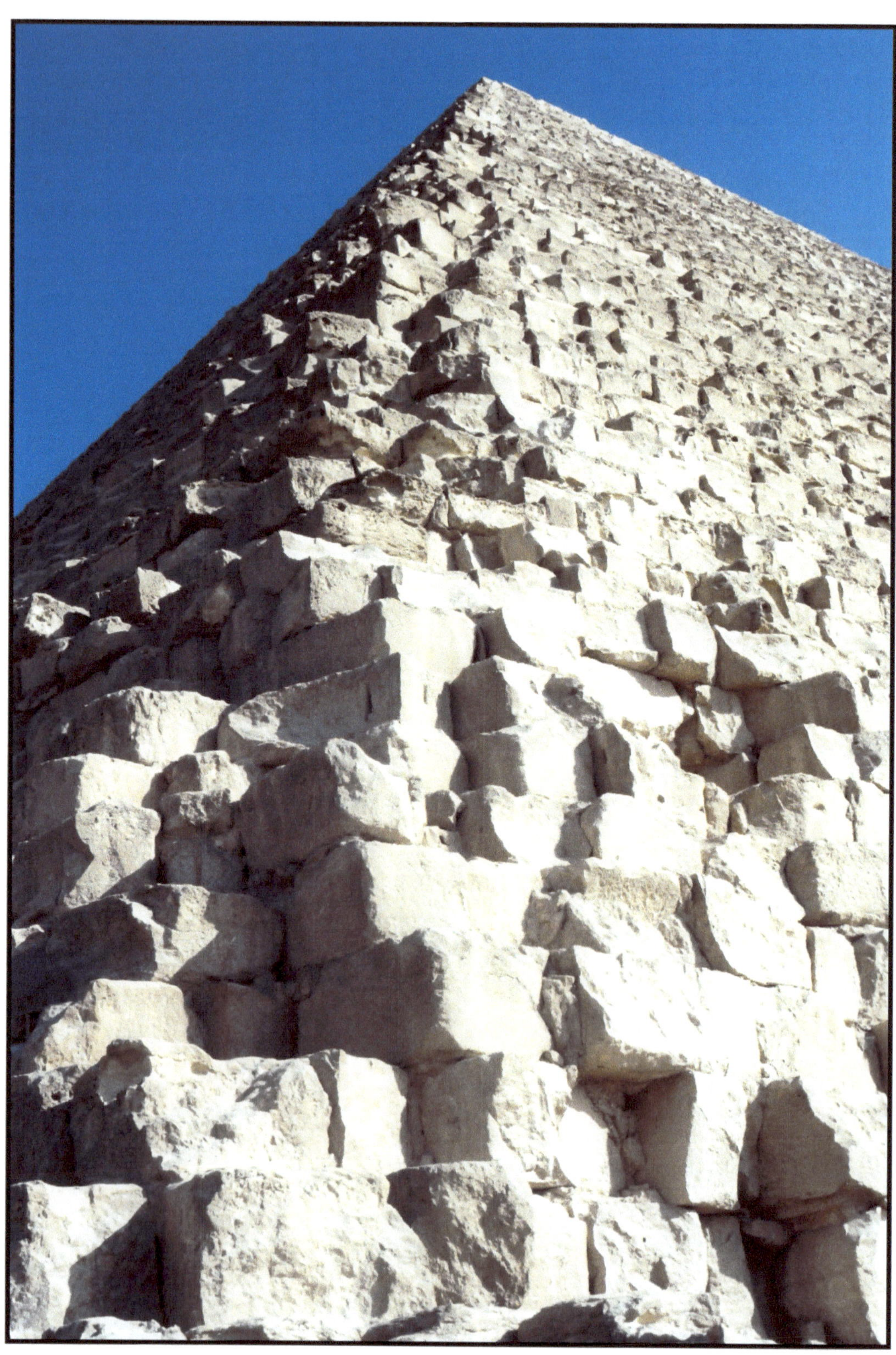

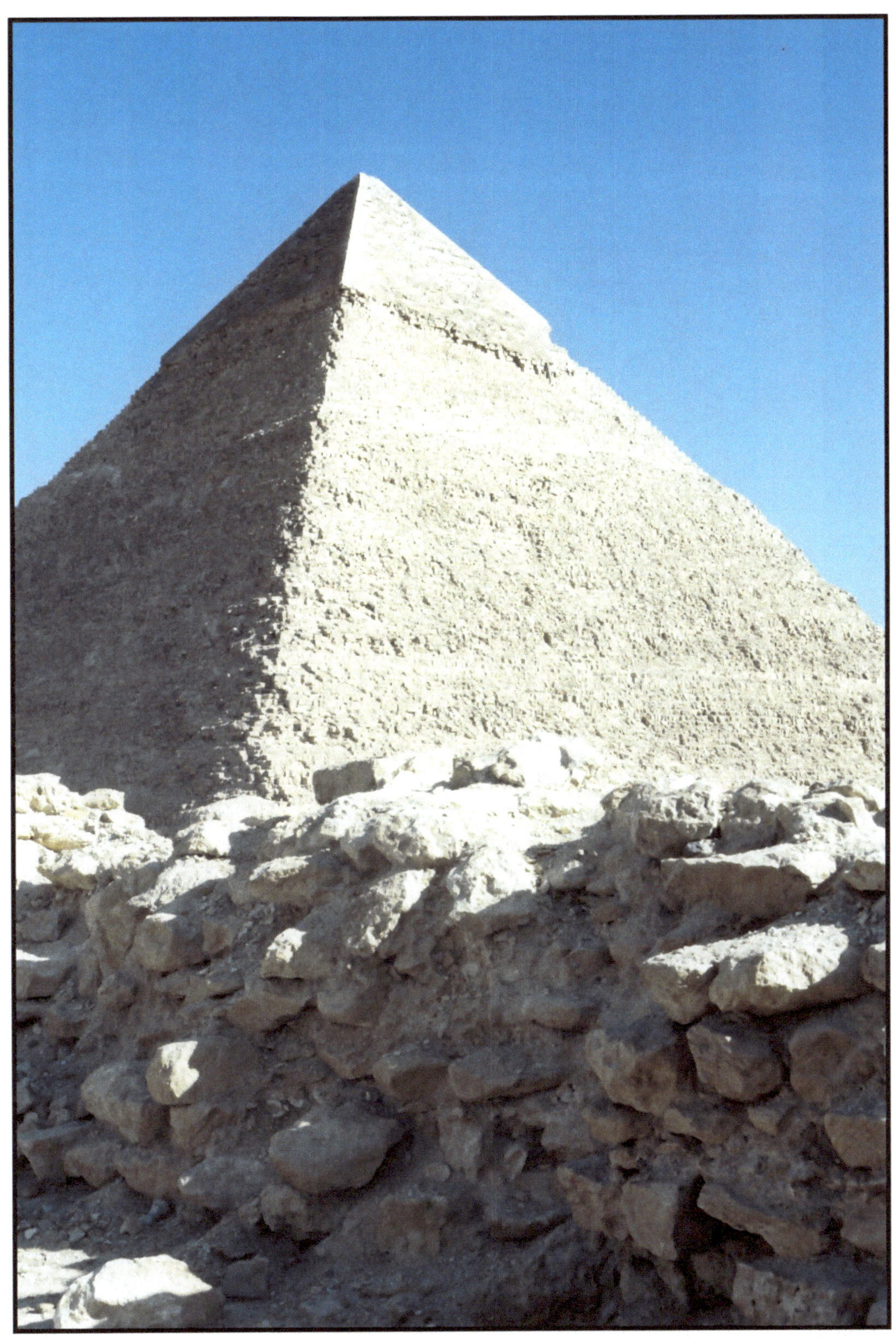

www.ingramcontent.com/pod-product-compliance
Lightning Source LLC
LaVergne TN
LVHW070120110826
845147LV00002B/160